This chart can help you find specific topics in the chapters of the text and in the handbook. Items in **boldface** will be especially helpful to you in writing and revising. Your instructor may use the chart in marking your work for correction or revision. ~~Th~~ ~~if~~ ~~he~~ on a paper, he is referring you to item 3 under Organizat~~ion~~ which begins on page 12. Some instructors use these refere~~nces~~ prefer abbreviations, such as "dg" for dangling modifier. ~~C~~ of such abbreviations, with page references, and also a~~~~ writing process.

Some Practical Hints

H	H1 **Testing an Outline** **71**	H2 **Style** **169**	H3 **Taking Examinations** **177**	H4 **The Critical Paper** **231**	H5 **The Research Paper** **283**	H6 **Persuasion** **335**

Handbook

Sentence Structure S	S1 Fragment 354	S2 Fused Sentences 355	S3 Run-on Sentence 356	S4 Comma Splice 357	**Diction** **D**	
	S5 Parallel Structure 359	S6 Dangling Modifier 361	S7 Shifts in Subject-Verb 363	S8 Incomplete Constructions 365	D1 Using a Dictionary 367	
Word Order **WO**	WO1 Normal Order 373	WO2 Ambiguous Order 375	WO3 Awkward Separation 376	WO4 Unemphatic Order 377	D2 Word Analysis 370	
Grammatical Forms F	F1 Principal Parts 380	F2 Tense 380	F3 Case 383	F4 Agreement (Subject-Verb) 386	**Glossary**	
	F5 Agreement (Pronouns) 392	F6 Reference 394	F7 Faulty Complement 396	F8 Adjective Adverb 398	gloss Glossary 438	
Punctuation P	P1 Uses of Comma 400	P2 Misuse of Comma 408	P3 Uses of Semicolon 409	P4 Misuse of Semicolon 410	P5 Period 411	P6 Question and Exclamation Marks 411
	P7 Colon 412	P8 Quotation Marks 413	P9 Punctuation with Quotation Marks 415	P10 Apostrophe 416	P11 Ellipsis and Dash 417	P12 Parentheses and Brackets 418
Mechanics	sp Spelling 422	abr Abbreviations 428	caps Capitals 429	hyph Hyphen 431	ital Italics 433	no Numbers 434

Writing with a Purpose

FIFTH EDITION

Houghton Mifflin Company
Boston
Atlanta
Dallas
Geneva, Illinois
Hopewell, New Jersey
Palo Alto
London

**FIFTH
EDITION**

1974 Impression

James M. McCrimmon

Florida State University

WRITING WITH A PURPOSE

Preface

This impression of *Writing With a Purpose* follows the text of the fifth edition except for Chapter 10, *The Critical Essay,* which has been considerably expanded to meet the needs of classes which make writing about literature a major part of the work in composition. This chapter, now subtitled "Writing About Literature," recognizes that a discriminative reading of the text is a prerequisite for even the *pre*writing of an essay responding to a literary work. To provide a basis for such reading, the chapter discusses nine major elements in the structure of a piece of literature: *situation, character, action, theme, structure, symbol, irony, point of view, and voice.*

Those who are familiar with the fifth edition know that it has been extensively influenced by the suggestions of critics made both in the planning stage and during the revision, suggestions which led to five main kinds of changes:

1. Simplification of content and style.
2. Greater attention to the prevailing interests and preoccupations of students today.
3. An even wider application of the concept of purpose as a guide through the composition process, especially with reference to the writer's awareness of his obligation to his readers.
4. More opportunity for classroom analysis of models and exercises so that instructors and students need depend less on the author's analysis.
5. More direct advice to the student to help him apply the principles of composition to his own writing.

I acknowledge with gratitude the help of the following consultants for the fifth edition: Beth Barnes of the University of North Carolina; Jean H. Bitner of Keystone Junior College; George W. Boyd of Millsaps College; Fay Chandler of Pasadena City College; Homer C. Combs and members of the English staff of Florida Technological University; Edward P. J. Corbett of The Ohio State University; Soren F. Cox of Brigham Young University; James W. Culp of Texas Tech; Nancy Hilts Deane of the University of New Hampshire; Charles O. Ham, Jr., of McHenry County College; William C. Hamlin of the University of Missouri; John Igo of San Antonio College; Mel McKee of DeKalb College; Adam David Miller of Laney College; Duane C. Nichols of Salisbury State College; Woodrow Ohlsen of Pasadena City College; James Olson of Wisconsin State University; Neal Resnikoff of Providence College; David Skwire of Cuyahoga Community College; Robert K. Stone of the University of Wisconsin; Jon C. Stott of Western Michigan University; Stafford H. Thomas of the University of Illinois; Jack W. Weaver of Winthrop College; Richard Young of the University of Michigan.

I am also indebted to the following student readers: John Neal, De Kalb

College; Ulla Johnson, Laney College; Nancy McCoy, Pasadena City College; Christine Doyle, Western Michigan University; and Donna Topolewski, Keystone Junior College.

I wish particularly to thank the following professors for their help in obtaining student essays: Webb Salmon and his associates in the composition program at Florida State University; Robert E. Burkhart of Eastern Kentucky University; Ralph L. Corrigan of Sacred Heart University; and Florence Trefethen of Tufts University.

For useful criticisms of the expanded Chapter 10, I am indebted to Beth Barnes of the University of North Carolina; Nancy Hilts Deane of the University of New Hampshire; and Duane C. Nichols of Salisbury State College.

Finally, I am again indebted to my wife, Barbara S. McCrimmon, for her help in proofreading at all stages.

James M. McCrimmon

Tallahassee, Florida

Contents

Part Two   Writing and Rewriting

Part Four   Handbook of Grammar and Usage

Part One
Prewriting

Chapter 1

Purpose: An Overview

Do you sometimes find writing a frustrating experience? If you do, you have something in common with many professional writers, including some of the best. The job of transforming a blank page into a piece of effective communication is a complex one. If it were not, there would be no need for teaching composition. But the complexity can be made more manageable as you acquire techniques for handling it. Writing is a process that can be learned and used; it is not, like height, a product of the genes about which little or nothing can be done. Increased proficiency in the process will not in itself make a great writer, but it can make a much better one.

We shall begin by breaking the whole writing process into three stages: *prewriting, writing,* and *rewriting.* Simply stated, prewriting is what the writer does before he begins his first draft; rewriting is what he does when he is revising that draft into a finished essay. In prewriting he is trying to get clearly in mind what he wants to do and how he wants to do it. In writing he works out these decisions in detail through the first draft. In rewriting he reconsiders what he has done and tries to improve it.

These stages are not always so separate as this division may imply. In some short papers, especially in examination essays, all three stages merge into a continuing operation—planning, writing, and revising. In long papers, especially those based on reading or research, one will usually not start to write until he has gathered his material and organized it by a satisfactory outline, and he may revise his first draft two or three times. But because of the importance of prewriting to your work in composition, we suggest that you think of it as a necessary, separate stage, at least until you have made it a habitual way of starting to write. For this reason we devote Part One of this book to prewriting.

BASIC DECISIONS

Two relationships dominate the act of writing, one between the writer and his *subject,* the other between the writer and his *reader.* The first of these is concerned with the writer's own understanding of what he wants to do with his subject. Since he cannot say everything about it, he must explore it to find out what possibilities are open to him, and which of these are most to his liking. In short, he is trying to discover his own dominant interest in the subject. The second relationship is concerned with the reader. Here the writer is trying to decide how his knowledge of his reader influences what he should do and how he should do it. Obviously these two sets of decisions are interrelated. We begin with the writer and his subject.

Your View of Your Subject

Suppose a student given a choice of subjects picks "the generation gap." His first step is to find out what he might say about it. He does not start with a blank mind. From reading, radio, television, conversation—simply from living in a society in which the generation gap is of public concern—he already commands a body of information and opinion, but he has probably never sorted it out, or organized it into a complete and consistent statement. He might begin by jotting down the first things that come to mind, something like this:

1. Generation Gap – What is it?
2. Depression vs. Affluent Society
3. War – the Bomb – the draft
4. Effect of TV
5. Adult hypocrisy

These jottings are not a preliminary organization of an essay, not even a scratch outline, just a list of topics on which something might be said. Their chief value is that they offer some starting points for thinking. Once the writer has written "Generation Gap—What is it?" he has found something to think about, and the blank page is not quite so frustrating as it was.

As he explores each of these topics, his thinking may go like this:

```
     1. Generation Gap. Not necessarily bad. Always
gap between father-son, mother-daughter because of
experience. Greatest when children are young,
decreases later. Gap also between people of same age
(hawks and doves, conservatives and liberals). Gap
between 10 yr. olds and 20 yr. olds greater than
```

between 20 and 40. Different points of view not just matter of age. Trouble with metaphor is that it distorts the situation.

    2. <u>Depression</u> <u>vs</u>. <u>Affluent</u> <u>Society</u>. Consider when Dad was my age. Depression. No jobs. Little money. Worked way through college, night job. No time to worry about politics. Little money or time even for dates. Main drive for economic security. My situation quite different. More time, more money, more opportunity to worry about other things. Effect of difference on his point of view and mine.

    3. <u>War, etc</u>. No declaration of war. Defoliation. Destruction of villages, whole population, women and children. "Necessary to destroy village in order to save it." Division within this country. Attitude toward U.S. abroad. Cost of war. To what end? Effect on college students.

    4. <u>Effect</u> <u>of</u> <u>TV</u>. Violence as way of life brought into living room. Riots, burnings, assassinations (Martin Luther King and two Kennedys). We <u>see</u> violence; our fathers, when they were growing up, only <u>read</u> about it. Big difference. Cumulative effect of this on young people. No wonder we protest. TV shows violence as effective protest. Talking gets you nowhere. Burn, baby, burn. Marshall McLuhan on the effect of TV.

    5. <u>Adult</u> <u>hypocrisy</u>. Inconsistency between what they say and what they do. Sex, religion, racial tolerance, business ethics, Bill of Rights. Difference between private and public morality. Reaction of youth to all this.

At this stage the five topics begin to take shape as ideas. The writer is finding out what he could say about them, and the more he explores, the more thoughts he uncovers. His notes still fall far short of being finished papers, but they are growing. He may even have gone far enough to commit himself to one of the following five papers:

1. A paper which seeks a better understanding of the generation gap by showing that the differences in point of view are more complex than the term makes them seem. The writer is moving toward an informal definition of the generation gap. If he continues in this direction, he could have two or three pages that would be worth writing and reading.

2. A paper which traces the difference in attitudes between young people and their parents to the economic conditions in which they grew up. Such a paper would contrast the importance of material possessions and economic security to the two generations. Later you will see a passage developing this contrast.

3. A paper which narrows the topic to the war in Indochina and sees it as a decisive factor in splitting the generations.

4. A paper which develops the idea that today's college students are the first generation to mature in a television environment and shows the effects of that influence on their attitudes.

5. A paper which contrasts the professed code of behavior of the older generation with their actual behavior on matters of sex, religion, racial tolerance, and business ethics.

Any one of these five ideas could be developed into a good paper, but an attempt to treat them all in one paper of 600 words or so would be a serious mistake, since the paper would be superficial and would lack focus. The writer must therefore decide which topic is closest to his main interests and experience. He may even combine two of these topics in one paper. But unless he can merge them into a unified essay he runs the risk of writing a paper that splits into two unrelated parts.

Whatever his decision, he must select some of the material he has uncovered and reject the rest. The following excerpt from a magazine develops the second of our five topics. Rightly or wrongly, the man being discussed is taken as representative of modern parents.

It's really sad. He's so lonely and unsure, and can't understand why his children have rejected him. And the saddest thing of all is that there are so many insecure uptight parents like him in this country, parents who fought so hard for what the System told them was good; and the Depression created such an intense desire to possess material goods that they've forgotten there are other values in life. It's always what you don't have as a kid that's important when you're an adult. They had families but no money, so they want a Better Homes and Gardens house; we had Better Homes and Gardens houses and wanted a family and love. I can understand how my father's generation got the way it is, why material things are so important—I'd probably have ended up the same way. I just wish they'd step into my life for a while and see what I didn't have, and why I want the things I do. My father belongs to the last of the generations to believe in the Great American Promise that material goods will make you happy, while I belong to the first of the generations which has discovered that not only do material goods not bring heaven on earth, they can turn it into an absolute hell. They found the answers to life in the traditional American ideals—all they needed was the money; we've got the money, and found out that the old ideals aren't worth having anymore.[1]

[1] From Kate Haracz, "The Education of Kate Haracz," *Change*, May–June 1970. Reprinted by permission of *Change* magazine and Miss Haracz.

EXERCISE

Take part of any of the other four sets of notes on page 5 and expand it to include your further thoughts on the topic. Then write at least a page which develops the ideas you think most important.

Your View of Your Reader

You know from experience that what you say and how you say it depend in part on whom you are talking to and on the situation of the moment. A student complaining about a grade on a paper will talk very differently to his roommate and to his instructor. These differences apply equally in writing. A writer must think of his reader long before he begins to write, and that concern affects his choice of subject, the tone and organization of his work, the kinds of illustrations and examples he uses, his sentence structure, and his choice of words. Writing is not good or bad in itself, but as it succeeds or fails in getting the response intended.

Considering your reader in a composition class is fairly easy, since you have a constant audience in your instructor and classmates and can soon learn what is appropriate to them. Most of your problems will come from your failure to realize that a statement that seems clear to you may not be clear to them because they cannot always see from the words alone just what you have in mind. In conversation you can easily adjust your response to a puzzled look or a "What do you mean?" But there is no such direct feedback in writing. If a writer is to avoid such troubles he must anticipate the reader's needs. If a statement is abstract, he must give supporting or clarifying details to make it concrete. If his diction is vague, he must choose a more precise term. The one thing he must not do is to think he need satisfy only himself. In prose, at least, he must try to see his work through his reader's eyes.

EXERCISES

A. Reread the Kate Haracz paragraph on page 6 and discuss your answers to the following questions:

1. Is the paragraph appropriate for this class as audience, even though it was written for the readers of Change, *a journal many people would describe as "liberal"?*

2. Is there anything in the paragraph that would be objectionable to a general audience of educated adults?

B. Now read the following paragraphs, which immediately preceded that paragraph in the same article. Apply questions 1 and 2 above to these paragraphs and discuss your answers. If you find differences in the content and style of the two passages, can you explain them?

Man, a really classic case of generation gap tonight: Cathy and I were interviewing three RA candidates, and we went bopping out to the Hospitality

Inn's coffee shoppe (that extra *pe* is for extra class). We'd been there about two hours and had almost finished the interviews (as well as our food; the poor waitress was dismayed when I ordered pecan pancakes, a chocolate shake and onion rings—I'm sorry but dinner in the dorm really lost tonight: we played name it and claim it—and she's lucky I didn't order a pistachio shake and chili like I usually do) when the father figure walks in, plops his bod down next to us, and announces that he's all for us doing our own bag (*doing our own bag?* Well, that's what he said), and all parents want is for their children to be happy. Aha, I thought, an enlightened adult. *Wrong, Katie, wrong.*

This guy was almost the compleat adult which we kids have come to know and despise (not despise really, just want to avoid at all costs). His major hang up was sex; the conversation (monologue, actually) oscillated between tirades against "cheapie girls" and "I could lay you tomorrow." (We all sat there, repulsed at the thought.) Next, he came out with "America is the best country on earth." (Did you know that the Constitution, Bill of Rights and Declaration of Independence contain the sacred justification for the American business system? Neither did I, but being the respectful, well-brought-up child that I am, I listened to and heeded my elder's words of wisdom.) "And we've left it to you kids, and you're going to give it all away with your pot and free love and wake up and find the communists ruling and, boy, then won't you be sorry." (We tried to point out that while we agreed with American democratic principles, we'd just like to see them practiced for a change. No soap.) And then came the final, incredible statement that "everything we did was right at the time." Now, I'm not one to categorically knock people of my father's generation; I think that the majority of them did what they thought was right at the time, but there's a big difference between what you *think* is right and what turns out to be the best thing. It's just a minor human failing which we're all, even my father's generation, even or especially my generation, subject to. He started on the "youth today has too much money" bit, but dropped it when we nailed him with, "Who gave it to us?" Then, as we left, he said he hoped we would all marry Republicans. Marry a Republican? *Yecch.*

Your View of Your Purpose

By "purpose" we mean *the controlling decisions a writer makes when he determines what he wants to do and how he wants to do it.* We do *not* mean anything so general as deciding to "inform," "persuade," or "amuse," since these terms can mean so many different things that they give almost no help. Decisions about purpose establish guidelines to follow in working out the content and style of a paper. These guidelines include the writer's particular and personal view of his subject, his view of his reader, and his view of the impression he wants to give that reader.

You have seen a preliminary attempt to determine purpose by our hypothetical student groping toward what he wanted to say about the generation gap. By exploring possible approaches to the subject and deciding which one he preferred, he was finding out his views. He was making a partial decision about his purpose. You also saw in the Kate Haracz excerpt (pages 7–8) how the style of the first two paragraphs was chosen to appeal to a certain kind of reader. That style was the result of a decision about purpose.

The following student essay is a fine example of how a clear sense of purpose controls content and style. The author's general subject is TV westerns. Out of all the things she could have done with that subject she chose to write an ironic criticism. That decision about her approach to the subject (made, of course, with an eye to her classroom audience) directed her through the complex task of poking fun at westerns while pretending to admire them.

Why We Need More Westerns on Television

The other night I saw a wonderful western on television. It had just about everything you'd want—fast horses, handsome men, beautiful women, mean outlaws, sneaky Indians, waving grass, rolling plains, covered wagons, smoking pistols, hard liquor, torrid love, bitter tears, bloody death—just about everything you could ask for, all packed together into one little hour, and early enough for the kids to see it, too. This program was really something and I think we need lots more just like it, because programs like that teach lots of things that everybody ought to know—things that help us in our everyday life, and at other times, too. I'll tell you what I mean.

Take making friends, for instance. Most people are pretty slow at this, but they don't have to be. This program showed that a person can make friends quickly if he really tries. There was a trail scout in this story and a Russian countess, and at the beginning, they didn't even know each other, but before the first commercial, which came about four minutes after they met, they were already lying in the grass and kissing, just as if they'd known each other for years. I think we should all take a lesson from this—it's sort of a symbol. A Russian and an American making love on the prairie under the sky. It has a lot of meaning to it.

Another thing about westerns is that they show the difference between good and bad people. After you watch a few westerns, it's pretty easy to tell which is which. The good men, for instance, seldom have beards or whiskers, and most of the bad men do. Also, the good man never shoots a person in the back—he waits until the person turns around to face him, which is the decent thing to do. On the other hand, bad men will shoot a man anywhere and will even shoot a woman or a dog sometimes. Speaking of women, there are good ones and bad ones, just like men. The good ones are usually married, while the bad ones usually aren't. The bad women usually wear real low-cut dresses or short ones, and the good women usually have on aprons; they might wear pretty tight dresses (the young good ones, that is; the old good women wear loose dresses), but they're hardly ever cut low. All these things are very helpful to people watching the program, because they know right away whose side to be on. And just like knowing how to make friends quickly, it's very helpful in life to know whose side to be on.

One of the best things westerns teach is our country's history. I'll bet people with television sets know lots more about history than people without television sets, because westerns on television are just crammed with history. They tell how we had to fight the pagan Indians every step of the way to get them to give us this land so that we could really make something out of it. (We let them go on living here, after we won the land fair and square, and we even gave them special areas called "reservations" to live on. They're real nice places—sort of like wild game preserves to keep animals from becoming what they call "extinct.")

When you start thinking about all the advantages of watching westerns, it's pretty plain to see that we ought to have more of them. There has been a lot of progress made toward getting more westerns on television, and you can see a good western almost any time except Sunday. Unfortunately, on Sunday afternoons there are things like symphony orchestras, documentary films, and panel discussions—real dull, long-hair stuff that most Americans wouldn't be interested in. The only good thing about Sunday is that before you know it, it's Monday again, and the beginning of a whole new week of interesting, educational, realistic, historical westerns. But friends, we've got to do something about Sunday afternoons.

1. When do you first sense the author's purpose? What sentence or sentences give you the first clue?

2. The paper consists of an opening and a closing paragraph and three middle or body paragraphs, on making friends, telling good people from bad, and learning our country's history. How are the examples in these paragraphs related to the writer's purpose? Pick out the most successful and discuss their appropriateness. Is there any material in the essay that conflicts with or does not advance the purpose?

3. What is the author's attitude toward her audience—distant or intimate? On what evidence do you base your answer? Is this relation with the audience a suitable one for the girl's purpose?

4. In the fourth paragraph what evidence is there of irony in the treatment of the American Indian?

5. Consider the diction. Some people object to such contractions as *I'll, don't, aren't* and such colloquial expressions as *kids, lots of, sort of, pretty slow, real low-cut* in a paper for an English class. Do you object to them in this essay? Why or why not?

6. Is the statement in the final paragraph that most Americans are not interested in symphony orchestras, documentary films, and panel discussions a digression, or does it have a function in this essay? Explain your answer.

A good deal of careful thinking has to go into a clear decision about purpose, but that thinking pays off in surer and more consistent development of the paper. All through the process of writing, a writer faces a series of choices: of material, organization, diction, and style. If he has no firm understanding of purpose, his decisions can work against each other so that his writing lacks consistency. A sense of purpose makes it easier to decide what kinds of choices are appropriate and what ones are not. Moreover, a writer who knows his purpose has a channel through which his ideas can flow as he writes; he is not at the mercy of every thought that pops into his head. Purpose charts his course and keeps him from aimless drifting.

EXERCISE

Discuss some of the differences you would expect to find in content and style between two papers, one to be written as an editorial in the student newspaper urging the abolition of rules about when women students must return to their dormitories, the other to be written to persuade the Dean of Women to take the initiative in bringing about a more liberal policy regarding such rules.

Your View of Yourself as a Writer

Every writer presents some view of himself to his readers. By his attitude toward them, his approach to his subject, and the tone and style of his writing, he creates an impression whether he intends to or not. For example, contrast the following statements:

1. There are major disagreements about the effects of marijuana. Many serious and intelligent people are convinced that it is not only harmful in itself but can lead to the use of harder drugs. Others, equally serious and intelligent, feel that these beliefs are not justified and that marijuana is less harmful than alcohol. I don't know which side is right, if either is, but I do think we should make an honest attempt to find out the truth. Surely this is a question on which competent medical authorities could give us advice. I know I would like to hear the question fully discussed by a panel of qualified experts in an atmosphere unpolluted by emotional assertions.

2. All this jive about the dangers of pot makes me sick. It's just another attempt by the establishment to make us conform to their life style. There's no proof that a little pot ever did anybody any harm. Some kids may start with pot and go on to the hard stuff, like some start with beer and go on to become alcoholics. So what? Are the rest of us to be legislated against because some neurotics drift into excesses? You can build a better case against tobacco, alcohol, overeating, sex, or the automobile as potentially dangerous pleasures than you can build against pot. Sensible people make a distinction between use and abuse. It takes a special kind of feeblemindedness to believe that the way to stop an occasional abuse of something is to prohibit it entirely.

Whatever the merits of these statements as arguments, there is no doubt that the two writers are very different personalities. The first gives the impression of being open-minded, fair to both sides, cautious, maybe a bit dull, uncertain about the facts but confident that a reasonable decision could be made if we had more light on the subject and less heat. The second is cocksure, contemptuous of his opponents, decisive, forceful, and belligerent.

The personality a writer reveals or assumes in his work is usually called his *persona*. This term originally meant a mask and referred to the practice in ancient Greek drama of actors wearing different masks when they played different roles. Applied to writing, the term *persona* is a recognition that different writers reveal different personalities and that the same writer may adopt different personalities for different purposes. Thus the girl who wrote "Why We Need More Westerns on Television" deliberately represents herself as naive and easily taken in. Obviously she is not at all that kind of person in real life. She adopts the role to suit her purpose, and the role or persona is part of the fun of her paper.

Whatever persona a writer adopts, he should know what he is doing. It can be most unfortunate to reveal a persona that one did not intend and that works against his purpose. Since a persona that appeals to some audiences will be unattractive to others, the writer's decision about the effect he wants to create must be geared to his understanding of his audience. To some readers Kate Haracz's persona will be appealing. Others will see girlish silliness in her digression on her eccentric eating habits. Still others will react indignantly to her assumption that the man she tells about is typical of adults in general.

EXERCISE

If a student paper is badly organized, carelessly written, or messy in appearance, will these weaknesses have any influence on the reader's impression of the writer's persona? Discuss your answer.

FROM SUBJECTS TO THESES

Our student exploring the generation gap gave us a useful case history of the purposeful approach to a writing problem. Listing its possibilities and limiting his attention to one phase of it led him to the main idea he finally chose to develop. We are now ready to look further into this process and the various parts of it.

Choosing and Restricting a Subject

The subjects of some of your papers will be decided for you by the wording of the assignment. But when you have a choice, don't shuttle indecisively among alternatives. Pick a subject that lies close to your interests and experience and start to explore it. No amount of thinking will give you a subject that has never been used before. Nevertheless, a paper that expresses *your* observations, *your* ideas, and *your* values, even on a commonplace subject, will be original in the sense that it has never been written before and only you can write it. It is not the subject that counts, but what you do with it.

Almost any subject you choose will at first be too big for a single essay and will have to be *restricted,* as the generation gap was finally restricted to one of five topics. It is sometimes useful to distinguish between the *general subject* and what we may call the *real subject*. The general subject is an area for investigation, like "The Generation Gap." The real subject identifies what you really want to do within the general subject area, like the five different approaches to the generation gap that we saw on pages 4–5. The real subject is, of course, a restriction of the general subject, but it goes beyond restriction by identifying the kind of content to be used. For example, "Main Street" is a restriction of "Our Town," but the restriction does not suggest what the writer is going to say about Main Street. Only when he goes one step further—to show, for example, that Main Street is a symbol of the small businessman's commitment to private enterprise—does he have his real subject. The distinction can be further illustrated by the following contrasts. The arrows indicate that the real subject emerges from the general one.

General Subject	Real Subject
TV Westerns ⟶	An ironic and amusing spoof of TV westerns
College Education ⟶	The irrelevance of freshman comp.
Studying ⟶	How to get maximum results with minimum efforts

Until you have found your real subject you have no course for your ideas to follow, because there are no paths through a general subject until you make one. Such general subjects as pollution, student protest, and our space program do not suggest what you are to do with them, and so you have nothing specific to write about. It is only when you restrict the general subject to one of its subtopics that you begin to think efficiently about what you might do. The restriction forces you to concentrate on a narrower topic. As you do so, illustrations and examples begin to come to mind and you will have specific material to use.

Probably the best way to find a real subject for a paper on pollution, for example, is to ask, "What examples of pollution do I know from my own experience?" Recalling actual cases may lead quickly to a restricted subject that can be handled with confidence. Thus a student who lives on the Gulf coast and knows the damage done to birds, sea life, and property by oil slicks will probably restrict his subject at once to "The Effects of Oil Pollution on Beach Resorts." One who lives near the Hudson and knows the damage done by the Consolidated Edison Company to the fish in that river may find that his real subject is "Look What Nuclear Pollution Has Done to Fish in the Hudson River." In both cases remembered experience in examples provides a short cut to the real subject.

A student who needs to restrict his subject before he can think of examples may have to follow a more methodical route, like the one shown below. In the diagram, the general subject of pollution is first broken down into two main types. Then the causes of the types are identified and examples come to mind.

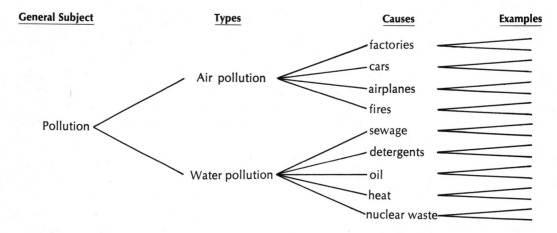

| **General Subject** | **Types** | **Causes** | **Examples** |

In this diagram the examples are not filled in, because the examples most useful to a writer are those he has himself experienced. But finding examples is the most important part of restriction. First, because they come to mind while he is thinking about causes, they will probably determine the exact kind of restriction he chooses. Second, it is the examples that convey most of the specific meaning. Notice how much it is the details in the following extract that affect you as reader.

Starting early in 1963, a new small nuclear plant at Indian Point on the Hudson began killing fish by the ton. The exact number killed probably will never be known . . . but the toll must have run into millions. The exact cause of the 1963 kill has never been made precisely clear. . . . But apparently the fish were attracted by hot water discharged from the plant after it had been used to cool the condenser. Swimming in to investigate the hot water, the fish were then trapped underneath a pier which had sheathing partly down the sides to keep debris away from the nearby intake pipe. As they jammed into the space under the pier, they could not find their way out. Some swam inside the bowels of the plant to meet their death; others milled around hopelessly, crowding all the closer as new recruits swam in under the boarding. Many apparently became enervated and diseased. This went on for at least six months, and Con[solidated] Ed[ison] operated a huge wire basket elevator to remove the dead and the dying.

Fishermen learned of the kill when great numbers of crows began concentrating at the plant dump to feast on the vast piles of rotting fish. On June 12, 1963, Dom Pirone, consulting biologist to the Long Island League of Salt Water Sportsmen; Harvey Hauptner, then the league's conservation chairman; Fred Luks, an outdoor columnist; and Art Glowka, an Eastern Airlines captain and angler, visited the Indian Point plant. Of that visit Pirone said: "We saw 10,000 dead and dying fish under the dock. We learned that Con Ed had two trucks hauling dead fish to the dump when the plant was in operation."[2]

EXERCISES

A. *As an exercise in restriction to find a real subject, take one of the following general subjects (or provide your own) and reduce it to a topic that might be treated thoroughly in two or three pages. State the real subject and indicate the content of the paper by notes similar to those used for the generation gap.*

Student Protest
Women's Liberation
College Education

B. *After discussing your notes with your instructor or your classmates, write the paper you have prewritten.*

Stating the Thesis   A writer who has discovered his real subject by prewriting has reached a decision about the content of his paper. In many though not all essays, that decision can be summarized in a brief statement, *preferably one sentence*. For example, the real subjects of the first two papers on the generation gap may be summarized as follows:

1. The so-called generation gap is more complex than the name suggests.

2. Differences in the values of young people and their parents are a result of their economic backgrounds.

Such a summary sentence is called a *thesis*. It usually appears at or near the beginning of the finished essay and thus tells the reader what main idea the essay is going to develop. It serves the same function in an essay as a topic sentence in a paragraph, that of an introductory summary of what is to come. The following sentences could be either topic sentences or theses, depending on whether they were to be developed through one paragraph or several.

[2] From Robert H. Boyle, "The Hudson River Lives," *Audubon*, March 1971. Reprinted from *Audubon Magazine* of the National Audubon Society © 1971 and with the permission of John Cushman Associates, Inc. Copyright © 1971 by Robert H. Boyle.

It's always what you don't have as a kid that's important when you're an adult.

Women drive as carefully as men do.

A policeman's lot is not a happy one.

Since the thesis states the main idea an essay will develop, it is used only in essays restricted to one idea. Many quite purposeful papers do not develop a main idea. A report of an event may have a purpose—to make the reader see what happened. A directive about how to do something may have a purpose—to show the reader how to do it. But such papers do not develop one dominant idea. The thesis essay is only one of several types of exposition, but it is the type usually emphasized in composition classes.

If your paper is not going to develop one main idea, there is no point in pretending it does by giving it a thesis. If you wish only to explain the T-formation in football, any attempt to begin with such a thesis as "The T-formation is the best all-purpose attack in football" distorts your purpose, since all you want to do is to explain how the formation works. The suggested thesis will confuse your reader about your intentions; worse, it may confuse you by causing you to digress from your purpose.

Good and Bad Theses

A good thesis is *restricted, unified,* and *precise.* To be restricted it must show what one idea the paper is going to develop. It thus limits the scope of the paper to what can be discussed in detail in the space available. For example, such a thesis as "If our civilization is to survive we must solve the interrelated problems of overpopulation, pollution, and war" might be suitable for a 10,000-word article in a magazine, but how could it be treated in meaningful detail in a three-page essay? This thesis is too big for any paper a student is likely to write. His three pages would give room for only a general summary of so broad an idea. He would be wise to restrict the thesis to something he can treat with some thoroughness, perhaps one of the following:

The invasion of Fort Lauderdale by hundreds of college students during the spring vacation results in pollution of that city's beaches.

A good part of the smog problem in Los Angeles is caused by the increased number of people who must drive considerable distances to and from work in the city.

The army's need to find some place to dump its accumulation of chemicals presents a serious pollution danger.

The procedure for restricting a thesis is the same as that for restricting a general subject. You break the unrestricted thesis into its parts and concentrate on a part you know about. For instance, almost any student could write an effective paper on the thesis, "I am a polluter," since he has only to look into the pollution he himself causes to find specific material for his paper.

EXERCISE

The unrestricted thesis, "There are serious objections to college systems of grading," can be broken into at least four sub-theses:

1. *The grading system is an inefficient way of evaluating a student's perform-ance.*
2. *The grading system emphasizes grades rather than learning.*
3. *The grading system leads to the unhealthful practice of cramming.*
4. *The grading system leads to cheating.*

Take any one of these sub-theses, concentrate on it, and jot down the kinds of illustrations and evidence that come to mind. Keep at this until you have more material than you could use in a three-page paper.

A good thesis is *unified* as well as restricted. It must express only one idea. The thesis "Flights to the moon are thrilling adventures which also produce practical benefits, yet it is difficult to justify their costs" says three things about moon-flights: (1) they are thrilling, (2) they produce prac-tical results, (3) it is difficult to justify their costs. If the student takes up these ideas in turn, he can easily emerge with a three-part paper which does not center on any one of the ideas. He could also write three different papers. If he wants to emphasize costs, he must make them the dominant part of his thesis by subordinating the other ideas, thus: "The costs of moon-flights are too great to be justified by the thrills and practical results we get from them."

EXERCISE

In the following examples the lack of unity at the left is removed by the re-vision at the right. Study the contrasted samples and explain why the first ver-sion lacks unity and how unity has been achieved in the second.

Not Unified	**Unified**
The United Nations Organization has major weaknesses and cannot prevent a major war.	The organization of the UN makes it incapable of preventing a war be-tween the major powers.
Printing has had a long and complex history during which it has brought about social and cultural reforms.	The development of printing has brought about social and cultural re-forms.
Mutual funds have grown rapidly in this country and offer advantages for the small investor.	Mutual funds have grown rapidly in this country because they offer ad-vantages for the small investor.

Finally, a thesis should be *precise*. It should be so stated that it can have only one interpretation. For example, the thesis "My home town is one of the most interesting in the state" does not indicate the content of the essay, since "interesting" is vague and can mean many things. A reader will want to know *in what way* the town is interesting. If he has to read the whole essay to find out, the thesis does not help him. Moreover, its vagueness exerts no control over the writer and does not suggest what kinds of material he needs.

Words such as "interesting," "colorful," "exciting," "inspiring," "unusual," "difficult" are too vague for a thesis. So are metaphors. The thesis "Where instructors are concerned, all that glitters is not gold" may seem clever, but what does it mean? The best scholars are not always the best teachers? Instructors who put on a good show in the classroom do not always help students to master the subject? Or something else? The precise meaning of a thesis should be immediately clear. Metaphors may be effective in the text of an essay, but they can be dangerous in a thesis.

EXERCISES

A. *Some of the following statements would make acceptable theses and some would not, because they lack restriction, unity, or clarity. Reject those that are not acceptable and explain your rejection.*

1. In the following essay I would like to tell you about VISTA.
2. Quaker education is essentially a religious education.
3. U.S. involvement in Indochina has had unfortunate results.
4. This essay will deal with the differences in salaries between teachers and professional athletes.
5. Our accomplishments in the space program are out of this world.
6. The popular conception of a schizophrenic as a person with a "split personality" is inaccurate.
7. Compared with other languages, English has a relatively simple grammar, but its spelling is complex and confusing.
8. Hawaii has a great future.
9. Student writing would be considerably improved if more attention were paid to prewriting.
10. The use of drugs has increased significantly in the last ten years. Some drugs, such as LSD, are admittedly dangerous, but there is considerable disagreement about marijuana.

B. *Take the thesis "My home town is interesting" and list all the things that might be considered interesting about your town. Would one or two of them make a good short paper? If so, what thesis would you write for that paper?*

C. *Take any campus problem that interests you and prewrite it so as to find a thesis that you feel confident you could develop adequately in about three pages.*

D. *As a final test of your ability to see the relation between purpose and development, read the following student essay and answer the questions that follow it.*

On Your Own

[1] Before I came to this campus I knew things would be rough. I had heard from friends ahead of me in high school how big the U was and that a new freshman was sure to feel lost and lonely for a time. I had also been told that the work would be much harder than I was used to and that students got less help from the teachers. All this advice got summed up in the phrase, "At the U you're on your own." Now after three weeks here I know what the older fellows meant.

[2] During Freshman Week I didn't know whether I was coming or going. I never had so many different activities crowded into one week. The first thing I did when I arrived on campus was to go to the dormitory and get my room. There I met my roommate, whom I had written a couple of times to during the summer. He introduced me to some of the other fellows in the dorm, and we compared notes about what we had done in high school and what we wanted to do here. It was a nice beginning for college, for I got to know several students who have been my good friends ever since.

[3] During the next three or four days we had something scheduled every minute. We took physical examinations and scholastic tests and I had to take an extra math test because I did not have enough math in high school. After the tests we went to see our advisers, who told us what subjects we should take and helped us plan our programs. I didn't have too much trouble because one of the older boys in the dorm had briefed me on the courses I'd have to take, although the adviser almost refused to OK my program because I had forgotten to bring the slip showing I had taken my physical.

[4] Registration wasn't as bad as I had been told. I came early in the alphabet, so I was able to get all of the classes my adviser had approved, except that I had to switch hours for my PE section. Those who came later were less lucky. By then classes were pretty well filled up and some students practically had to tear up their programs and start over again.

[5] My real troubles began when classes started. Where my most difficulty was was the assignments. I thought I understood the work as it was being taken up in class, but it was a different story when I tried to do the assignments. Worst of all, every one of my instructors seemed to have the idea that his class was the only one I was taking. I had more homework for each course

than I had for all my courses together in high school. Fortunately several of us in the dorm studied together and were able to help each other out.

1. What is the thesis of this essay as it is revealed in the first paragraph?

2. Taking each of the numbered paragraphs in turn, decide whether they do or do not consistently develop that thesis. Explain your judgment by reference to the text.

3. After studying the emphasis within the essay, decide what its real subject is. What is the student really trying to show?

4. If you find a conflict between the real subject and the student's thesis, what thesis would you suggest to remove that conflict?

5. What is the minimum revision you would suggest to make the essay a consistent development of the real subject?

6. What lesson, or moral, do you draw from your study of this essay about the relation between purpose and development?

Chapter 2

Sources of Material

A writer's material consists of the facts, examples, and opinions he uses to make his real subject clear to himself and to his readers. It comes from two general sources: from what he has experienced at first hand, and from what he has learned through conversation and reading. Such material is stored in his memory and can be recalled and used as needed. He selects what is pertinent and adapts it to his purpose. In this chapter we will deal with four main sources: *personal experience, observation, interviews,* and *reading.*

PERSONAL EXPERIENCE

It can reasonably be said that what one hears and reads is as much a part of his personal experience as what he sees or does, but here we are going to limit "personal experience" to one's memory of events, people, and places that one knows at first hand, or to the feelings one has had in particular situations, or to ideas suggested by these experiences and feelings considered in retrospect.

The following student essay is drawn from a girl's experience and her reactions to it.

Places of Pleasure

One night, because we had nothing better to do, my roommate and another girl and I hopped in the car and set off for a grand tour of the campus dives. On my journey I found neither dens of iniquity nor glimpses of a promised land, but merely the mildly amusing sequence of scenes I had expected. I say amusing, for nothing is more a point of gentle laughter than a child; no one can help smiling when he sees a youngster mimicking the ludicrous actions of his elders in all seriousness; and at every place I went I saw children playing at being adults.

I saw children smoking in every way they had ever seen: in a nervous, endless chain; languidly as Cleopatra; in the fashion of underworld characters; or with a pseudo-sophisticated flick of the wrist.

I saw children talking in every tone imaginable: boisterously, pretentiously in earnest, in the manner of men and women of the world, or with an air of boredom.

I saw children drinking beer: they drank it from bottles, from glasses, from pitchers; they sipped it, they gulped it, they studied it; they adored it.

And all the time I felt I was in a land of Lilliputians with everything built to size: there were small rooms, cozy seats, tiny bottles, pint-sized ash trays, baby-faced proprietors, and little boy waiters. What could be more charming! And yet after a few moments of amusement I found myself becoming absolutely bored. . . .

My feeling of boredom melted to pity and I felt moved to cry out in a ringing voice with dramatic pauses—"Unhappy generation! You are right in your unhappiness. Your pleasures are not dictated to you. There is more joy to living than this. Rise up! Go forth!"—when suddenly it occurred to me that perhaps I was the odd personality, unable to enjoy standard entertainment. Maybe they were really having a good time.

In a cloud of uncertainty I followed my friends back to the dorm and got into the shower, the only place where my powers of reasoning function properly, and began to talk to myself.

"Jane," I said, "you have smoked L & M, Lucky Strike, Viceroy, Marlboro, Winston, Kentucky Brand, Camel, Chesterfield, and homemade cigarettes. You have talked to priests, psychiatrists, businessmen, teachers, teenagers, Chinese, Czechoslovakians, Japanese, Hawaiians, Germans, Hungarians, Swedish, English, and Americans about life, death, philosophy, sex, politics, morals, religion, and the future of America. You have drunk whiskey, vodka, rum, gin, vermouth, champagne, and your father's wine in bedrooms, barrooms, bathrooms, bowling alleys, basements, cocktail lounges, cars, and swimming pools. Have or have not all these things been fun?"

"Yes," I sighed, remembering.

"And have you or have you not enjoyed, along with smoking, jabbering, and drinking, the pleasures of reading, listening to music, watching plays, and praying on your knees to a hidden God?"

"I have," I replied, beginning to see the light.

"Then what right have you to laugh at, sneer at, pity, or judge the people you saw in the places you went to tonight?"

"No right at all," I whispered, scrubbing my ears.

But as I turned on the cold water all my confidence and defiance came back to me and "There was something sad and wrong in those places!" I cried to my departing self.

The things this writer saw and heard on her visit to the campus spots—people drinking beer, smoking, and talking—are not unusual. Many students have similar experiences. What transforms this experience into an effective paper is the girl's attitudes and reactions. Her reactions change as she reconsiders what she has seen, and it is the record of this change, not of the things she saw, that impresses and interests a reader. The success of the paper lies in the girl's *evaluation* of her experience.

The ability to evaluate experience is what gives writing its character, because the evaluation produces a personal view of the subject. Since each personal view is unique, it gives the writer something original to say. In the following extract from a book by James Baldwin, the impact on a reader comes not from the report of what happened to the author, but from the significance he attaches to what happened, to his evaluation of his experience.

... Negroes in this country—and Negroes do not, strictly or legally speaking, exist in any other—are taught really to despise themselves from the moment their eyes open on the world. This world is white and they are black. White people hold the power, which means that they are superior to blacks (intrinsically, that is: God decreed it so), and the world has innumerable ways of making this difference known and felt and feared. Long before the Negro child perceives this difference, and even longer before he understands it, he has begun to react to it, he has begun to be controlled by it. Every effort made by the child's elders to prepare him for a fate from which they cannot protect him causes him secretly, in terror, to begin to await, without knowing that he is doing so, his mysterious and inexorable punishment. He must be "good" not only in order to please his parents and not only to avoid being punished by them; behind their authority stands another, nameless and impersonal, infinitely harder to please, and bottomlessly cruel. And this filters into the child's consciousness through his parents' tone of voice as he is being exhorted, punished, or loved; in the sudden, uncontrollable note of fear heard in his mother's or his father's voice when he has strayed beyond some particular boundary. He does not know what the boundary is, and he can get no explanation of it, which is frightening enough, but the fear he hears in the voices of his elders is more frightening still. The fear that I heard in my father's voice, for example, when he realized that I really believed I could do anything a white boy could do, and had every intention of proving it, was not at all like the fear I heard when one of us was ill or had fallen down the stairs or strayed too far from the house. It was another fear, a fear that the child, in challenging the white world's assumptions, was putting himself in the path of destruction. A child cannot, thank Heaven, know how vast and how merciless is the nature of power, with what unbelievable cruelty people treat each other. He reacts to the fear in his parents' voices because his parents hold up the world for him and he has no protection without them. I defended myself, as I imagined, against the fear my father made me feel by remembering that he was very old-fashioned. Also, I prided myself on the fact that I already knew how to outwit him. To defend oneself against a fear is simply to insure that one will, one day, be conquered by it; fears must be faced. As for one's wits, it is just not true that one can live by them—not, that is, if one wishes really to live. That summer, in any case, all the fears with which I had grown up, and which were now a part of me and controlled my vision of the world, rose up like a wall between the world and me, and drove me into the church.[1]

Baldwin does not claim that the things that happened to him were unique. He assumes, as his purpose requires, that they happen to most young blacks. It is his evaluation of his experience—the significance he generalizes from it —that produces its effect on the reader. The author's real subject is not what happened to James Baldwin, but what it is like to grow up as a black boy in a society dominated by white people.

The two passages you have just read suggest the wide range of possible papers that can be written from personal experience. Within that range each writer has ample room to choose what he wants to do. There is no such person as the student who has "nothing to write about"; there are only students who have not evaluated their experiences acutely enough to find real subjects in them.

EXERCISE

Look back on some part of your own life—for example, your changing attitudes toward your parents, the other sex, school, adolescence, maturity—and try to evaluate it. Do not write, but think about what you might say about that subject. Then pick the train of thought which seems most promising to you. Stay with that train of thought until you begin to see a possible paper emerging. When you are satisfied, write a memorandum to yourself about what you want to say and how. Keep it for future use.

OBSERVATION

A second major source of material is the sensory impressions we get when we examine anything closely and carefully. Most of us, most of the time, notice only a little of what we see, hear, feel, taste, and smell. This is natural, because much of the time these impressions do not interest us. When we are looking for a golf ball that we drove into the rough we are not going to distract ourselves by examining the trees. But when our interest is aroused, or we feel a real need to observe, we can readily train ourselves to do so. One student reported that during initiation, when he had to shine the shoes of all the upperclassmen in his fraternity, he learned to identify every pair by

[1] From *The Fire Next Time* by James Baldwin. Copyright © 1962, 1963 by James Baldwin. Reprinted by permission of the publisher, The Dial Press.

its peculiar wrinkles and scuffs. From these observations he wrote an amusing little paper in which he imagined the characters of his brothers from their shoes and then showed how wrong these imaginings were. Another, visiting an old house which had been vacant for some time, noticed that a cane had stood in a corner so long that its shaft had bent. Later he was able to use this observation to great effect in a paper he was writing, as a symbol of the passage of time.

Interpreting Observations

Usually observations become important to us only when we can attach some significance to them. A footprint on a crowded beach would not normally arouse strong emotions, but to Robinson Crusoe on his desert island a naked footprint became tremendously important, because it meant (that is, he interpreted it to mean) that there was someone else on the island, someone who could be a source of danger.

Basic to interpretation is inference-making. An *inference* is a conclusion or judgment which expresses some significance or attitude suggested by what is seen, heard, or read. We see the sky clouding up and infer that rain is coming, or we hear a noise outside the kitchen door and infer that some animal is at the garbage can. Sometimes a single observation may trigger a chain of inferences. Thus Robinson Crusoe saw a footprint and inferred (1) that somebody else was on the island, (2) that there was a possibility of danger from that person, (3) that he should take precautions against that danger. In all such instances the thing observed becomes a sign of something, and the inference interprets the sign.

The following dialogue is an amusing example of drawing inferences from observations.

The Camera Eye[2]
by Newman Levy

We were seated in the lobby of the hotel as she walked swiftly by us, turned a corner sharply, and was gone.

"That's an uncommonly good-looking girl," I said to my wife, who was deep in a crossword puzzle.

"Do you mean the one in that imitation blue taffeta dress with the green and red flowered design?"

"The girl that just walked by."

"Yes," said my wife, "with that dowdy rayon dress on. It's a copy of one I saw at Hattie Carnegie's, and a poor copy at that. You'd think, though, that she'd have better taste than to wear a chartreuse hat with it, especially with her bleached hair."

"Bleached? I didn't notice her hair was bleached."

[2] From *The Atlantic Monthly*, December 1952. Copyright © 1952 by The Atlantic Monthly Company, Boston, Mass. Reprinted with permission.

"Good heavens, you could almost smell the peroxide. I don't mind a bit of make-up provided it looks fairly natural. But you could scrape that rouge off with a knife. They ought to add a course in make-up to the curriculum at Smith."

"Smith? Why Smith?"

"From her class pin, of course. You must have noticed it hanging from her charm bracelet."

"I wasn't looking at her wrist."

"I'll bet you weren't. Nor at those fat legs of hers, either. A woman with legs like that shouldn't wear high-heeled patent-leather shoes."

"I thought she was a very pretty girl," I said apologetically.

"Well, you may be right," said my wife. "I was busy with my puzzle and I didn't notice her particularly. What's the name of a President of the United States in six letters, beginning with T?"

All the husband sees is "an uncommonly good-looking girl." His wife sees the color and material of the girl's dress, her hat, hair, class pin, bracelet, legs, and shoes, and she interprets these details by drawing inferences from them ("imitation," "dowdy," "poor copy," "excessive make-up," "fat legs," etc.). We may wonder whether all her inferences were the result of unbiased observation, or whether they were tinged by disapproval of her husband's attention to the girl. But these inferences are required by the writer's purpose. He has to make the woman catty and her husband vague to establish the contrast he wants, just as he has to show that, for all her acute observation, she cannot think of a President whose name has six letters, beginning with T. Quite evidently she attaches more importance to some things than to others.

Next to indifference, the greatest obstacle to accurate observation is the willingness to settle for a general impression. It is easier to say that a girl is "uncommonly pretty" than to cite the details on which that inference is based. As a result we often state a general impression which makes too quick a leap from details to inference. A reader may have difficulty making that leap; he may need more information than he has been given. Teachers are inclined to diagnose this kind of over-generalization as a failure to use specific diction. But the trouble often lies in the student's failure to observe all the significant details of the subject before he rushes into a general impression. The student cannot know what specific diction to use until he knows what specific image to convey.

A general impression is important, since it is the pattern by which the specific details are finally organized. But the pattern should take shape in the observer's mind as a response to individual details; otherwise he may ignore details that are significant and jump to a mistaken interpretation or one that is only partly true. The following exercise is designed to make you study details *before* you make a comprehensive inference about the artist's purpose.

EXERCISE

On pages 28–29 are reproduced two engravings by the eighteenth-century artist, William Hogarth. The one at the left is entitled "Beer Street"; the one at the right, "Gin Lane." Study the pictures carefully and answer the following questions. Be sure you answer each question before you go on to the next.

1. What is the financial condition of the pawnbroker in each picture? What can you infer by looking at his house? What is the pawnbroker doing in each? List the details which lead you to your inference in each case.

2. Describe the physical, financial, and mental condition of the populace in each picture. Specify details in each picture which justify your inference. Discuss both foreground and background figures in each picture, their appearance, and their activities.

3. What is the status of housing and the building trades in each picture? Specify details which led you to your inferences.

4. Can you draw any inferences as to why Hogarth would have favored one beverage over the other? What class of society is he mainly depicting?

Observation and Discovery

The materials you get from observation will often be reshaped in your mind by the inferences you make about them. This reshaping will contain something of you and thus be your personal re-creation of the original material. Usually this re-creation grows out of the way you combine existing material. You discover a new relationship between A and B, and that relationship is an insight or an idea you have contributed. The following student essay illustrates the process.

Twinkletoes and the Tailback

Although Dame Margot Fonteyn, internationally famed ballerina, might not like being compared to Gale Sayers, running back of the Chicago Bears football team, some of the basic requirements of their respective professions are similar. A ballet buff may be inclined to scoff at the idea that the delicate beauty of the dance could be likened to the rough and tumble of football, but if one watches the game with discerning eyes, the moves and counter-moves of the opposing teams will gradually come to have a flow of movement which, in a broad sense, resembles a panorama of dancers. A player leaping to catch a forward pass needs the same sense of timing and agility as a ballerina executing a *grand jeté*.

Whether it is referred to as gracefulness in the ballerina or coordination in the football player, both expressions describe an ease of movement which is an absolute necessity for either profession. Along with this natural talent, emphasis is placed on physical fitness. Most of the training and exercises are

Beer Street, engraving by William Hogarth, 1697-1764, from the National Gallery of Art, Rosenwald Collection, Washington, D.C.

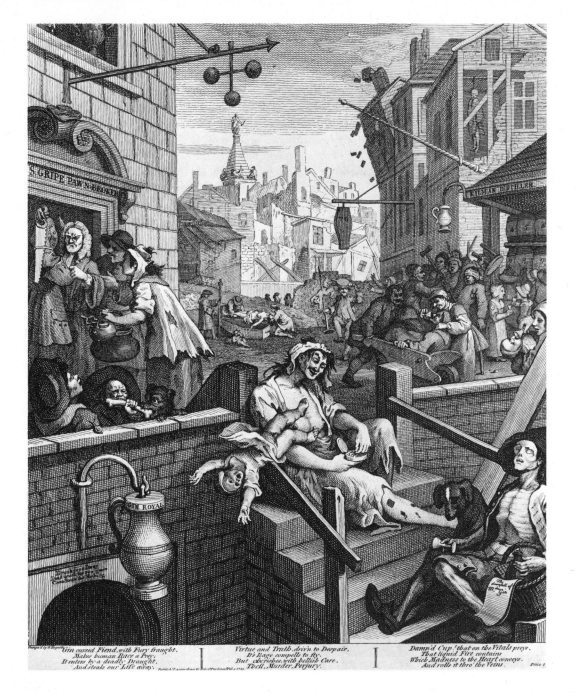

Gin Lane, engraving by William Hogarth, 1697-1764, from the National Gallery of Art, Rosenwald Collection, Washington, D.C.

concentrated on developing the muscles of the legs in order to strengthen them, for strong legs are required to sustain the performer until the final gun has been fired or the last note of music sounded.

Both professions also demand a deep emotional commitment. The depth of this commitment is often the only difference between being in the chorus or being the prima ballerina. A ballerina must remain on her toes, both literally and figuratively, or she will give a lackluster performance which separates a competent performance from a superb one. The football player must be "up" for each game or his playing will be mechanical and lack the "second effort" which is the mark of a good professional. Many players who were stars in their college days have failed to make the transition into the professional ranks because they were playing not for love of the game but only for money. The true professional in either field is one who would continue to give his best performance even if the financial rewards were not as great.

In both professions the pre-performance planning is carefully worked out. The choreography for a ballet has been composed before the ballerina goes on the stage. Her success in any particular role is not so dependent on any innovation she may bring to it as on the perfection with which she executes it. All the plays of any football team have similarly been worked out before the game, and victory is won by the concentrated and unified effort of all its members. Practice is therefore an essential ingredient of success. Daily practice, perfecting all the moves that have been planned, is indispensable to both groups.

It would be hard to think of any two groups more unlike than ballerinas and professional football players, but out of her observations of both, the writer of this paper made a discovery that they are surprisingly alike. The detailed explanation of the similarities she found produces an effective and highly original paper.

The ability to discover similarities between otherwise unlike things is an important source of creative thinking in all fields. The history of science shows many examples of an investigator finding a clue to the solution of his problem in the discovery of an analogy, the classic example being the relation Newton is alleged to have seen between the falling apple and the principle of gravity. In literature the ability to see similarities is a prerequisite for metaphors and puns and for much literary criticism. As "Twinkletoes and the Tailback" shows, this faculty can provide excellent material for an essay.

INTERVIEWS

Another good way to get material about a subject is to talk with someone who knows it at first hand. One approach to this source is through an interview. An interview is a planned conversation, usually prearranged, with an expert, an eyewitness, a participant, or someone with special information or a special point of view. You have probably heard dozens of such interviews on television programs like "Meet the Press," "Face the Nation," or the programs conducted by Dick Cavett and David Frost, and you have read others in a variety of magazines.

In conducting an interview the following advice may be helpful:

1. Before you seek an interview know as much as you reasonably can about the person you are to interview. Check the spelling and pronunciation of his name, the title of his present position, the experience that qualifies him to be an expert. If you cannot find that information in a standard biographical reference work,[3] consult someone who knows him well enough to give it to you.

2. Decide what information you want and prepare questions that will get this information. Be sure the questions are as clear as you can make them.

3. Do not limit your questions to those that invite "Yes" or "No" or simple factual answers. Your informant may have valuable insights to offer which will not be encouraged by such restricted questions. Let him answer the questions in his own way. But if he leaves part of a question unanswered, repeat it in a more restricted form—for example: "Mr. Johnson, from what you have said would I be correct in assuming that you think colleges should admit students only on the basis of an entrance examination?"

4. If his answers are too general or are not clear to you, follow them up with a request for further information. Notice how David Frost does this in an interview with Truman Capote.

FROST: You . . . said once, when you were analyzing whether you would have gone to a psychiatrist, that it might "have lessened the penalties I pay." I can't imagine you ever paying penalties. Have you?

CAPOTE: Sure, everybody pays penalties.

FROST: What sort of people pay?

CAPOTE: In the process of maturing, if you mature at all, one has to pay a certain price.

FROST: What do you mean?

CAPOTE: I don't think it's possible to go through life, unless you're a complete idiot, without being continuously hurt one way or another. The only thing that doesn't hurt me is to pick up a newspaper and read some libelous thing about me or some bad review of something. That doesn't bother me at all. But if I feel somebody has betrayed me in some way or been disloyal or something, I get terribly upset about it.[4]

---

[3] Such as *Who's Who in America* or more specialized references such as *Who's Who in Education* or the *Directory of American Scholars*.

[4] From David Frost, *The Americans* (New York: Stein and Day, 1970).

5. Take adequate notes, not during the interview, but immediately afterward, while your informant's comments are still fresh in your mind. There is no objection to jotting down an occasional brief note during the interview, but any attempt to get down everything that is said will slow the conversation. Your informant will then begin to dictate his answers so that you can get them on paper, and that will inhibit both what he says and how he says it. Of course, a tape recorder offers an excellent and usually acceptable means of recording the whole interview. But if you do not have one, take only enough notes to let you summarize the interview immediately after it is finished. You will see an example of such a summary at the end of the following published interview.

The following selection is an extract from an account of an interview with David Ben-Gurion.[5] Because the whole interview is too long to print here certain parts have been omitted and the omissions indicated by ellipses (. . .). The omitted material is essentially background information and additional comments that Ben-Gurion makes later in the interview. These omissions do not distort the content of his comments on the conditions necessary to a permanent peace.

Amid the imponderables of a Middle East thrown violently out of focus by the death of President Nasser, one towering personality remains—Israel's legendary elder statesman, David Ben-Gurion, father of the Jewish state, for fifteen years its ironhanded first Prime Minister, author of its declaration of independence, creator of its incomparable armed forces, and possibly the closest our age has come to the "philosopher-king" concept immortalized by his favorite author, Plato. . . .

Recently I spent an afternoon with this remarkable man at his desert retreat —kibbutz Sde Boker—deep in the Negev. With Nasser's funeral rites in Cairo still a vivid memory, I wanted to know how Nasser's long-time rival envisaged the future of the Middle East. I was also anxious to probe the questing mind that, during early Egyptian air raids, immersed itself in the Greek and Chinese classics, to see if there might be found wisdom to illumine some of the confusions of the world scene. . . .

What did Ben-Gurion think about it all? The stocky figure, encased in a huge, gray turtle-neck sweater against the desert's winter chill, shot upright in his chair. . . . The blue eyes blazed as a stabbing forefinger punctuated his fluent, heavily accented English.

"Peace, *real* peace, is now the great necessity for us," he said. "It is worth almost any sacrifice. To get it, we must return to the borders before 1967. If I were still Prime Minister, I would announce that we are prepared to give back all the territory occupied in the Six-Day War except East Jerusalem and the Golan Heights—Jerusalem for history's sake, the Golan for security."

[5] From John McCook Roots, "Peace Is More Important Than Real Estate," *Saturday Review*, April 3, 1971. Copyright 1971 Saturday Review, Inc.

These were startling and controversial views. With the future of his country at stake, and considering the tough public line of his own government, did he really wish to go on record as strongly as this?

"Certainly," he shot back. "I am a realist and see things as they are. When I think of the future of Israel, I only consider the country before the Six-Day War. We must return to 1967. We should give all gains back, except Jerusalem and the Golan, and these we should negotiate about." Then, as if anticipating the obvious query: "Sinai? Sharm el Sheikh? Gaza? The West Bank? Let them go. Peace is more important than real estate. We don't need the territory. With the proper irrigation we now have enough land right here in the Negev to care for all the Jews in the world—if they come. And they certainly will not all come. No, we don't require more land.

"As for security, militarily defensible borders, while desirable, cannot by themselves guarantee our future. *Real* peace with our Arab neighbors—mutual trust and friendship—that is the only true security. . . ."

"Of course," he conceded, gesturing toward a picture of Abraham Lincoln on the wall, "these frontiers I have indicated would be, from our point of view, far from ideal. But a bad peace is better than a good war." . . .

What is important in this part of the interview is Ben-Gurion's judgment of what Israel should do to encourage an enduring peace. To make sure that he has that position down in a form that will permit easy and accurate recall, the interviewer might summarize the content of Ben-Gurion's remarks as follows:

Ben-Gurion believes compelling necessity in Middle East is lasting peace between Arabs and Israeli: Such peace impossible by military means: must rest on mutual trust and friendship. To help establish this relationship, Ben-Gurion says Israel should return all territory occupied at end of 1967 war. Admits return of occupied territories not ideal solution from Israeli view, but insists Israeli do not really need these lands: "Peace is more important than real estate."

Such a summary serves two purposes. It records the gist of the interview, and the very act of summarizing clarifies and reinforces the interviewer's memory of what was said. The summary makes it certain that he can recall accurately, even some time later, the main point Ben-Gurion made.

EXERCISE

Select two people to interview on one of the following general subjects. Explain why you chose these particular people and write out the chief questions you would ask each of them.

1. The response of the college to the request for more emphasis on black studies.

2. Student attitudes toward the use of marijuana.

3. The advisability of appointing a student representative to the Board of Trustees of your college.

READING

A major source of material for college writing is reading—not only reading done for course work, but general reading, including newspapers and magazines. Some of this reading will be purposeful, in a search of material for immediate use. Some of it will be recreational, done with no present intention of use. In either case the information and attitudes you encounter will become part of your total experience and will be subject to recall and use when some purpose makes them relevant.

The following passage develops a thesis which is stated in the first paragraph. The material supporting the thesis is drawn from general reading. The inference expressed in the thesis is probably based on a great variety of sources, but when the writer comes to develop that inference in his essay he illustrates it by three specific references to things he has read. First, identify these references. Second, discuss their appropriateness to the thesis. Third, from your own reading suggest at least one more reference that might be used to support this thesis.

"It's not my fault! it's not my fault! Nothing in this lousy world is my fault, don't you see that? I don't want it to be and it can't be and it won't be." This outcry comes from Kerouac's Sal Paradise, but it expresses the deep conviction of multitudes of irresponsibles in the age of self-pity. It is a curious paradox that, while the self is the center of all things, the self is never to blame for anything.

The fault is always the fault of someone or of something else. This is implicit in all the letters which are addressed to Abigail Van Buren. "Dear Abby: This is my problem . . . My husband . . ." "Dear Abby: Here is my problem . . . My wife . . ." Or it may be my son, my daughter, my mother-in-law, my neighbors. It is never Me.

Blame it on God, the girls, or the government, on heredity, or on the environment, on the parents, on the siblings, on the cold war, on the pressures toward conformity, on being unloved and unwanted. But don't blame it on me, the very center around which the whole universe revolves. This me is like the innocent and apparently unmenacing Dennis, who stands before an accusing mother, in the middle of the parlor, with his body twisted about as he looks back on the carpet at some curious mud tracks which lead right up to his heels. Says Dennis, in bewilderment, "I don't know what that stuff is . . . it just keeps following me."[6]

Notice the process by which the specific references are generalized into the inference stated in the thesis. Presumably the writer encountered his three illustrations in different contexts serving different purposes. As these and other references accumulated in his mind he began to fit them into a pattern: "I am never to blame; it is always somebody else." This pattern gave him his thesis, a generalization from numerous bits of reading. The process involves three stages: first, acquiring bits of apparently unrelated material from reading; second, seeing a common element in them and recognizing that they fit into a pattern and illustrate an idea; third, expressing the idea as a thesis, thus establishing the controlling idea of a piece of writing.

Some of the material you use in class papers will come from reading on an assigned or chosen subject. The following two paragraphs, which state and begin to develop a thesis, are from a student paper based on special reading.

The habits of careful research and independent thinking characteristic of Thomas Jefferson's writings in his adult life were established when he was a student of law. It was during his student years that Jefferson developed what he termed his "canine appetite" for reading. It was also during this time that his almost belligerent demand to the right to do his own thinking and his habit of freely exercising that right were formed.

As a boy, at the Reverend Dr. Maury's school, Jefferson was considered a superior student, although he sometimes got behind in his assignments and had to depend on occasional holidays to allow him to catch up. During his first year at William and Mary he allowed social activities to take more of his time, attention, and money than he later thought wise. Since he was an ardent horseman, a competent violinist, a good dancer, and an easy and pleasant conversationalist who was popular with the young ladies of Williamsburg, he might have been expected to continue his college career as he had begun it, but in his second year he reduced his social activities and devoted himself more intensively to his studies. The following year, at the age of nineteen, he began to read law under George Wythe, one of the ablest lawyers in

[6] From Robert Elliot Fitch, *Odyssey of the Self-Centered Self* (New York: Harcourt, Brace & World, Inc., 1961).

the colonies. Under Wythe's influence his scholarly habits were firmly established. Jefferson himself described these years as "a time of life when I was bold in the pursuit of knowledge, never fearing to follow truth and reason to whatever results they led, and bearding every authority which stood in their way."

These two paragraphs are based on considerable reading in several sources. The writer made notes as she read, inferred a thesis from her notes, selected and reorganized them to support her thesis, and then summarized the material in her own words. All her information came from reading, but not in the form shown here. This form was *her* contribution. By selecting and reorganizing her notes to suit her purpose and then working them into a unified composition, she gave her materials new shape. The process was not basically different from that used in the selection on pages 34–35 and in the Ben-Gurion interview.

Your main source of published material will be your college library. Somebody once said that if he wanted to found a college and had only a limited amount of money, he would first build a library. If he had any money left, he would then build a dormitory. If he still had money, he would build a place where students could come together to talk. Such a college would have serious deficiencies, but the priority which puts the library first emphasizes its importance to college education.

There is not space in this chapter to discuss the resources of a library; that subject is postponed to Chapter 11. But four points can be made here. (1) Every effective writer is informed, at least on the subject he is writing about. (2) Personal experience, however rich, is sharply limited, and reading is the quickest and easiest way to extend it. (3) Your best source of reading material is the nearest good library. (4) The more you explore that library and learn of its resources, the better informed you will be.

Interpreting Reading

Although all reading requires interpretation of printed symbols, some kinds of reading are more difficult to interpret than others. Poetry is usually more difficult than nonfiction prose, partly because a poet is less interested than a prose writer in conveying one specific meaning. The essayist tries to convey information or control the reader's responses, thus limiting him to one clear interpretation. The poet often invites a variety of responses to the same symbols. For this reason the interpretation of a poem is not an unquestionable decision about what the poem "means"; it is a revelation of how the reader reads the poem. The same is true for much fiction.

Literary interpretation begins with close examination of the text. Some students may be tempted by a general impression into making a superficial interpretation. Or they may feel frustrated and give up too quickly when the writing seems "hard." To avoid errors, examine the text piece by piece and let successive observations suggest a pattern for the whole. If you begin with observations about individual words and gradually larger units, you may achieve a valid cumulative understanding of the whole.

On first reading the following poem by Emily Dickinson, some readers assume that they grasp its meaning immediately: "It's just a poem about flowers and how soon they die." But only careful observation can lead to a more satisfying interpretation.

> Apparently with no surprise
> To any happy Flower
> The Frost beheads it at its play—
> In accidental power—
> The blonde Assassin passes on—
> The Sun proceeds unmoved
> To measure off another Day
> For an Approving God.

1. Note how simple is the poem's form—two quatrains with a rhythm found often in poems for children. A reader might assume that any idea embodied in so simple a form must be equally simple.

2. Note the use of capitals to personify and vitalize the "characters."

3. At first reading, the poem seems merely to describe frost nipping the head of a flower which has bloomed too early—or too late.

4. On closer observation, one expression emerges as unusual and arresting. Why is the frost personified as a *blonde* Assassin"? "Assassin" suggests evil; if the poet meant to provide merely a visual detail, why didn't she write "white assassin," since frost is more accurately white than blonde? Perhaps she intended some paradoxical fusion between the favorable connotations of "blonde" ("blondes have more fun") and the evil connotations of "assassin."

5. Once this curious collision of impressions is observed, other words assume new interest. The frost's power is "accidental," suggesting that it is an unintentional murderer, merely playing. The "happy" flower feels "no surprise" at becoming the victim of violence. In the human world, assassination is intentional, the victim is surprised, and a witness, unlike the "unmoved" Sun, is shocked. The poet describes actions in the natural world where there are no human feelings; but because she personifies Flowers, Frost, and Sun, we judge their actions by human standards. This device emphasizes two points: (a) that violence in nature seems like human violence, (b) but that, for non-human nature, our normal reactions and values are inappropriate.

6. The last line states that God approves the violence the poem describes. Our theologies predispose us to think of God as gentle, or at least just. Why, then, should He approve the destruction of a lovely flower, particularly one made to resemble an innocent human victim? It begins to seem that the poem is ironic.

7. Once you sense the irony, you will have a better idea of what the poem intends. There is a wide gap between man-made justice and morality and the world of nature, in which waste and violence are commonplace and imply neither good nor evil. Can these contradictory systems both be valid? You are allowed your own answer. You may interpret the poem to mean that man is not subject to the same indifferent waste and violence as the rest of nature, but lives by better values. Or you may infer that man's confidence in a moral order is shown to be a delusion because of what happens in nature.

By now you probably have an interpretation consistent with the full text of the poem. If so, you have come to realize that the poem is no simple description of a natural event, but a brief expression of a complex philosophical question. You also realize that the poem's simple form is deceptive, and the burden of meaning is greater than it suggests.

Whatever your interpretation, you now have something to say. You can show what the poem means to you, or you can evaluate the judgment you believe it makes about life. If the latter, you may raise and explore the question whether man's ethical standards are contradicted by nature; you may discuss the possible sentimentality which personification encourages; you may attack the poem as trivial, or you may praise it for its insight into man's relation to nature. Whatever your choice, you have found something to write about by close reading and interpretation. This discovery gives you the real subject of your paper and all the material you need to develop it.

EXERCISES

A. *The following selection offers an excellent example of the results of an observation on a mind equipped to explore its implications. Read the article and answer the questions that follow it.*

Driftwood on the Ice[7]

While on a voyage in the sealing ship *Viking* to the Arctic Ocean in 1882, Fridtjof Nansen, then an ambitious twenty-one-year-old naturalist, who had gone along to learn something at first hand about the methods of marine research, noticed a piece of driftwood on a floe off the coast of Greenland. To the rest of the ship's company, the log meant nothing. To an Eskimo, it might have meant an added stick of valuable firewood. But to young Nansen's mind it posed a problem: What kind of wood was it? Where had it come from? Before Nansen stopped thinking and investigating, he had become the last man in history "to discover an ocean"; he had come nearer the North Pole than any other human being up to that time; and he had helped mightily in the founding of a new science, that of oceanography.

[7] From Harold A. Larrabee, *Reliable Knowledge* (Boston: Houghton Mifflin Company, 1964).

His first question about the driftwood was easily answered: it was some sort of pine. That ended his concern with that particular log of wood. For this simple step of classification made available a large amount of accumulated botanical information concerning the localities where pine trees do and do not grow. Nansen now had a basis for framing a number of possible answers to his second question. He knew, for example, that there were no pine trees on Greenland, Iceland, or Spitzbergen; so those points of origin could be eliminated. There were, however, plenty of pine trees in North America, Norway, and Siberia. But the question remained: from which of these three countries could the driftwood have come by the aid of an ocean current and borne on top of a cake of floating ice? From his personal knowledge of the normal behavior of driftwood and floes, Nansen was reasonably sure that the log had not climbed aboard the floating ice. Therefore, it must have fallen upon the ice from somewhere along the shore. That meant, he deduced, that it had come from a land with pine trees growing near the shore, and with offshore formations of floating ice.

His next step was to try out successively in his mind the North America, the Norway, and the Siberia hypotheses. He knew that the Gulf Stream came northward from the southern coast of North America, where there were pine trees, but no ice. Norway's shores were likewise pine-clad but ice-free; so both of those hypotheses could be eliminated. That left Siberia, which had both pine trees and offshore floes. The log, he conjectured, must have been brought from the eastern Siberian coast to Greenland by a hitherto-unknown drift current across the Arctic regions, which might well be one great ocean. Nansen's theory was scoffed at as absurd, although it was soon powerfully reinforced by other evidence, especially by the finding of unmistakable relics, on floating ice off the southwest coast of Greenland, of the American polar ship *Jeanette*, which had been wrecked north of the New Siberian Islands three years before. In an address before the Christiania Geographical Society in February, 1890, Nansen summed up his reasons for believing that "a current flows at some point between the Pole and Franz Joseph Land from the Siberian Arctic Sea to the east coast of Greenland"; and announced his plan to prove his theory in a spectacular fashion by drifting across the polar sea in a ship carried only by the slowly moving ice pack. This "illogical scheme of self-destruction" was hailed as "sheer madness" by most of the contemporary authorities on Arctic exploration; but they were silenced by the famous voyage of the *Fram* (1893–96) from the coast of Siberia to a point near Spitzbergen, propelled solely by the ocean current beneath the ice in which the stout ship had been frozen fast. Few men have seen their theories more triumphantly vindicated than did Nansen. His train of thought and observation, starting from the driftwood on the ice, not only revolutionized the technique of polar exploration; but also established the essential characteristics of the Arctic Ocean, thus paving the way for wholly unforeseen results of great practical importance in solving the future problems of weather prediction, of the sealing industry, and of Arctic transportation.

1. Identify the main stages of Nansen's reasoning from his observation of the drifting log to the announcement of his theory at the meeting of the Christiania Geographical Society.

2. Why did Nansen alone, of all the people on the *Viking,* attach significance to the drifting log? What inference about response to observation do you draw from your answer?

3. What sources of information did Nansen bring to bear on his speculations about the origin of the log? Can you identify those that probably came from reading?

4. What inference do you draw from the scorn with which Nansen's theory was first met?

5. Try to put yourself in the shoes of those who protested that the projected voyage of the *Fram* was "sheer madness." Would you have made such a protest in this situation?

6. Admittedly there was danger in the voyage of the *Fram.* Do you think Nansen was aware of that danger? What encouraged him to persist?

7. Discuss the question whether Nansen's final success was a *technical* or an *imaginative* triumph. By a technical triumph we mean one like our landing men on the moon, an achievement dependent on technical know-how and equipment.

B. *The following article, written by a columnist for a news magazine, reveals material drawn from a variety of sources and shaped into a unified communication. Read it, then answer the questions which follow it.*

"The Cities Are Finished"[8]
by Stewart Alsop

"I can tell you one thing," said Henry Ford the First in the early 1920s. "The cities are finished."

After last week's meeting of the mayors here in Washington, it begins to seem that Henry Ford may have been right. Perhaps our cities really are finished, as places where any sensible person would wish to live, and thus as viable social institutions. Great social institutions do die, after all—the British Empire is dead, for example; and the family farm, the foundation stone of the old American way, is busy dying. To judge from the way the mayors talked, the cities are dying too. . . .

The rot of the cities really started back in the decades when Henry Ford made his prediction. Then a small minority of city dwellers—those rich enough to own a car—discovered that it was pleasanter to live out among the trees and the fields and to drive in to work. Nearby farm villages began to be transformed into bedroom towns—in the close-in suburbs, you can see the

[8] From *Newsweek,* April 5, 1971. Copyright Newsweek, Inc., 1971.

big houses of that era still, often transformed into funeral parlors or dreary rooming houses. Thus began, in a very small way, the erosion of the tax base that is causing such anguish to the mayors who gathered in Washington last week.

When the rich move out and the poor stay behind, the tax base is fatally weakened. More and more poor people need more and more welfare or other financial support, and there are fewer and fewer rich people to support those poor people with their tax money. The result is inevitable. All the mayors said about the same thing. Let New York's Mayor John Lindsay speak for them all:

"In New York we have a deficit of $300 million and face a deficit next year of $1 billion. Frankly, even with help in Washington, I'm not sure we can pull out of the urban crisis in time."

If money were the only problem, the urban crisis could be solved in one of two ways. One way is to obliterate the increasingly artificial dividing line between suburb and city and tax on the basis of a whole metropolitan area. This makes sense—except to the suburbanites, who consider their taxes exorbitant already, and who therefore bitterly resist incorporation into metropolitan areas. Suburbia, more than ever before, is where the votes are, as the politicians are well aware.

Thus, the more politically practical way is for the Federal government to overleap the ring of white suburbs around the central cities and provide the necessary tax money. This is what is now clearly going to be done, in one way or another, whether Richard Nixon or Wilbur Mills finally has his way on the details. Will it work?

The best answers seem to be "for a while," and "up to a point." One way or another, the Federal government will no doubt find a way to keep the cities ticking over. But that does not mean that Henry Ford was wrong. The cities may be "finished," not because they've lost their tax base, but simply because they've become unlivable. . . .

Newark, for example, is already a city without any white middle class, and middle-class Negroes are escaping to the suburbs too. "Wherever the cities are going," says the city's black mayor, Kenneth Gibson, "Newark's going to get there first. We have the worst infant mortality, maternal mortality and crime rate in the country." Who would want to live in Newark if he could help it? Federal money—even a lot of Federal money—may keep Newark ticking over, but it is not going to make Newark a nice place to live.

Richard Scammon, a brilliant statistician and former Census Bureau chief, has a grim vision of the American city of the future. The exodus of business offices and factories will accelerate, he thinks, along with the exodus of middle-class blacks as well as whites. Net population of the cities will continue to fall—Baltimore, for example, may be down from more than 900,000 to half a million by 1980. More and more of the population will be dependent on welfare or other support, so that the time will come when an actual majority of the big-city population will be publicly supported.

The cities, Scammon speculates, could then come increasingly to resemble urban models of the old Indian reservations, kept alive by the state, but ruled by a kind of internal jungle law. The surrounding middle-class suburbs would be heavily guarded (as some are already), the chief function of the guards being to protect the middle-class majority in the suburbs from marauding bands from the cities.

The vision may seem a bit too gloomy. Even so, a lot of people who know what is really happening to the cities suspect that Henry Ford was right. Mayor Moon Landrieu of New Orleans, for example, remarked last week that "the cities are going down the pipe." Cities have gone down the pipe before, after all. Rome in the Middle Ages was a village of 25,000 bedraggled survivors huddled around the Colosseum, and many other once great cities are "one with Nineveh and Tyre." There is no reason to suppose that our cities are immune. In fact, there is plenty of reason to think they are not.

1. Identify the major sources from which the writer got his information and try to decide which were probably personal experience and which probably came from reading.
2. What is the thesis of the article? What is the relation of thesis and title?
3. In your judgment has the author consistently and adequately developed that thesis, considering the space available to him? Discuss your answer.
4. Does this article have any impact on you as a reader? Does it give you information you did not previously have? Does it make you more aware of the problems of big cities? Does it influence your thinking about these problems?

C. *Read the following short story, answer the questions which follow it, and if possible discuss your answers.*

A Sum in Addition
by William March

Collins said: "Sure there's a corkscrew in there. You'll find it chained to the wall. All hotels have 'em." And Menefee answered from the bathroom: "Well, there's not one in *here*. Look for yourselves if you boys don't believe me."

"That's a fine way to treat drummers," said Red Smith. "I'll write and complain to the management." He got up and stretched himself. "I'll look in the closet," he said. "Maybe I'll find something to open it with in there."

Menefee came back into the room and put the unopened bottle on the dresser, his head drawn backward and turned at an angle, his eyes squinting up. He ground out the cigarette that had been burning between his relaxed lips. "You boys keep your pants on," he said; "I'll go down and borrow a corkscrew off a bellhop." He put on his coat and went into the hall, closing the door behind him.

Collins sat back and rested his legs on the vacant chair, looking lazily over his shoulder at Red Smith. Red was pulling out drawers noisily, or standing tip-toe to peer at shelves just above his head. Then he stopped, picked up something and came into the room with it. It was a sheet of hotel stationery covered with writing and it had been crumpled into a ball and thrown into the closet.

Red opened the sheet and smoothed it flat, and when he had read it, he passed it to Collins, a peculiar look on his face. "Read this, Wade," he said.

Collins read slowly, the paper held close to his eyes. At the right of the sheet, and commencing it, was the following entry: "Cash on hand $17.45."

Then, to the left, were the following entries:

```
Expenses babyies funerel (about) ........................$148.00
Wifes hospital bill (about) ...........................  65.00
Owe to grocery store ................................  28.17
Back Rent (2 mo.—make it 3) .........................  127.25
Incidentals  ........................................  25.00
                                                      ————————
                                                      $394.42
```

A little farther down the paper were the following words: "Will borrow four hundred dollars from Mr. Sellwood." This sentence was repeated, like an exercise in penmanship, over and over, until the paper was filled with it. At first the words were written boldly, heavily, and there were places where the pen had broken through the paper behind the determination of the writer; but as the writing progressed, the man seemed less sure of himself, as if his courage and his certainty were fading away. The sentences were more perfect here, with an occasional mended letter; they were written more slowly, as if each letter were pondered. The last sentence was not finished at all. It dwindled thinly into wavering illegibility.

Collins had read the thing through and sat with it in his hands. He said sympathetically: "Tough! Tough!" then added: "He knew he couldn't work it out. He knew he was fooling himself; so he crumpled up the paper and threw it in the closet."

Red Smith sat down, resting his elbows on his knees, his bright, coppery hair shining in the light. Suddenly he had a picture of a shabby little man sitting in this same cheap hotel room, going over his problem, over and over, and finding no answer to it. Finally he said: "Don't you suppose Mr. Sellwood let him have the four hundred bucks after all? Why not?"

Collins sighed, the masonic emblem resting on his fat stomach rising with his breath. He spoke mockingly: "Of course not, Little Sunshine. Of course not! Maybe our friend went to *see* Mr. Sellwood all right, but Mr. Sellwood said that times were hard right then and he had a lot of expenses of his own. I guess that's about the way it worked out."

Red lifted his alert face. "I think you're wrong, Wade, I think everything worked out all right."

But Collins shook his head. "Not a chance, young fellow!" he said. "Not a chance!"

Red replied: "Just the same, I think Mr. Sellwood let him have the four hundred bucks. He was an old friend of the family, you see. Then he got a good job for this fellow that paid more money, and this fellow came back home almost running. He came up the steps three at the time to tell his wife. Everything worked out fine for them after that."

"Maybe he met Santa Claus on the way home," said Wade heavily, "and old Santa slipped the money in his stocking." Then he said more seriously: "The fellow who wrote that is sitting in some other cheap hotel tonight still figuring, and still trying to find an answer, but he won't, because there isn't any answer for him to find."

The door opened then and Menefee stood before them, a corkscrew in his hand. "Everything's okay," he said. "Everything's all set."

"We'll leave it to Menefee," said Red Smith. "Give him the writing, Wade, and let's see what he thinks."

Collins passed over the paper and Menefee examined it carefully, as if he did not understand it, before he looked at the two men, puzzled a little.

"What's it all about? This don't make sense to me."

Collins shook his head. "Good old Menefee. Trust him."

Red laughed a little and said earnestly: "Don't you see the point, Menefee?"

Menefee read the thing through again, turned the paper over and examined the writing once more. "I'm damned if I do," he said helplessly. Then a moment later he added triumphantly: "Oh, sure, sure, I see the point now! Sure I do. It's added up wrong."

Red Smith looked at Collins and they both laughed. "It *is* added up wrong!" said Menefee, indignant and a little hurt. "Eight and five are thirteen and eight are twenty-one . . . seven makes twenty-eight, and five thirty-three—not thirty-four, like it is here."

But Collins and Red Smith continued to laugh and to shake their heads.

"All right," said Menefee. "I'm dumb; I admit it." He pulled in his lips and spoke in a high, quavering voice: "Come on, boys; let your poor old grandmother in on the joke!" He picked up the bottle and poured three drinks into three tumblers, grumbling a little to himself. "I never saw such superior bastards in all my life as you two are," he said.

1. What are "drummers" and why are they looking for a corkscrew? Is the corkscrew necessary to the story apart from the men's immediate need of one?

2. In the whole context of the story is it important whether Menefee or one of the other men goes out of the room to get a corkscrew?

3. The core of the story is the list of expenses, beneath which is written several times, "Will borrow four hundred dollars from Mr. Sellwood." What inferences do Red Smith and Wade Collins make from this document?

4. Red Smith later takes a more optimistic view of the unknown man's problem and suggests a happy ending. Collins disagrees. Since the story does not tell us what happened after the list was made, both Smith and Collins are stating unsupported opinions. Which opinion is more appropriate to the whole context of the story?

5. When Menefee is given the list he sees something the others missed. Does this show that he is more observant than they? What inference do Smith and Collins make about Menefee's discovery? In the context of the story is that a logical inference?

6. What significance do you attach to the title of the story?

7. Suppose you are asked on an examination question to discuss the relations of plot, character, and structure in this story. Prewrite the answer you would make.

D. *At first glance this poem by E. E. Cummings may seem meaningless to you. But stick with it for a while and see if you can give it meaning. If you can't, try reading it aloud. Does that suggest anything to you? The poem is not so difficult as it seems. See what you can make of it.*

---

un
der fog
's
touch

slo

ings
fin
gering
s

wli

whichs
turn
in
to whos

est

people
be
come
un

Chapter 3

Patterns of Organization

As you gather material and clarify your purpose, you will begin to discover the plan by which your paper can best be organized. Your notes, or any scratch outline you make from them, may suggest that you have one main point and five examples, or a contrast of two things, or three reasons to support a contention. Most materials naturally fall into one pattern of organization rather than another. This chapter deals with the patterns most commonly used: illustration, comparison and contrast, analogy, classification, process, and cause and effect. One other, argument, will be discussed in Chapter 13. If you master these, you can adapt and combine them to fit almost any kind of material you will be called upon to write about.

ILLUSTRATION

The simplest way to explain something is to say what it is and to give some examples of it. So the commonest and most useful pattern of organization consists of a general statement explained or illustrated by examples or details. This pattern is highly elastic—it can fill a sentence, a paragraph, or an essay of 4,000 to 5,000 words. The following takes one sentence:

Main idea followed by five examples

A trunk in the attic is often a treasure chest of things that once were deeply meaningful to someone—pictures of relatives no longer identifiable, faded newspaper clippings recording some triumph by one of the children, letters tied with ribbons or encased in boxes, old notebooks containing primitive stories or verses written in a child's hand, dresses that have been out of style for fifty years but are still lovely in a museum-like way.

The five details make a list: pictures, clippings, and so on—each an example of the opening general statement.

The structure of the following passage is revealed by the marginal notations:

Thesis stated and clarified

Birds reared in isolation from their kind do not generally know what species they belong to: that is to say, not only their social reactions but also their sexual desires are directed towards those beings with whom they have spent certain impressionable phases of their early youth. Consequently, birds raised singly by hand tend to regard human beings, and human beings only, as potential partners in all reproductive activities.

Example 1

A female barnyard goose which I now possess was the only survivor of a brood of six, of which the remainder all succumbed to avian tuberculosis. Consequently she grew up in the company of chickens and, in spite of the fact that we bought for her, in good time, a beautiful gander, she fell head over heels in love with our handsome Rhode Island cock, inundated him with proposals, jealously prevented him from making love to his hens, and remained absolutely insensible to the attentions of the gander.

Example 2

The hero of a similar tragi-comedy was a lovely white peacock of the Schönbrunn Zoo in Vienna. He too was the last survivor of an early-hatched brood which perished in a period of cold weather, and to save him, the keeper put him in the warmest room to be found in the whole Zoo, which at that time was in the reptile house with the giant tortoises. For the rest of his life this unfortunate bird saw only in those huge reptiles the object of his desire and remained unresponsive to the charms of the prettiest peahens. . . .

Example 3

Another tame adult male jackdaw fell in love with me and treated me exactly as a female of his kind. By the hour, this bird tried to make me creep into the nesting cavity of his choice, a few inches in width. He became most importunate in that he continually wanted to feed me with what he considered the choicest delicacies. Remarkably enough, he recognized the human mouth as the orifice of ingestion and he was overjoyed if I opened my lips to him, uttering at the same time an adequate begging note. This must be considered as an act of self-sacrifice on my part, since even I cannot pretend to like the taste of finely minced worms, generously mixed with jackdaw saliva. You will understand that I found it difficult to cooperate with the bird in this manner every few minutes! But if I did not, I had to guard my ears against him, otherwise, before I knew what was happening, the passage of one of these organs would be filled right up to the drum with warm worm pulp, for jackdaws, when feeding their female or their young, push the food mass, with the aid of their tongue, deep down into the partner's pharynx. However, this bird only made use of my ears when I refused him my mouth, on which the first attempt was always made.[1]

The basic structure of the illustrative pattern is clearly shown in this selection: thesis plus example, plus example, plus example—for as many

[1] Adapted from *King Solomon's Ring*, by Konrad Z. Lorenz. Copyright 1952 by Thomas Y. Crowell Company, New York, publishers.

examples as the writer thinks necessary. In this passage each example is a little story or case history used to illustrate the author's thesis about the unusual behavior of birds reared in isolation from their kind. In the earlier selection the five examples illustrated the kinds of articles often found in an old trunk. You can judge for yourself how well the examples in these passages add to and clarify the meaning.

EXERCISES

A. *Read the passage below and then answer the questions that follow it.*

There is always the miracle of by-products. Plane a board, the shavings accumulate around your toes ready to be chucked into the stove to kindle your fires (to warm your toes so that you can plane a board). Draw some milk from a creature to relieve her fullness, the milk goes to a little pig to relieve his emptiness. Drain some oil from a crankcase, and you smear it on the roosts to control the mites. The worm fattens on the apple, the young goose fattens on the wormy fruit, the man fattens on the goose, the worm awaits the man. Clean up the barnyard, the pulverized dung from the sheep goes to improve the lawn (before a rain in autumn); mow the lawn the next spring, the clippings go to the compost pile, with a few thrown to the baby chickens on the way; spread the compost on the garden and in the fall the original dung, after many vicissitudes, returns to the sheep in the form of an old squash. From the fireplace, at the end of a November afternoon, the ashes are carried to the feet of the lilac bush, guaranteeing the excellence of a June morning.[2]

1. What is the guiding generalization of this passage? Would you say that it is a thesis?
2. How many illustrations does the passage contain?
3. What is the relationship between the number of illustrations and the number of sentences? Explain.
4. In the passage about the trunk, the illustrations are descriptive details. In that about the behavior of birds, the illustrations are brief case histories. How would you describe the illustrations in this passage? Compare and contrast them with those in the two others. If possible, discuss in class.

B. *Write a paragraph developed with examples which illustrate one of the following generalizations or any other of your choice.*

1. People sometimes take affront when none was intended.
2. Some of the most valuable lessons are learned unconsciously.
3. Advertising often appeals to our vanity.

[2] From E. B. White, *One Man's Meat* (New York: Harper & Row, 1964).

COMPARISON AND CONTRAST

A second fruitful kind of organization and of thinking is the discovery and analysis of similarities and differences. Comparison stresses likenesses and contrast stresses differences, but as thought processes and as patterns of organization the two are often used together. There are two main ways of organizing materials for comparison and contrast. The simpler of these may be called the *divided* pattern, in which everything is first said about *A*, and then everything about *B*. This pattern is used in the following paper about two novels.

A Gimmick with a Difference

Introductory statement of the comparison

By coincidence, two novels that I have read in the last couple of months happened to be based on the same science fiction type of gimmick, the formation of a hitherto unknown crystal pattern which in an instant turned a liquid into a solid—with disastrous results.

A: The Andromeda Strain

The first of these novels was *The Andromeda Strain,* by Michael Crichton. In this book a satellite returning from space brings back a trace of a substance which at unbelievably slight contact can turn human blood into a crystallized solid, causing immediate death. Of course the characters in the novel don't know this, and the government organizes a team of scientists to find out what is happening. After a great deal of detailed description, most of it very interesting, and several hundred pages of suspense, the annihilation of the human race is narrowly avoided not by anything the characters are able to do, but because the virus which causes crystallization suddenly mutates back into something harmless so that blood is no longer turned into a solid.

B: Cat's Cradle

The other book, *Cat's Cradle,* by Kurt Vonnegut, used the same gimmick in a different way. Here it is something called "ice nine," a hypothetical isotope of ordinary ice, which imposes its solidifying crystal pattern on anything moist it touches. In this book, though, things happen for keeps. The ocean, the population of an island, and everything else in the world turns to "ice nine," and at the end of the book only two people seem to be still alive— and probably they won't be for long. While the other book is basically trivial, this one is not, but has a deeper meaning, because "ice nine" is the invention of a scientific genius who never cared about humanity, even his own children, who grow up emotionally warped and strange. He could have destroyed the "ice nine," but was too much interested in it as a scientific problem, so it destroyed him instead, and finally, everything else on earth. The book is thus against science, or at least against a certain type of inhumane scientist, and is serious and despairing about mankind and the modern world.

In this paper a brief introductory paragraph states the subject of the contrast and the remainder devotes one paragraph to *The Andromeda Strain* and a separate paragraph to *Cat's Cradle*. The structural pattern could be described as "all about *The Andromeda Strain* before anything about

Cat's Cradle." Or to say the same thing in more general terms, it is "all about *A*, then all about *B*." The body of the paper is thus divided into two roughly equal parts, each of which deals with one of the two topics being contrasted. Note that the writer makes no attempt to compare the two books point by point. This pattern is easy for the writer, since it lets him dispose of one topic before starting the other.

The second and more complex mode of comparison-contrast may be called the *alternating* pattern, since it takes up characteristics of the two topics one at a time and compares or contrasts them point by point: *A–B*, *A–B*, *A–B*, and so on, for as many pairings as the subject requires. The following student paper illustrates this method.

Chair One Is Not Chair Two

Introductory paragraph: both chairs

Chair One is not Chair Two. True, both are arrangements so similar in their concrete shapes that even a Martian on his first trip to earth could tell that these two objects serve the same purpose.

Chairs 1 and 2 contrasted in appearance: corresponding details in same sentence

The quick glance of an earth dweller would tell a great deal more—earth dwellers would notice the chipped layer of ivory paint and the crude hand-painted brown flowers across the top of the back of Chair One, and contrast this with the shining maple stain on Chair Two. Earth Dweller would reflect on the pleasures of foam rubber cushioning on Chair Two while wincing slightly at the taut caning criss-crossing the seat of Chair One. And the spindled banister back above the caning would add further thoughts of discomfort not evoked by the smooth maple slats of Chair Two.

Chairs contrasted in workmanship: first chair 1, then chair 2

The very observant earth dweller would not think of comfort at all when confronted with Chairs One and Two. Banister Back, he would conclude, is part of the past. Jack plane tracks score the underside, and the patina of venerable, unfinished wood lies almost hidden inside the frame. Not so Chair Two—its finish is unmarred, the veneer of its legs uncracked, the slats firmly glued. The calculatedly colonial patterned material that covers the seat is precisely nailed.

Chairs contrasted as products of craftsmanship and mass production: first chair 1, then chair 2

Chair One was not born as a piece of furniture alone. It was born in an age of little material wealth, and was treasured year upon year not only as a chair but also as a symbol of the different and more furnished world everyone strove for. The apprentice who warmed its burgeoning curves and the artisan who measured its fineness invested it with a value that increased as humans successively made it a part of their lives. As it passed from generation to generation, family legend passed with it. Chair Two is bloodless. Its sharply cut lines and exactly duplicated curves speak only of screaming machines spitting out legs, braces, slats, and seats. Its gleaming surface tells not of human hands, but of paint sprayers and dipping vats. Humanity touched it when the warehousemen stenciled "7042" under the seat.

Conclusion: chair 1, then chair 2

Chair One is not, indeed, Chair Two. Chair One is a talisman of the humanity by which America was hand-hewn. Chair Two is a trade-in on next year's French Provincial suite.

The alternating pattern is more difficult for the writer than the divided pattern, since it requires him to keep the details of both elements of his subject in mind all the time. But not all subjects lend themselves equally well to the two patterns. The two novels have different plots, different sets of characters, different points of climax, and so on, whereas both chairs have seats, backs, and finishes. Thus the divided method would have been less satisfactory for comparing and contrasting the chairs than it is for comparing and contrasting the books. But when there is a choice, the alternating pattern generally produces the more interesting results.

EXERCISES

A. *Reread "Twinkletoes and the Tailback" (page 27) and decide whether it shows a divided or an alternating structure.*

B. *Read the selection below and answer the questions which follow it.*

Presently it is a popular occupation among the computer fraternity to compare their mechanism to the human brain. The conclusions are not disheartening—marvelous as the machines are, the brain seems still a good deal more marvelous. Like the mills of the gods, it grinds slow compared to the machines, but it grinds exceeding fine—it is original, imaginative, resourceful, free in will and choice. The machine operates at a speed approaching that of light, 186,000 mi. per sec., whereas the brain operates at the speed at which impulses move along nerve fiber, perhaps a million times slower—but the machine operates linearly, that is, it sends an impulse or "thought" along one path, so that if that path proves to be a dead end the "thought" must back up to the last fork in the road and try again, and if the "thought" is derailed the whole process must be begun again; the brain operates in some mysterious multipath fashion whereby a thought apparently splits and moves along several different paths simultaneously so that no matter what happens to any one of its branches there are others groping along. And whereas even a transistorized computer has a fairly modest number of components, the brain, it seems, has literally billions of neurons, or memory-and-operation cells. To rival an average human brain a computer built by present techniques would have to be about as big as an ocean liner, or a skyscraper. And even then it would lack the capacity for originality and free will. To initiate free choice in a machine the operator would have to insert into its program random numbers, which would make the machine "free" but uncoordinated—an idiot.[3]

1. Does this selection follow the divided pattern, the alternating pattern, or some other? Explain your answer in detail.

2. Does this selection deal mainly with comparison or with contrast, or is it an even balance of the two? Explain your answer.

[3] From Gerald S. Hawkins, *Stonehenge Decoded* (New York: Doubleday & Company, Inc., 1965). Copyright © 1965 by Gerald S. Hawkins and John B. White.

C. *Prewrite a paper of comparison or contrast between any two members of the following lists. Or if you prefer, choose a topic of your own. After you have chosen your topic, determine which kind of structure is better for your purpose. If your instructor wishes, these prewriting activities may be developed into an essay.*

1. Music: hard rock, folk, jazz, popular dance music of the 1940's (1950's, etc.), symphonic music, medieval church music, etc.

2. Yankees, Southerners, Westerners, Midwesterners, etc.

3. The ideas, attitudes, beliefs symbolized in the dress of modern young people, members of a religious order, the military, older people.

4. Some beliefs and values of your generation and another generation.

ANALOGY

A related kind of organizational pattern based on a special form of comparison is *analogy.* In analogy, a striking likeness between two things is made the basis of an extended comparison even though the two things may be unlike in many other ways. Analogy is akin to metaphor (page 145), and is useful in exposition to clarify an abstract concept or process by comparing it to something familiar and concrete. In the following paragraph the analogy with pitching and catching helps to clarify the abstract concept that both sending and receiving messages are active processes in communication.

Let me use the example of baseball. Catching the ball is just as much of an activity as pitching or hitting it. The pitcher or batter is the *giver* here in the sense that his activity initiates the motion of the ball. The catcher or fielder is the *receiver* in the sense that his activity terminates it. Both are equally active, though the activities are distinctly different. If anything is passive here, it is the ball: it is pitched and caught. It is the inert thing which is put in motion or stopped, whereas the living men are active, moving to pitch, hit, or catch. The analogy with writing and reading is almost perfect. The thing which is written and read, like the ball, is the passive object in some way common to the two activities which begin and terminate the process.[4]

Note that the structure of this analogy follows that of the alternating comparison. Note also that the analogy is used entirely for the benefit of the reader. There is no implication that it helped the writer clarify his own thinking, only that it helps him to make an abstraction concrete and clear.

[4] From Mortimer J. Adler, *How to Read a Book* (New York: Simon and Schuster, 1940).

The following somewhat longer analogy, on the other hand, gives evidence of having helped to advance the author's thinking.

Scientists visiting South America often came to see our laboratory and our forest stations. It was while showing the forest to one of these visitors, a botanist, that the idea of the biological similarity between the forest and the sea first occurred to me. We had lunch beside a little stream in a ravine where the forest was dark and quiet, singularly lifeless. Later I persuaded the botanist to climb the ladders on one of the trees, a dizzying experience avoided by many of our visitors. We rested at the 14-meter platform and then climbed on to the 24-meter platform, which was well up in the forest canopy at that particular point. . . .

In the course of our mosquito studies we had found that each different species had its characteristic flight habits. Some kinds were found only near the ground, others only high in the trees; some that were most common high in the trees in the morning or afternoon would come down near the ground during the midday hours, showing a sort of daily vertical migration.

While I was explaining this to my friend, it struck me, that this is just the way animals act in the sea. Most life is near the top, because that is where the sunlight strikes and everything below depends on this surface. Life in both the forest and the sea is distributed in horizontal layers.

The analogy, once thought of, was easily developed. The vocabulary for life in the sea could be transferred to the forest. In the treetops we were in what marine students call the pelagic zone—the zone of active photosynthesis, where sunlight provides the energy to keep the whole complicated biological community going. Below, we had been in the benthos, the bottom zone, where organisms live entirely on second-hand materials that drift down from above—on fallen leaves, on fallen fruits, on roots and logs. Only a few special kinds of green plants were able to grow in the rather dim light that reached the forest floor.

My mosquitoes acted in some ways like the microscopic floating life of the sea, the plankton. Each species among the plankton organisms has a characteristic vertical distribution: some living only near the surface, others only at considerable depths, and so forth. The plankton organisms in general show a daily vertical migration, coming to the surface at night and sinking during the day: a migration to which my mosquitoes were only a feeble counterpart. But insects on land are only partially analogous with the plankton of the sea. A major portion of the plankton consists of microscopic plants, busy using the energy of the sun and the dissolved carbon dioxide of the water to build up starch and thus provide the basis for all the rest of the life of the sea. These microscopic plants would correspond not to the insects of the forest, but to the leaves of the trees. The forest insects would correspond only to the animal component of the plankton: to the copepods and tiny shrimp and larval fish which live directly on the plants or on each other at the very beginning of the endless chain of who eats whom in the biological community.

The real basis of the analogy is that both the forest and the sea are three-dimensional. The students of the sea have always been keenly aware of this, but the students of the forest have paid less attention to problems of depth. Of course the scale is utterly different. To compare the "gloomy depths of the forest" with the "gloomy depths of the sea" is so far-fetched as to be ludicrous—though each phrase is apt enough in its own context. The analogy is closest if we compare shallow tropical seas with tropical forests, especially with the great rain forests of the Amazon, the Congo and southeast Asia.[5]

The author's use of this analogy is of particular interest. Whereas Adler says his analogy is "almost perfect," Bates says his should not be pushed too far: that to compare the "gloomy depths" of the forest and the sea would be far-fetched and ridiculous. Rather, its use to him was to point out that the forest and the sea are both three-dimensional, and that certain implications of this fact are useful in studying such phenomena as the habits of different species of mosquitoes in comparison with different species of plankton.

Both authors are thus keenly aware of what might be called the *logical fit* of an analogy. They know how far to push it and where to stop: that is, what points of comparison in the analogy hold true, and what other possible points would be exaggerated or unfruitful.

EXERCISES

A. *Analyze the analogy in the following passage for (1) aptness as the basis of an explanatory comparison; (2) logical fit.*

To get the effect of running into a stationary truck at 15 m.p.h. picture a concrete floor with your steering wheel stuck into it by its column, projecting about a foot. Imagine yourself lying face down on the floor with your stomach draped over the steering wheel. Four very large men pick you up by your arms and legs and raise you in the air until you are suspended horizontally 7½ feet up. Then they let go and you fall spread-eagled on to the wheel and the concrete. If you think glass might be kinder to your face than concrete, there's no objection to putting a sheet of glass on the floor to represent the windscreen; or add any other of the dash fittings in the appropriate positions.

Those who feel they could protect themselves with their hands and arms in a crash should try to visualize to what a limited degree they could break their fall under the above conditions. The forces and masses are strictly comparable in the two cases, and the hands and arms are not nearly strong enough to provide any protection except as a piece of padding.

A pedestrian hit by your car at 15 m.p.h. gets approximately the same impact that you yourself would receive in the above case.

[5] From Marston Bates, *The Forest and the Sea* (New York: Random House, 1960). © Copyright 1960 by Marston Bates. Reprinted by permission of Random House, Inc.

To get the effect of hitting the stationary truck at 30 m.p.h. do the same thing, except that you are raised 30 feet up (rooftop of a two-story house) before they let you drop on to the wheel. For 60 m.p.h. the distance is 120 feet —say the 14th floor of an apartment building.

To get the effect of a safety belt, picture one of these on strong supports slung just above the wheel to break your fall.

This analogy explains rather vividly why, after you have helped get the spokes of a broken steering-wheel out of a corpse's stomach, you tend to drive slowly for a while, and become irritable when someone talks of "just crawling along, my dear, at 45."[6]

B. *Find analogies to explain the following topics: (1) Time; (2) Guilt; (3) Waste.*

CLASSIFICATION

Classification is the process of grouping together things perceived as being alike in some particular way. Draft boards classify as 1A young men who are considered as being alike in specific ways, and as 2S, 1Y, or 4F those who are considered as being alike in other specific ways. Classifications are man-made. Young men are not 1A or 4F until the draft board says so. Any individual may be, and usually is, classified in a number of ways: John Jones, college junior, honor student, chemistry major, 2S, Methodist, redhead, tenor, bachelor, and so on. None of these classifications is a complete description of John Jones, but each describes the classifier's interest in him at the moment.

When a classification is used as a tool of thought, the categories established impose a form and a meaning on material that would otherwise lack both. Classification is thus a valuable route to new knowledge and insight. For example, after each italicized word below are two meanings: first the original meaning, then the modern one. Try to find a pattern by which you can classify the words to show how their meanings have changed.

1. *acorn* (various kinds of nuts—the seed or nut of oak trees)
2. *bonfire* (a fire for burning bones or corpses—any large outdoor fire)
3. *boor* (a farmer—an ill-mannered person)
4. *boycott* (an Irish captain who was ostracized by his neighbors—refusal to associate with any person or group)
5. *cad* (a younger son of an aristocratic family—an ill mannered fellow)
6. *cattle* (property or wealth—cows, bulls, and steers)
7. *champagne* (wine from a French district—any wine resembling French champagne)

[6] From T. S. Skillman, *Road Safety* (New York: David McKay Company, Inc., 1966).

8. *corn* (a hard particle—the seed of a particular cereal crop)

9. *cunning* (knowing or skillful—tricky or meanly clever)

10. *dean* (an officer in charge of ten people—a major college administrator)

11. *deer* (any small animal—a particular animal with antlers)

12. *discard* (reject a card—throw something away)

13. *ferry* (travel—travel by boat)

14. *gossip* (a godparent—a spreader of rumors)

15. *hussy* (a housewife—a woman of low morals)

16. *knave* (a boy—a villainous man)

17. *knight* (a young male servant—a titled person)

18. *lady* (a breadmaker—a woman of quality)

19. *martinet* (a French general who was a stickler for discipline—any rigid disciplinarian)

20. *minister* (a servant—a clergyman or statesman)

21. *pedagogue* (a slave—an educator)

22. *shibboleth* (a password used in the Bible—any word or phrase that identifies a particular group)

23. *shirt* (a loose outer garment worn by either sex—a garment worn by a man)

24. *skirt* (a loose outer garment worn by either sex—a garment worn by a woman)

As here written, the list is simply in alphabetical order. But as you study the words you notice that *acorn* has changed from a name for various kinds of nuts to a name for one kind: its meaning has become more specialized or restricted. Then you look at *bonfire* and decide that its meaning has changed in just the opposite way: once specialized, it has become broader or more general. This discovery, coupled with the previous one, suggests two possible kinds of change and two groupings—from broad to narrow and from narrow to broad, or restriction and extension.

You then note that *boor* does not fit into either of these groups, but seems to have acquired less pleasant connotations. You see that the same is true of *cad* and some other words. So you now have three groups, and you may guess that there will probably be another, one with *more* favorable connotations to contrast with the third group—a guess you find verified by *knight, lady,* and some others. With these clues you should be able to establish the categories and fit each word into the appropriate one.

When you have finished this classification, you will have not only a new way of looking at these words, but a pattern into which you can fit many others. Moreover, you have the general statement, basic organization, and supporting details for at least a paragraph. To develop the idea and organization into an essay would require enough additional material to illustrate each of your four types of changes through a complete paragraph. Regardless of its length, this example shows the close relationship among the general idea, the organization, and the supporting details. It also illustrates that when the basic thinking is done in prewriting, an essay can be structured before writing begins. Observation and study of material lead to a chain of prewriting activities. Finally, this example illustrates that classification has much in common with comparison and contrast.

Classification appeals to many students. In the following essay, the student generalizes from her experience to establish three kinds of teachers. Her classification is not meant to be all-inclusive; rather, she deals only with the types that interest her and as she has seen them. Nevertheless her types allow her to compare teaching styles and to make significant comments on their similarities and differences.

The Thought-Promoters

Introduction announcing the types

Some teachers rush through their lectures, trying to give students as much information as possible to memorize. Others plan their presentations so as to make students think about the subject. These latter teachers may be called Thought-Promoters. Most of them can be grouped into three types according to their teaching methods: *Outline-Givers, Opinion-Askers,* and *Game-Players.*

Characteristics of Type 1

The Outline-Givers begin by giving their students an outline of the subject which they are to follow in conducting their own research and analysis. This outline shows the main headings of the subject, but the students are expected to provide the detailed information to develop the outline. In a sense, they use the outline as a map for the territory they are going to explore in the laboratory or library.

Example of Type 1

This method is a favorite of many science teachers. During lecture Mrs. D. Bacillus, a biology teacher, sketches the principle of diffusion; then in the lab the students conduct a variety of experiments to identify and describe examples of diffusion. In preparing their lab reports they are expected to use the original outline, but they are also expected to go beyond it and through their laboratory findings to come to some sort of conclusion about the principle of diffusion.

Second example of Type 1

Mr. A. Lincoln, a history professor, uses a variation of this method. In class he presents a subject with two points of view: during the Civil War the North and South both felt their cause was just. Mr. Lincoln sets up these conflicting opinions and suggests sources to read for a fuller understanding of the conflict. The students consult these sources, sift out the relevant material, and organize and write a summary analysis of the two points of view. Like the biology students, they go beyond the material that the teacher originally gave them by their independent study of the subject.

Characteristics of Type 2

The next group, the Opinion-Seekers, prefers in-class thinking. The main objective of these teachers is to involve their students in individual and group responses. This objective is achieved by asking questions which require evaluation of material being presented in class.

Two examples of Type 2

Miss Vera Gabby is a speech teacher. When she has trouble getting students to be attentive while one of their classmates is speaking, she solves the problem by asking for constructive criticism at the end of each speech, thus promoting critical listening and judgment. A theology teacher, Mr. G. Angel, encourages class participation by working questions into his discussion of a topic. In attempting to show the relation of the word "hallow" to the concept of "god," he will ask students where they heard "hallow" before and what they understand it to mean. In the process of defining the word the students become cooperatively involved in a concept that the teacher wants them to understand.

Characteristics of Type 3

The Game-Players start their students thinking in a subtler manner than either of the other types of thought-promoters. Their method is to put students in situations in which they are required to do something: to describe what they see, to draw a conclusion from given data, to compare two things, or to "role-play" a problem. The students are expected to learn something from the experience, though what is to be learned is usually not announced in advance.

Example of Type 3

When the students of Mr. Rhetoric's class first play one of his games they wonder what the man is up to. He gives them little problems of watching and describing. Gradually the games become more complex; they require sorting observations into categories and describing the special features of each category. At first the students may not grasp the purpose of these games, but soon they begin to see that they are finding out ways of thinking about things, and their experience gives them confidence in their ability to lay out an approach to a problem and to do their own thinking about it.

Concluding statement

All three types of thought-promoters are really doing the same thing in different ways. They are leading students into a more mature attitude toward study by giving them responsibility for their own education. Their students learn the facts of the subject but, more important, they learn how to get the facts and what to do with them when they have them.

The following rules for classification should be kept in mind.

1. Every classification must be made on one clear and consistent basis. Tools may be classified as machine tools and hand tools. Hand tools may be classified by function as cutting, striking, and assembling tools. It would not be logical to cross categories, such as machine tools, cutting tools, and hammers, since a machine tool may be for cutting, striking, or assembling and a hammer may be a machine tool or a hand tool.

2. If a class is divided, there must be at least two subclasses. Unless there are at least two subclasses, there is no need to subdivide a main class.

3. A classification set up to handle a body of data must include all items to be classified: all power tools, all hand tools, etc. A paper like "The Thought-Promoters" is an exception, since it discusses types observed but makes no pretense of treating all types which exist.

EXERCISES

A. *Determine the basis for each of the following classifications, and point out any in which one category is selected on a different basis from the others.*

1. Automobile, boat, carriage, chariot.
2. Freighter, liner, sailboat, tanker.
3. Cow, panther, pig, sheep.

B. *The passage on page 56 classifies words according to changes of meaning. Can you think of other possible classifications of words? For what purposes would these other classifications be useful?*

C. *Using "The Thought-Promoters" as a model, set up a classification including at least three types of students, dates, personalities, insults, or excuses; or pick a topic of your own.*

1. State the basis of your classification and explain why you chose it.

2. Write a general introductory statement and list your categories. You now have a written plan for an essay.

3. If your instructor wishes, write the essay.

PROCESS

A process is a sequence of operations or actions by which something is done or made. The development of the human embryo from conception to birth is one process; the procedure by which the citizens of the United States elect a President is another.

To describe a process, a writer must first know it thoroughly. Second, he must divide it into its steps or stages. Third, he must explain each step in enough detail so a reader can "see" it and if necessary perform it himself. Following are the most common types of process essay:

1. The "how-to-do-it" essay, which gives directions for doing something, in the manner of a recipe.

2. The "how-it-works" essay, which shows an operation in its successive stages. This type usually follows a time order and thus resembles narration.

3. The "how-it-is-organized" essay, which shows how a complex organization (business, university, political party) functions by breaking it into departments and showing what each does. Here the order is functional or spatial.

4. The "how-did-it-happen" essay, or causal process, which seeks a cause for a known effect.

Here is an example of a process narrative of Type 1—"how-to-do-it." Read it carefully in preparation for the exercise which follows it.

Contour Drawing[7]

Sit close to the model or object which you intend to draw and lean forward in your chair. Focus your eyes on some point—any point will do—along the contour of the model. (The contour approximates what is usually spoken of as the outline or edge.) Place the point of your pencil on the paper. Without taking your eyes off the model, *wait* until you are *convinced* that the pencil is touching that point on the model upon which your eyes are fastened.

Then move your eye *slowly* along the contour of the model and move the pencil *slowly* along the paper. As you do this, keep the conviction that the pencil point is actually touching the contour. Be guided more by the sense of touch than by sight. THIS MEANS THAT YOU MUST DRAW WITHOUT LOOKING AT THE PAPER, continuously looking at the model.

Exactly coordinate the pencil with the eye. Your eye may be tempted at first to move faster than your pencil, but do not let it get ahead. Consider only the point that you are working on at the moment with no regard for any other part of the figure.

Often you will find that the contour you are drawing will leave the edge of the figure and turn inside, coming eventually to an apparent end. When this happens, glance down at the paper in order to locate a new starting point. This new starting point should pick up at that point on the edge where the contour turned inward. Thus, you will glance down at the paper several times during the course of one study, but do not draw while you are looking at the paper. As in the beginning, place the pencil point on the paper, fix your eyes on the model, and wait until you are convinced that the pencil is touching the model before you draw.

Not all of the contours lie along the outer edge of the figure. For example, if you have a front view of the face, you will see definite contours along the nose and the mouth which have no apparent connection with the contours at the edge. As far as the time for your study permits, draw these "inside contours" exactly as you draw the outside ones. Draw anything that your pencil can rest on and be guided along. *Develop the absolute conviction that you are touching the model.*

This exercise should be done slowly, searchingly, sensitively. Take your time. Do not be too impatient or too quick. There is no point in finishing any one contour study. In fact, a contour study is not a thing that can be "finished." It is having a particular type of experience, which can continue as long as you have the patience to look. If in the time allowed you get only halfway around the figure, it doesn't matter. So much the better! But if you finish long before the time is up, the chances are that you are not approaching the study in the right way. A contour drawing is like climbing a mountain as contrasted with flying over it in an airplane. It is not a quick glance at the mountain from far away, but a slow, painstaking climb over it, step by step.

[7] From Kimon Nicolaides, *The Natural Way to Draw* (Boston: Houghton Mifflin Company, 1941).

Do not worry about the "proportions" of the figure. That problem will take care of itself in time. And do not be misled by shadows. When you touch the figure, it will feel the same to your hand whether the part you touch happens at the moment to be light or in shadow. Your pencil moves, not on the edge of a shadow, but on the edge of the actual form.

At first, no matter how hard you try, you may find it difficult to break the habit of looking at the paper while you draw. You may even look down without knowing it. Ask a friend to check up on you for a few minutes by calling out to you every time you look at the paper. Then you will find out whether you looked too often and whether you made the mistake of drawing while you were looking.

This exercise should be used in drawing subjects of all sorts. At first, choose the contours of the landscape which seem most tangible, as the curve of a hill or the edge of a tree-trunk. Any object may be used, although those which have been formed by nature or affected by long use will offer the greatest amount of variation, as a flower, a stone, a piece of fruit, or an old shoe. Draw yourself by looking in the mirror, your own hand or foot, a piece of material. It is the experience, not the subject, that is important.

EXERCISE

With drawing pencil and paper before you, reread the foregoing selection one step at a time and make a contour drawing of a subject of your choice. Are there any steps in the process which are not in the best order? Are there any steps in the process which are not absolutely clear? (Make your answers as specific as possible.) How practical is this recommended process?

The following essay is an example of Type 2—the "how-it-works" process.

The Spider and the Wasp[8]

[0] In the adult stage the [Pepsis] wasp lives only a few months. The female produces but a few eggs, one at a time at intervals of two or three days. For each egg the mother must provide one adult tarantula, alive but paralyzed. The tarantula must be of the correct species to nourish the larva. The mother wasp attaches the egg to the paralyzed spider's abdomen. Upon hatching from the egg, the larva is many hundreds of times smaller than its living but helpless victim. It eats no other food and drinks no water. By the time it has finished its single gargantuan meal and become ready for wasphood, nothing remains of the tarantula but its indigestible chitinous skeleton.

[1] The mother wasp goes tarantula-hunting when the egg in her ovary is almost ready to be laid. Flying low over the ground late on a sunny afternoon, the wasp looks for its victim or for the mouth of a tarantula burrow, a round

---

[8] From Alexander Petrunkevitch, "The Spider and the Wasp," *Scientific American*, August 1952. Copyright © 1952 by Scientific American, Inc. All rights reserved.

hole edged by a bit of silk. The sex of the spider makes no difference, but the mother is highly discriminating as to species. Each species of Pepsis [wasp] requires a certain species of tarantula, and the wasp will not attack the wrong species. In a cage with a tarantula which is not its normal prey the wasp avoids the spider, and is usually killed by it in the night.

[2] Yet when a wasp finds the correct species, it is the other way about. To identify the species the wasp apparently must explore the spider with her antennae. The tarantula shows an amazing tolerance to this exploration. The wasp crawls under it and walks over it without evoking any hostile response. The molestation is so great and so persistent that the tarantula often rises on all eight legs, as if it were on stilts. It may stand this way for several minutes.

[3] Meanwhile the wasp, having satisfied itself that the victim is of the right species, moves off a few inches to dig the spider's grave. Working vigorously with legs and jaws, it excavates a hole 8 to 10 inches deep with a diameter slightly larger than the spider's girth. Now and again the wasp pops out of the hole to make sure that the spider is still there.

[4] When the grave is finished the wasp returns to the tarantula to complete her ghastly enterprise. First she feels it all over once more with her antennae. Then her behavior becomes more aggressive. She bends her abdomen, protruding her sting, and searches for the soft membrane at the point where the spider's leg joins its body—the only spot where she can penetrate the horny skeleton. From time to time, as the exasperated spider slowly shifts ground, the wasp turns on her back and slides along with the aid of her wings, trying to get under the tarantula for a shot at the vital spot. During all this maneuvering, which can last for several minutes, the tarantula makes no move to save itself.

[5] Finally the wasp corners it against some obstruction and grasps one of its legs in her powerful jaws. Now at last the harassed spider tries a desperate but vain defense. The two contestants roll over and over on the ground. It is a terrifying sight and the outcome is always the same. The wasp finally manages to thrust her sting into the soft spot and hold it there for a few seconds while she pumps in the poison. Almost immediately the tarantula falls paralyzed on its back. Its legs stop twitching; its heart stops beating. Yet it is not dead, as is shown by the fact that if taken from the wasp it can be restored to some sensitivity by being kept in a moist chamber for several months.

[6] After paralyzing the tarantula, the wasp cleans herself by dragging her body along the ground and rubbing her feet, sucks the drop of blood oozing from the wound in the spider's abdomen, then grabs a leg of the flabby, helpless animal in her jaws and drags it down to the bottom of the grave. She stays there for many minutes, sometimes for several hours, and what she does all that time in the dark we do not know. Eventually she lays her egg and attaches it to the side of the spider's abdomen with a sticky secretion. Then she emerges, fills the grave with soil carried bit by bit in her jaws, and finally tramples the ground all around to hide any trace of the grave from prowlers. Then she flies away, leaving her descendant safely started in life.

The selection begins with an introductory summary of the process, then each paragraph takes up a separate stage, so that, beginning with the first stage in the paragraph numbered 1, the six stages are described in six paragraphs, as follows:

Stage 1. The wasp flies over an area looking for the right kind of tarantula.

Stage 2. When she discovers one, she lands and examines it to be sure that it is the right kind.

Stage 3. When satisfied, she digs the hole in which she intends to bury the spider.

Stage 4. She re-examines the spider—this time more aggressively—looking for a vulnerable spot.

Stage 5. She attacks the spider and, after a struggle, paralyzes it.

Stage 6. She drags the paralyzed spider into the hole, affixes her egg on its abdomen, fills the grave, and leaves.

This analysis by stages is a paragraph summary. The structure of the summary shows the structure of the essay, which could also be shown by short headings, if each heading described one of the stages:

I. Looking for a victim
II. Checking to be sure
III. Digging the grave
IV. Circling for an attack
V. Paralyzing the spider
VI. Burying the spider and the egg

CAUSAL ANALYSIS

A process broken into parts to establish a causal relation among the parts may be called a *causal process* or a *causal analysis*. Such a process may move from cause to effect or from effect to cause. When the former, it begins with a known cause and shows the stages by which that cause will produce effects. For example, a doctor may predict the course of a disease once he has established that the disease (cause) is present.

Conversely, the process may go from effect to cause, as when a doctor tries to identify the cause of a patient's symptoms. The procedure may include a chain of reasoning in which finding a cause leads to a prediction of other effects: if the lights have gone out ($effect_1$) because the power is off (cause), then the refrigerator won't work ($effect_2$) and the perishable food in the refrigerator will spoil ($effect_3$).

A common writing problem is to discover the causes of given effects. Such a problem is diagnostic: what's wrong with the car? why are we in Vietnam? why isn't he speaking to me? Sometimes a definitive answer can be given to such a question, but often we have to settle for an answer which cannot be positively proved.

The following selection, the conclusion to the essay about the spider and the wasp, illustrates the kind of causal analysis which seeks, not certainty, but what the writer thinks is the best answer. In the part you have read, the author showed how the mother wasp provided for her offspring. As a result, we know how the operation was carried out. But we are still left with the puzzling question: why does the tarantula, which could kill the wasp, allow itself to be treated so? The following part shows the author's attempt to find the cause of the spider's strange conduct.

[1] In all this the behavior of the wasp is qualitatively different from that of the spider. The wasp acts like an intelligent animal. This is not to say that instinct plays no part or that she reasons as man does. But her actions are to the point; they are not automatic and can be modified to fit the situation. We do not know for certain how she identifies the tarantula—probably it is by some olfactory or chemo-tactile sense—but she does it purposefully and does not blindly tackle a wrong species.

[2] On the other hand, the tarantula's behavior shows only confusion. Evidently the wasp's pawing gives it no pleasure, for it tries to move away. . . . That the spider is not anesthetized by some odorless secretion is easily shown by blowing lightly at the tarantula and making it jump suddenly. What, then, makes the tarantula behave as stupidly as it does?

[3] No clear, simple answer is available. Possibly the stimulation by the wasp's antennae is masked by the heavier pressure on the spider's body. . . . But the explanation may be much more complex. Initiative in attack is not in the nature of tarantulas; most species fight only when cornered so that escape is impossible. Their inherited patterns of behavior apparently prompt them to avoid problems rather than attack them.

[4] For example, spiders always weave their webs in three dimensions, and when a spider finds that there is insufficient space to attach certain threads in the third dimension, it leaves the place and seeks another, instead of finishing the web in a single plane. This urge to escape seems to arise under all circumstances, in all phases of life, and to take the place of reasoning. For a spider to change the pattern of its web is as impossible as for an inexperienced man to build a bridge across a chasm obstructing his way.

[5] In a way the instinctive urge to escape is not only easier but often more efficient than reasoning. The tarantula does exactly what is most efficient in all cases except in an encounter with a ruthless and determined attacker dependent for the existence of her own species on killing as many tarantulas as she can lay eggs. Perhaps in this case the spider follows its usual pattern of trying to escape, instead of seizing and killing the wasp, because it is not aware of its danger. In any case, the survival of the tarantula species as a whole is protected by the fact that the spider is much more fertile than the wasp.[9]

[9] From Alexander Petrunkevitch, "The Spider and the Wasp," *Scientific American,* August 1952. Copyright © 1952 by Scientific American, Inc. All rights reserved.

Here the author begins by stressing the intelligent conduct of the wasp in order to emphasize the apparent stupidity of the tarantula. He thus shows the need to discover why the spider acts as it does. Second, he shows two possible causes disproved by the facts. Third, he suggests a hypothesis—that the spider's actions reflect an instinctive behavior pattern. Fourth, he supports that hypothesis with supplementary evidence from the way spiders build their webs. Finally, he tries to show that the suggested cause is sufficient to explain the spider's behavior. The stages in his causal process can be summarized thus:

I. Introduction to provide contrast and thus pose the problem (¶1)

II. Refutation of possible but false causes (¶2)

III. Hypothesis suggesting the real cause (¶3)

IV. Support of hypothesis from web-building evidence (¶4)

V. Further support for hypothesis by showing that it offers what seems to be a sufficient cause to explain the spider's actions (¶5)

This structure may be simplified still further:

I. Introduction to pose the question

II. Refutation of unsatisfactory answers

III. Discovery and support of a satisfactory cause

EXERCISE

Analyze the structure of the following selection by first making a paragraph summary, then converting the summary to a simple outline, as was done with the causal process essay about the spider and the wasp. Then explain how the three paragraphs of the selection are related.

What we know of prenatal development makes all this [attempts made by a mother to mold the character of her unborn child by studying poetry, art, or mathematics during pregnancy] seem utterly impossible. How could such extremely complex influences pass from the mother to the child? There is no connection between their nervous systems. Even the blood vessels of mother and child do not join directly. They lie side by side and the chemicals are interchanged through the walls by a process that we call osmosis. An emotional shock to the mother will affect her child, because it changes the activity of her glands and so the chemistry of her blood. Any chemical change in the mother's blood will affect the child—for better or worse. But we cannot see how a liking for mathematics or poetic genius can be dissolved in blood and produce a similar liking or genius in the child.

In our discussion of instincts we saw that there was reason to believe that whatever we inherit must be of some very simple sort rather than any complicated or very definite kind of behavior. It is certain that no one inherits a knowledge of mathematics. It may be, however, that children inherit more or less of a rather general ability that we may call intelligence. If very intelligent children become deeply interested in mathematics, they will probably make a success of that study.

As for musical ability, it may be that what is inherited is an especially sensitive ear, a peculiar structure of the hands or of the vocal organs, connections between nerves and muscles that make it comparatively easy to learn the movements a musician must execute, and particularly vigorous emotions. If these factors are all organized around music, the child may become a musician. The same factors, in other circumstances, might be organized about some other center of interest. The rich emotional equipment might find expression in poetry. The capable fingers might develop skill in surgery. It is not the knowledge of music that is inherited, then, nor even the love of it, but a certain bodily structure that makes it comparatively easy to acquire musical knowledge and skill. Whether that ability shall be directed toward music or some other undertaking may be decided entirely by forces in the environment in which a child grows up.[10]

[10] From William H. Roberts, *Psychology You Can Use* (New York: Harcourt, Brace & World, Inc., 1943).

Chapter 4

Shaping and Testing An Outline

For many of the papers you write, the nature of your material and your purpose will determine your pattern of organization. When your purpose requires you to explain or illustrate a general statement by details or examples, you will use some variant of the illustrative pattern. Other kinds of materials lead to organization by comparison or contrast, analogy, classification, or process. The pattern of organization you follow for any unit of material is determined by the nature of the material and what you plan to do with it.

For short papers, a clearly stated thesis and a few notes may provide all the written plan you need. But for longer papers, especially critical and research papers, you may be asked to present an extensive outline at the end of the prewriting stage so that you and your instructor can check the plan before you begin to write the paper.

TOPIC AND SENTENCE OUTLINES

In a *topic outline* the entries are not complete sentences but headings consisting of single words or phrases which identify the topic to be discussed under each heading. You have seen such an outline on pages 63 and 65 and will see a more fully developed one on page 74.

In a *sentence outline* each entry is a complete sentence. It not only identifies the topic to be dealt with; it states what is to be said about the topic. Thus:

Topic entry: Population growth

Sentence entry: Population growth is a consequence of two main factors: increasing birth rate and decreasing death rate.

The difference between topic and sentence outlines is as much one of use as one of form. The topic outline is convenient for setting down stages in a process—e.g., tee shots, fairway shots, approach shots, putting strokes—or the categories of a classification. It allows the writer to block out his subject matter. But it does not tell him, or his reader, what is to be done with these parts. The sentence outline is the better form when the content is not a label but an idea. It is more restricting than the topic form, and as we saw in studying the thesis, this restriction helps the writer by controlling him. The decision about which form to use depends on what the essay is to do. If it is going to develop a thesis, the sentence outline will be safer; otherwise, the topic outline will be more convenient.

In practice, most sentence outlines emerge from preliminary topic outlines. The first step is usually to block out the areas of the subject:

> I. Population growth
> A. Birth rate
> B. Death rate

Such headings are useful, but they are a long way from saying anything specific about the topics. The writer then asks what he wants to say about the topics, and his answers convert the headings into sentences:

I. The growth of human population is a function of two main factors.

    A. The birth rate has been steadily increasing over the past century.

    B. The death rate has been steadily decreasing over a much longer time.

Each of these sentences can become the topic sentence of a paragraph or a thesis for a series of paragraphs comprising a larger unit of composition. The writer then develops each unit.

SHAPING THE OUTLINE

If a writer begins to outline before he has clearly established the purpose of his essay, he will have to experiment with trial outlines in order to find out how his material should be shaped. He will be like the student trying to see what patterns of semantic change are illustrated by the list of words on page 55. As long as he understands that he is groping for a plan, these trial outlines will help him discover what his essay should do. The danger is that he may settle too soon for an inefficient plan. It is always safer to postpone the formal outlining until the controlling decision about purpose has been firmly made. But if tentative or trial outlines are necessary, the final plan should be carefully checked before the writing is begun.

The following sequence shows an outline emerging through successive stages. It is assumed that the writer has already made a serious study of the influence of heredity and environment on the individual and has concluded that neither can be proved to be more important than the other. This conclusion is the *thesis* of his essay.

Stage I
Simple topic out-
line establishes
over-all organiza-
tion by identifying
major topics to be
discussed

Thesis: It is not possible to prove that either heredity or environment is the more important influence on the individual.

   I. Difficulties of defining "heredity" and "environment"
  II. Difficulties of studying cases of the past
 III. Difficulties of experimental studies

Stage II
Major topics of
earlier outline are
further subdivided
and entries begin
to take shape as
sentences. These
are not always
finished sentences,
but they begin to
convert topics into
statements of ideas
and thus indicate
what is to be said
about the topics.

Thesis: It is not possible to prove that either heredity or environment is the more important influence on the individual.

   I. Terms "heredity" and "environment" not definable.
     A. Heredity and environment cannot be separated.
     B. "Environment" too vague a term.
  II. Studies of famous and infamous people are not decisive.
     A. Famous people: Shakespeare, Newton, Lincoln.
     B. Infamous people: the Jukes family.
 III. Heredity and environment cannot be isolated in studies of children.
     A. Newborn babies have already had nine months of prenatal environment.
     B. Fraternal twins have different inheritances, and may or may not have significantly different environments.
     C. Identical twins do have the same inheritance, but we cannot be sure they have the same environment.

Heredity vs. Environment

Stage III
This final stage in-
cludes the follow-
ing revisions:
1. The subdivision
of previous entries
is completed.
2. All entries are
expressed as fin-
ished sentences
and these are re-
vised, if necessary,
so that all sen-
tences are as par-
allel in form as
they can be made.
3. As a result of
these revisions,
each entry be-
comes a potential
topic sentence for
one or more para-
graphs of the
essay, and the out-
line also serves as
a paragraph sum-
mary of the whole.

Thesis: It is not possible to prove that either heredity or environment is the more important influence on the individual.

   I. In practice we are not able to define "heredity" or "environment" with precision.
     A. We are not able to define "heredity" except in terms of characteristics which may have been influenced by environment.
       1. Some inherited characteristics of fruit flies appear only when the environment encourages their appearance.
       2. An acorn will never grow into anything but an oak tree, but whether it becomes an oak tree or not depends on environmental conditions.
     B. We are not able to define "environment" with precision.
       1. The environment of individuals in a society is so complex that we cannot define it rigorously.
       2. Except in very limited laboratory experiments, the word "environment" is so vague that it is useless for serious discussion.
  II. We cannot reach any trustworthy conclusions about the relative influences of heredity and environment by studying the histories of famous or infamous people.

A. A study of Shakespeare, Newton, and Lincoln provides us no answer.
 1. If their greatness was due to inheritance, why were other members of their families not distinguished?
 2. If their greatness was due to environment, why did others in the same environment not achieve greatness?
B. A study of the notorious Jukes family provides no conclusive answer.
 1. We know that the Jukes family had a bad inheritance and a record of delinquency, but we cannot be sure that the inheritance caused the delinquency.
 2. The Jukes family members had each other as part of their environment, and it is probable that any child brought up in that environment would have become a delinquent.

III. We cannot experimentally study heredity or environment apart from each other.
A. We cannot do it by studying newborn babies.
 1. They have had nine months of prenatal environment.
 2. They may or may not later display characteristics which are assumed to be inherited.
B. We cannot do it by studying fraternal twins.
 1. Such twins come from different eggs and have different inheritances.
 2. Such twins may have quite different environments; for example, a boy twin has a different environment from a girl twin, even when brought up in the same family.
C. We cannot even do it by studying identical twins because, although they have the same inheritance, we cannot be sure that they have the same environment.

In planning such an outline it is wise to lay out the main divisions before worrying about subdivisions. Establish all Roman-numeral headings first; then break down each Roman-numeral heading into capital-letter entries, and so on, following the principle of completing one level of division before starting the next lower level. This way you remain in control of your outline: you will not be likely to distort the organization by developing some headings too much and others too little. Since any change in the content of the main headings (though not necessarily in the style) will probably require changes in the subheadings, too early attention to subheadings may be time wasted. Finally, when a careful outline is required, keep the thesis and main headings in your mind and reconsider them at convenient intervals. Especially try to avoid finishing the outline at a single sitting. Second thoughts are often better than first, and you want to be sure about the over-all structure of your ideas before you begin to develop them in detail.

TESTING THE OUTLINE

As a check of the structure, it is usually wise to test the outline by asking the following questions:

1. Is the thesis satisfactory?
2. Is the relation among the parts clear and consistent?
3. Does the order of the parts (sequence) provide a logical progression from the thesis?
4. Is the outline complete?
5. Can each entry be developed in detail?

Is the Thesis Satisfactory?

Since the thesis controls the whole outline, a faulty statement invites trouble all along the way. As we have seen, the thesis should be restricted, unified, and precise. A poorly stated thesis can lead to a badly organized or a pointless paper. A rigorous checking of the thesis is therefore the first and most important step in testing the usefulness of a tentative outline.

As an additional illustration of what may develop from an unsatisfactory thesis, consider the following:

The purpose of this paper is to provide a better understanding of the American Indian by revealing a few facts about his everyday life and customs.

The author of this statement has not really restricted his topic or clarified his purpose, and any paper he writes is likely to be scattered and superficial. Why does he think that "a few facts" about the everyday life and customs of the Indian will help us to understand him better? What kind of facts? What will be his criterion for using some facts and omitting others? When we look at his outline we see, as his thesis suggests, that he is going to write a pointless paper "about" the American Indian.

I. The Indian's religion differs from the white man's.
   A. The Indian's religion is complicated.
   B. His conception of the supernatural has a strong influence on his everyday life.
II. The Indian medicine man is one of the most important people in the tribe.
   A. The training of the medicine man begins at an early age.
III. Dancing is of great importance in the life of the Indian.
   A. There are many classes of dancing.
   B. The instruments used to accompany the dancers are of a wide variation.
IV. The education of the Indian was not very extensive.
   A. There were several Indian colleges built.
V. The government of the Indian was simple.
   A. There were four divisions in the government.

The vagueness of the thesis encouraged the student to tack on anything that had any connection with his general subject. This example is an unusually bad one, but it shows what can happen when a student bases an outline on a fuzzy, pointless thesis.

Is the Relationship Among the Parts Clear and Consistent?

In a good outline one can see how each main unit brings out an important aspect of the thesis and how each subdivision helps to develop its main heading. If there is any doubt about the relation of any heading to the thesis, that heading is either poorly stated or is a potential trouble spot in the outline. Whatever the reason, the difficulty should be removed before writing is begun.

Notice how clear is the relation among all parts of the following outline. Each Roman numeral shows a distinct relation to the thesis; each capital letter is a logical division of its Roman numeral. No entry in the outline fails to advance the purpose, and each introduces, at its proper place, a significant part of the argument.

Thesis: The development of the community college as an alternative to the traditional four-year college has provided a necessary extension of opportunity in higher education.

  I. The traditional four-year college system was discriminatory.
    A. It discriminated in favor of wealth.
    B. It discriminated in favor of special preparation.
    C. It discriminated in favor of special ability.

  II. The four-year system was geared to a few specialized interests.
    A. It was geared to liberal arts education.
    B. It was geared to a limited number of professions, e.g., law, medicine, and engineering.
    C. It was geared to the training of teachers.

  III. Community colleges, largely a development of the '60's, admit many persons formerly excluded from higher education.
    A. They admit many who could not afford a four-year college.
    B. They admit many who could not meet the entrance requirements of a four-year college.
    C. They admit many whose interests could not be met by a four-year college.

  IV. Community colleges provide education in professional, semi-professional, and vocational areas not served by the traditional four-year college system.
    A. They offer training for newer professions such as police science, firefighting, and paramedical specialties.
    B. They offer training for vocations such as auto mechanics, keypunch operation, and electronics.

A good way to test an outline is to ask, for every entry, whether it points back to the one it is developing. The capital-letter entries should point back to the Roman-numeral entry they are developing:

II. The four-year system was geared to a few specialized interests.

    A. It was geared to liberal arts education.

    B. It was geared to a limited number of professions, e.g., law, medicine, and engineering.

    C. It was geared to the training of teachers.

Notice also that inconsistency in the form of the entries or parts will make their relationship less clear.

II. The four-year system was geared to a few specialized interests.

    A. It was geared to liberal arts education.

    B. Professions such as law, medicine, and engineering were served by the system.

    C. The training of teachers was one of its main activities.

In this version, where A, B, and C are no longer parallel in form, their parallel relationship to their main heading is obscured. Consistency in the form of topics is not just a matter of style; it emphasizes their relation to each other and to the topic they develop.

Does the Order of the Parts Provide a Logical Progression?

Just as the sentences within a paragraph must follow a logical order, so must the parts of an outline. If any of the parts are out of order, the disorder will be magnified in the essay, and a reader will be confused or irritated. In the pair of outlines in parallel columns on page 74, compare the faulty version at the right with the more logical one at the left.

The outline at the left follows a *before-during-after* order. Part I describes the condition in which Elizabeth found the fleet, part II shows her support of the new naval leaders, part III deals with the immediate results of that support, and part IV summarizes all the results in a contrast with part I. Within these main units there is a logical progression of ideas. Within II the order goes from why Elizabeth acted (A) to what she did (B). In III the order is a succession of related consequences of her actions, which builds up to the contrast between I and IV. Throughout the outline the emphasis is on Elizabeth's contribution, as the purpose requires.

The order in the outline at the right follows no evident logical progression from the purpose statement. Elizabeth is mentioned only once, late in the outline in a minor heading (II C 1), and then without suggesting her contribution. In the main units the order seems to be haphazard. Part II —

Purpose: To show Elizabeth's contribution to the development of the English navy

I. Condition of navy prior to Elizabeth's reign
   A. Its size compared with first-rate navies
   B. Its lack of government support
   C. Its inefficient use

II. Elizabeth's support of the "Sea Dogs"—Drake, Frobisher, Howard, Raleigh, and Grenville
   A. Political and economic reasons for her support
   B. Nature and extent of her support

III. Results of Elizabeth's support of Sea Dogs
   A. Economic rivalry with Spain
   B. Defeat of Armada and new prestige of English navy
   C. Extensive shipbuilding program to forestall Spanish retaliation
   D. More efficient design for ships
   E. Improved theory of naval warfare
   F. Foundation of English naval tradition

IV. Summary of condition of navy at end of Elizabeth's reign in contrast to condition described in I above

Purpose: To show Elizabeth's contribution to the development of the English navy

I. Condition of navy prior to Elizabeth's reign
   A. Navy relatively small in comparison with other first-rate powers
   B. Inadequate government attention to fleet

II. Development of naval warfare during the period
   A. Importance of battle with Spanish Armada
     1. Types of warfare used by both sides
     2. Defeat of Armada a turning point in English history
   B. Brief description of offensive and defensive forces of English navy
     1. Classification of ships as to size and armament
     2. Location of forces
   C. Work of Elizabethan Sea Dogs
     1. Influence upon Elizabeth
     2. Sea Dog fighting tactics
       a. Work of Drake
       b. Treatment of Spanish ships

III. Comparison of formation and battle tactics of Elizabethan and modern navies
   A. Factors of formation and battle tactics
   B. Closing paragraph

the largest unit — is limited to naval warfare, and part III is a wholly irrelevant comparison between Elizabethan and modern navies. Within the big central part II the organization is puzzling. What is the relation between types of warfare used by both sides (A 1) and the importance of the battle with the Armada? Does B 2 overlap A 1? Why does C shift the emphasis from Elizabeth to the Sea Dogs, when she is the subject of the paper? And if C is concerned with the Sea Dogs, why is only Drake mentioned?

The contrast between the logical order of these two outlines will be easier to see in the following simplification.

Logical Progression	Illogical Progression
I. Conditions existing before Elizabeth acted	I. Conditions existing before Elizabeth acted
II. What she did, and why	II. A collection of material, including types of warfare, significance of the Armada's defeat, the work of the Sea Dogs (chiefly Drake), treatment of the Spanish ships
III. The results of her action	
IV. Contrasted summary of the situation in I and III	III. Comparison of Elizabethan and modern navies

A careful comparison of these two outlines should suggest two conclusions. First, unless a writer seeks a logical progression, he can drift into a plan which does not organize, but merely ties material into bundles without regard to why things are put in one bundle rather than another, or even why the bundles were made up in the first place. Second, if the progression of ideas or materials is confused in the outline, it will be worse in the essay. The writer then simply passes his confusion along to the reader.

It will be obvious that the chief trouble in the outline at the right lies in the second main heading. The profitable question to consider is: How can a student detect such errors before they are allowed to give a faulty organization to his paper? Some general answers are possible. First, it will be easier to see the faults of an outline on the day after it has been constructed, when the student can approach the task with more objectivity. Second, when faced with what is possibly just a collection of material, the student can ask himself: What is the common subject of this material: What precise contribution to the navy did Elizabeth make here? Notice that a sentence outline might have saved the writer from trouble by restricting the things he could do under a sentence entry. Third, since this section is presumably dealing with Elizabeth's contribution, the writer could ask himself, at each subheading: Is this clearly a contribution that Elizabeth herself made? If it is a contribution, but the contribution is obscured by the heading, then the correction lies in revising the heading to make it show what it is intended to show. If this cannot be done, then the material is probably irrelevant to the purpose. Finally, these suggestions can be summed up in one piece of general advice: ask yourself, *What answer will I give the instructor if he thinks the progression of ideas here is not clear or not logical?* That question will force you to challenge the structure of the outline.

Is the Outline Complete? This is really not one question but two: first, are all major units of the subject represented; second, is each major unit subdivided far enough to guide the development of the essay? In college essays, the second consideration is the more important. Obviously, if we are going to divide Gaul into three parts, we should deal with three parts. It is less obvious, but not less important, that if we are going to discuss the work of the Elizabethan Sea Dogs, we must not stop with Drake.

If you compare the two outlines we have just considered, you will see that part III of the left-hand outline provides a fuller subdivision of the material inadequately suggested in II C of the right-hand version. As a plan for a paper, the six headings under III at the left provide a fuller plan than the two headings under II C at the right. Of course, a writer may compensate for incomplete subdivision in the outline by complete development in the essay. But that requires him to do better planning while writing than he did when he was concerned only with planning. *In practice, students almost never correct the deficiencies of an outline during the composition of an essay.* Flaws in the outline are almost certain to be preserved.

Can Each Entry Be Developed in Detail?

Each entry in the outline should be fully developed when the essay is written. Every instructor has known students who construct outlines containing entries for which they have no material, so that all they have to say about these entries is what they have already said in the outline. *Every entry in an outline should be adequately developed, and no entry should appear unless the author has the material to develop it.* There can be no rigid rule about how much development each entry should receive. Sometimes a single entry will require two or three paragraphs in the essay; occasionally several minor entries may be dealt with in a single paragraph. For inexperienced writers, *a useful rule of thumb is that each entry will usually be developed into at least one paragraph.*

SUMMARY

1. In a topic outline the entries are expressed in words or phrases; in a sentence outline each entry is a complete sentence. The topic outline is better for an essay which does not develop a dominant idea; for a paper that does develop an idea (thesis), the sentence outline is preferable. In practice, most sentence outlines evolve out of preliminary topic outlines.

2. The conventions of outlining require that all headings be given an appropriate symbol and be indented to show the degree of subdivision. They also require that the outline distinguish major and minor divisions and keep the grammatical structure of all headings parallel.

3. In preparing an outline, finish the major divisions before you touch minor ones. Do the Roman numerals before you begin the capital letters, and the capitals before the Arabic numerals. This will insure that you work out the outline in a series of stages.

4. When you think your outline is complete, test it by considering the following questions: (*a*) Is the thesis satisfactory? (*b*) Is there a clear and

consistent relationship between the thesis and each main division, and between the main and minor entries? Do the Roman numerals point back to the thesis, and the capital letters to the Roman numerals? (*c*) Does the order of the parts provide a logical progression from the thesis? (*d*) Is the outline complete? Have all the major units been presented, and have the subdivisions been carried far enough to provide a reliable guide for the actual composition?

EXERCISES

A. *Below are the thesis and Roman numerals of a sentence outline. Beneath these are sixteen statements that comprise the capital letters and Arabic numerals. From these data, reconstruct the complete outline.*

Thesis: Plastic surgery for veterans attempts to improve both function and appearance.

    I. The plastic surgeon is primarily concerned with restoring function.

    II. The plastic surgeon is also interested in improving the appearance of the scarred and the wounded.

1. The hands and arms are among the first portions of the body to be restored.
2. The plastic surgeon can rebuild an entire new face for the patient.
3. Noses are rebuilt to enable patients to breathe and to improve appearance.
4. New eyelids are made to protect eyes.
5. Leg and arm stumps may be made healthy and alive by plastic surgery before artificial limbs are applied.
6. Scars that make veterans hideous are removed.
7. Patients are restored to their former appearance as nearly as possible.
8. Ears are restored by plastic surgery.
9. New tendons are put into fingers so they can move.
10. Skin grafts are done on visible burns.
11. Thumb and forefinger are most important to save so that the hand can function.
12. Lower jaws are rebuilt so that a patient can eat, drink, and speak naturally.
13. Entire forearms are rebuilt by plastic surgery.
14. Scars that are opened and undermined, then sewed together, heal neatly without scarring.
15. Hands are most important for the veteran to help himself.
16. Surgeons connect live tissue to a paralyzed area to heal it almost without a defect.

B. *Make a topic outline of "Twinkletoes and the Tailback" (page 27).*

C. *Study the following notes carefully and group like information together—for instance, all the good things about technology on one page and all the bad things on another. Second, within each of these groups, arrange the notes under topic headings: health, transportation, pollution, and so on. When you have done this, write an outline to show the relations among your groups. Finally, write any thesis that you think your outline develops, and revise the outline if necessary to show clear relationships between the main headings and the thesis, and between the main headings and the subheadings. You may ignore any notes in the list which are not relevant to your thesis, but if you do, be sure that you can justify your rejection of them.*

1. Many once-common diseases, such as tuberculosis, diphtheria, and small-pox, have been substantially brought under control.

2. For the first time in history man could now produce enough food to eliminate hunger from the world.

3. The death rate from automobile accidents in this country is approaching 50,000 a year.

4. Among the triumphs of technology are modern plumbing, heating, and air conditioning.

5. One of our great problems today is air pollution from industrial smoke, heating fuels, and automobile exhausts.

6. Beginning in 1347, the plague known as the Black Death wiped out at least one-fourth the population of Europe.

7. Given present atomic weapons, World War III could mean the end of the human race and life on earth.

8. In the late nineteenth century the lumber industry in this country denuded millions of acres of land.

9. Largely through improved diet and medical care, the death rate in the United States has been cut almost in half since 1900, and the rate of live births has almost doubled.

10. Improvements in grains, livestock, and other agricultural products have quadrupled the productivity of the American farm in the last fifty years.

11. Noise pollution is increasingly serious, especially near airports, highways, construction sites, and some factories.

12. Some people blame the weakening of family ties on the telephone, the automobile, and television.

13. Planned obsolescence, the making of products so that they will wear out quickly and will soon be replaced by newer models, is being increasingly criticized.

14. Where we now have sixty commuters in sixty automobiles with sixty exhaust pipes, one bus can carry sixty people—with only one exhaust pipe.

15. Antibiotics, vaccines, and antiseptics have saved countless lives.

16. In 1900, 60% of the U.S. population was agricultural. Today that figure has declined to about 20%.

17. The automobile has given us previously unknown opportunities for travel, commuting, pleasure, and daily activities of all kinds.

18. On the once-famous train the Wabash *Cannonball* it took eight hours to go from St. Louis to Detroit. It now takes one hour to fly.

19. The increase in size and weight of the Japanese population since World War II is striking evidence of the effects of improved food and medical services.

20. The lumber industry developed the practice of reforestation on the concept of "perpetual yield." Other national resources would benefit by application of this principle.

21. Instead of abandoning an old car on the street, one can sell it for $20 to a company that "squashes" it to a manageable cube so that the metal can be reused.

22. The upper and middle classes have left the cities for the suburbs, and at the same time displaced workers have flocked to the cities and created ghettos.

23. When we have sent surplus food to a foreign country, that country's agricultural economy has sometimes suffered from the loss of its own natural market.

24. For many, the automobile is a symbol of false values, an opportunity for illicit activities, a means of escape from responsibility, and an aid to crime.

25. At the present rate of growth, the world's population will have doubled by the year 2000.

26. Many people think cancellation of plans for the supersonic transport plane is a victory in the war against pollution.

Part Two
Writing and Rewriting

Chapter 5

Paragraphs: Compositions in Miniature

So far we have dealt with prewriting—with choosing and restricting a subject, formulating purpose, finding and organizing material. We turn now to the actual process of writing, and we begin with the largest unit within the whole composition, the paragraph.

The usual paragraph within the body of a piece of writing can be thought of as a composition in miniature. On a smaller scale, it requires much the same process of organizing and developing as a whole essay. It has a dominant idea, sometimes implied, but often expressed in a topic sentence (thesis). This idea is *developed* by examples, comparisons, explanations, or arguments to make the meaning of the topic sentence clear. There is often a concluding restatement of the topic idea, similar to the concluding paragraph of an essay.

The following paragraph starts with a topic sentence, develops it through two explanatory sentences and two examples, and ends with a summary conclusion. In the marginal notations at the left, *T* stands for topic sentence, *E* for examples, and *C* for conclusion or restatement of the topic sentence.

T

Explanation of topic sentence

By a strange perversity in the cosmic plan, the biologically good die young. Species are not destroyed for their shortcomings but for their achievements. The tribes that slumber in the graveyards of the past were not the most simple and undistinguished of their day, but the most complicated and conspicuous.

E_1 The magnificent sharks of the Devonian period passed with the passing of the period, but certain contemporaneous genera of primitive shellfish are still on

E_2 earth. Similarly, the lizards of the Mesozoic era have long outlived the dinosaurs who were immeasurably their biologic betters. Illustrations such as these

C could be endlessly increased. The price of distinction is death.[1]

[1] From John Hodgdon Bradley, "Is Man an Absurdity?" *Harper's Magazine*, October 1936.

The topic of this paragraph is the survival of species, and the thesis is that highly developed species tend to die out. This idea is stated in the opening sentence and explained in the second and third sentences. The fourth and fifth sentences each give an example; the sixth indicates that other examples are legion; and the final sentence rephrases the topic idea. The paragraph thus has the structure of an essay on a small scale: introduction, body, and conclusion.

DEVELOPING PARAGRAPHS: FOUR REQUIREMENTS

To be a composition in miniature, a paragraph must meet certain requirements. It must discuss one topic only; it must say all its reader needs to know about it; it must adopt an order easy to follow; and it must hang together. In other words, it must have *unity, completeness, order,* and *coherence.*

Unity

Unity in a paragraph is internal consistency. Anything that does not further the purpose of a paragraph destroys its unity. You saw an example of broken unity in the student paper "On Your Own" (page 19), which drifted away from the announced purpose and wound up saying nearly the opposite. Reread the second paragraph of that paper and note that in the third sentence the author was trapped into a digression when he wrote, "The first thing I did when I arrived on campus was to go to the dormitory and get my room." At that point the reader expects an account of some difficulty which illustrates the topic sentence, "During Freshman Week I did not know whether I was coming or going." But "the first thing I did" suggests to the writer the second and third things, so that he drifts into an account of his actions, almost none of which illustrate the confusion he had promised to reveal. He lost control simply by forgetting what he set out to do. For such a paragraph, the only cure is rewriting to make the paragraph consistently develop its topic sentence.

EXERCISES

A. In the following paragraph, first find the start of the digression, then rewrite to give unity. Assume that your reader is a high school student who will be going to college next year.

In college writing the main emphasis is on content. It is what you have to say that counts most, and you are expected to think out the content of a paper before you begin to write. Mechanical correctness is still important, but you are supposed to have learned about that in high school. Such things as period faults, comma splices, dangling modifiers, faulty pronoun references, and bad spelling can fail a paper. So be sure that you can recognize these errors and correct them. I have found that it pays to go over my first drafts carefully to catch such mistakes, and I often wish we had spent more time on proofreading in high school. Believe me, it is a discouraging experience to plan carefully what you want to do in a paper and then have it returned with the comment, "The content of this essay is pretty good, but the grammar and spelling are atrocious."

B. *The following paragraph lacks unity for a different reason. It does not change its direction, but one sentence is off the topic. As you read it, see if you can tell which one.*

It is a good thing that we learn to speak as children. If the learning were postponed until we were adults, most of us would be too discouraged by the difficulties to persevere in the task. Perhaps, in that event, our political campaigns would be conducted in sign language and our radio broadcasters would be required to learn the Morse code. We take a child's learning to talk for granted, and not infrequently parents grow worried when their four-year-old stumbles over his consonants or becomes snarled in his syntax. Yet compared with the intellectual achievement of learning to talk, the discovery of the theory of relativity is a trifling accomplishment.

Completeness Completeness is relative. How much development an idea requires depends on how much a reader needs to be told in order to understand it. The following gives almost a minimum answer to a question:

Does it ever get too cold to snow? It never gets too cold to snow, but it frequently gets too cold for snow to fall in flakes, because at subzero temperatures the air is too dry to produce snowflakes.

The second sentence answers the question asked by the first, but not in detail. Most readers want to be told *why* subzero air is too dry to produce snowflakes. The paragraph is therefore not complete. This is what the author actually wrote:

Too cold to snow? It never gets too cold to snow, but it frequently gets too cold for snow to fall in flakes. *Flakes fall when the air through which they pass is 32° Fahrenheit or slightly lower. At this temperature the air usually holds enough moisture to allow the flakes to become fat and mat together, and the fall is likely to be heavy. As the temperature sinks lower, the air becomes drier, the snowfall lighter and more powdery. At temperatures below zero a heavy fall of snow is rare. The snow that does fall takes the form of ice spicules, ice needles, or fills the air with fine, glittering, diamond-like dust.* The air at these subzero temperatures is usually too dry to produce flakes.[2]

---

[2] From *The World Almanac.*

Here the italicized explanation is the real substance, or development, of the paragraph, and the original becomes the topic and concluding sentences. This detailed version provides a more complete answer.

The following paragraphs are incomplete for any reader who does not have from experience the detailed information their writers had in mind. Assuming that your reader has not had this experience, complete the paragraphs by providing details. Remember that it is the reader, not the writer, who has to be satisfied.

1. It used to be that when I had to write a paper for English class, I would sit and stare at a piece of blank paper for hours, and then wring out sentences one at a time until I had the number of words I needed. I have now begun to see that there is a better and an easier way. I still have a lot to learn, but I can't tell you how much easier the process seems already.

2. To excel in any skill, talent alone is not enough. Every kind of worthwhile activity has its special technique. Talent *and* technique is my motto from now on.

Order

Like structure in a larger composition, order in a paragraph grows partly out of the material and is partly imposed by the writer. A narrative process (see pages 59–62) follows a time order; some descriptions must be arranged spatially, from left to right, bottom to top, or near to far. Most expository materials fit best into one of four patterns: (1) from *general to particular;* (2) from *particular to general;* (3) from *whole to parts;* and (4) from *question to answer* or *effect to cause.*

General to Particular. This most popular order for expository paragraphs begins with a topic sentence which serves as an introductory summary of the topic. The remaining sentences explain or illustrate this statement, so that the idea becomes increasingly clear as the paragraph progresses. The paragraphs about the extinct species (page 83) and snow (page 85) both follow this pattern, the first with a series of examples, the second with an explanation. The nature of the development depends on the nature of the topic. While some topics need examples or explanation, others require comparison or contrast to develop similarities or differences, and still others call for description of a process or proof of a conclusion. The writer must decide, but if he knows his material the decision should not be difficult.

The following cites a battery of details to illustrate the opening generalization about the "miracle" of New York.

Topic sentence (thesis)	It is a miracle that New York works at all. The whole thing is implausible.
Subtopic 1	Every time the residents brush their teeth, millions of gallons of water must
Example 1	be drawn from the Catskills and the hills of Westchester. When a young man
Example 2	in Manhattan writes a letter to his girl in Brooklyn, the love message gets

It is a miracle that New York works at all. The whole thing is implausible. Every time the residents brush their teeth, millions of gallons of water must be drawn from the Catskills and the hills of Westchester. When a young man in Manhattan writes a letter to his girl in Brooklyn, the love message gets blown to her through a pneumatic tube—*pfft*—just like that. The subterranean system of telephone cables, power lines, steam pipes, gas mains and sewer pipes is reason enough to abandon the island to the gods and the weevils. Every time an incision is made in the pavement, the noisy surgeons expose ganglia that are tangled beyond belief. By rights New York should have destroyed itself long ago, from panic or fire or rioting or failure of some vital supply line in its circulatory system or from some deep labyrinthine short circuit. Long ago the city should have experienced an insoluble traffic snarl at some impossible bottleneck. It should have perished of hunger when food lines failed for a few days. It should have been wiped out by a plague starting in its slums or carried in by ships' rats. It should have been overwhelmed by the sea that licks at it on every side. The workers in its myriad cells should have succumbed to nerves, from the fearful pall of smoke-fog that drifts over every few days from Jersey, blotting out all light at noon and leaving the high offices suspended, men groping and depressed, and the sense of world's end.[3]

This paragraph begins with a topic sentence which has two subtopics. Each subtopic is clearly stated, and each is developed by a series of examples.

A common variation of the general-to-particular order is the paragraph that not only begins but also ends with a general statement. Until the last sentence, such a paragraph follows a general-to-particular order; then the topic idea is restated, usually in different words, as a concluding sentence. The specimen paragraph on page 83 is an example of this variation.

Particular to General.   One may reverse the order shown above and begin with particulars that lead to a general statement or summary, as in the following:

If you enjoy working out the strategy of games, tit-tat-toe or poker or chess; if you are interested in the frog who jumped up three feet and fell back two in getting out of a well, or in the fly buzzing between the noses of two

---

[3] From *Here Is New York* by E. B. White. Copyright, 1949 by E. B. White. Reprinted by permission of Harper & Row, Publishers, Inc.

approaching cyclists, or in the farmer who left land to his three sons; if you have been captivated by codes and ciphers or are interested in crossword puzzles; if you like to fool around with numbers; if music appeals to you by the sense of form which it expresses—then you will enjoy logic. You ought to be warned, perhaps. Those who take up logic get glassy-eyed and absent-minded. They join a fanatical cult. But they have a good time. Theirs is one of the most durable, absorbing and inexpensive of pleasures. *Logic is fun.*[4]

Here the examples come first: strategy of games, tit-tat-toe, and so on, in a series of *if*-clauses for over two-thirds of the paragraph. The writer then begins to generalize, and ends with his topic sentence, "*Logic is fun.*"

Whole to Parts.   Sometimes the purpose of a paragraph is not to explain an idea but to identify the parts or divisions of a topic. Thus a paragraph on the writing process might identify and define its three stages, prewriting, writing, and rewriting. Such a paragraph would have only a nominal topic sentence, such as "Usually the writing process goes through three stages." It would move not from general to particular or from particular to general, but from one stage or division to the next.

This kind of paragraph is sometimes called *enumerative,* because it lists or enumerates the parts of a topic. It is useful in summaries which show only the headings under which a topic is to be discussed. It is used in argument to list the issues to be considered, or as a conclusion to sum up what has been done. In the body of an essay its lack of detail can be a weakness, especially in a paragraph which becomes merely a list of subtopics.

The following paragraph illustrates the whole-to-parts order but goes beyond simple identification to suggest reasons for the objections it enumerates. It is still a summary of an argument that would need more space to be fully persuasive.

There are three objections to having students confer in small committees on their plans for projected papers. The first is that each set of conferences would require a full class hour. If a composition class meets three times a week, then one-third of the instructional time would be lost in each week in which conferences were held. The conferences would have to be very valuable to justify that expenditure of time. The second objection is that the conferences would weaken individual responsibility and initiative. Students would begin to depend on committee members to plan their papers for them, and the weakest or laziest students would become dependent on that assistance. Finally, the conference system would be a terrible waste of time for superior students, who could expect no constructive criticism of their plans and would simply be devoting a class hour as unpaid teaching assistants.

[4] From Roger W. Holmes, *The Rhyme of Reason* (New York: Appleton-Century, 1939).

Question to Answer, Effect to Cause. A paragraph may begin with a question and give the answer, or with an effect and explain the cause. Such a paragraph may have no specific topic sentence beyond the opening question, problem, or dilemma. The answer or cause is given by the rest of the paragraph. The following paragraph goes from question to answer.

Why does Socrates appeal to contemporary students? They respond to his fearless assertion of his right to determine his own conduct despite powerful opposition from the majority of his fellow citizens. The conflict between individual freedom and sociopolitical authority which he dramatizes expresses their own central dilemma. These students have outgrown the disciplines of parents. In college, various authorities—the college administration, campus mores, and student cliques—vie for their allegiance. They are also uneasily conscious of the different standards of the professional and business worlds they are about to enter. The sensitive student, confused by these uncertain values, is thrilled when Socrates, the original rebel who became the "father" of philosophy, tells his fellow Athenians that he loves and cherishes them, but chooses to obey only his own vision of the right and good. Socrates' example can still engender a revolutionary fervor in youthful hearts. It was hardly an accident that the campus rebellions at Berkeley and earlier at the University of Colorado were led by philosophy majors.[5]

In the following paragraph the first sentence states an effect and the rest analyze its causes. The final sentence sums up the causes.

While the revolutionary remains the hero of our times, no other revolutionary hero will supplant Che. The rapid development of his cult after his death was the logical outcome of the end of his life, which had been spent in an atmosphere of secrecy, mystery, potency, and combat. Che's cowardly murder brought him instant consecration, because his death made certain all the qualities ascribed to him. His choice to leave Cuba and his martyrdom for his cause set him above Fidel Castro or Ho Chi Minh or Mao Tse-tung as a symbol of revolution, even though his talents as a guerrilla leader may have been inferior. If Che had remained in Cuba or had died accidentally like Camilo Cienfuegos, his portrait would not be paraded by students all over the world, his example would not be quoted everywhere, his works would not be so widely read. Not only Marxists, but almost all progressives, and even pacifists who qualify their admiration for Che by warning that they disagree with some of his methods, would agree with Fidel's praise of Che's qualities as a man: "If we wish to express what we want the men of future generations to be, we must say: 'Let them be like Che.' "[6]

[5] From J. Glenn Gray, "Salvation on the Campus: Why Existentialism Is Capturing the Students," *Harper's Magazine*, May 1965.
[6] Andrew Sinclair, *Che Guevara* (New York: The Viking Press, 1970).

SUMMARY: SOME KINDS OF PARAGRAPH MOVEMENT

General to Particular

(From general statement to supporting details which explain or illustrate.
Topic sentence at or near beginning
of paragraph.)

Conclusion or general statement
followed by details of explanation or
proof

(Variation. Topic sentence restated
as conclusion at end of paragraph.)

Details

Particular to General

(From a series of explanatory or illustrative statements to the conclusion
drawn from them. Topic sentence at
or near end of paragraph.)

Details leading up to concluding
topic sentence

Whole to Parts

(Paragraph moves through a succession of parts or stages of the whole.
Often a first, second, third order.)

1. _____
2. _____
3. _____

Question to Answer; Effect to Cause

(Paragraph begins with question or
effect, then answers the question or
shows the cause. Usually no topic
sentence.)

Question or effect

Answer or cause

EXERCISE

*Analyze the structure of the following paragraphs, answering these questions
about each.*

1. Does the paragraph have a topic sentence?

2. Does it have a concluding sentence?

3. In what order is it developed?

*4. With what kind of material is it developed, i.e., one or many examples,
explanation, other?*

(1)

Man sees the world not as it is, hard, purposeless, indifferent, but as he wishes it to be, a place where everything will somehow come out for the best and he will triumph ever after. For he will somehow find the perfect mate, the perfect work, the perfect home: the perfect life from which boredom, injustice, and imperfection magically disappear and all is like an idyll. Can man rise above this sentimental fantasy? If so, he may grow up. If not, he will remain a child forever.

(2)

Compared with some other historical civilizations, the ritualized violence of the American gladiatorial arts is pretty thin. There are no Carthaginian or Aztec human sacrifices to watch, no Latin bullfights, no guillotinings such as once sickened Tolstoy in Paris, no public hangings such as the British once had, no cockfights or bear fights (except on the early frontier or as survivals in the mountain areas today), no battles to the death between Roman gladiators, no mangling of men by lions. What cruelty there is in American culture is reflected less in its spectator sports than in any other of the pugnacious civilizations of history. Only wrestling, boxing, and (to some extent) football and ice hockey remain brutal, and the most ruthless of these—wrestling—has been converted into a TV buffoonery. The prize fights have had their murderousness muted since the days when frontier bullies fought catch-as-catch-can or two toughs pounded each other with bare knuckles for as many as fifty or sixty rounds. As the gladiatorial arts have become big industries the brutal in them has been diminished and the spectacle accented.[7]

(3)

The fall of Rome was not an event, like the fall of Fort McHenry or the Bastille. It was a slow process of disintegration which came from many causes, some so gradual and so pervasive that they were scarcely noticeable to the most acute observers of the time. Because of high taxes and resistance to harsh laws forbidding workmen to change their trades, the population of the cities slowly melted away. Many who fled the cities were drawn to the great country houses, the villas or estates which became the nucleus of the medieval manor, the central social institution of feudalism. As the imperial treasury grew lean, it became harder to man and pay the legions; and there were generals in the provinces who found a march on the capital too great a temptation to resist. Thus slowly the machinery of government and of empire fell into disuse. And when the barbarians came, there was no power to resist.

[7] From Max Lerner, *America as a Civilization* (New York: Simon & Schuster, Inc., 1957).

Coherence   Coherence means sticking together. A paragraph is coherent when the sentences are woven together or flow into each other. The reader then moves easily from one sentence to the next and reads the paragraph as an integrated unit, not a collection of separate sentences.

Coherence Within the Paragraph.   The best way to get coherence in a paragraph is to think in paragraphs. A writer with a clear idea of what he wants to do is not likely to have serious trouble with coherence. Most incoherent paragraphs come from thinking out the implications of the topic one sentence at a time. A writer who works this way will write one sentence, stop, think a minute, write a second sentence, stop, and continue in a series of spurts and pauses. Paragraphs written this way are almost sure to lack coherence, for the writer is starting afresh at every sentence. He loses the sense of continuity with the last sentence before he begins the next, and the hesitation in his thinking is reflected in the jerkiness of his writing.

A paragraph that lacks unity or orderly movement will not be coherent, since a reader cannot move easily from one sentence to another if he has trouble seeing the relation between them. But coherence is not simply a matter of unity and order. Read the following paragraph aloud and you will see that it jerks from one sentence to the next.

[1] I was accepted and started work. [2] My experience had been derived chiefly from books. [3] I was not prepared for the difficult period of adjustment. [4] I soon became discouraged with myself and so dissatisfied with my job that I was on the point of quitting. [5] My employer must have sensed this. [6] He called me into his office and talked to me about the duties of my position and the opportunities for advancement. [7] I realized that there was nothing wrong with me or the job and I decided to stay.

This writer omitted small but important links or details of her thought and thus left gaps in her writing. In sentence 2 she is contrasting her previous experience with her present one and needs to make the point that *now* her experience has changed. This gap can be filled by adding "Until that time" at the beginning of the second sentence. When she wrote, in sentence 3, that she was not prepared "for the difficult period of adjustment," she had in mind the particular adjustment "that every inexperienced secretary must face in a new position." But she did not say so. Again, she skipped a thought between sentences 5 and 6: her employer must have called her in for a talk *because* he sensed her dissatisfaction. In sentence 7 she jumped from the talk to her change of attitude, a gap she could have bridged by the remark "That talk helped me." Finally, she omitted a necessary qualification in her last sentence. There *was* something wrong with her, but nothing "that experience could not cure." Perhaps no one of these gaps is serious in itself, but their cumulative effect is to make the reader's job more difficult than it needs to be.

Now read the revised version aloud, paying particular attention to the italicized additions, and see if closing the gaps makes the reading easier.

I was accepted, and started work. *Until that time* my experience had been derived chiefly from books, *and unfortunately* those books had not prepared me for the difficult period of adjustment *that every inexperienced secretary must face in a new position. Consequently* I soon became *so* discouraged with myself and so dissatisfied with the job that I was on the point of quitting. *I think* my employer must have sensed this, *for* he called me into his office and talked to me about *both* the duties of my position and the opportunities *it offered* for advancement. *That talk helped me considerably.* I realized that there was nothing wrong with me or the job *that experience could not cure*, and I decided to stay.

Some Transitional Devices

In addition to closing gaps in thought, the following transitional devices help to provide coherence in a paragraph in other ways.

Pronoun reference. Because it refers to an antecedent, a pronoun points back and gives a simple and natural connection. In the following paragraph the pronouns *they* and *he* are valuable links.

Most people use a lot of words to express their ideas. They talk at us by the hour to explain just one thought. They lecture from platforms, from pulpits, from soapboxes, from armchairs. They toss around the same idea on the radio, in town hall, at a conference table, at a club meeting. One good idea may certainly be worth all those words, but when they come our way too fast— sometimes twisted, emotion-packed, ill-assorted—they are meaningful to us only if we can see the idea bare as bones. No matter how many words are used, a listener should be able to sum up the idea in one sentence or less. If he can do that, he can understand what is being talked about. If he can't, he is hazy about the controlling idea that all those words refer to.[8]

To see how important pronouns are as transitions, try reading the paragraph aloud, substituting the antecedents for the pronouns—"Most people," "those words," and "a listener." How does the paragraph sound?

Repetition. Though careless repetition is awkward, deliberate repetition (page 122) of key words, phrases, or sentence patterns can connect sentences in a paragraph. The repetition of *Gibson-Fonda* and the repetitive structure of key sentences supplement pronoun references as binding elements in the following paragraph.

[8] From Bess Sondel, "Everybody's Listening," *National Parent-Teacher*, January 1951.

[1] The protagonist and antagonist are William Gibson, the author, and Henry Fonda, the star. [2] Gibson is motivated by a conviction of the integrity of his characters. [3] If his hero, Jerry, is a confused character, then Jerry's confusion must become explicit in the play, even though that confusion may, in turn, confuse the audience. [4] If Gittel, his heroine, is a profane, promiscuous, but endearing little Brooklyn gamin, she has to be profane and promiscuous in the play, even at the risk of alienating the audience. [5] Fonda is motivated by a sense of what an audience will accept, of what constitutes good theatre. [6] He wants the characters to be "likable"; therefore he wants potentially objectionable traits toned down. [7] But there is an ironic twist to the conflict between these two points of view. [8] Gibson and Fonda cannot simply slug it out to decide whose play is to be produced. [9] They are committed to a two-million-dollar business enterprise, the success of which demands their complete cooperation.

[2] parallel with [5]

[3] parallel with [4]

These repetitions of structure are deliberate

Contrast.   When the topic sentence calls for comparison or contrast, the alternation between the compared or contrasted elements, *A* and *B,* provides some coherence. This is especially true with the alternating contrast pattern (pages 50–51). The Gibson-Fonda contrast above, with its *A* + *B* development, gives structural coherence by stating the contrast in the first sentence, illustrating it in the next three, and repeating it in the last two.

Transitional Markers.   These are words or phrases often placed at or near the beginning of a sentence or clause to signal the relationship between a new sentence and the one before it. The commonest markers are the conjunctions *and, or, nor, but, for.* Others—sometimes called transitional connectives—also indicate the direction which the new sentence is about to take. The commonest transitional connectives may be classified as follows:

1. To introduce an illustration: *thus, for example, for instance, to illustrate.*
2. To add another phase of the same idea: *secondly, in the second place, next, moreover, in addition, similarly, again, also, finally.*
3. To point a contrast or qualification: *on the other hand, nevertheless, despite this fact, on the contrary, still, however, conversely, instead.*
4. To indicate a conclusion or result: *therefore, in conclusion, to sum up, consequently, as a result, accordingly, in other words.*

Coherence Among Paragraphs.   The following series of five paragraphs illustrates a variety of transitional devices: repetition of key words, use of pronouns, transitional connectives, references to events in preceding paragraphs, keeping a common subject running through a series of paragraphs, repetition of a significant idea either within a paragraph or among several paragraphs, and restatement of the thesis. All these devices weave sentences into paragraphs, and paragraphs into a unified composition.

Repetition of "city" keeps emphasis on Hamburg, which is the subject of this paragraph

[1] On three nights late in July and at the beginning of August 1943, the heavy planes of the RAF Bomber Command droned in from the North Sea and subjected the city of Hamburg to an ordeal such as Germans had not experienced since the Thirty Years' War. A third of the city was reduced to a wasteland. At least 60,000 and perhaps as many as 100,000 people were killed—about as many as at Hiroshima. A large number of these were lost one night when a ghastly "fire storm," which literally burned the asphalt pavements, swept a part of the city and swept everything into itself. Adolf Hitler heard the details of the attack and for the only known time during the war said it might be necessary to sue for peace. Hermann Goering visited the city with a retinue to survey the damage and was accorded so disconcerting a reception that he deemed it discreet to retire.

Points contrast with preceding paragraph

Reference to the bombing in previous paragraph

Pronoun references

[2] Yet this terrible event taught a lesson about the economics of war which very few have learned and some, indeed, may have found it convenient to ignore. The industrial plants of Hamburg were around the edge of the city or, as in the case of the submarine pens, on the harbor. They were not greatly damaged by the raids; these struck the center of the city and the working class residential areas and suburbs. In the days immediately following the raids production faltered; in the first weeks it was down by as much as 20 or 25 per cent. But thereafter it returned to normal. By then the workers had scanned the ruins of their former homes, satisfied themselves that their possessions and sometimes their families were irretrievable, had found some rude clothes and the shelter of a room or part of a room in a still habitable house, and had returned to work. On these three nights of terror their standard of living, measured by houseroom, furnishings, clothing, food and drink, recreation, schools, and social and cultural opportunities, had been reduced to a fraction of what it had been before. But the efficiency of the worker as a worker was unimpaired by this loss. After a slight period of readjustment, he labored as diligently and as skillfully as before.

Reference to "three nights" of first sentence in paragraph 1

Signals addition to what has been said

Reference to paragraph 1

Transition to content of paragraph 2

[3] There is a further chapter to the story. Before the attacks, there had been a labor shortage in Hamburg. Afterward, despite the number killed and the number now engaged on indispensable repairs, there was no shortage. For, as a result of the attacks, thousands who were waiters in restaurants and cafés, attendants in garages, clerks in banks, salesmen in stores, shopkeepers, janitors, ticket takers, and employees in handicraft industries (which, being small and traditional, were more likely to be in the center of town) lost their places of employment. They had previously contributed nothing to war production. Their contribution to the standard of living proved dispensable. Now they turned to the war industries as the most plausible places to find employment.

Pronoun references

Contrast with paragraphs 1 and 2

[4] Even in the presumptively austere and dedicated world of the Third Reich, in the third year of a disastrous war, the average citizen had access to a wide range of comforts and amenities which habit had made to seem essential. And because they were believed to be essential they were essential. On such matters governments, even dictatorships, must bow to the convictions of the people even if—the exceptional case—they do not share them. The

Repetition of "essential," a key term

*"In doing so"
connects last two
sentences in
paragraph*

*Restatement of
thesis which was
first stated at be-
ginning of para-
graph 2*

German standard of living was far above what was physically necessary for survival and efficiency. The RAF broke through the psychological encrustation and brought living standards down somewhere nearer to the physical minimum. In doing so it forced a wholesale conversion of Germany's scarcest resource, that of manpower, to war production.

[5] In reducing, as nothing else could, the consumption of nonessentials and the employment of men in their supply, there is a distinct possibility that the attacks on Hamburg increased Germany's output of war material and thus her military effectiveness.[9]

EXERCISE

Analyze the two following paragraphs for the use of transitional devices. Mark them in detail to show use of pronouns, repetition, transitional connectives, and any other devices you find in them.

(1)

One of the functions of a society is to make its inhabitants feel safe, and Americans devote more of their collective resources to security than to any other need. Yet Americans do not feel safe, despite (or because of) shotguns in the closet and nuclear bombers patrolling overhead. With each decade we seem to accumulate more fears, and most of these fears seem to be about each other. In the fifties we were afraid of native Communists, and although we now feel sheepish about *that* moment of panic we express today the same kinds of fear toward blacks, hippies, and student radicals; and in our reactions to all of these fears we have created some very real dangers.[10]

(2)

While black students seize buildings and demand separate living and eating facilities, Negro students urge that students, all students, be allowed to live and eat as they choose; and further, that university officials refrain from making concessions to blacks which would result in the creation of an atmosphere in which Negro students might be forced because of social pressure into making "choices" which could only limit, only divert them from achieving those skills without which no revolution is possible: knowledge, ability, and character. In the fullest sense, these fundamentals can only be obtained through a college experience as broad gauged, as free as possible. . . . And the revolution, the real revolution, the one that takes long hard preparation, unshackled ability, tireless effort, and much time is not coming tomorrow. While black students have copped out of this revolution, Negro students know that for them it has only begun. While black students busily issue "demands," hold rallies, indulge in countless meetings, attract publicity and foundation and university funds, Negro students deeply committed to the real task find

[9] From John Kenneth Galbraith, *The Affluent Society* (Boston: Houghton Mifflin Company, 1958).
[10] From Philip Slater, *The Pursuit of Loneliness* (Boston: The Beacon Press, 1971).

themselves in an unenviable position, for they must struggle for the real revolution against university administrators who, pandering to the whims of the moment, capitulate to the "demands" of blacks which delimit not only themselves, but all students. Negro students must fight for the real revolution against white students who, paralyzed by guilt complexes, countenance anything, any idea espoused by the loudest, the most boorish black. Finally, they must oppose their brethren who have, though emotionally committed, not only lost sight of the real goal, but who have rejected either consciously or unconsciously the prerequisites to its achievement.[11]

REVISING PARAGRAPHS

This section is a practical application of what has been said about the requirements of a good paragraph. We shall begin by analyzing two unsatisfactory paragraphs and revising them. Before a writer can revise a paragraph he must first see clearly what is wrong with his first draft. Each revision will therefore be preceded by a criticism of the deficiencies of the original. After studying these revisions, you will be asked to criticize or revise some other paragraphs.

Case 1

In considering both the original and the revised version of the following paragraph, do not let your agreement or disagreement with the argument affect your judgment. We are criticizing only the *structure* of the paragraph. If you want to refute or support the argument, you can do so later.

Original paragraph

[1] Young women who respond to the problem of overpopulation by vowing that they will never have children are making a dramatic but futile gesture. [2] Most of them won't keep that vow. [3] It is easy to say you won't have children when you are eighteen. [4] Who wants them then? [5] The few who practice what they preach will be insignificant. [6] The problem is too global to be affected by a few women who don't have children. [7] It's going to take something like the United Nations to reduce the birth rate in India and China and countries like these.

Criticism.   1. The second, third, and fourth sentences move away from the topic sentence, which emphasizes the futility of the vow, not the likelihood of its being broken. Thus three of the six sentences following the topic sentence interrupt its development.

2. The global nature of the problem is dismissed too quickly and too generally in sentences 6 and 7. This is the main point of the argument and needs more explanation to be persuasive.

[11] From Oliver Henry, "A Negro Student's Observations of Blacks," *Columbia Daily Spectator*, March 11, 1969.

3. The fifth sentence distorts the writer's idea. It is not the girls who are insignificant, but their contribution to a solution of the problem. Moreover, the "practice-what-they-preach" cliché is inappropriate. The girls aren't preaching; they are making a promise.

4. The reference to India and China in the last sentence suggests that the problem is caused by some countries, not by all. This weakens the argument that it is a global problem.

Revised paragraph   Young women who respond to the problem of overpopulation by vowing that they will never have children are making a dramatic but futile gesture. Even if they keep that vow—a hundred, a thousand, or ten thousand of them— it will make little difference in the total situation. Overpopulation is not an individual problem, not even a national one; it is a global problem. Its solution requires that the fast-rising curve of the world's population be halted and flattened out. That requires a global effort, not to make our best stock renounce the right to have children, but to persuade people all over the world to restrict the size of their families.

Case 2   In the play *Antigone,* Polynices, the brother of Antigone and Ismene, is killed while leading a rebellion against the state. Creon, the king, decrees that the corpse shall be denied the burial which the practices of religion require. Ismene accepts this decree, but Antigone defies it and buries her brother at the cost of her own life. After reading the play, a student writes an essay containing the following paragraph.

Original paragraph   It is not surprising that Antigone and Ismene react quite differently to Creon's ban on the burial of their brother. Antigone has spent much of her life with death, misfortune, and hardship. It wasn't an easy task, I'm sure, for her to look after her blind father, Oedipus, during the wanderings of his exile, no matter how much she loved him, but during these years she learned a sense of responsibility to one's family which Ismene was not required to learn. Oedipus was constantly talking about the will of the gods and the importance of putting religious duties first. He talked frequently, too, about death as a release from pain. He had a temper that would fly up suddenly and cause him to act impulsively and rashly, without thinking about his own safety. And he despised Creon and his concern with only political considerations. It is only natural that some of this temperament would rub off on Antigone—like father, like daughter—and cause her to defy Creon's order. Ismene has been less influenced by Oedipus. She has been brought up by Creon and taught to obey him.

Criticism.   1. The contrast is lopsided. Ismene's side of it gets only the last two sentences. The revision should pay more attention to her.

2. Too much space is given to Oedipus. He is the subject of four of the ten sentences and is prominent in two more; thus he is the main character in

about half the paragraph. His influence should be discussed in less space, and he should be subordinated to Antigone.

3. Conversely, Creon does not get enough space. He is as important to the contrast as Oedipus. When Ismene's side of the contrast is expanded, it should do more with Creon's influence on her.

4. Since the reason for the different actions of the two sisters is that they are the products of different experiences, that reason should be clearly stated at the beginning, preferably as part of the topic sentence.

5. Since this is to be a divided contrast, the shift from Antigone (*A*) to Ismene (*B*) will be made clearer if it is signaled by an appropriate transitional marker—"On the other hand," "By contrast," or at least "But."

Revised paragraph   It is not surprising that Antigone and Ismene react quite differently to Creon's ban on the burial of their brother. The two sisters are products of different experiences. As the constant companion of Oedipus, Antigone has acquired from her father a strong sense of religious and family obligation and a conviction that divine laws take precedence over human laws. She has also learned to subordinate personal considerations of security and happiness to her religious duties. Perhaps she has also acquired something of her father's contempt for Creon as a person and for the narrow political values which he represents. It is natural, therefore, for her to reject Creon's authority when it clashes with her religious conviction that her brother must be given a burial service. Ismene, by contrast, has been little influenced by her father's religious values. She has grown up safely and securely in Thebes as a member of Creon's household. In her environment the values were political rather than religious, and the emphasis was on unquestioning obedience to political authority, to Creon as the ruler of the state and the ruler of the household. In accepting Creon's decree she merely did what she had been brought up to do. It is not necessary to assume that she loved Polynices less than Antigone did. Given their different backgrounds, it was as natural for Ismene to obey Creon as it was for Antigone to defy him.

EXERCISES   **A.** *In note form, as in the criticisms already made, point out the defects of the following paragraph. Without rewriting the paragraph, suggest how it might be revised.*

Isn't it silly how much fuss some people make about a boy who wears his hair long? Long hair on men is nothing new. In Samson's time it was a sign of masculinity, but nowadays it is thought of as effeminate. You can't tell the boys from the girls, they say. It is the same with beards. Personally, I think a beard is manly, especially if it is not too scraggly. Look at pictures of Lincoln and Grant and some of our other great Presidents. But some people think that long hair is a sign of poor grooming. They don't know how much time some of the boys spend shampooing their hair and combing their beards, even using an eyebrow pencil to fill in the vacant spots. Others think long hair is a sign of protest. Protest against whom? The barbers? You can't tell a person's political ideas by the length of his hair.

B. *Write a substantial paragraph evaluating the strengths and weaknesses of the following paragraph.*

There is much talk today about "the new morality." People who use that term mean the new *immorality.* But what's new about immorality? Like the poor, immorality has always been with us since Eve ate the apple and Cain slew Abel. Young people today are no worse than their parents or their grandparents, and probably no better either. As in other generations, some do and some don't. They may do it more openly, some of them, but then again maybe they don't. It's hard to judge the morality of a whole generation, especially when you want to think the worst of young people anyway. My guess is that young people today are pretty moral, but not always.

C. *Both versions of the paragraph that follow begin with these lines from Richard Lovelace's poem, "To Althea from Prison":*

> *Stone walls do not a prison make,*
> *Nor iron bars a cage;*
> *Minds innocent and quiet take*
> *That for an hermitage . . .*

Choose the version you think is the more effective paragraph and explain your choice.

---

(1)

[1] These lines by Richard Lovelace express a basic truth: that freedom is a state of mind. [2] The world of the mind is wide and roomy, and a man who can move around in it can tolerate the cramped quarters of a prison cell and resign himself to being cut off from the outside world, as monks and mystics have often proved. [3] It is intellectual imprisonment that rusts a man. [4] Eldridge Cleaver says that when he was in jail he wrote *Soul on Ice* to save himself. [5] In his writing he could re-enter the world of events and ideas and thus, in a sense, escape into a fuller life. [6] Although his mind was neither innocent nor quiet, Folsom Prison became a hermitage to him. [7] It was a place in which he could think out and resolve his conflicts.

(2)

[1] These lines by Richard Lovelace express a basic truth: that freedom is a state of mind. [2] Neither stone walls nor iron bars can contain a mind. [3] A man who can move around in his mind is not cramped by them. [4] Monks

and mystics voluntarily choose to cut themselves off from the outside world, with all its distractions, in order to meditate. [5] It is intellectual imprisonment that rusts a man. [6] If we really want to rehabilitate prisoners, we should encourage them to use their minds. [7] Many of them have gained the equivalent of a college education while they were in jail. [8] Eldridge Cleaver says he wrote to save himself. [9] His years in Folsom Prison became tolerable while he was writing *Soul on Ice*. [10] Not every prisoner has his potential, but many could broaden their minds and become useful citizens when they were released. [11] Criminals have to be put away for the good of society, but that's no reason why their lives should be wasted.

SPECIAL PARAGRAPHS: INTRODUCTIONS, TRANSITIONS, CONCLUSIONS

All we have said so far in this chapter applies to body paragraphs, those which develop parts of a topic within the body of a composition. In most short papers all paragraphs are of this kind, except that first and last paragraphs introduce and round out the discussion as a whole. But longer pieces often have special paragraphs which open or close them, or link the parts. Such paragraphs are interest-getters, pointers, or clinchers, not fully developed units of a discussion. They therefore need special mention.

Introductory Paragraphs

An introductory paragraph gets the reader started and often makes a special effort to interest him. Journalists call interest-getters "hooks," and there are many kinds. Here are a few.

1. To announce a topic in the form of a challenging question and to hint at its importance:

Into what is a modern girl to grow? Many a psychologist or educator today will find few questions more recurrent or more troubling than this one, if he stops to consider it.[12]

2. To announce a topic and describe a problem in the form of a brief representative incident.

A group of youngsters—the oldest was 14—formed a circle and solemnly inhaled on a Turkish water pipe until their eyes were glazed and distant. All of them were deep-tanned, sun-bleached, sports-playing California-affluent junior-high-schoolers, good students and normal children whose parents thought they were on a picnic.[13]

[12] From Bruno Bettelheim, "Growing Up Female," *Harper's Magazine*, October 1962.
[13] From Albert Rosenfeld, "Marijuana: Millions of Turned-on Users," *Life*, July 7, 1967.

3. To announce a topic and indicate the two subtopics which are to be discussed:

This book is a collection of short stories by Southern writers. And that involves two questions which more than once had to be considered in the making of this book. What is a Southern writer? And what is a short story?[14]

Transitional Paragraphs

Occasionally a whole short paragraph will serve as a transition. Such a paragraph always comes at a point where the author has finished one main unit and is about to start another. The paragraph may sum up what has been said before beginning the new unit. It may introduce one or more illustrations of a point already made. Or it may state what comes next.

1. To sum up before beginning a new unit:

Well, that's how it was before "she" came into my life. Now let me tell you what it's like to be married to a Honda.

2. To provide a transition from a general statement to a discussion of specific examples or applications:

I know of course that all this still sounds vague. But don't worry. From this point on we are getting down to brass tacks.[15]

3. To show what the writer intends to do next:

Now, you may admit all these things and yet inquire what can be done about them without sacrificing values that have become precious to us all. Since I realize that this question is a just one, I shall outline briefly the organization of the University of Utopia. It will be seen that not all the features of this university are new and original. At Wisconsin, Harvard, Swarthmore, and numerous other places, many phases of its plan have been tried and have succeeded. Much of the rest of the program has been under discussion at the University of Chicago and elsewhere for some years.[16]

Concluding Paragraphs

A conclusion never has to be a mere dry summary. It may restate or sum up, make a prediction or plead for action, be quiet or climactic. The following conclusions are representative.

[14] From Robert Penn Warren, *Southern Harvest* (Boston: Houghton Mifflin Company, 1937).
[15] From Rudolph Flesch, *The Art of Plain Talk* (New York: Harper & Row, 1946).
[16] From Robert M. Hutchins, "The University of Utopia," *Yale Review,* March 1931.

1. To sum up and make a plea for careful thought and possible future action:

It seems to me that there is one clear lesson to be drawn from the story of a girl pursued and murdered while thirty-four neighbors looked on. It is this: Lest we too become like the neighbor who wanted to "forget the whole thing," we must have the courage to become involved, to act when the need is clear. Unless we do, the blood of the victim will be on our hands for the rest of our lives.

2. To summarize and to point forward:

Antwerp was good, bad, beautiful and crass—truly Europe's greatest center of civilization up to the closing of the Scheldt River. Even then the city did not die. There were still Breughels who painted and Plantin offspring who printed. Since then it has borne the armies of the French and the rockets of the Nazis, with enemy occupation in between. It has continued to survive, in spite of man as well as because of him. It has rebuilt where vandals have destroyed, and if need be, in an age of destruction for destruction's sake, it could build again.[17]

3. To restate the main argument and imply a personal application to the reader:

To say, then, that "metaphor is of no particular relevance" to prose, seems to me stupefying. My conclusion is that those who have no gift for metaphor and imagery are doubtless wise to keep clear of it; but that those who have it, whether in writing or in speech, will find few qualities that better repay cultivation.[18]

EXERCISES

A. *Comment on the following introductory paragraphs. How do they announce the topic? What do they do to arouse your interest and make you want to go on reading? How well do they succeed?*

1. Have you had the eerie feeling that you are *not* being left alone? That somebody unknown and unseen is spying on you? You were not imagining things. Our privacy is up for sale.[19]

[17] From John J. Murray, *Antwerp in the Age of Plantin and Breughel* (Norman: University of Oklahoma Press, 1970).
[18] From F. L. Lucas, *Style* (New York: The Macmillan Company, 1955).
[19] From Myron Brenton, *The Privacy Invaders* (New York: Coward-McCann, 1964).

2. "Remember, you're future people. You're not here-and-now people. You may not want to build a city as you know it today." With that admonition architect Frank Gehry led a group of 11- and 12-year-olds into an experiment in city building.[20]

3. For three thousand years, poets have been enchanted and moved and perplexed by the power of their own imagination. In a short and summary essay I can hope at most to lift one small corner of that mystery; and yet it is a critical corner. I shall ask, What goes on in the mind when we imagine? You will hear from me that one answer to this question is fairly specific: which is to say, that we can describe the working of the imagination. And when we describe it as I shall do, it becomes plain that imagination is a specifically *human* gift. To imagine is the characteristic act, not of the poet's mind, or the painter's, or the scientist's, but of the mind of man.[21]

B. *Comment on the following transitional paragraphs. For each, name the topic which has gone before, that which is to follow, and the relationship between the two.*

---

1. Such, then, seems to me a preferable pattern to use when thinking about literature, and even, for that matter, about art in general. Let me point out some of its advantages.

2. So much, then, for the woodwinds. Let us turn next to their nearest sister instruments in the orchestra, the brasses.

3. I shall discuss the theory and practice of persuasion later on. First, however, I wish to offer an alternative model of factual exposition to the one we have seen. I shall do so at some length, but it will make for economies later.

C. *Comment on the following conclusions. How well do they give a sense of completeness? How do they achieve it? Do they summarize? point forward? give a warning? express a hope?*

---

1. The procession which marked the conclusion of the ten-month Constitutional Convention set a symbolic seal on the long process and thus had the effect which many public ceremonies have of making it all seem a real and believable event. In the words of Benjamin Rush, the Philadelphia physician and signer of the Declaration of Independence, " 'Tis done. We have become a nation."

---

[20] From a newspaper story.
[21] From J. Bronowski, Address to the American Academy of Arts and Letters, May 1966.

2. And if indeed men do achieve that victory [of social conscience over materialism], they will know, with the greater insight they will then possess, that it is not a human victory, but nature's new and final triumph in the human heart—perhaps that nature which is also God. "The rationality of man," a great theologian once wrote, "is the little telltale rift in Nature which shows there is something beyond or behind her." It remains for man, in his moral freedom, to prove that statement true.[22]

3. The light which puts out our eyes is darkness to us. Only that day dawns to which we are awake. There is more day to dawn. The sun is but a morning-star.[23]

SUMMARY EXERCISES

For each of the two exercises below, write a paragraph of your own, using the materials given. Make your paragraphs complete, unified, and coherent. Do not feel that you have to use all the material given unless it is appropriate to your purpose.

A. *The following statistics on the apportionment of personal income tax to various national uses is an estimate for 1971 based on the expected national budget for that year. Study the figures carefully and write a paragraph using the material as you see fit to develop or support a thesis of your own based on this information.*

A married man with a taxable income of $20,000 after deductions and exemptions will be taxed $4,800 by the federal government. This figure will include old-age tax but not gasoline, cigarette, liquor, and other federal taxes. The following breakdown of this amount is based on the proposed presidential budget for the fiscal year.

Defense, war and war preparations, $1,620. War veterans, $220. Interest on debt, mostly to pay for past wars, $412. Foreign aid and propaganda, $86. Space research and technology, $67. Total for those items, a little over $2,400 . . . about half the total tax.

The other half goes as follows: to old-age pensions, welfare, and other social services, $1,271. Health services, including medicare, research, consumer protection, disease prevention and hospitals, $335. Price supports for farmers, rural electrification, conservation, $120. Work on rivers and harbors, environment, parks, other outdoor projects, $91. Housing, urban renewal, community programs, $96. Education aid, $130. Manpower training, $52. Airports, highways, mass transit, mail service, help for small business, $230. All other government functions, $70.

[22] From Loren C. Eiseley, "An Evolutionist Looks at Modern Man," *Saturday Evening Post*, April 26, 1958.
[23] From Henry David Thoreau, *Walden*.

B. *The following table shows a relationship between the number of years American males go to school and the amount of money they earn afterwards. In each line there are three figures, an income range, the percentage of people in that range, and the number of school years they have completed. Study the figures carefully and write a paragraph on some inference you draw from them.*

Education and Income

Source: U.S. Bureau of the Census (based on 1969 data)

Income Levels	Percent of Male Earners	School Years Completed (Median)
$1,500 to $1,999	3.4	8.4
$2,000 to $2,499	3.6	8.6
$2,500 to $2,999	3.0	8.7
$3,000 to $3,999	6.9	9.2
$4,000 to $4,999	7.2	10.3
$5,000 to $5,999	8.9	11.6
$6,000 to $6,999	9.6	12.1
$7,000 to $7,999	10.3	12.3
$8,000 to $9,999	15.2	12.4
$10,000 to $14,999	16.9	12.8
$15,000 to $24,999	5.6	15.3
$25,000 and over	1.8	16.3

Chapter 6

Effective Sentences

The sentences in a paragraph are not isolated statements but steps in a continuum. They are related to what has gone before and to what will follow. While it is traditional to call them units of composition, they are units only in the grammatical sense, that each sentence has its own subject and predicate and is not a part of some other sentence. The Handbook (pages 347 ff.) deals with the conventions of usage within the sentence. Here we are concerned with rhetorical effect, with the ways sentences are constructed and revised to make them effective expressions of ideas.

CONSTRUCTING SENTENCES

In this section we shall examine four types of sentences: *standard, parallel, balanced,* and *periodic.* These are not mutually exclusive types, since a standard sentence often contains parallel elements, and since both balanced and periodic sentences depend on parallelism. But each type has its own characteristic structure. A knowledge of that structure will allow you to choose the form that best suits your needs for any particular sentence.

The Standard Sentence

The standard sentence, sometimes called the "loose" or "cumulative" sentence, is considered standard partly because it is by far the most common, and partly because all other types are derived from its basic subject-predicate pattern. The writer of a standard sentence begins with the main clause and expands it by adding further information. In the following examples, the main clause is italicized to set it off from the added elements, which are here spaced out to suggest the cumulative effect of the sentence.

The missing boy was found   unharmed   in a gravel pit   late this afternoon.

I was rehearsing my speech   as I walked across campus   on my way to class   when my thoughts were distracted   by the sight of a girl   in the briefest of miniskirts.

The pavements were slick with leavings   mainly cast-off, rotten leaves, fruits   and vegetables . . .[1]

In such a sentence the content unfolds a bit at a time. The writer begins with the main clause, then adds whatever information he thinks will complete the statement he wants to make. He is the judge of how much or how little information he wants to include in a particular sentence. Thus the second example could have been written:

I was rehearsing my speech as I walked across campus on my way to class. Suddenly I saw a girl in the briefest of miniskirts. I forgot about my speech.

The core of a standard sentence is its main clause expressed in its simplest form. This core, kernel, or basic sentence consists of a subject followed by any one of three constructions: (1) an intransitive verb (The children + *were playing*); (2) a transitive verb followed by its object (The children + *found* + *a robin*); (3) a linking verb followed by its complement (The children + *were* + *unhappy*).

Modification.   Each of these basic sentences can be expanded by modifying any of its parts. The effect of the expansion is to increase the *density* of the sentence—that is, to increase the information and therefore the meaning it conveys. In the following sentences the modifiers are in parentheses and are connected by arrows to the words they modify.

The (neighbors') children were playing (noisily) (in our yard).

(This afternoon) the children found a (wounded) robin (on the sidewalk).

The children (in the fourth grade) were unhappy (with the teacher's decision).

By modifying any part or all of a main clause a writer can enrich a sentence with specific details. You saw in earlier parts of this book that such details help to improve the quality of the writing by making it less general and more concrete. This kind of concreteness can be introduced into the

[1] James Baldwin, *Giovanni's Room.*

sentence through modification, as the italicized modifiers in the following sentences show.

The missing ten dollar bill was found *between the pages of a book that my father had been reading.*

I was walking across the campus rehearsing my speech, *head down, muttering to myself, completely oblivious of the people passing,* when for some reason I looked up and saw, *coming toward me,* a girl in the briefest miniskirt I've ever seen.

The game was delayed by a bomb scare, *which halted play in the fourth inning for 45 minutes while police cleared the stands and searched in vain for a bomb reported to be there.*

No matter which direction they move, few travelers will find a better-appointed airport than Amsterdam's Schiphol—*clean, white, modern, un-crowded,* and *equipped with one of the best-appointed, free-port shopping areas in the world.*[2]

EXERCISE

The following statements are main clauses that would be more meaningful to a reader if illustrative or explanatory details were added. Provide such details as you can within a single sentence. The comments within the brackets suggest a procedure.

1. There are several things I don't like about her. [Such as?]
2. I am homesick. [For what? Specify.]
3. I am in favor of equal rights for women. [What particular rights or why?]
4. An old man approached us. [How?]
5. I did not feel like going to the party. [Why not?]

Coordination. The density of a sentence may be increased by two other methods: coordination and subordination. *Coordination* is the process of combining similar elements into pairs or series. Instead of saying

The woman looked tired. Her children also looked tired.—

we combine these two basic sentences into one

The woman and her children looked tired.—

[2] Horace Sutton, in *Saturday Review.*

by retaining the common predicate, *looked tired,* and combining the two subjects into a compound subject. Similarly we can combine

> She looked tired. She looked frustrated. She looked disgusted.—

by retaining the common subject and linking verb and by arranging the adjectives in a series:

> She looked tired, frustrated, and disgusted.

By this process we can combine a number of sentences (or pieces of information) into a single sentence.

When two or more basic sentences are combined by coordination, the joined elements are usually linked by a coordinating conjunction—*and, but, for, or, nor, either-or, neither-nor, yet.* The coordinate elements may be single words, phrases, subordinate clauses, or main clauses:

Noun subjects	The *woman* and her *children* stood in the doorway of the waiting room.
Verbs	They *blinked, looked* around, and *shuffled* to the nearest bench.
Noun objects	They took off their *caps, coats,* and *mufflers.*
Phrases (used as adverbs)	They threw them *on the bench, on the floor, on top of each other.*
Adjective clauses	The woman, *who talked loudly* and *scolded constantly,* looked exhausted.
Predicates	She *sorted out the clothing* and *made the children as comfortable as possible.*
Main clauses	*The children fell asleep,* and *the woman laid her head back against the wall and closed her eyes.*

Coordinate elements always have the same form and grammatical function. Literally, they are "of the same order." We cannot compound nouns with adjectives, or finite verbs with infinitives, or phrases with clauses. The requirement that coordinate elements have the same form will be important in our study of parallel constructions.

Subordination. Of equal importance in sentences is *subordination,* the process of reducing the grammatical rank of a basic sentence or main clause so that it can be included as a subordinate construction in another sentence. For example, the second of the two basic sentences

> He was absent. *He was sick.*—

may be combined into the first by making it a subordinate clause:

> He was absent *because he was sick.*

Or a basic sentence may be reduced to a phrase, or even to a single word, as in

The man walked across the room. *He walked with a limp.*

The man walked across the room *with a limp.*

The man *limped* across the room.

Subordination increases the density of one sentence by embedding in it the content of another. Thus the second version reduces a clause to a phrase and avoids repeating subject and verb. And the third version merges the second idea into the original verb. The revisions add no information, but they provide greater economy.

In combining basic sentences into denser patterns, we have a considerable choice of combinations. Suppose we have five pieces of information to include in a sentence:

a. A railroad signal was faulty.

b. An express plunged into the rear of a freight train.

c. Five people were killed.

d. Forty-seven people were injured.

e. This accident happened last night.

We can begin with any one of these basic sentences, and for each beginning we will have several ways of arranging the other information. How we actually combine the sentences is determined less by what orders are possible than by what order best suits our purpose. A writer who wanted to establish a causal sequence might follow a time order:

Last night a faulty signal caused an express to plunge into the rear of a freight train. Five people were killed and forty-seven were injured in the crash.

In this version, *a, b,* and *e* are combined into one sentence, in which *a* becomes the subject and *b* the object of the main clause, and *e* becomes an adverbial phrase telling when the action occurred. Then *c* and *d* are combined as coordinate clauses in the second sentence.

But a newspaper reporter who wants to get down first the information readers will think most important may use this sequence:

Five people were killed and forty-seven injured last night when an express plowed into the rear of a freight train because of a faulty signal.

Here *c* and *d* are combined into a compound main clause, and the other sentences are reduced to modifiers—one adverbial clause and two adverbial phrases.

EXERCISE   *Following are nine pieces of information. By coordination and subordination combine them into one sentence, or at most two. You may leave out any information you think unnecessary or repetitive. For example, you may leave out Minnesota and Boston if you think that "Twins" and "Red Sox" are sufficient identification. But try to include all the information essential to an accurate report of the incident.*

1. Last night the Minnesota Twins and the Boston Red Sox were playing a baseball game at the Twins' park.
2. An unidentified person phoned the police.
3. He reported that a bomb had been placed under the stands.
4. In the middle of the fourth inning the game was stopped.
5. An announcement of the bomb report was made to the crowd.
6. The police cleared the stands and searched for the bomb.
7. They did not find one.
8. The fans were allowed to return to their seats.
9. The game was resumed after a total delay of 45 minutes.

The Parallel Sentence

On page 110 the following sentence was used to illustrate the combining of three basic sentences into one:

> She looked *tired, frustrated,* and *disgusted.*

In this combination the three italicized predicate adjectives are arranged in a series of coordinate elements. These elements all have the same form (adjectives) and the same grammatical function (complements). Because of this similarity of form and function they are said to be *parallel constructions.*

A parallel sentence is one that *emphasizes* parallel constructions. The word "emphasizes" is necessary in this definition. A standard sentence containing two or more coordinate constructions may be said to be parallel with respect to these constructions. But here we are concerned with the kind of parallelism that goes beyond simple combining and achieves rhythm and emphasis through the repetition of parallel structures.

Many standard sentences can be made parallel sentences by emphasizing the parallel ideas inherent in them. For example,

> I am in favor of equal rights for women, especially the right to compete on equal terms for jobs for which they are qualified.—

is a standard sentence in which the opening main clause is modified by the words following "women." But if we rewrite that sentence to read

I am in favor of equal rights for women, especially *the right to compete on equal terms for jobs for which they are qualified, the right to get the same pay as men for the same job,* and *the right to equal opportunities for promotion.*—

the repetition of the pattern "the right to . . ." so emphasizes the parallelism of the italicized phrases that the sentence can now be considered a parallel sentence.

The following examples illustrate a variety of parallel constructions.

1. Robert E. Lee was ___ a foe without hate,
        a friend without treachery,
        a soldier without cruelty. . . .[3]

    (*a series of noun phrases acting as matched complements of "was"*)

2. . . . a new genera-
   tion of Americans ___ born in this century,
        tempered by war,
        disciplined by a hard and bitter peace,
        proud of our ancient heritage . . .[4]

    (*a series of modifiers of "generation of Americans"*)

3. On his way to some peak
   of purity, Stravinsky _____ resuscitated classical form,
        introduced startling new concepts of rhythm
         and sonority,
        gave the intellect parity with emotion.[5]

    (*a series of predicates*)

4. Throughout the country,
   the major cities are in
   trouble _____ scarred by slums and ghettos,
        threatened by racial strife and
        crippled by inadequate finances.[6]

    (*a series of phrases in apposition with "trouble"*)

5. I came, I saw, I conquered.   (*a series of main clauses*)

[3] Benjamin H. Hill, *A Tribute to Robert E. Lee.*
[4] John F. Kennedy, *Inaugural Address.*
[5] Herbert Saal, in *Newsweek.*
[6] Whitney M. Young, Jr.

All these sentences have two things in common: first, a repetitive structure which gives similar form and emphasis to similar ideas; second, a rhythm which reinforces the parallelism, especially when the sentence is read aloud. Because this regularity of structure and rhythm sets a pattern which is both visual and audible, any conspicuous interruption of the parallelism will introduce a shift which is noticeably awkward. Thus Example 1 above would be spoiled if the third phrase had been written "a kind soldier."

As the examples show, a parallel sentence is an effective way to say a number of similar things about a subject. Similarity of meaning calls for similarity of form, and the parallel sentence provides that similarity. Thus the girl who wrote the ironic essay about TV westerns (page 9) naturally turned to a parallel sentence when she needed to illustrate what she meant by "everything you'd want":

It had just about everything you'd want—*fast horses, handsome men, beautiful women, mean outlaws, sneaky Indians, waving grass, rolling plains, covered wagons, smoking pistols, hard liquor, torrid love, bitter tears, bloody death*—just about everything you could ask for, all packed together in one little hour, and early enough for the kids to see it, too.

The cumulative effect of this long list suited her purpose exactly, and the parallel sentence was a fine way for her to achieve that effect.

When parallelism is extended through a paragraph, each sentence becomes an element in the series of parallels and states one phase of the idea in the chosen form. The repetitive pattern provides the coherence that ties the separate sentences into a unified whole. In the following paragraph notice the similarity of idea and form in each of the five sentences that develop the opening topic sentence.

America, the richest and most powerful nation in the world, can well lead the way in this revolution of values. There is nothing to prevent us from paying adequate wages to schoolteachers, social workers and other servants of the public to insure that we have the best available personnel in these positions which are charged with the responsibility of guiding our future generations. There is nothing but a lack of social vision to prevent us from paying an adequate wage to every American citizen whether he be a hospital worker, laundry worker, maid or day laborer. There is nothing except shortsightedness to prevent us from guaranteeing an annual minimum—and *livable*—income for every American family. There is nothing, except a tragic death wish, to prevent us from reordering our priorities, so the pursuit of peace will take precedence over the pursuit of war. There is nothing to keep us from remolding a recalcitrant status quo with bruised hands until we have fashioned it into a brotherhood.[7]

[7] From Martin Luther King, Jr., *Where Do We Go From Here: Chaos or Community?* (New York: Harper & Row, 1967).

EXERCISE	*The following excerpt is from a paragraph on the topic that in the writer's first weeks of college everything was so new that he could see no pattern in his experiences. He then illustrated his topic sentence by a long parallel sentence having a series of eight predicates, each showing one difficulty caused by the newness of the experience. He completed the paragraph by restating the topic idea in different words. The excerpt here given contains the topic sentence, the first four of the parallel predicates, and the concluding sentence. Complete the paragraph by providing four additional parallel predicates. You can draw them from your own experiences during the first weeks of school. The structure of the paragraph is shown below.*

Topic sentence	During the first weeks of college everything is so new that we are aware only of individual experiences, not of the pattern of these experiences. We
Predicates of the subject "we." *You are to provide four others.* ——▶	move into a new home, live with strangers, try to find our way around an unfamiliar campus, plan academic schedules we do not understand, . . .
Restatement of topic sentence	In all these activities we have no habit patterns to guide us in relating one experience to another, so that we seem to be living in a world of separate and unrelated events.

The Balanced Sentence

A balanced sentence is a special kind of parallel sentence, in which two parallel elements are set off against each other like equal weights on a balance or scale. In each of the following sentences the underlined parts illustrate the balance:

1. You do your thing, and I'll do mine.
2. Man is mortal, but humanity is not.
3. I come to bury Caesar, not to praise him.
4. His experience suggests that he can do the job; his character assures that he will do it well.

In reading these sentences aloud, one tends to pause between the balanced parts. That pause is often marked by a coordinating conjunction (*and* in 1 and *but* in 2), but sometimes by a negative particle (*not* in 3), and sometimes by punctuation alone (the semicolon in 4). Whatever the marker, it serves as a fulcrum, the point at which the two parts balance against each other.

As sentence 4 shows, a balanced sentence can be used to state an idea in the first half and then support or reinforce it in the second. But the most common use of the form is to set up a contrast. Notice how the contrast in the following passage is developed through a sustained series of balanced sentences.

I felt myself in rebellion against the Greek concept of justice. That concept excused Laius for attacking Oedipus, but condemned Oedipus for defending himself. It tolerated a king's deliberate attempt to kill his baby son by piercing the infant's feet and abandoning it on a mountain, but later branded the son's unintentional killing of his father as murder. It held Oedipus responsible for his ignorance, but excused those, including Apollo, who contributed to that ignorance.

The structure of this paragraph can literally be diagrammed as a scale, with the contrasted parts balanced on the fulcrum of the repeated conjunction *but*.

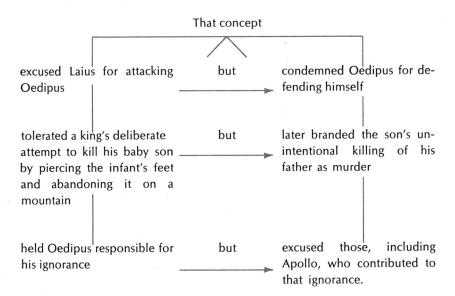

Such a balanced structure points up the contrast in the thought so that the rhetorical pattern reflects and supports the logical pattern. Moreover, the regular rhythm of the matching clauses is itself attractive to a reader. But notice it is the *repeated* contrast in the example that gives the sense of balance. If, instead of following the arrows across the scale, you read down the left side before reading the right, much of the balanced effect is lost. This experiment should suggest to you that when you are contrasting two things you will get better balance by contrasting them a part at a time, as in the alternating contrast pattern you studied in Chapter 3.

The Periodic Sentence

A periodic sentence is one which builds up, often through two or more parallel constructions, to a climactic statement in the main clause. The following sentence, which comments on the constitutional rights of life, liberty, and the pursuit of happiness, illustrates the pattern.

But if life hardly seems worth living, if liberty is used for subhuman purposes, if the pursuers of happiness know nothing about the nature of their quarry or the elementary techniques of hunting, *these constitutional rights will not be very meaningful.*[8]

Here the writer moves through a series of conditional "if" clauses to the concluding statement of the italicized main clause. If we use *C* for subordinate clause and *M* for main clause, the structure can be diagrammed as *C, C, C, M.* In the following quotation from *Hamlet,* the opening series consists of four infinitive phrases and can be diagrammed *P, P, P, P, M.*

> To die, to sleep; to sleep, perchance to dream;
> Aye, there's the rub.

EXERCISE

Using P, C, M for phrase, subordinate clause, and main clause respectively, diagram the structure of each of the following periodic sentences.

1. Over the river and through the woods, to grandmother's house we go.
2. To praise with a small voice and a restraining hand, to follow with reservations and a feeble heart, is to serve Peter while in the pay of Paul.
3. As long as politicians talk about withdrawal while they attack, as long as government invades privacy while it discusses human rights, as long as we act in fear while we speak of courage, there can be no security, there can be no peace.
4. Whether we stand or fall, whether we succeed or fail, we shall have given to the cause our hands, our heads, our hearts.

The prime difficulty of the periodic sentence is that the writer must see its whole pattern before he begins to write it. In a standard sentence he has much more freedom to continue or to stop after the main clause; he can compound main clauses or add subordinate clauses or phrases as he writes. But a periodic sentence has to be thought out in advance, and the longer it is, the more prewriting it requires. For this reason periodic sentences are less common than standard or parallel sentences. Yet they can have powerful effect when a writer wants to emphasize a main clause by holding it back until the end of the introductory parallel structure. In the following sentence

From breakfast to lunch, from lunch to dinner, from dinner to midnight snack, *she is thinking of only one thing, the next meal.—*

the introductory phrases, by postponing and leading up to the italicized main clause, give it an emphasis it would not have at the beginning. The whole sentence is thus tied together and resolved by the final main clause.

[8] Aldous Huxley, "Education on the Nonverbal Level."

EXERCISE   *Study the sentences in the following paragraph and pick out those that seem to you clear examples of parallel, balanced, and periodic sentences.*

To think of Chaplin is to think of the movies. Yet this unique actor, director, and producer has added little to movie technique or movie form. He has not been a technician but a pantomimist, a commentator, a satirist, a social critic. His artistic problems have not been cinematic; they have been personal, always being solved by feeling. His importance lies not in what he has contributed to film art, but in what he has contributed to humanity. If he is negligible as a movie craftsman, if he has evolved no new formal aspects to enrich the medium, he has created many monuments to enrich society. Chaplin will always be known for his social outlook, his insight into human nature, his pantomimic skill, his ingenious development of the incident, and his evocation of mood. It is these qualities rather than any plastic contributions which have made him significant as a screen artist.[9]

REVISING SENTENCES

Truly effective sentences are more often rewritten than written. Certainly our first expression of an idea is often not the best we can do and can be much improved by revision. It makes no difference to the reader when the revision takes place. It may come during the first draft, as the writer tries alternate forms to see which he prefers; it may come after the first draft is completed; most frequently, it comes both during the first draft and afterwards, when the writer has time to concentrate on the details of expression.

This section discusses revising sentences for four main qualities: *clarity, emphasis, economy,* and *variety.*

Revision for Clarity

The first requirement of a good sentence is that it be clear. Most failures in clarity come from three sources: (1) from such errors as misleading word order, confused pronoun reference, omission of necessary words, and inadequate punctuation; (2) from vague diction; (3) from over-involved sentence structure. Errors of the first kind are treated in the Handbook. Problems of diction are discussed in Chapter 7. Here we shall deal with the lack of clarity that comes from trying to handle too many ideas in one sentence. The following example introduces the problem.

His mother, who had been living in Ohio, where she had been keeping house for her nephew who lost his wife in a car accident and needed help in bringing up his three small children, having been in poor health since her husband died, because she suffered from chronic asthma, had to move to Colorado.

[9] From Lewis Jacobs, *The Rise of the American Film* (New York: Harcourt, Brace, 1939).

As written, this sentence consists of a main clause (*His mother had to move to Colorado*) interrupted by five subordinate clauses, some referring to the mother and some to the nephew. This involved structure is hard going for both writer and reader. Any revision should aim to simplify the structure by reducing the number of clauses per sentence. The number of clauses can be reduced by either or both of two methods: by distributing the clauses into two sentences, or by omitting information not necessary to the statement. The second method, of course, depends on the writer's view of what is necessary.

There are several ways of revising the sentence above. Let us consider just two.

1. His mother had been suffering from chronic asthma since her husband died and finally had to move to Colorado to relieve it. Before going to Colorado, she had been keeping house in Ohio for a nephew who was left with three small children when his wife was killed in an automobile accident.

This revision assumes that all the information in the original version is necessary and distributes it through two sentences. The first has a compound main clause and one subordinate clause. The second has a simple main clause and two subordinate clauses. Neither the information nor the number of clauses is significantly reduced, but the passage is clearer because the clauses are easier to assimilate in two sentences, one emphasizing the mother's problems, the other the nephew's.

Now consider this version:

2. Because of her chronic asthma, his mother had to move from Ohio to Colorado. In Ohio she had been keeping house for a widowed nephew and his three small children.

This revision leaves out several pieces of information presumably not necessary. It reduces the original six clauses to two, both main clauses. And it reduces the number of words from 55 in the original and 52 in the first revision, to 30.

Both revisions are clearer than the original. The first revision may be considered minor, since it makes less change in the content. The second revision is major, since it selects and reorganizes the content. Between these minor and major revisions, others are possible. Try a few variations to see which you prefer.

The first requirement in any revision is to see that revision is necessary. The writer must get away from his own involvement in the sentence and see it as his reader will. If he cannot do that, he is likely to leave the sentence as he first wrote it. But once he appreciates the need for revision he has such a choice of alternatives that he can easily improve the original. Notice that the revisions above reduce the density of the original sentence. This statement may seem to contradict what was said earlier about combining sentences. But there is no contradiction. Some sentences should be combined to achieve greater density; others should be simplified by rewriting one sentence as two or three. The decision to combine or to separate, to simplify or to enrich, depends on the writer's material and his best judgment of how to present it to his reader.

EXERCISE   *Simplify the structure of the following sentences to make them easier to read.*

---

1. Democracy is the easiest form of government from the point of view of the ordinary citizen, leaving him free to think, talk, and worship as he pleases, but also requiring him to be sufficiently informed about local, national, and international events to weigh and decide policies which may affect the security and welfare of his children and grandchildren, thus making it the most difficult form of government.

2. The reason it is difficult to see while driving in a fog is that the headlights hit the small particles of water of which the fog is composed so that they block the beam of light and reflect it back to the driver's eyes, and the denser the fog is the more light is reflected, because there are more water particles, until the driver cannot see beyond his headlights.

Revision for Emphasis

Emphasis is a reflection of purpose through style. There are usually several ways of expressing any idea, and if one way gives greater emphasis than others to what a writer wants to stress, that is the best way for his purpose. Here we shall discuss three ways of obtaining purposeful emphasis: *emphatic word order, emphatic repetition,* and *emphatic voice.*

Emphatic Word Order.   The way a writer uses word order to obtain emphasis in a sentence depends on two considerations: What words does he wish to emphasize? What positions within a sentence provide the most emphasis?

Take the sequence: event—the shooting of Abraham Lincoln; place—Ford's Theater; time—the evening of April 14, 1865; assassin—John Wilkes Booth. Normally we would consider the name of the President the most important part of the sentence and would put it in the subject position. Then we would be required to follow with the verb. With that start, we could arrange the three other elements in any order we pleased, though there probably would be a normal preference for naming the assassin next. To indicate the flexibility of the last three elements, we shall arrange them vertically:

	by John Wilkes Booth
Abraham Lincoln was shot	in Ford's Theater
	on the evening of April 14, 1865

But if the sentence occurred in a biography of the actor, he would probably be made the subject:—*John Wilkes Booth shot Lincoln . . . .*

And if the author were writing a history of Ford's Theater, he might order the sentence thus:—*It was in Ford's Theater that Booth shot Lincoln on the evening of April 14, 1865.*

In a longer sentence, both the beginning and the end are emphatic positions. The most important material is put in these positions, and less important material is placed in the middle. If unimportant details pile up at the end of a sentence, they may get more emphasis than they deserve, and the reader may feel that the sentence is "running down," because he expects important information at the end and does not get it. Notice the difference between the following statements:

Unemphatic Order	Emphatic Order
It was necessary to notify the fans that because of a bomb threat the stands would have to be cleared and searched in the fourth inning.	The bomb threat made it necessary to notify the fans in the fourth inning that the stands would have to be cleared and searched.

The version at the left puts the announcement to the fans and the time at which it was made in the most emphatic positions in the sentence, and the dramatic information about the bomb threat and the clearing of the stands in the least emphatic position. The sentence is both unemphatic and ambiguous. The version at the right puts the bomb threat and the clearing of the stands in the emphatic positions and the announcement and the time in the middle.

EXERCISE

Revise the following sentences to put the least important information in the middle and thus emphasize the elements placed at the beginning and the end.

1. In a magnificent stretch run the favorite overtook six horses and won by a nose, thrilling the crowd.

2. Patrick Henry said "Give me liberty or give me death" in an incendiary speech before the Virginia House of Burgesses.

3. It is entirely possible that morality consists only in the courage of making a choice, I have sometimes thought.

Climactic Order. Climax arranges the material of a sentence so as to build up to a major idea. We have seen that the force of the periodic sentence derives from this order, but climax may also be used in standard sentences. The following examples contrast anticlimactic and climactic order. Study both versions of each sentence and explain what changes were made in the revisions.

Anticlimactic Order	Climactic Order
The prosecution asked in its summing up that the jury bring in a verdict of guilty, which was the only possible verdict considering the violence of the crime and the lack of provocation.	In summing up, the prosecution asked the jury to consider the lack of provocation and the violence of the crime and then bring in the only possible verdict—guilty.
He said that the U.N. had failed in its chief function to preserve the peace of the world, although it had done much of which it could be proud and was still performing valuable services in many areas.	He said that, though the U.N. had done much of which it could be proud and was still performing valuable services in many areas, it had failed in its chief function, to preserve the peace of the world.

In general, any acceptable inversion of normal word order tends to emphasize the inverted word. In *Slowly and sadly we laid him down* and in *Right you are*, the modifiers are emphasized by being moved from the ends of the sentences to the beginnings. The following sentence would normally begin with *Time* as the subject—*Time is the leading idea. . . .* But notice the emphasis obtained by making it the complement and holding it till the end:

The leading idea which is present in all our researches and which accompanies every fresh observation, the sound which to the ear of the student of Nature seems continually echoed from every part of her works, is—Time!

Emphatic Repetition.　More often than not, unintentional repetition weakens a sentence:

All uniforms must be of absolutely uniform quality.

The palatial palace was brilliantly lighted with many brilliant lights.

Intentional repetition, however, can produce desired emphasis. We have seen (page 93) that repeated words can help knit a paragraph together. We have also seen that the repetition of necessary structure words helps maintain and emphasize parallel and balanced elements. Deliberate repetition of key words can also give strong emphasis. Consider the following:

It was an act of senseless *brutality, brutally* planned and *brutally* executed, serving no purpose except to indulge a *brute* passion.

It is easy to find scapegoats for the pollution problem: to *blame* the industrialist, to *blame* the chemist, to *blame* advertising or capitalism, or, in one comprehensive condemnation, to *blame* society; but everyone who drives a car or burns electricity or flushes a toilet has a share of the *blame;* it is not *blaming* that is needed, but a conscientious and consistent attempt to make *blame* unnecessary.

Emphatic Voice. It is common in composition courses to urge students to use verbs in the active rather than the passive voice. This advice is generally sound, because the active voice is usually more natural and the so-called "weak passive" often leads to wordiness and awkward shifts in structure.

Weak Passive	More Emphatic Active
A final examination was failed by both starting halfbacks.	Both starting halfbacks failed a final examination.
He was not prepared for the test and so only half the questions were answered.	Because he was not prepared for the test he answered only half the questions.
Looking through the binoculars, the ship was sighted.	Looking through the binoculars, I sighted the ship.
In a fit of temper his clubs were thrown in the lake.	In a fit of temper he threw his clubs in the lake.

But there are situations in which the passive is more accurate and even more emphatic than the active voice. The beginning of a sentence is, as we have seen, a position of stress, and putting a word there tends to emphasize it—sometimes unwisely. For example:

The *legislature* founded the university ninety years ago.

Some *persons* left two suitcases and four parcels on the train to Brooklyn.

The *people* elected Lincoln President although he did not have a majority of votes in 1864.

You should not take antibiotics without a prescription.

In these sentences the stress should not fall on the grammatical subjects, which are of almost no interest to the thoughts conveyed. Passive constructions, ignoring these subjects entirely, give more accurate emphasis:

The *university was founded* ninety years ago.

Two *suitcases* and four *parcels were left* on the train to Brooklyn.

Lincoln was elected President in 1864 although he did not have a majority of the votes.

Antibiotics should not be taken without a prescription.

The choice between active and passive forms is like any other choice a writer has to make. It is to be judged by results. The preferred form is the one that does best what the writer wants to do. When in doubt he can try both voices and then decide. If he does, he will usually, but not always, choose the active verb.

EXERCISE	*Revise the following sentences to provide better emphasis.*

1. A speech cannot be prepared and a history lesson studied by me in one short hour.

2. An official stood at the gate staring down all comers with an unpleasant official stare.

3. Sandwiches and ice cream were offered to and enjoyed by all those who attended the Chancellor's reception.

4. Three policemen policed the dance, but several magnificent jewels and an assortment of less valuable jewelry were stolen by some skillful thieves despite the determination of the police to protect the guests' jewels and other valuables.

5. The ROTC was legislated into existence by our national legislature by the Land Grant Act of 1863.

6. Wounded and bleeding, somebody dragged me to shelter just as it began to rain, as it continued to do for the next several hours.

7. "I have considered the arguments for and against a stay of execution, and I still favor mercy," the governor said, "when all is said and done."

8. To protest is to be part of one's time and generation. To take part in protests is a duty one cannot ignore. Protesting is experiencing a fierce joy one can scarcely deny.

9. The ball was hit so hard by Johnson that when it was found later outside the fence, it was discovered that the cover had been split.

10. But all of this was hardly news to John Parks, whose love for nature has always been matched by a deep and informed concern for its well-being for many years.

Revision for Economy	Economy is a relation between the number of words used and the amount of meaning they convey. A sentence is not economical because it is short, or wordy because it is long. The test is not the number of words but the amount of information they convey. Consider these two statements:

Although I cannot truthfully say that I was acclaimed during my high school career as a prodigy, being what is generally known as an average student, yet I was able to survive the rigors of academic pursuits and to achieve graduation without ever having received a failing grade in any subject.	Although I was only an average student in high school, I never failed a course.

The version at the right says all the author wants to say, and from the reader's point of view, says it better. The version at the left obscures the meaning by trying to be "literary." It is not only wordy but pretentious.

But now consider the two following statements:

Unfortunately, the rules of spelling do not solve my problems.	Unfortunately, the rules of spelling do not solve my problems: *i* before *e* except after *c* leads me into trouble with *counterfeit* and *seize,* and the rule about dropping a silent *e* before a suffix beginning with a vowel makes me want to spell *mileage* without an *e*.

The version at the left has fewer words but much less meaning. The illustrative details at the right provide a fuller message. If these details are needed, it would be foolish to omit them simply to get a shorter sentence. Decisions about economy must always be made in relation to meaning.

Wordiness—the opposite of economy—is common in student writing. When a whole essay is wordy, the trouble may lie in scanty prewriting or in a monotonous style that could be tightened up by better use of coordination and subordination. Revision of these weaknesses requires complete rewriting. Here we are considering only wordiness *within* a sentence, and revision is relatively easy. The two most common methods are cutting out useless words and substituting more economical expressions for wordy ones. Both methods are illustrated below.

Cutting out a useless introductory phrase

~~It is interesting to observe that~~ Students are generally better prepared for college than they were twenty years ago.

~~With reference to the question of equal rights,~~ I think women should have equal rights.

Cutting out useless words within the body of a sentence

The people ~~who stood around outside~~ in the street had a better view than those ~~who stayed~~ inside.

~~At an~~ Early ~~stage~~ in his career, Yogi encountered a coach who kept ~~constantly~~ urging him to analyze his motions ~~while he was up~~ at the plate.

Substituting a word for a phrase or a clause

She looked ∧*sick.* ~~as though she was not feeling very well~~.

He sold several of his ⌐paintings. ~~of the~~ (Impressionist) ~~School~~.

She is the girl ∧*in* ~~who is wearing~~ the red sweater.

I do not approve of ~~the~~ *his* methods. ~~he employs~~.

EXERCISE

Revise the following sentences to reduce wordiness.

---

1. With respect to that question there is, in my opinion, no one answer that is generally acceptable.

2. As far as the average student is concerned, the proposal is one that does not interest us in any way.

3. The plot of the book is full of all kinds of exciting actions but, as for the characters, they do not seem to be the kind of people that one could believe in.

4. Although there is a wide diversity of opinion about the war in Vietnam, there is nevertheless a general feeling among most people that the sooner it is brought to a conclusion, the better off everyone will be.

5. I think that most people, including faculty members, agree that while book learning is important, there is a great deal of useful information that one can learn from the extracurricular activities that exist in such abundance on every college campus.

6. The Dean said that statistics show that in most cases the students who do not make their grades and have to withdraw from college do so because they have not learned to discipline themselves to serious study for a whole semester. He said that most students who come to college have the ability to do successful work if they would only apply themselves.

7. I can only hope that I derive as much benefit out of my years of college work and study as I got from the four years which I spent in high school.

8. Concerning the relationship between the laws of today and the laws of ancient times, I think that the author is wrong in stating that the laws of today are based on ancient laws.

9. They live in the city of Eau Claire, which is in the state of Wisconsin.

10. The attempts of the administration to instill confidence in them among the people have met with mediocre success, to say the least.

**Revision for
Variety**

Logically, a discussion of variety in sentence structure belongs in a chapter on the paragraph. Variety is not a characteristic of single sentences but of a succession of sentences. We consider it here because it is useful to discuss variety *after* parallel and periodic sentences, word order, and subordination. Consider the following contrasted passages:

---

1. John Stuart Mill was born in 1806 and died in 1873.

2. He was famous as a child prodigy.

3. His fame continued through his life.

4. He was a logician and a political economist and a man of letters.

5. He was one of the most influential thinkers of the nineteenth century.

John Stuart Mill (1806–1873) was a child prodigy whose fame did not cease at maturity. As a logician, political economist, and man of letters, he was one of the most influential thinkers of the nineteenth century.

The revision at the right was achieved by the following operations:

a. Sentences 1 and 2 were merged by combining the subject of 1 and the complement of 2 into a simple sentence and putting the dates in parentheses.

b. Sentence 3 was reduced to a subordinate clause and embedded in the combined sentence so that 1, 2, and 3 form a complex sentence.

c. Sentence 4 was reduced to a phrase and placed at the beginning of 5 to make a short periodic sentence.

These revisions not only provide variety but also cut the number of words by nearly 30 per cent without reducing content.

EXERCISE

As an exercise in using the above procedure, first consider the possible revisions which follow the paragraph about Henry V. Then decide which of these possibilities you want to use in rewriting the paragraph. It is not necessary to use all the possibilities. Use those that give you the best paragraph. For ease of reference the sentences are numbered.

[1] Shakespeare's chronicle history of *Henry the Fifth* is a drama of kinghood and war. [2] It is essentially a play about a young king's coming of age. [3] Henry V had been an irresponsible young prince before his accession to the throne. [4] He had to prove his worthiness as king by leading his army in war. [5] He invaded France and captured Harfleur, and then tried to withdraw his troops to Calais. [6] He and his men were confronted by a numerically superior French army at Agincourt. [7] In a famous passage in Shakespeare's play, Henry urges his soldiers on to an incredible victory. [8] The superior mobility and firepower of the English proved too much for the heavily armored French.

1. Combine 1 and 2 by omitting "is" in 1 and with necessary punctuation omit "It" at the beginning of 2, thus making "a drama of kinghood and war" a phrase within the combined sentence. Write the sentence so formed.

2. Combine 3 and 4 by inserting a comma + "who" after "Henry V," substitute a comma for the period at the end of 3, and omit the "He" in 4. Write the sentence so formed.

3. Reduce the first half of 5 to a phrase "After invading France and capturing Harfleur," and substitute "he" for "and then."

4. Join 6 with 5 by "but" and change the "He" of 6 to "he." Write the sentence thus revised.

5. Combine 8 and 7 by inserting "in which" after "victory" and making the necessary change in capitalization. Write the revised sentence.

6. Now, using any of these revised sentences, or any revisions of your own, rewrite the complete paragraph.

REVIEW EXERCISES

A. *First read the following paragraph, then make notes on how you would revise it to achieve greater sentence variety. Finally make the revision by rewriting the paragraph from your notes.*

American romanticism has many articles of faith. One article of faith is what we might call the "one-person" theory. This is the theory that for each individual there is a "right one." This right one is also "the only one in the world." It is the task of every unmarried person to wait, or to search, for that one. It is his duty. "Somewhere I'll find you." "Somewhere in the world she is waiting for you." These are familiar expressions of the belief. Yet Americans are not fools. They know that for a boy in Iowa the "only one" is not in Calcutta. They know that the "only one" is not even in California. Surveys were made not many years ago. Sociologists found that half the people applying for marriage licenses lived within twenty blocks of each other. Somewhere in the world she is waiting for you. Probably you can walk to her house in time for lunch.

B. *The following extract is the first page of a paper written by an education major and revised by her instructor. Study the changes he made. Does his condensation as printed below the revision omit significant content from the original, or is the content slight in the revision because it was slight in the paper? If you think the instructor has been too harsh, write an alternative revision which will get rid of the wordiness. By "process of creation" the student means the process of discovering ideas for the real subject. "Invention" is another name for this process. The lines have been numbered for ease of reference.*

Invention

1 The goal of every English teacher is to help

2 ~~develop in the~~ students, / ~~the ability~~ to understand

3 ~~and~~ communicate *in* their native language. ~~For the~~

4 ~~teacher~~ To achieve this goal ~~he must also acquaint~~

5 ~~the students with the process of creation that each~~

6 ~~of us uses.~~ The teacher must present the students

7 with opportunities to analyse *and use the creative* ~~the process of creation~~

8 ~~that is employed when each of us communicates and~~

9 ~~apply this process effectively.~~

10 *The trend today is to emphasize* ~~The idea of communication has led the vanguard~~

11 ~~of the "New English." The emphasis now placed on~~ the

12 teaching of linguistics *as an aid to communication.* ~~ties into the importance im-~~

13 ~~plied in teaching children to communicate effectively.~~

14 ~~But communication without cognizant knowledge of~~

15 ~~how the process works is not enough.~~ *But* ~~Effective commu-~~

16 ~~nication involves the speaker's or writer's knowledge~~ *requires an understanding of invention*

17 ~~of the use of language and how language is used to~~ *as well as of linguistics.*

18 ~~"invent" communication.~~

After the instructor's revision

The goal of every English teacher is to help students to communicate in their native language. To achieve this goal the teacher must present the students with opportunities to analyze and use the creative process.

The trend today is to emphasize the teaching of linguistics as an aid to communication. But effective communication requires an understanding of invention as well as of linguistics.

C. *Check the following words in your dictionary: ambivalent, blatant, enigmatic, furbish, garrulous, myopic, sanctuary. Then choose any four, and for each of these make brief notes on its source, original meaning, one present meaning, and an illustration of its use. For each word work all this information into a single sentence, as illustrated in the following example:*

Synchronize, from the Greek words for "together" and "time," originally meant "contemporaneous," but now means "to cause to move at the same time," as in "The sound track was synchronized with the film."

D. *Study the following passages and underline those sentences or parts of sentences that show parallel, balanced, or periodic structures.*

1. Young men are fitter to invent than to judge, fitter for execution than for counsel, and fitter for new projects than for settled business. *(Francis Bacon)*

2. But I doubt that there have been many chapters in the story of the American Republic where the incongruous has appeared so stark, the irrational so irresistible, and the clearly improbable so eventually certain. *(Emmet John Hughes)*

3. For words, like people, are born and die, are changed and weathered by the seasons, and, passing, do not altogether disappear, but leave their imprint in the language.

4. A man dies on the shore: his body remains with his friends, and the mourners go about the streets; but when a man falls overboard at sea and is lost, there is a suddenness in the event, and a difficulty in realizing it, which gives it an air of awful mystery. *(Richard Henry Dana)*

5. There was no day for him now, and there was no night; there was but a long stretch of time, a long stretch of time that was very short; and then— the end. Toward no one in the world did he feel any fear now; and toward no one in the world did he feel any hate now, for he knew that hate would not help him. *(Richard Wright)*

6. Now, when I read a novel of American campus life, or see a Hollywood version with its fair maidens in lovers' lane, dreamy-eyed youth in white flannels lolling under leafy boughs or lustily singing, arms about one another's shoulders, of their school's immortal glories and their own undying loyalty—when I come across all this, I am astonished and unbelieving, or I have a faint twinge of nostalgia for a beautiful something I never knew. *(Eric Sevareid)*

Chapter 7

Right Words

Words are not right or wrong in themselves but as they succeed or fail in doing what the writer wants them to do. A word is "right" in a sentence when it expresses the writer's meaning and is appropriate to the situation in which it is used. This chapter will first discuss those qualities which generally make words effective, and then consider how undesirable qualities may be removed in revision.

QUALITIES OF GOOD DICTION

In choosing your words, keep these four things in mind. The right word is always *accurate* and *appropriate*. Your diction should be as *concrete* as your purpose demands. And a telling *image,* or *figure of speech,* can often do more than a paragraph of literal prose.

Accurate Diction   A word is accurate when, in its sentence, it has both the right *denotation* and the right *connotations*. The denotation of a word is its *explicit* meaning. It is the thing, event, or concept to which the word refers. Thus the denotation of "desk" is that piece of furniture you sit at when you study or write. This denotative use of "desk" is sometimes called its "dictionary meaning," but that is misleading, since dictionaries record connotations as well as denotations. The denotative use of a word is simply its use to name something, without suggesting any emotional reaction to the thing being named.

The *connotation* of a word is its *implicit* meaning. In addition to naming something, the connotations suggest or imply some association with or attitude toward the thing being named. Thus in the questions

Who is that *girl* with Bill?

Who is that *dog* with Bill?

Who is that *chick* with Bill?—

all three italicized words refer to a relatively young human female, but "dog" suggests an unfavorable attitude toward the girl, and "chick" a favorable one. In these sentences "girl" is used denotatively; "dog" and "chick," connotatively. You can easily think of other sentences in which "dog" and "chick" are used denotatively to refer to nonhuman creatures. Thus it should be clear that denotations and connotations are not inherent in the words themselves, but in the way we use them.

Some words, such as *brave, efficient, valuable,* and *love,* generally carry only favorable connotations. Others, such as *absurd, callous, vicious,* and *lust,* usually have only unfavorable connotations. Still others have favorable connotations in some contexts and unfavorable ones in others. Compare "a *fat* check" and "a *fat* girl." The following verses aptly contrast favorable and unfavorable connotations:

> Call a woman a kitten, but never a cat;
> You can call her a mouse, cannot call her a rat;
> Call a woman a chicken, but never a hen;
> Or you surely will not be her caller again. . . .
>
> You can say she's a vision, can't say she's a sight;
> And no woman is skinny, she's slender and slight;
> If she should burn you up, say she sets you afire,
> And you'll always be welcome, you tricky old liar.[1]

EXERCISE

In each of the following sentences, the contrasted elements refer to the same situation. First discuss the different connotations of the contrasted terms in each sentence. Then write three sentences of your own to show similar contrasts.

---

1. He said he was *firm of purpose;* his wife said he was *stubborn.*
2. Helen thought he was *shy;* I thought him *sullen.*
3. The difference between *a boyish prank* and *an act of vandalism* depends on whose children do the mischief.
4. I am *portly,* Harold is *chubby,* but Charles is *obese.*
5. Some critics said he gave a *popular performance;* others said he *catered to vulgarity.*

Choosing the right denotation is usually easier than choosing the right connotation. Most errors in denotation come from three sources: confusion of words with similar forms (*affect–effect, respectful–respective, stationary–stationery*); confusion of antonyms—words with opposite meanings (*antag-*

---

[1] John E. Donovan, "Semantics," *The Saturday Evening Post,* July 13, 1946. Reprinted by permission of Mrs. Gertrude D. Crane and *The Saturday Evening Post.*

onist–protagonist, port–starboard, urban–rural); and the failure to express the exact meaning intended. The first of these mistakes is often considered an error in spelling. The second is usually a temporary confusion which will disappear as the writer gains experience with the terms that cause trouble. This kind of error can easily be corrected by checking a questionable word in a dictionary. The third error is the most difficult to recognize and to correct. More attention to concrete diction will often help (page 138), but the only sure cure is to develop the habit of concern for accurate statement. There is no formula for developing that habit, but reading over your first draft slowly and checking doubtful words in a good dictionary is a constructive approach.

EXERCISE

For each of the following sentences, first select the word in parentheses which most accurately expresses the writer's thought. Then write another sentence using the rejected word. If you cannot be sure which meaning was intended, write a separate sentence for each word.

1. She makes all her own clothes. She is quite (adapt, adept) at tailoring.
2. The committee passed a resolution (censoring, censuring) the film.
3. The instructor said the remark was (irrelevant, irreverent) to the discussion.
4. The colonel was concerned about the (morals, morale) of his troops.
5. There is no truth in her story. It is all a (fragment, figment) of her imagination.
6. The President was asked to issue an (official, officious) explanation.
7. His reasoning was completely (fallacious, fictitious).
8. The noise made by the construction workers (detracted, distracted) the class.
9. He felt that he had no more (illusions, allusions) about anything.
10. Your remarks (infer, imply) a very low opinion of space exploration.

Most choices of diction are choices of connotation. When a word has obviously wrong connotations, as "skinny" for "slender" in an otherwise complimentary context, the fault is easy to spot and correct. Less obvious are the distinctions between words which are near synonyms (have similar meanings) but may have important differences in particular contexts. For example, "dawdle," "procrastinate," and "vacillate" all have the general meaning of not getting on with the job, but they suggest different kinds of inaction. Hamlet vacillates, and his vacillation leads to procrastination, but he does not dawdle. "Untidy" and "disorderly" can be used as near synonyms to describe a room, but it would be a major error to describe a house as "disorderly" if you meant that it was "untidy."

In the following list, all the words in each line have roughly the same general meaning as the italicized word at the left; yet they cannot always be used interchangeably. Distinguish their differences by showing how they would affect the meaning of the phrase if they were substituted for the italicized word.

An *angry* remark: annoyed, belligerent, indignant

A *careful* answer: cautious, deliberate, painstaking

An *embarrassed* speaker: abashed, chagrined, flustered

An *odd* costume: bizarre, unconventional, quaint

To *plead* for a favor: beg, coax, wheedle

To *reprimand* an offender: admonish, rebuke, scold

A *tired* man: exhausted, sleepy, weary

Appropriate Diction

Words are appropriate when they are suited to the situation in which they are used. A doctor explaining a disease at a medical convention would speak quite differently than he would in reporting a diagnosis to a patient. One explanation might be as accurate as the other, but each would be influenced by the situation in which it was made.

In choosing appropriate diction the two main considerations are the kind of language required by the situation, including the audience, and the distance the writer wants to maintain between himself and his reader. The above example about the doctor in two speaking situations illustrates both considerations. At a medical convention he would use the technical terms of his profession. He would call cancer "carcinoma," and instead of saying "heart attack" he would use the scientific name for the particular kind of heart attack—for example, "coronary thrombosis." His attitude toward his audience would be objective, impersonal, and distant in the sense that he was speaking from a platform to a mass audience, not sitting by a bedside talking to a patient. On the platform he would not have to worry about possible connotations of "carcinoma"; at the bedside he would be sensitive to the emotional disturbance that might result from telling a patient he had cancer. In this chapter we will deal with the kind of language the situation requires. The distance between writer and reader will be discussed in the next chapter.

The Kind of Language Required: Levels of Usage. The "English language" is a general term for the speaking and writing habits of all the people—several hundred millions of them—who use English as their native tongue. No two of these people speak the language in exactly the same way, but by ignoring individual differences and emphasizing group similarities, we can recognize certain subclasses of English which we call *dialects*. For example, there are national dialects (American, Australian, British English) and regional dialects (New England, Southern, Midwestern). Although the people who use each of these varieties of English tend to think of their own brand as "normal," no one dialect can be proved superior to others. Each belongs to a group, and serves that group well.

The dialect which the schools have historically taught is called *standard English*. *Webster's Third New International Dictionary* defines this term as

the English that with respect to spelling, grammar, pronunciation, and vocabulary is substantially uniform though not devoid of regional differences, that is well-established by usage in the formal and informal speech and writing of the educated, and that is widely recognized as acceptable wherever English is spoken and understood.

We can simplify this definition by saying that standard English is the usage of educated speakers and writers of English. The schools, which are committed to helping young people to educate themselves, generally stress this dialect. It is the standard by which expository writing in schools and colleges is usually judged.

Within the standard dialect there is a wide range from formal to quite informal diction. We can identify main segments of that range by a diagram.

Formal	Informal	Colloquial

We can best explain these segments by postponing "informal" until we have discussed "formal" and "colloquial."

Formal Diction. Formal diction has two conspicuous characteristics. It usually avoids contractions (*I've, can't, won't*) and clipped words (*exam* for *examination, auto* for *automobile, phone* for *telephone, ad* for *advertisement*). It makes considerable use of "learned" words. These are words mostly borrowed from a foreign language, often for use in some field of learning (the law, medicine, psychology) and are much used in professional writings in these fields. Some of these words have become so useful that they are used by educated people generally, but seldom by uneducated people.

Contrasted with learned words are "popular" words, which are used by the whole populace, educated and uneducated. These words are the basic elements of the vocabulary. By their use people from widely different social levels are able to speak a common language. The following list illustrates learned and popular pairs having the same denotations.

Learned	Popular	Learned	Popular
abdomen	belly	granular	grainy
capitulate	surrender	imminent	near (in time)
carcinoma	cancer	mendicant	beggar
corpulent	fat	myopic	shortsighted
decapitate	behead	psychotic	insane
facilitate	make easy	terminate	end

Colloquial Diction. The term *colloquial* is defined by *The American Heritage Dictionary* as "characteristic of or appropriate to the spoken language or to writing that seeks its effect; informal in diction or style of expression." Colloquial diction is not "incorrect" or "slovenly." It is conversational, using the kinds of words and expressions educated people use when they are speaking together quite informally. Such a style is used in writing when the writer wants to give the impression of talking directly and intimately to his reader. When he does so, he will generally avoid all formal terms and use contractions and clipped words generously. The effect he is aiming at is as much informality as he can get in writing.

Slang. The *Oxford Dictionary* defines slang as "language of a highly colloquial type." Notice that the adjective is *colloquial*, not *vulgar, incorrect,* or *nonstandard.* Slang is used at all social levels. Its use is less frequent and more discriminating among educated speakers, but though a college president would usually avoid slang in a public address, he might well use it in many informal speech situations.

Slang has its origin in a desire for novelty. Much of it is borrowed from the special vocabularies of particular groups or activities: *zero in* (gunnery), *on the beam* (aerial navigation), *behind the eight ball* (pool), *raise the ante* (poker), *pad* (rocketry), *offbeat* (music), *tuned in* and *turned off* (radio). Some of it comes from the underworld (or underground): *snow, grass, joint, mainliner, stoned.* Many slang expressions are borrowed from the standard vocabulary and given different meanings: *no sweat, flipped, cool, cat, soul, rap, high.*

Slang terms sometimes serve a continuing purpose and become established usage. The words *bus, cab, canter, hoax,* and *mob* were once slang but are now accepted in formal English. But most slang is soon so dated that it becomes a little funny. Here are a few expressions from earlier times.

World War I: gee whiz, oh, you kid!, doughboy, Heinie

The '20's and '30's: flivver, lounge lizard, sugar daddy, caught with the goods, get next to

World War II: milk run, whiz bang, goldbrick, over the hill, can do, Roger

The freshness that makes slang effective at first is soon worn off by overuse, and what was once creative becomes lazy borrowing. This is the chief reason why instructors often object to slang in college writing. If the slang words were carefully chosen and if they were appropriate to the purpose and style of the paper, they would be effective. But if slang were so chosen, there would be much less of it in student compositions.

EXERCISE

Write down a dozen slang terms now current on your campus. For each term write a definition and a sentence illustrating its use. Then for any three of these terms write popular and learned synonyms, as in the following example.

Slang	Popular	Learned
to split	to leave	to depart

Informal Diction. Informal diction occupies the broad range between formal and colloquial usage. It may include some formal terms, some contractions and clipped words, some slang, but in general it stays away from the extremes at both ends of the scale. It thus has the broadest scope and the greatest variety and versatility of the three ranges we have been studying. For this reason informal standard usage has become the preferred mode in modern English, even in serious writing on significant subjects.

EXERCISE

In George Bernard Shaw's play Pygmalion *(perhaps better known by its musical and film versions as* My Fair Lady*), Liza Doolittle, a cockney flower girl who is being taught by Professor Higgins to talk like a lady, meets her first test at a small party at the home of Mrs. Higgins, the professor's mother. Here is a fragment of the conversation. Read it and contrast Liza's first remarks about the weather with her account of her aunt's death. How is this contrast consistent with Shaw's purpose in this scene?*

MRS. HIGGINS. Will it rain, do you think?

LIZA. The shallow depression in the west of these islands is likely to move slowly in an easterly direction. There are no indications of any great change in the barometrical situation.

FREDDY. Ha! Ha! How awfully funny!

LIZA. What is wrong with that, young man? I bet I got it right.

FREDDY. Killing!

MRS. EYNSFORD HILL. I'm sure I hope it won't turn cold. There's so much influenza about. It runs right through our whole family regularly every spring.

LIZA. My aunt died of influenza: so they said. . . . But it's my belief they done the old woman in. . . . Why should she die of influenza? She come through diphtheria right enough the year before. I saw her with my own eyes. Fairly blue with it, she was. They all thought she was dead; but my father he kept ladling gin down her throat til she came to so sudden that she bit the bowl off the spoon. . . . What call would a woman with that strength in her have to die of influenza? What become of her new straw hat that should have come to me? Somebody pinched it; and what I say is, them as pinched it done her in.

Concrete Diction The following diagram illustrates the meaning of "concrete" in relation to its opposite, the term "abstract."

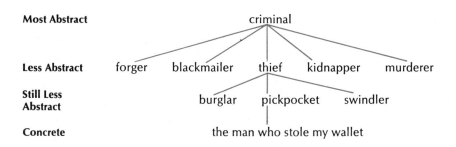

Most Abstract				criminal		
Less Abstract	forger	blackmailer	thief	kidnapper	murderer	
Still Less Abstract		burglar	pickpocket	swindler		
Concrete		the man who stole my wallet				

The word "criminal" refers to a general class and can be subdivided into the more specific classes on the second line of the diagram. "Criminal" does not specify which of these subclasses is being referred to; rather, it points to what they all have in common. Such words as "criminal" are said to be *abstract* or *abstractions*. The phrase "the man who stole my wallet" refers to a particular individual, someone who could be identified by a photograph or picked out of a police lineup. As contrasted with "criminal," "the man who stole my wallet" is said to be *concrete*. The diagram also shows that abstractions are relative. The words on the third line are more abstract than the term on the fourth line, but less abstract than those on the second, which are still less abstract than "criminal."

This diagram could also be arranged horizontally, with the most abstract terms at the left and the most concrete at the right.

Most Abstract	Less Abstract	Still Less Abstract	Concrete
criminal————	thief————	pickpocket————	the man who stole my wallet
athlete————	football player————	halfback————	Gale Sayers

Arrange the following sets of terms from left to right in order of decreasing abstraction.

freshman, college student, member of Dr. Jones's composition section, Bill Mason

Senator Mansfield, politician, leader of the majority party in the Senate, senator

winner of the Kentucky Derby, horse, Canonero II, racehorse, animal

Neither abstract nor concrete words are good or bad in themselves. There are purposes which require abstractions. For example, a President's inaugural address cannot deal with concrete particulars; it can be only a general statement of policy or intention. But when a writer is trying to translate an experience into words that will help the reader to share that experience, his success will depend largely on his ability to make the reader see and feel. For this purpose concrete words are more helpful than abstract words. Notice the concreteness of the diction in the following paragraph, and underline the words and phrases that help you to share the writer's experience with water.

The scullery was a mine of all the minerals of living. Here I discovered water —a very different element from the green crawling scum that stank in the garden tub. You could pump it in pure blue gulps out of the ground; you could swing on the pump handle and it came out sparkling like liquid sky. And it broke and ran and shone on the tiled floor, or quivered in a jug, or weighted your clothes with cold. You could drink it, draw with it, froth it with soap, swim beetles across it, or fly it in bubbles in the air. You could put your head in it, and open your eyes, and see the sides of the bucket buckle, and hear your caught breath roar, and work your mouth like a fish, and smell the lime from the ground. Substance of magic—which you could tear or wear, confine or scatter, or send down holes, but never burn or break or destroy.[2]

Sensory Words. As the preceding paragraph illustrates, some words refer to sensory experiences: to what we see, hear, touch, taste, and smell. Because these words call up sensory images, they are particularly effective in description. In the following list, some words could fit into more than one sensory category.

Touch: chill, clammy, cold, corrugated, grainy, gritty, harsh, jarring, knobby, moist, nubby, numb, plushy, rough, satiny, slimy, slithering, smooth, sting, tingle, tickly, velvety

[2] From Laurie Lee, *The Edge of Day* (New York: William Morrow and Company, 1959).

Taste: bland, biting, bitter, brackish, briny, metallic, minty, nutty, peppery, salty, sour, spicy, sweet, tainted, vinegary, yeasty

Smell: acrid, fetid, greasy, mouldy, musky, musty, pungent, putrid, rancid, rank, reek, stench, sulphurous, woodsy

Sound: bellow, blare, buzz, chatter, chime, clang, clatter, clink, crackle, crash, creak, gurgle, hiss, hum, murmur, pop, purr, rattle, rustle, screech, snap, splash, squeak, swish, tinkle, whine, whisper

Sight: blaze, bleary, bloody, burnished, chalky, dappled, ebony, flame, flash, flicker, florid, foggy, gaudy, glare, glitter, glossy, glow, golden, grimy, haze, inky, leaden, lurid, muddy, roiled, sallow, shadow, smudged, spark, streak, tawny, turbid

Sensory words help the reader re-live the experience the writer is recording. Notice how the following description helps you to feel, hear, see, and smell the details of ploughing.

The ploughing, now in full swing, enveloped him in a vague, slow-moving whirl of things. Underneath him was the jarring, jolting, trembling machine; not a clod was turned, not an obstacle encountered, that he did not receive the swift impression of it through all his body; the very friction of the damp soil, sliding incessantly from the shiny surface of the shears, seemed to reproduce itself in his finger-tips and along the back of his head. He heard the horse-hoofs by the myriads crushing down easily, deeply, into the loam, the prolonged clinking of trace-chains, the working of the smooth brown flanks in the harness, the clatter of wooden hames, the champing of bits, the click of iron shoes against pebbles, the brittle stubble of the surface ground crackling and snapping as the furrows turned, the sonorous, steady breaths wrenched from the deep, laboring chests, strap-bound, shining with sweat, and all along the line the voices of the men talking to the horses. Everywhere there were visions of glossy brown backs, straining, heaving, swollen with muscle; harness streaked with specks of froth, broad, cup-shaped hoofs, heavy with brown loam; men's faces red with tan, blue overalls spotted with axle-grease; muscled hands, the knuckles whitened in their grip on the reins, and through it all the ammoniacal smell of the horses, the bitter reek of perspiration of beasts and men, the aroma of warm leather, the scent of dead stubble—and stronger and more penetrating than everything else, the heavy, enervating odor of the up-turned, living earth.[3]

The effect of this paragraph depends on two things: first, the writer's keen observation of horses ploughing, and, second, his choice of concrete words to describe the scene. These two qualities go together. Without close observation he would not have had such detailed information. Without the concrete words the details could not have been so vividly expressed.

[3] From Frank Norris, *The Octopus*.

EXERCISE

The following pairs of statements convey the same information in different ways. From each contrasted pair, choose the one which you think is the more concrete and justify your choice.

1A

In the past, girls in rural communities had no facilities for bathing except those offered by some neighboring stream. In such circumstances a bathing suit was not always a necessity, but if one was worn it was likely to consist of nothing more than some discarded article of clothing tailored to fit the occasion.

1B

Forty years ago if the farmer's daughter went swimming she swam in the crick below the pasture, and if she wore a bathing suit, which was not as customary as you may think, it was likely to be a pair of her brother's outgrown overalls trimmed with scissors as her discretion might suggest.

2A

Suddenly I felt something on the biceps of my right arm—a queer light touch, clinging for an instant, and then the smooth glide of an oily body. I could feel the muscles of the snake's body slowly contract and relax. At last I saw a flat, V-shaped head, with two glistening, black protruding buttons. A thin, pointed sickening yellow tongue slipped out, then in, accompanied by a sound like that of escaping steam.

2B

Suddenly I felt the snake moving over my arm. I felt the contraction of its muscles as it moved. Then I saw its ugly head and its evil-looking eyes. All the time its tongue kept moving in and out, making a kind of hissing noise.

Imagery

"Imagery" is another term for "figurative language"—that is, language which uses metaphor, simile, and other "figures of speech." The chief element of such figures is a striking comparison between two things which are not usually thought of as similar, but which in the imagination of the writer become similar in some way important to him.

An example will make this imaginative comparison clearer. Consider the following line from "The Highwayman," a poem by Alfred Noyes.

The moon was a ghostly galleon tossed upon cloudy seas.

The basic comparison in this line is of the moon and a sailing ship. Now in most ways the moon is quite unlike a ship. But as Noyes watches it alternately emerging from behind the clouds and disappearing into them again, this alternation between appearance and disappearance reminds him of the way a ship disappears from view as it goes down into the trough between two waves and then comes into view again as it rises on the next crest. In Noyes's imagination the moon is seen as being *tossed* by the clouds as a ship is tossed by the waves. This similarity can be diagrammed thus:

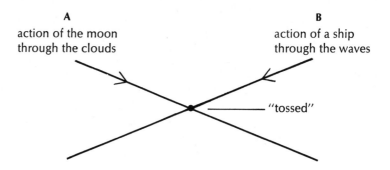

A
action of the moon
through the clouds

B
action of a ship
through the waves

"tossed"

The unifying element is the tossing that alternately brings the object into view and takes it out again.

The comparison made in this figure of speech has two effects on a reader. First, it gives him a visual image of the action described and therefore makes that action concrete. Second, it stimulates the reader's own imagination to make other associations between the moon and a ship—both are beautiful, graceful, and romantic; both are often thought of as feminine; both have a kind of grandeur because of their remoteness from the humdrum concerns of daily living. This double effect is often emotionally satisfying, so that the reader gets pleasure in sharing the writer's discovery of an unexpected similarity, and still further pleasure from his own associations.

Test these observations about the effect of imagery and the associations it suggests on this figure by W. B. Yeats:

> An aged man is but a paltry thing,
> A tattered coat upon a stick . . .

This figure may seem to express a harsh judgment of old men. In what sense does it apply? The dominant image or picture is that of a scarecrow: "a tattered coat upon a stick." Surely the poet is not thinking about the *uses* of a scarecrow. Of what, then? Are old men less vital than young men? If so, how—physically or mentally? What kinds of interests are more likely to dominate young men than old? The following lines precede this figure of speech in Yeats's poem, "Sailing to Byzantium":

> That is no country for old men. The young
> In one another's arms, birds in the trees,
> —Those dying generations—at their song,
> The salmon-falls, the mackerel-crowded seas,

Fish, flesh, or fowl, commend all summer long
Whatever is begotten, born, and dies.
Caught in that sensual music all neglect
Monuments of unageing intellect.[4]

Does the emphasis on sexual activity in this context make the figure less harsh and more meaningful?

In expository writing the chief use of figures of speech is to make the abstract concrete and vivid by helping the reader to visualize it. This visualization is assisted by likening a difficult or obscure subject to one that is well known. You have seen (page 52) the relation between writer and reader compared to that between a pitcher and a catcher in baseball. In the following paragraph the differences between the problems of a physical scientist and those of a social scientist are clarified in an analogy between swimmers and runners.

In discussing the relative difficulties of analysis which the exact and inexact sciences face, let me begin with an analogy. Would you agree that swimmers are less skillful athletes than runners because swimmers do not move as fast as runners? You probably would not. You would quickly point out that water offers greater resistance to swimmers than the air and ground do to runners. Agreed, that is just the point. In seeking to solve their problems, the social scientists encounter greater resistance than the physical scientists. The conditions under which the social scientists must work would drive a physical scientist frantic. Here are five of those conditions. He can make few experiments; he cannot measure the results accurately; he cannot control the conditions surrounding the experiments; he is often expected to get quick results with slow-acting economic forces; and he must work with people, not with inanimate objects.[5]

The figures of speech most frequently used are *analogy, simile, metaphor, personification,* and *allusion.* Each of these types uses some kind of comparison, but each has its own characteristic form and use, as explained below. In this section we deal with the *use* of these figures. Later, when we come to revising ineffective diction, we shall consider the *abuse* of figures of speech.

Analogy.   An analogy is an extended comparison of two things which explains one by means of the other. If *A* and *B* are in some way alike, our knowledge of *A* can be used to explain *B*. Thus we can explain that reading is an active, not a passive, experience by likening the reader to a catcher in

[4] Reprinted with permission of The Macmillan Company, Mr. M. B. Yeats, and Macmillan & Co. Ltd., from *Collected Poems* by William Butler Yeats. Copyright 1928 The Macmillan Company, renewed 1956 by Georgie Yeats.
[5] From Donald L. Kemmerer, "Are Social Scientists Backward?" *American Association of University Professors Bulletin,* Autumn 1948.

baseball; or we can suggest differences between social and physical scientists by comparing them respectively to swimmers and runners. Analogy uses a familiar example to help explain a more complex and difficult one. The following analogy from Old English literature compares the brevity of man's life to the flight of a sparrow through a house.

> Such appears to me, O king, this present life of man on earth in comparison with the time which is unknown to us, as though you were sitting at the banquet with your leaders and thanes in winter and the fire was lighted and the hall warmed, and it rained and snowed and stormed outside; and there would come a sparrow and quickly fly through the hall, come in through one door and go out through the other. Now in the time that he is inside he is not touched by the storm of winter; but that is only the twinkling of an eye and the least interval, and at once he comes from winter back to winter again. So this life of man appears save for but a little while; what goes before or what follows after we do not know.[6]

A second use of analogy is as a type of reasoning. If we know that *A* and *B* are alike in several respects, and if we know that something is true of *A*, we assume that the corresponding thing will be true of *B* also. Thus because human babies and baby apes are alike in many ways, we can assume that we can feed a baby ape as we would feed a human baby.

Simile. A simile compares two things by asserting that one is like the other. A simile usually contains the word "like," "as," or "so," and is used to transfer the qualities or feelings we associate with one to the other. Thus in

> My love is like a red, red rose,[7]

the beauty we see in the rose is imaginatively transferred to the girl. She is not like a rose in all respects (thorns, for example), but in her beauty and in the pleasure her beauty gives to an observer. Similarly, in

> As a dog returns to his vomit, so a fool returns to his folly,[8]

the disgust caused by the image of the dog's action is transferred to the fool. The simile invites the reader to respond to the repeated folly of a fool as he would respond to the sight of a dog eating its own vomit.

In general, a simile compares *A* and *B* in such a way that the reader responds to *A* as he would to *B*, where *A* is the thing being talked about and *B* is the thing to which it is being compared. Thus in the examples above, "love" and "fool" are *A*, and "rose" and "dog" are *B*.

[6] Translated from Bede, *The Ecclesiastical History of the English People.*
[7] Robert Burns, "A Red, Red Rose."
[8] Proverbs 26:11.

EXERCISE *In the following similes mark the compared parts A and B.*

1. Going up the river was like traveling back to the beginnings of the world. (*Joseph Conrad*)

2. . . . the evening is spread out against the sky
   Like a patient etherized upon a table . . . (*T. S. Eliot*)

3. As cold waters to a thirsty soul, so is good news from a far country. (*Proverbs 25:25*)

4. The Assyrian came down like the wolf on the fold . . . (*Lord Byron*)

5. I saw eternity the other night,
   Like a great ring of pure and endless light. (*Henry Vaughan*)

Metaphor. A metaphor compares two things by identifying one with the other. It does not say that *A* is like *B*, but that *A is B*. Thus Yeats's aged man (*A*) *is* a tattered coat upon a stick (*B*), and Noyes's moon (*A*) *is* a ghostly galleon (*B*). The two subjects are merged into one in the writer's imagination, and the reader is invited to see *A* as *B* and thus to transfer the associations of *B* to *A*.

EXERCISE *In the following metaphors mark the two things being compared as A and B, and explain in what respect they are alike for the purpose of the metaphor.*

1. Idealism is the noble toga that political gentlemen drape over their will to power. (*Aldous Huxley*)

2. Hiroshima was no longer a city but a burnt-out prairie. (*Michihiko Hachiya*)

3. Communism is not love. Communism is a hammer which we use to crush the enemy. (*Mao Tse-tung*)

4. Middle-class America is the condition of mind which supposes that a new, plastic Eden has been descried on a calm sea off our bow. (*Carl Oglesby*)

5. The incandescent quality of his [Winston Churchill's] words illuminated the courage of his countrymen. (*John F. Kennedy*)

Many words and phrases no longer thought of as figures of speech were originally metaphors and similes. Thus *foil* and *parry* derived from the sport of fencing; *checkmate* was a metaphor from chess; *rosy red* and *sapphire blue* were similes, as were *dirt cheap* and *silver hair*. *At bay* once described a hunted animal when it finally turned to face the baying hounds; a *crest-fallen* cock was one which had been injured in a fight; and an *alarm* was a call to arms. Many other expressions retain their metaphorical appearances, but are so common that we no longer think of them as figures of speech—expressions such as the mouth of a river, the face of a clock, the front (originally "forehead") of a house, the brow of a hill, the top of the morning.

EXERCISE

It has often been remarked that we think in metaphors (and similes) and that the metaphors we use shape our view of a subject. For example, to speak of death as "sleep" calls up quite different associations than death as a "grim reaper," and to consider light as "particles" leads to a different view than to think of light as "waves." Choose one of the following terms, or take one of your own choosing, and write two different metaphors or similes for it. Then jot down the kinds of association each metaphor or simile suggests. Finally, using some of these associations, write a paragraph developing one of your metaphors into an analogy.

time, spring (the season), war, liberty, education

Personification. **Personification is the device of endowing animals, inanimate objects, abstractions, and events with human qualities and abilities:**

The eagle, perched on his mountain throne, surveyed the far reaches of his kingdom.

The flames ate hungrily at the wooden foundations.

The once proud trees bent meekly before the storm.

Take a bath in the dark tonight and let the water make love to your skin. (*Lanvin Perfumes and Soaps*)

It may be that we shall by a process of sublime irony have reached a stage in this story where safety will be the sturdy child of terror, and survival the twin brother of annihilation. (*Winston Churchill*)

Personification, like analogy, simile, and metaphor, implies and pictures a similarity. But whereas metaphor and simile may compare any two things, one of the elements of personification must be a human characteristic. The subject must be described in terms of human appearance, actions, attitudes, feelings, or responses. The only exception is that inanimate objects may be described as having qualities that are common to human beings and animals, as in the second example above.

As we shall see later, the effectiveness of any figure of speech depends on its appropriateness and its freshness. Time is often personified, especially at the end of a year, as Father Time, a much overused figure. Here is a fresher image of time, as a charioteer relentlessly pursuing the speaker.

> But at my back I always hear
> Time's wingèd chariot hurrying near.[9]

[9] Andrew Marvell, "To His Coy Mistress."

EXERCISE

Discuss the personification in the following verses. What things are being compared and how? In the second example, do you find other figures of speech in addition to personification?

> Loveliest of trees, the cherry now
> Is hung with bloom along the bough,
> And stands about the woodland ride
> Wearing white for Eastertide.[10]

> Out of us all
> That make rhymes,
> Will you choose
> Sometimes—
> As the winds use
> A crack in the wall
> Or a drain,
> Their joy or their pain
> To whistle through—
> Choose me,
> You English words?[11]

Allusion.   An allusion is a reference to some historical or literary event or person having a striking resemblance to the subject under discussion. Thus the sentence "Drivers who drink keep Charon working overtime" refers to a figure in Greek mythology whose duty it was to ferry the dead across the River Styx into Hades. To call David Ben-Gurion the George Washington of Israel is to compare his contributions to his country with those of Washington to the United States; each is "the father of his country." A sports reporter watching a favored team being upset by a weak one may suggest the effect on the spectators by saying, "The crowd couldn't have been more shocked if the Christians had started to eat the lions."

A successful allusion provides a flash of wit or insight, and gives the reader the pleasure of recognition. But if the reader does not recognize an allusion, it will mean nothing to him and may annoy him and leave the meaning obscure. Rather than blame his own ignorance, he will then label the allusion "pedantic"—that is, so erudite that no "normal" reader should be expected to understand it. For this reason, a writer should always be reasonably sure that his allusions will be familar to the audience he is writing for.

[10] A. E. Housman, "Loveliest of Trees."
[11] Edward Thomas, "Words."

EXERCISE *Can you identify the allusions in the following sentences? If not, consult your dictionary. Then explain the comparisons.*

1. Citizens of Atlanta, Georgia, like to call it the Athens of the South.
2. When the lieutenant was convicted of killing Vietnamese civilians, some people said he was being made a scapegoat for all our sins.
3. For anyone who has slept in a Navy hammock the bed of Procrustes would have no terrors.
4. Vidkun Quisling's betrayal of his countrymen to the Nazis made him the Benedict Arnold of Norway.
5. Though I have seen my head (grown slightly bald) brought in upon a platter
   I am no prophet . . . (*T. S. Eliot*)
6. Living metaphor is a kind of two-headed Janus, looking two ways at once, and making us see two things almost simultaneously. (*F. L. Lucas*)
7. To those beautiful and idyllic islands of the South Pacific, civilization has brought its Pandora's box.
8. After such losses, the best that could be claimed was a Pyrrhic victory.
9. A high-level persuader will begin by hints, and rich stimulating morsels. . . . Slowly, slowly, he will lead his Sanchos farther into the Impossible. (*Gilbert Highet*)
10. . . . a kind of Gargantuan and bizarre playfulness at once humorous and terrifying, as if the settlement had fallen, blundered into the range of an idle and whimsical giant. (*William Faulkner*)

REVISING DICTION

The preceding section dealt with qualities of good diction. This section discusses undesirable qualities that should be removed in revision—chiefly *vagueness, jargon, triteness,* and *inappropriate figures of speech.*

Vagueness Words are vague when they do not convey a precise meaning. Consider the following sentence:

That kind of publicity is always *bad business* for an *organization,* and the men in our *house* felt *pretty bad* about it.

What does "bad business" mean here? Does it cause the "organization" to lose prestige on campus? Does it invite administrative interference in personal living? If the organization is a fraternity, why not say so? When the men feel "pretty bad," how do they feel—frustrated, angry, ashamed, embarrassed, resentful?

The italicized words are so vague—that is, they could mean so many different things—that the sentence communicates no precise meaning. The vagueness may come from either or both of two causes: failure to think out (prewrite) the intended meaning before writing the sentence, or failure to choose words that clearly convey that meaning. These faults can easily be corrected in revision if the writer will ask himself, "What will this mean to the reader?" In asking that question, he is also asking himself, "What do I mean here?"

In checking for vagueness, be alert for "utility words" such as the following.

affair	fine	lovely	regular
awful	freak	marvelous	scale
big	funny	matter	silly
business	fuss	nature	situation
circumstance	gadget	nice	smooth
condition	glamorous	organization	sort of
cool	goods	outfit	state
cute	gorgeous	peculiar	stuff
fantastic	great	person	terrible
field	like	pretty	thing
fierce	line	process	weird

These are all useful words—sometimes too useful. In ordinary speech, which does not usually permit deliberate choice and gives no chance for revision, these utility words are common and often go unnoticed. In writing they may be used precisely if the context limits them to one interpretation, as in the following sentences:

Ted and Mary are having an *affair.*

Stop acting *like* a child.

The new parking law has hurt *business.*

The *organization* of your essay needs revision.

But because they so readily come to mind, these words are often used as easy substitutes for more precise diction. Their *deliberate* use in a sentence needs no apology, but when revising you would be wise to challenge them even then, to be sure they do express your meaning precisely.

EXERCISE *Revise the following sentences to provide more precise substitutes for the italicized utility words. Since the meanings of some of the sentences will be doubtful, you will have to decide what meaning you want them to convey. One sentence is revised to illustrate the procedure.*

Example: It gave me a *funny feeling* to hear my father use such *awful* language.
Revised: I was embarrassed by my father's use of profanity.

1. It was a *nice* thing to do. It made me feel *great* that my friends took time off during exams to throw me a *fantastic* birthday party.

2. The *person* across the hall has some *odd* kind of canine roommate—*like* that's one really *weird* dog.

3. Today she wore a *lovely* outfit which was a *nice* shade of blue, and a *sort of* a *cute* hat with a *pretty* ribbon on it.

4. It's *cool* the way E. E. Cummings doesn't use any capital letters and has *funny* spaces between words.

5. She's *great,* she's *fantastic,* she's *gorgeous.* What more can I say?

Jargon

The word *jargon* originally meant meaningless chatter. It later came to mean the specialized language of a group or profession, as in "habeas corpus" (law), "top up the dampers" (British for "fill the shock absorbers"), and "stand by to come about" (sailing). A third meaning, used in this chapter, is suggested by the following definition from *Webster's Third New International Dictionary,* which says jargon is "language vague in meaning and full of circumlocutions and long high-sounding words."

The following paragraph both illustrates jargon in this sense and translates it:

"In conformity with the preceding point, if all the interacting parties (in marriage, in minority-majority groups, in different occupational, religious, political, economic, racial, ethnic and other interacting groups and persons) view the given overtly similar (or dissimilar) traits: A, B, C, D, N (physical, biological, mental, socio-cultural) as negligible values or as no values at all, as comprising even no similarity (or dissimilarity), such overt similarities-dissimilarities are innocuous in the generation of either solidarity or antagonism." This is a "scientific" way of saying that if we are unconcerned about our differences or similarities, they are not the sources of friendship or hostility.[12]

The three chief characteristics of jargon are:
1. Highly abstract diction, often technical, with a fondness for "learned" rather than "popular" words: *have the capability of* for *can, facilitate* for

[12] Sidney Hook, review of P. A. Sorokin's *Society, Culture, and Personality,* in *The New York Times Book Review.*

make easy, implementation of theoretical decisions for *putting a theory to use, maximize productivity* for *increase production,* and *utilization of mechanical equipment* for *using machinery.*

2. Excessive use of the passive voice: If machines break down they *are found to be functionally impaired.* If a plan does not work, *its objectives were not realized.* If management failed to consider the effects of certain changes on the workers, the error is reported as *"With respect to employee reactions to these changes, management seems to have been inadequately advised.* If more than half the students in a class did not make an outline before writing an essay, *It was discovered that on the part of a majority of the class population the writing of the essay was not preceded by the construction of an outline."*

3. Conspicuous wordiness, as illustrated in the examples given above.

Jargon does not come naturally to freshmen. When they use it, it is because they believe that there is something dignified or scholarly about such language, or that using it makes their message somehow more important or impressive. Nothing could be more mistaken. Any attempt to magnify one's style at the expense of the reader confuses or even denies the purpose of communication.

EXERCISE   *Contrast the two following passages for readability and concreteness or abstractness.*

---

(1)

To be, or the contrary? Whether the former or the latter be preferable would seem to admit of some difference of opinion; the answer in the present case being of an affirmative or of a negative character according as to whether one elects on the one hand to mentally suffer the disfavor of fortune, albeit in an extreme degree, or on the other to boldly envisage adverse conditions in the prospect of eventually bringing them to a conclusion. The condition of sleep is similar to, if not distinguishable from that of death; and with the addition of finality the former might be considered identical with the latter: so that in this connection it might be argued with regard to sleep that, could the addition be effected, a termination would be put to the endurance of a multiplicity of inconveniences, not to mention a number of downright evils incidental to our fallen humanity, and thus a consummation achieved of a most gratifying nature.[13]

(2)

To be, or not to be: that is the question.
Whether 'tis nobler in the mind to suffer
The slings and arrows of outrageous fortune,

[13] Sir Arthur Quiller-Couch, "Interlude: On Jargon."

Or to take arms against a sea of troubles,
And by opposing end them? To die, to sleep;
No more; and by a sleep to say we end
The heart-ache and the thousand natural shocks
That flesh is heir to, 'tis a consummation
Devoutly to be wish'd. . . .[14]

Triteness

The terms *trite, hackneyed, threadbare,* and *cliché* are used to describe phrases and expressions, once colorful and apt, which have been used so much that they have lost their freshness and force. Like outdated slang, trite expressions once called up original images and conveyed a sense of excitement and discovery. But the very qualities which make a phrase striking when it is new work against it when it has been used too much. Here are a few examples of triteness:

---

apple of her eye	hook, line, and sinker
birds of a feather	lock, stock, and barrel
black sheep	mountains out of molehills
blind as a bat	raining cats and dogs
budding genius	sober as a judge
cool as a cucumber	teeth like pearls
diamond in the rough	thick as thieves
fly in the ointment	water over the dam

Trite diction blocks thought. A writer who uses a ready-made phrase instead of fashioning his own soon has no thought beyond the stereotyped comment which his trite diction suggests. Consequently his ideas and observations follow set patterns: any change in personnel becomes a "shakeup"; all hopes become "fond," "foolish," or "forlorn"; standard procedure for making a suggestion is to "drop a hint"; defeats are "crushing"; changes in the existing system are "noble experiments" or "dangerous departures"; unexpected occurrences are "bolts from the blue"; and people who "sow wild oats" always have to "pay the piper" even though they are "as poor as churchmice."

Whenever it can be recognized, triteness should be removed during revision. Unfortunately, what is recognized as trite by an instructor may seem original, or at least effective, to a student. He may not have had enough experience with a cliché to recognize its triteness, and therefore it may not occur to him to revise it. The student who wrote the paper in the following exercise probably did not realize that much of her diction was trite until a more experienced critic pointed it out to her.

[14] Shakespeare, *Hamlet*, **III**, i.

EXERCISE

Discuss the following essay carefully in class. Underline all expressions that you would label "trite." There is sure to be some disagreement, but your class should be able to reach a majority decision on many terms. When you find clear examples of triteness, suggest a revision to get rid of them. Often the best revision is a restatement of the idea in simple, nonfigurative language. For example, "Money doesn't grow on trees and how well I've learned that" can be rewritten, "I have learned to live within my income."

To be taken out of a little world, high school, and placed on a large university campus was a big step in my life. From the first day I arrived at the University, I changed. I could no longer be "mother's little girl" and run to her for advice on what to do about this and how to do that. I had to change.

I am, from all outward appearances, the same person I was when I left home in September and yet, I'm not. Being with people who are more mature has helped me grow up. I've developed a more grown-up idea of life. I've had to make decisions and judgments I've never before been faced with. I've had to give my own opinions and as the old saying goes, "fend for myself." Life isn't a bower of roses, and I've learned it. I've learned to think more seriously of why I'm at school and what I'm deriving from it. Am I doing my best down here? If not, I'd better get busy. People depend on me and I've had to shoulder responsibility. I've grown up a lot. I'm on my own. I have to be able to prove to myself and my parents I can take my place in the world.

Money doesn't grow on trees and how well I've learned that. What a rude awakening, when I finally realized all the odd change I used to ask for at home wasn't with me at school. I had thought my allowance was an enormous amount and, before I knew it, it was gone. College has taught me "a penny saved is a penny earned." I've learned to live within my allowance and have some left to store in my bank for a rainy day.

College has helped me to become a more mature person who has the ability to make decisions for herself. It's not all in the books, what you learn at college. It's your everyday existence with different people and situations that gives you something more, perhaps helps you grow up a little. It's made me a better person and more able to cope with any situation which is to come.

Inappropriate Figures of Speech

The concreteness of figures of speech make them conspicuous. Therefore if a figure is faulty for any reason, its blemishes will also be conspicuous, and the writer will lose, not gain, by having used it. The following inaccurate simile, instead of clarifying the meaning, obscures it.

He felt as uncomfortable and out of place in a room full of women as a wolf in a sheepfold.

This simile distorts the idea by introducing an inept comparison. The only discomfort a wolf is likely to feel in a sheepfold would come from indigestion, and that is not the kind of discomfort the writer had in mind. The reader may be amused by the incongruous images this simile suggests, but he will be amused by the writer's incompetence, not by his skill. The writer would have been wiser to resist the simile and simply say, "He felt uncomfortable and out of place in a room full of women." As a student once wrote, "Is it not better to call a spade a spade than to cover it with a beautiful but deceptive cloth which will come off and reveal it in the end?"

Figures of speech can be inappropriate in two ways: when the image does not fit the writer's meaning, as in the example above; or when the figure calls up images which are inconsistent or *mixed,* as in this example:

The President's ill-advised action has thrown the ship of state into low gear, and unless congressmen wipe out party lines and carry the ball as a team, it may take the country months to get back on an even keel.

This mixed metaphor tries to combine in one image a ship, a car, some lines that can be erased, a football game, and a ship again. These subjects will not combine. What the writer probably meant to say was that the President had made a serious mistake and that, unless Congress rectified it, the country would suffer. He would have been wiser to say just that. By plunging into a metaphor he had not thought out, he lost his thought in a confusion of images.

Figures of speech should be carefully chosen to support the writer's tone and intent, and they should be worked out (prewritten) before they are written down on paper. During revision their logic should be checked and their effectiveness should be reconsidered. If they survive this double analysis, they should be well worth the trouble it takes to create them.

EXERCISE

Analyze the following figures of speech and revise any that are inappropriate or mixed.

---

1. Like the foolish virgins in the Bible, the politicians have been asleep at the switch and have allowed a glorious opportunity to go down the drain.
2. When spring comes, the face of old Mother Earth is arrayed in garments of breathtaking beauty.
3. His words fanned the flame of her indignation and caused it to boil over.
4. Efforts to help the veterans were sidetracked by a bog of red tape.
5. Into this great forest the hand of man has never set foot.
6. The huge rock went crashing down the hill like a lover hurrying to meet his lass.

7. Schwarz's meat balls have won their niche in the hall of fame.

8. I decided to unleash upon a too-indifferent world my whole Pandora's bag of virtues and vices.

9. He is as hard-hearted as the man who peeled his apple with a dull knife, so it wouldn't hurt too much.

10. The grandfather was bursting with pride over the child's wit, like a ripe tomato on a sunny shelf.

REVIEW EXERCISES

A. *Study the following student paper with a view to revising it. First consider the appropriateness of the introductory analogy. Then consider the relative space devoted to the analogy and to the subject with which the writer is dealing. Finally make specific suggestions about how the paper could be improved.*

A Serious Problem

Seven years ago a neighbor of mine married a very beautiful woman. When they were married, everyone exclaimed how her youth radiated beauty. The husband felt very fortunate in being able to marry such a beautiful woman. He bought her fine clothes and would take her out in public, feeling great pride. The husband, coming from a large family, also wished to have a large family, and in the seven years of their marriage the couple bore six children. Recently he noticed that he no longer received compliments on his wife's beauty. Upon looking and studying his wife, he realized that she showed signs of old age and yet, she was actually still quite young. Just as the timeworn woman showed signs of decline from constant childbearing, our rivers, lakes, and streams show signs of old age and infection, caused mostly by their continual use as outlets for the disposal of production wastes by our factory systems. Daily, tons of waste materials are dumped into our rivers and lakes making them unfit as a source of drinking water or a habitat for marine life. Each year cities spend an increasing amount of money for the sanitation of their drinking water, and each year thousands of fish can be seen floating at the surface of lakes and rivers, choked or poisoned by pollution. Some time ago, people praised the presence of beautiful lakes and rivers, and now, complain how the rivers and lakes are choked with industrial wastes. So now the question arises as to which is more important, the future of our water supply on which much of our future depends or the manufacture of products that we use today.

We *can* have both.

B. *The student author of the following paragraph tried too hard to achieve an elevated style, and instead wrote jargon. Read the paragraph carefully to get the gist of the message. Then rewrite it to communicate that message in simpler language.*

It was fortunate, or unfortunate, depending on the circumstances and the evaluation thereof, that I had no formulated or precise conceptions when I left high school and commenced work as a telegraphist in the Public Service. While on duty one evening, a colleague, who was interested in weight-lifting, allowed me to peruse a book on the subject, entitled *Big Arms,* by Bob Hoffman. Not having yet realized my latent interest in athletic endeavors, I was surprised at the manner in which the book held my interest. This I only realized after a while. It was that book which stimulated me to make a purchase of a weight-lifting set, and despite the inhibiting influences of long work hours, little sleep, and irregular meals, to exercise in my free moments.

C. *Advertising often makes use of an implied comparison between the product and something else which has favorable associations in the public mind: the taste of a cigarette is likened to the freshness of springtime, or an automobile is called a cougar to suggest strength and speed. Select a half-dozen such advertisements and use them as the raw material for a short paper on metaphor in advertising.*

Chapter 8

Style: The Way It Is Written

The word "style" has many meanings, ranging from the way a man lives to the latest cut in women's clothes. Even applied to writing it can refer to anything from the philosophy and personality of the writer ("Style is the man himself") to his choice of words and the way he combines clauses into sentences. This chapter considers the question, "What constitutes the style of a piece of writing?"

THE COMPONENTS OF STYLE

We can begin with the preliminary statement that "style is the way it is written." To find out what that statement means, let us examine a student essay to see what specific traits make up "the way it is written." First read the essay, then answer the questions that follow it and discuss them in class.

The Snake in the Garden

Mother and I always seemed to have different perspectives about her garden. She had a kind of refracted vision caused by her adult point of view, which saw the garden from the top down; whereas I, who did the weeding, always saw it from the bottom up. Most of the charm and warmth she found there seemed oddly at variance with my own appreciations of the garden.

It was neither well kept, nor very artful; instead it was what Mother called a "natural" garden, which meant that only country flowers grew there, and such order as could be perceived was all that a small boy could be coerced into keeping. Bushes and shrubs grew shaggy and undisciplined, spreading out into hedges or thickets as the notion struck them. Flowers grew generally at random, venturing out of their original plots and wandering off to visit one another all over the yard. My notion of order in a garden ran to geometric patterns and tidy straight lines, mostly derived from magazine pictures and a belief that such gardens were easier to maintain. Mother planted things where they would be happy, which always meant next to something else so that they could be company for each other.

Everything in the garden Mother found enchanting. The lightning bugs, she said, were winking and sending messages, like little ships floating in a dark sea. Perhaps they were, but my interest in them was proprietary. The role of the lightning bug was to be pursued, captured, and sealed up in a mason jar with holes punched in its zinc alloy lid. Sometimes the little ships would get their lights pinched off so I could see if they still worked without their bodies: murder among the dogwoods.

Overwhelming the back fence of the garden was a mob of lilacs. Though the bushes were tall and droopy, bending under the weight of the lush blossoms, Mother would not consider trimming them. Their deep blues and fiery lavenders flecked with white were not unattractive, but the odor of lilac when I was pulling weeds around them was overpowering. Every brush against them brought down a shower of tiny petals, which had to be raked up (or under). And if it had rained or the branches still held dew, every brush brought down a real shower on my head and shoulders. Besides, the honeybees, flies, mosquitoes, and occasionally a wasp found the cool dark fragrance under the lilacs irresistible.

Behind the lilacs lived a company of sunflowers, the only things in the garden taller than the lilacs. The big round heads were every shade of yellow from garish to shriek. The sunflowers grew straight up five or six feet and gave off no perfume. Though the stems and leaves were coarse and rough to work among, I found the sunflowers a thoroughly admirable flower; not because they were beautiful or stately as my mother said, but because when broken off close to the ground, the strong flexible stem with its firm head became a serviceable weapon, good for knocking cans off the fence or the heads off other sunflowers.

The hollyhocks—a crazy quilt of yellows, indigos, pinks, crimsons, and oranges—we both valued, but for different reasons. Mother saw them as frail and delicate, dainty feminine things radiant with color, and she liked to pick bouquets of the blossoms to set afloat in a bowl of water. But I knew that in the fall, when the blossoms and leaves had fallen, the inner resin of the stalks toughened into a tasteless gum which could be chewed with great satisfaction. And furthermore, the straight hollyhock stems, when thoroughly dry, made the very best lightweight spears and arrows.

In all the whirrs and clicks and ratchets of the insects of the garden, Mother heard only the music of summer. The morning glories were little blue trumpets twining around the fence slats, and these too she counted as part of summer's music. But close to the ground, among the shoots and tendrils of the morning glories, one silent inhabitant of the garden was dedicated to only the grimmest business. She was a huge garden spider, shiny black, vividly marked with yellow rays. Her long black legs looked like brittle glass wires; she was as big as my hand, eerie and fierce. Her network ran all through the morning glories, and it was difficult to know where it was safe to work without encountering her. Worrying her or tearing at the web with a twig was exciting business. She would turn slowly, symmetrically arranging each leg until she faced the twig, and then she would spring to the attack. I always retreated; she never did. Where Mother saw the beauty of the pale blue flowers, white-ribbed and fluted out into trumpet shapes, I knew there lurked a spider whose sole interest in life was in sacking up alive all the other insects of the garden and hanging them in their little silk coffins everywhere throughout the morning glories.

We never did get very close together in our appreciation of the garden, Mother and I. Most of the things I liked about it were nonexistent for her. Most of the things she liked were obviously flawed to me. The tea-rose had twice the number of thorns found on any other kind of rose. The dark violets growing under bushes in moist places out of the reach of the sun, she liked to show off to the neighbors. But I knew the cool moisture harbored slimy fat slugs as well as violets. The little weeds she permitted to grow by the porch steps she called quaint and natural, but every child called them snot-flowers in reference both to their odor and the unhappy result of picking them. The only kinds of flowers I cared about were the regular kinds that came from the seed packets they sold at school each spring, flowers like zinnias, marigolds, bachelor-buttons. Mother said I was only interested in the prize for selling the most seed packets. Naturally I thought then, and still think, mine was the more accurate perspective. But sometimes I think there is a view of the garden, and perhaps of other things, from which Mother derived a good deal of satisfaction, despite my secret knowledge of the truth.

Now that you have read the essay, discuss the following questions as thoughtfully as you can.

1. The title is "The Snake in the Garden," yet there is no mention of a snake within the piece. Who or what is the snake? Does the title contain an allusion to any other snake in another garden? If so, how are the two snakes related?

2. The essay describes various features of the garden, but is it only about the garden? What dominant contrast runs through the essay? Do you think this contrast is part of the writer's purpose?

3. If style is "the way it is written," does the writer's purpose influence the style of this essay? If so, how?

4. If you were asked to write a characterization of the mother as she is represented in this essay, what traits would you stress? Do you think these traits give you a "true" picture of her, or are they chosen to suit the author's purpose? Discuss your answers.

5. If you were to write a characterization of the boy, what traits would you emphasize? Do you think these traits accurately describe the author as a boy, or are they chosen to characterize the boy as he has to be for the writer's purpose? Discuss your answers.

6. Considering your answers to questions 4 and 5, do you think the author succeeds in assuming a personality in keeping with the purpose of the

essay? Such a personality is usually called the author's *persona*—the personality or character he assumes for purposes of the work, whether or not that personality accurately reflects his own. (Reread the section entitled "Your View of Yourself as a Writer," pages 11–12, where the concept of *persona* is introduced.)

7. If style is "the way it is written," is the persona of the writer part of his style? Discuss.

8. For what kind of audience is this essay written? Would it be appropriate for grade-school children, for college freshmen, for educated adults generally? Does the writer's view of his audience affect the way he writes his essay?

9. In the order given here, the author describes the general arrangement of the garden, lightning bugs, lilacs, sunflowers, hollyhocks, insects, and in the final paragraph, a series of specific contrasts between the mother's view of the garden and the boy's. Are the descriptive details chosen because they provide an unbiased view of the garden or because they suit the author's purpose?

10. Does the writer's use of some kinds of details and his omission of others influence the way the essay is written? In other words, is there a relation between his choice of content and his style? Explain.

11. Now look at individual sentences to see how they relate to purpose and persona. The contrast between the mother's and the boy's views of lightning bugs in paragraph 3 is a good starting point. Select any sentence or combination of sentences which seem to you especially effective and explain why you think so.

12. Can your class agree that if style is "the way it is written," any full description of the style of this essay must include the writer's purpose, persona, and his choice of material, organization, and diction, including figures of speech?

If there is general agreement on question 12, the following definition of style will identify its main components:

A definition of style

Style is a product of all the choices a writer makes in working out the implications of his purpose. If his choices are consistent they reveal (1) his view of his real subject, (2) his view of his readers, (3) his persona, (4) the kind of materials he selects, and (5) the way he structures and expresses his ideas, including the tone of his writing. The sum of these components constitutes "the way it is written." A description of the style of any piece of writing is therefore an explanation of the means by which the writer works out his purpose.

This definition relates purpose and style as cause and effect. Purpose is the writer's controlling decision about what he is going to do and how he is going to do it. Style is the result of that decision. Whether we say that purpose controls style or that style reveals purpose depends on whether we are emphasizing the writer's concerns or the reader's. For the writer, purpose controls style, because his decision about purpose controls all his other choices: he makes those choices that advance his purpose and rejects those that do not. To the reader, style reveals purpose, for only from the way a piece is written can he guess what the writer had in mind. This inference is perhaps most clearly seen in irony, where the writer pretends one purpose and counts on the reader to see that the style implies another. Thus the author of "Why We Need More Westerns on Television" (page 9) pretends to admire westerns, but she writes her paper in such a way that the reader quickly sees that she is making fun of them.

Since purpose and style are interrelated, any comprehensive judgment about the style of a paper must consider the writer's purpose. It would be foolish, for example, to criticize the colloquial diction of "Why We Need More Westerns on Television" without first considering whether that kind of diction was appropriate to the author's ironic intent.

Just as a football coach can stop the film of a game to study the mechanics of a particular play, so can a critic focus his attention on any one of the particular components of a writer's style. He can concentrate on paragraph structure, on use of illustrative detail, on length or complexity of sentences, on concreteness or abstractness of diction. In doing so, he is, for reasons that are important to him, dealing for the moment with one component of style to the exclusion of others. What he discovers by this analysis will often be useful, but it relates to only one aspect of a style. The whole style includes all the parts we have identified and their interrelationship, just as a football game includes the whole sequence of plays made during the game.

STYLE AND LANGUAGE

If by "language" we mean not only diction and sentence structure but the whole verbal context of a piece of writing, the language a writer uses provides the clues for a description of his style. To illustrate this statement we will take selected samples of writing and see what inferences about style can be made from their language. But before we do so, it will be useful to consider two terms, "tone" and "distance."

Tone

You are familiar with tone as a component of style from such statements as "Don't speak to me in that tone" and "I resented the tone of his remarks." These statements suggest that we object to something in language which implies an undesirable attitude toward us. But the attitude can also be a desirable one, as in "When she uses that tone, she can get away with anything." Tone, then, is a quality in language that expresses an attitude toward the listener or reader, as in

You can say that again! (agreement or approval)

Oh, come off it! (disapproval and annoyance)

Nonsense! (blunt rejection)

There may be something in what you say. (tentative acceptance)

Distance   We have already introduced distance by contrasting the manner of a doctor when addressing a medical convention and when talking at the bedside of a patient (page 134). The language a writer uses may suggest aloofness or intimacy. Compare the difference between a statement printed in a syllabus that "Students are expected to hand in their assignments on the dates stipulated" and an instructor's after-class remark to a student, "Joe, you've got to get your papers in on time." In the first statement the writer is impersonal and distant; in the second the speaker is personal and close. The distance a writer establishes between himself and his reader becomes an important element of his style.

You are now ready to study the following six examples and the accompanying analyses of the first three of them for *sentence structure, diction, tone,* and *distance*.

Example 1   You're going to paint that picturesque old barn. All right. One vertical line (better use charcoal) will place the corner of the barn, another line the base. A couple of lines for the trunk of the tree, and maybe a branch or two. Then a line to indicate the horizon—whatever divides the sky from whatever meets it (tree, barn, hill). That's all! No leaves, doorknobs, cats, mice, or daffodils. It's the painting that's fun, and any time wasted in getting into a mess of details is to be deplored. As we start to paint, anything resembling a real drawing on our canvas is purely accidental. . . .

Now squeeze out little blobs of color on your palette, and a big blob of white. And take a look at that sky. It is, let's say, cloudless. And it really is blue. Still not as blue as Uncle Ed's shirt. Take a half of a butter ball of white on your palette knife and plaster it on the front of your palette. Careful now! Just a pinch of blue and mix with the white until there are no streaks. Not blue enough? All right, just a tiny bit more—but easy! Satisfied? Dip your brush in the turpentine, then in the paint and slap it on! Boldly—never mind if you slop over the barn a bit.[1]

Sentence Structure.   The twenty-two sentences of this passage average only ten words in length, and over half of them are fragments. Most of the sentences which are complete consist of a main clause or two compound main clauses. There are only two subordinate clauses, no inverted constructions or periodic sentences, and few parallel structures. Sentences usually follow a straight subject-verb-object order.

Diction.   In the whole passage there are fewer than a dozen words more than two syllables long—*picturesque, accidental,* and *turpentine* are the most notable. Except possibly for *palette,* there are no "learned" words. Most of the diction is quite concrete. Contractions are numerous—*you're, that's, it's, let's.*

[1] From "Get in There and Paint" by Joseph Alger, in *Recreation*, November 1944. Reprinted by permission of the National Recreation Association.

Tone. The attitude toward the reader is friendly, almost chummy, perhaps a little bossy in an unobjectionable way. It is an informal teacher-pupil relationship, with the teacher talking simply and directly to the pupil.

Distance. The writer and the reader are as close together as they can be. The writer gives the impression of looking over the reader's shoulder, advising him and correcting him at every step of the painting process.

Summary. All the components blend into a consistent, conversational style which aims at ease of communication through simple sentences and simple diction. The writer gives the impression of talking in print. This is the kind of style we have called *colloquial* (page 136). It is not a style encountered frequently in this book, but it is by no means an uneducated style. It is conversational standard English, and it is perfectly suited to this writer's purpose, which is to persuade the reader that painting is fun and that anyone can do it.

Example 2   Now contrast the following example with the one you have just studied.

From those high storied shelves of dense rich bindings the great voices of eternity, the tongues of mighty poets dead and gone, now seemed to speak to him out of the living and animate silence of the room. But in that living silence, in the vast and quiet spirit of sleep which filled the great house, amid the grand and overwhelming stillness of that proud power of wealth and the impregnable security of its position, even the voices of those mighty poets dead and gone now seemed somehow lonely, small, lost and pitiful. Each in his little niche of shelf securely stored—all of the genius, richness, and whole compacted treasure of a poet's life within a foot of space, within the limits of six small dense richly-garnished volumes—all of the great poets of the earth were there, unread, unopened, and forgotten, and were somehow, terribly, the mute small symbols of a rich man's power, of the power of wealth to own everything, to take everything, to triumph over everything—even over the power and genius of the mightiest poet—to keep him there upon his little foot of shelf, unopened and forgotten, but possessed.[2]

Sentence Structure. This paragraph has only three sentences. There are no fragments and the sentences are long—38, 55, and 104 words respectively, or an average of 66 against 10 in the preceding example. The sentences are involved, none are simple, and none start with the subject. Subjects and verbs are often separated—sometimes widely—by intervening modifiers. The last sentence, as the punctuation shows, is extremely involved. Throughout the paragraph parallel and periodic structures are used for rhythmic and other effects.

[2] From Thomas Wolfe, *Of Time and the River* (New York: Charles Scribner's Sons, 1935).

Diction. Nineteen words are more than two syllables long, and there is a smaller proportion of monosyllables than in Example 1. The diction is less concrete and there are more learned words—*animate, impregnable, niche, compacted, garnished, mute.* Several phrases have a lofty, poetic ring—*high storied shelves, great voices of eternity, living and animate silence, proud power of wealth, the mute small symbols of a rich man's power, unopened and forgotten, but possessed.*

Tone. The tone is high-sounding, dignified, rhythmic, and eloquent. The writer evidently assumes that he is addressing readers who value these qualities and can respond to his own love of books.

Distance. There is considerable distance between writer and reader. Nowhere is the reader addressed directly. Nowhere does the writer refer to himself as "I" or "we." He is clearly more interested in his subject than in his readers. He expects his readers to rise to his level and feels no obligation to bridge the distance between himself and them.

Summary. As in the first example, all these components blend into a consistent style, but what a different style! This one aims at eloquence, not ease or familiarity. It is not the kind of style one would use to give directions, explain a process, or answer a question on an examination. It is not a style that a reporter or an editorial writer might use in a newspaper, or a presidential candidate in seeking the votes of the electorate. It is a style for special occasions and special audiences. We could call it a *grand* style, but the usual name for it is *formal*. In the hands of a writer like Thomas Wolfe or Winston Churchill this degree of formality can be eloquent and satisfying. In the hands of a lesser writer it can result in stiffness or even jargon. It is certainly not the style that one would recommend for freshman English.

Example 3   Our third example is a paragraph from an article by a college professor writing for an educational journal whose readers are chiefly teachers.

We also speak of attention as *noticing*. To notice is to select, to regard some bits of perception, or some features of the world, as more noteworthy, more significant, than others. To these we attend, and the rest we ignore—for which reason conscious attention is at the same time *ignore*-ance [i.e. ignorance] despite the fact that it gives us a vividly clear picture of whatever we choose to notice. Physically, we see, hear, smell, taste, and touch innumerable features that we never notice. You can drive thirty miles, talking all the time to a friend. What you noticed, and remembered, was the conversation, but somehow you responded to the road, the other cars, the traffic lights, and heaven knows what else, without really noticing, or focussing your mental spotlight upon them. . . .[3]

[3] From William G. Moulton, "Linguistics," *NEA Journal*, January 1965.

Sentence Structure. The six sentences of this paragraph are all standard sentences. They are more complex than those in Example 1, but less complex than those in Example 2. They vary in length from 7 to 36 words and average 22 words, more than twice the average length of those in Example 1, but only a third of those in Example 2. Their structure is more complex than in 1, less complex than in 2. In length and complexity, the sentences are about midway between those of the other two examples.

Diction. There are almost as many words of more than two syllables as there were in Example 2, but, except possibly for "perception," they are all "popular" words. The diction is less concrete than that in the first example, but more concrete than that in the second.

Tone. There is a clear relationship with the reader, who is addressed directly as "you" and is brought into partnership with the writer by the pronouns "we" and "us." But there is nothing of the chumminess we saw in Example 1. Neither is there the distance and impersonality of Example 2. The writer is clearly conscious of his readers and identifies with them, but not with the intimacy of the painting lesson.

Distance. As suggested above, in distance between writer and reader this passage is about midway between the two previous examples.

Summary. In formality the style is obviously somewhere between that of Examples 1 and 2. It is a middle style, which overlaps each of the others slightly but avoids the extremes of both. It could be used in a college lecture, a textbook, a student essay, a newspaper column, or a serious television commentary, and would be easily understood by educated adults generally. It is a multi-purpose style, called *informal* standard English.

Example 4

The informal style is much broader in range than either the formal or the colloquial. Toward one pole the writing shows definite colloquial characteristics, as does the following:

It's Friday afternoon, and you have almost survived another week of classes. You are just looking forward dreamily to the week end when the English instructor says: "For Monday you will turn in a five-hundred word composition on college football."

Well, that puts a good big hole in the week end. You don't have any strong views on college football one way or the other. You get rather excited during the season and go to all the home games and find it rather more fun than not. On the other hand, the class has been reading Robert Hutchins in the anthology and perhaps Shaw's "Eighty-Yard Run," and from the class discussion you have got the idea that the instructor thinks college football is for the birds. You are no fool, you. You can figure out what side to take.

After dinner you get out the portable typewriter that you got for high school graduation. You might as well get it over with and enjoy Saturday and Sunday. Five hundred words is about two double-spaced pages with normal margins. You put in a sheet of paper, think up a title, and you're off.[4]

Example 5

Toward the other pole informal writing makes extensive use of parallelism and the rhythmic quality noticed in Example 2:

This is man: a writer of books, a putter-down of words, a painter of pictures, a maker of ten thousand philosophies. He grows passionate over ideas, he hurls scorn and mockery at another's work, he finds the one way, the true way, for himself, and calls all others false—yet in the billion books upon the shelves there is not one that can tell him how to draw a single fleeting breath in peace and comfort. He makes histories of the universe, he directs the destiny of nations, but he does not know his own history, and he cannot direct his own destiny with dignity or wisdom for ten consecutive minutes. . . .

This is man, and one wonders why he wants to live at all. A third of his life is lost and deadened under sleep; another third is given to a sterile labor; a sixth is spent in all his goings and comings, in the moil and shuffle of the streets, in thrusting, shoving, pawing. How much of him is left, then, for a vision of the tragic stars? How much of him is left to look upon the everlasting earth? How much of him is left for glory and the making of great songs? A few snatched moments only from the barren glut and suck of living.[5]

Example 6

In the middle of the informal range the writing may be like this:

The possible advantages of space can be best appreciated if we turn our backs upon it and return, in imagination, to the sea. Here is the perfect environment for life—the place where it originally evolved. In the sea, an all-pervading fluid medium carries oxygen and food to every organism; it need never hunt for either. The same medium neutralizes gravity, insures against temperature extremes, and prevents damage by too-intense solar radiation—which must have been lethal at the Earth's surface before the ozone layer was formed.

When we consider these facts, it seems incredible that life ever left the sea, for in some ways the dry land is almost as dangerous as space. Because we are accustomed to it, we forget the price we have had to pay in our daily battle against gravity. We seldom stop to think that we are still creatures of the sea, able to leave it only because, from birth to death, we wear the water-filled space suits of our skins.[6]

[4] From Paul Roberts, *Understanding English* (New York: Harper and Brothers, 1948).

[5] From Henry David Thoreau, *Journal*.

[6] From *Astronautics and Aeronautics*, published by the American Institute of Aeronautics and Astronautics, New York.

EXERCISE   *For each of the last three Examples, make notes on sentence structure, diction, tone, and distance, following the analysis of the first three Examples. Then use your notes for either a class discussion or a paper, whichever your instructor prefers.*

We can now illustrate the approximate range of styles shown in our six Examples, from most formal to most colloquial, by the following diagram.

Formal	Informal				Colloquial
2	5	6	3	4	1

There could be disagreement about the relative positions of 6 and 3, which are both close to the middle of the informal range. Otherwise the scale is reasonably accurate.

The characteristics of formal, informal, and colloquial styles are summarized in the following table.

Formal	Informal	Colloquial
Paragraphs		
Relatively long.	Moderately long.	Usually short.
Sentences		
Relatively long, complex in structure; extensive use of parallel and periodic structures; no fragments.	Of medium length, 20 to 30 words; chiefly standard sentences; frequent parallel and some periodic sentences; fragments rare but occasional.	Short, simple structures; mainly subject-verb-object order; few inversions; frequent use of fragments.
Diction		
Extensive vocabulary, "learned" words; often abstract; avoidance of contractions and clipped words; observes fine grammatical distinctions often ignored in informal style.	Ranges from "learned" to colloquial, but mostly "popular"; from abstract to concrete; occasional contractions and clipped words; some inconspicuous slang.	Simple, mostly popular and colloquial; frequent contractions and clipped words; usually quite concrete; some slang.
Tone		
Impersonal, dignified; few references to reader.	Ranges from personal to impersonal; writer usually identifies with reader and often addresses him as "you."	Quite personal, often intimate; writer gives impression of talking directly to reader.
Distance		
Considerable.	Moderate.	Small.

EXERCISE *The following passages were written by a student as an experiment to show how different people might review the same book. First, for each passage infer the persona of the imagined author from the style (pages 11–12; page 160), and explain the evidence on which you base your judgment. Second, evaluate the student's experiment: how successful was she in making the other components of the style match the persona?*

(1)

I think *The Old Man and the Sea* is a good book for anybody to read because it is deep and tells about life. It says life is a sea full of dangers and big fish that are really chalanges for a person. When a person gets aholt of a big chalange he should stay with it even if he is scaret and tired and not let it beat him. I think this is a brave way to be and I would like to do it but my father says this is pretty dumb. He says if you want to get ahead in this world you have to sway with the wind.

My father says this is a dumb story. Because the old man is suppost to know his busniss and then goes fishing away out like he doesnt know anything. My mother doesnt think this is a good book for kids to read because it says about bladders and whores and making love but I think this is alright.

I like this book because it is short.

THE END

(2)

Ernest Hemingway, the great American author who lived in exile because Big Business was out to get him, outsmarted the Bosses when *Life* published his book *The Old Man and the Sea*. This is not the story of "man's futile and heroic struggle, a testament to man's indestructible spirit," as the bourgeois bubble-head from *Business World* reported at the time. It is a story which cries to the heavens for justice. It is the story of the plight of The People wherever they are oppressed. The sea and the land are the private domains of the Capitalist-Imperialists and the old man is Cuba, struggling, starving Cuba. Whatever the old man wins by the work of his hands is torn from him by the sharks of Big Business which bloat themselves in the Capitalist-Imperialist sea. All that is left to the old man is his dream of the day when The People will be strong and like a lion.

Your day will come, old man. OUR DAY WILL COME.

(3)

Well, I finally got around to reading *The Old Man and the Sea,* and Girls, as an amateur psychologist, all I could say when I finished it was, "Ernest Hemingway, your defense mechanisms are showing!" This book is just packed with psychology about the author.

Now, Ernest Hemingway follows the phenomenologist school of psychology, just like we do.—Mary, *most* of us do. I know *you're* Freudian but there's hardly any of *that* in *this* book.—Girls, remember the first principle of phenomenology? Acceptance without moral judgment. Well, I knew that Ernest Hemingway was a phenomenologist when I read *one sentence!* The old man, Santiago, is talking to himself and he says—Listen now, Girls—he says, "Old man, you were born to be a fisherman as the fish was born to be a fish." Isn't that beautiful? That's *real* acceptance—without moral judgment, of course.

Then there's the second principle of phenomenology. (What did you say, Gertrude? Refreshments are ready?) Well, Girls, read the book for yourselves. It's just *full* of psychology. And Ernest Hemingway's operational dynamics are just fascinating.

SOME PRACTICAL ADVICE ABOUT STYLE

So far in this chapter we have examined the styles of other writers in the belief that this analysis will give you background for making your own decisions about style. We now offer suggestions that may be useful to you in stylistic choices of your own.

1. Since style is a product of purpose, *the best way to control the style of a paper is to have a firm understanding of your purpose* and trust that understanding to guide you through all the choices you must make. If you are clear about what you want to do, you have a standard by which to test every choice. That standard will usually keep your choices consistent and all aspects of your style in harmony. You may slip now and then, but you will have a chance in revision to find your slips and correct them.

2. *In general, use an informal style* that will be appropriate to your class as audience. Keep your audience in mind at all times, and test the clarity and appropriateness of your statements by the way you think your audience will respond. This practice, consistently followed, will help you to see your writing as your reader will see it, and will tend to prevent vagueness and generality.

3. *Don't try to read your instructor's mind about the kind of style he wants.* What he wants is honest writing—writing that shows your unique view of the subject worked out for your classroom audience. Worry first about your real subject, then about how best to present it to your classmates. Above all, don't start with the notion that college English requires big words and flowery sentences or that there is some special kind of style appropriate to an English class.

4. *Be as specific as you can.* At best, language is a difficult medium—witness the Chinese proverb that "One picture is worth more than ten thousand words." Try always to pin down your general statements with specific examples or details. If you do not have specific details ready to use, you are not ready to make a general statement, for generalizations are inferences drawn from particulars. The realization that you are not ready to be specific may force you to study your subject in greater depth, and this will contribute to fuller understanding of it. This is what Francis Bacon meant when he said, "Writing maketh an exact man." Using vague words or undeveloped statements to conceal a lack of information cheats the writer as

much as the reader. The function of a composition course is not only to help you explain your ideas to others; it is also to help you understand the ideas you want to explain.

5. *Next to examples and explanatory details, the best way to be specific is to use concrete nouns, verbs, and modifiers.* These create images for the reader. In "The man walked down the street," the verb *walked* is general. When it is changed to *limped, lurched, staggered, strode,* or *meandered,* it suggests a more specific action. Of course, the action suggested must suit your purpose. It would be a mistake to write "The blind man strode down the street" if the context of your paper required him to move cautiously, feeling his way with a white cane that swept a path before him. Whenever possible, make your diction help the reader see the precise action you have in mind. But having an action in mind requires that you "see" it yourself. Only when you do so will you be able to choose the right words to describe it.

Concrete modifiers also help. You saw in Chapter 6 that the main clause of a standard sentence is often an abstract statement and that its meaning can be made clearer by adding specific modifiers, such as those italicized in the following sentence:

The blind man moved cautiously down the street / *feeling his way with a white cane / that swept a path before him.*

In the following sentence notice how the series of italicized phrases after the colon both extends and illustrates the meaning of the opening main clause:

Muskie fishing has its exciting moments: *the sudden thrill of a hard strike, / those delicious seconds when you wait for the muskie to turn the bait in his mouth before you set the hook, / the singing of the reel as he tears off in his first long run, / his final desperate dive as you bring him near the boat, /* and *the gleam of his brownish white belly as you pull him up to the net.*

Revision gives you an opportunity to add details. If you feel that a sentence is too abstract, you can extend it as in the example above, or you can open it up and insert concrete details wherever they belong, thus:

*slosh cold water on a temperamental
on our faces, kerosene stove*

We would get up before daylight, and prepare breakfast.

6. *Use figures of speech cautiously.* When they are right for your purpose, figures can be helpful (see pages 141–47). But if they are inappropriate or confused or trite, they will do more harm than good. For this reason it is a wise practice to visualize the image a figure suggests before you present it to a reader. This advice is just a specific application of the general advice to try to see your writing as a reader will see it.

7. *Revise individual sentences as necessary to give them the emphasis your purpose requires.* As you saw in Chapter 6, the chief means of getting appropriate emphasis are word order, deliberate repetition, parallelism, and position within a sentence. In general, use the active voice in preference to the passive, keep modifiers close to the words they modify, use parallel structures to establish similarity in a series of ideas or to present an alternating contrast, and put main ideas at or near the beginning, as in the standard sentence, or at the end, as in the periodic sentence. There is no one way in which a sentence must be written, except a way that really helps you tell a reader what you want to tell him. You are the sole judge of what you want to emphasize. Try to be sure the structure of a sentence supports the emphasis you want.

8. *If the sentences in a paragraph or an essay tend to be monotonous in length or structure, it is relatively easy to give them more variety.* The chief requirement for getting rid of monotony is to know it when you see it. Sometimes reading a paper aloud is the best way to sense it. Indeed, reading your work aloud, as though you were preparing to read it to your class, is an excellent way to tell whether it is ready for a reader. If reading aloud shows that your sentences are too much alike, you can vary their length and structure by several means. You can combine simple sentences by coordination and subordination as shown on pages 109–11. You can break up an unchanging subject-verb-object order by putting one or more adverbial clauses or phrases at the beginning of a sentence, within it, or at the end. And you can increase the length and density of a sentence by these same means.

But don't try too hard for variety. Most of your sentences should be standard, ranging in length from twelve to thirty words. If you depart from that pattern you should do so because the change makes for more effective communication, not just for variety. Changing two sentences in a paragraph, or even one, will often provide all the variety you need. Too much change can result in affectation. Too many periodic sentences are worse than too many standard sentences. The periodic sentence calls attention to itself, and overuse of it suggests self-conscious striving for a "literary" style.

9. Finally, remember that, *from the reader's point of view, the cardinal sins are vagueness and wordiness.* Of these two, wordiness is the less excusable. A writer may be vague because he is still trying to understand what he wants to do with his subject. Until he finds out he will have trouble communicating to a reader. But he can soon learn to detect wordiness, especially if some helpful critic draws it clearly to his attention. If, when he removes the wordiness, it is obvious that he has little to say, the reader will at least appreciate that the little has been simply and clearly stated.

But don't make the mistake of reducing the number of words by cutting out content. The space it takes to expand a general statement by examples and details is not wordiness; it is development of an idea. Wordiness is an excess of words over content (page 124). The extra words add nothing to the meaning; they merely stretch it thin and make the reader's job harder.

REVIEW EXERCISES

A. *The two paragraphs below express the same ideas. Discuss their styles by contrasting them for sentence structure, diction, and distance between writer and reader.*

There are, indeed, other objects of desire that if attained leave nothing but restlessness and dissatisfaction behind them. These are the objects pursued by fools. That such objects ever attract us is a proof of the disorganization of our nature, which drives us in contrary directions and is at war with itself. If we had attained anything like steadiness of thought or fixity of character, if we knew ourselves, we should know also our inalienable satisfactions.

We all have foolish desires. We want things which do not satisfy us when we get them. The fact that we want these things is evidence of our inconsistent nature. We are subject to conflicting desires and want to go in opposite directions at the same time. If we had a clearer understanding of our own needs and purposes, we would know what course was best for us.

B. *Both of the passages given below show marked inconsistencies in style. For each, identify the diction that is inappropriate to the rest of the context and suggest a revision. Then discuss your answers in class.*

(1)

To say that all goods become worthless in possession is either a piece of half-baked bunk that intentionally denies the normal in order to make the abnormal seem more shocking, or else it is a confession of frivolity, a confession that, as an idiot never learns what the score is, so we have never learned to distinguish true goods amid our extravagances of whim and passion. That true goods exist is nevertheless a fact of moral experience. "A thing of beauty is a joy forever"; a great yen, a bright idea, a profound and well-tried faith, are eternal possessions. And this is not merely a fact, to be asserted upon the say-so of those who know it by experience. It is a psychological necessity.

(2)

Have you ever tried to quit smoking? It's quite simple. I know. I have achieved abstinence thousands of times already. In fact, I quit every day. I awaken in the morning—my nose and throat dry and parched. Then, I decide to renounce all further association with the weed. But it's a terrible vice over which I no longer have any control. I've got to have a smoke. Just one. Then I'll refrain from further indulgence the rest of the day. Just one to take care of my terrible longing. I can go without food, without drink. But I must have a cigarette. Just one.

So I smoke one before going to school. Only that one. I promise myself, I'm not going to smoke any more today. I'll leave my cigarettes home today.

Yeh, that's what I'll do. And since I have no cigarettes, I shall be unable to make even a momentary concession to appetite.

C. *For each of the following passages, first infer the writer's purpose and the kind of audience he is addressing. Then select and discuss the components of his style in relation to his purpose and audience.*

---

(1)

Partly, young American political radicals now are merely conforming to the two-centuries-old Enlightened tradition of how to rebel. But most of the inappropriateness of their behavior and rhetoric derives, I believe, from their not admitting what they are most opposed to. If you accuse a manifestly flexible government of rigidity, cry out against the evils of a society and deny its goods though one of those goods is your right to cry out, and urge your faction to tear it apart NOW though it is manifestly too strong for you to tear apart, then, no matter whether you are sane or insane, what you really want must be something other than what you say you want. A true, whole revolution consists of the violent and illegal destruction of a government by a group out of power which then sets up a new government. But our nihilistic anarchists appear to want only the first, destroying, easy half of revolution. They say they are against Injustice and for Freedom, but they do not devote their energies to remedying specific injustices in one of the freest—maybe it would be more accurate as well as more unpleasant to say one of the most permissive—countries in the world; they would destroy this government without having a new system of government to put in its place. This can only mean that what they really want is to remove every restraint on impulse, to abolish governing itself.[7]

(2)

On the oily surface of the pond, from time to time a snout thrust upward, took in air with a queer grunting inspiration, and swirled back to the bottom. The pond was doomed, the water was foul, and the oxygen almost gone, but the creature would not die. It could breathe air direct through a little accessory lung, and it could walk. In all that weird and lifeless landscape, it was the only thing that could. It walked rarely and under protest, but that was not surprising. The creature was a fish.

In the passage of days the pond became a puddle, but the Snout survived. There was dew one dark night and a coolness in the empty stream bed. When the sun rose next morning the pond was an empty place of cracked mud, but the Snout did not lie there. He had gone. Down stream there were other ponds. He breathed air for a few hours and hobbled slowly along on the stumps of heavy fins.

[7] From George P. Elliott, "Revolution Instead—Notes on Passions and Politics," *The Public Interest*, Summer 1970.

It was an uncanny business if there had been anyone there to see. It was a journey best not observed in daylight; it was something that needed swamps and shadows and the touch of the night dew. It was a monstrous penetration of a forbidden element, and the Snout kept his face from the light. It was just as well, though the face should not be mocked. In three hundred million years it would be our own.[8]

(3)

In the long history of the world, only a few generations have been granted the role of defending freedom in its hour of maximum danger. I do not shrink from this responsibility—I welcome it. I do not believe that any of us would exchange places with any other people or any other generation. The energy, the faith, the devotion which we bring to this endeavor will light our country and all who serve it—and the glow from that fire can truly light the world.

And so, my fellow Americans, ask not what your country can do for you: Ask what you can do for your country.

My fellow citizens of the world: Ask not what America will do for you, but what together we can do for the freedom of man.

Finally, whether you are citizens of America or citizens of the world, ask of us the same high standards of strength and sacrifice which we ask of you. With a good conscience our only sure reward, with history the final judge of our deeds, let us go forth to lead the land we love, asking His blessing and His help, but knowing that here on earth God's work must truly be our own.[9]

(4)

When things get so balled up that the people of a country have to cut loose from some other country, and go it on their own hook, without asking no permission from nobody, excepting maybe God Almighty, then they ought to let everybody know why they done it, so that everybody can see they are on the level, and not trying to put nothing over on nobody.

All we got to say on this proposition is this: first, you and me is as good as anybody else, and maybe a damn sight better; second, nobody ain't got no right to take away none of our rights; every man has got a right to live, to come and go as he pleases, and to have a good time however he likes, so long as he don't interfere with nobody else. That any government that don't give a man these rights ain't worth a damn; also, people ought to choose the kind of government they want themselves, and nobody else ought to have no say in the matter.[10]

---

[8] From Loren Eiseley, *The Immense Journey* (New York: Random House, 1957). Copyright © 1957 by Loren Eiseley.

[9] John F. Kennedy, *Inaugural Address.*

[10] From *The American Language*, 3rd ed., by H. L. Mencken. Copyright, 1924, by Alfred A. Knopf, Inc., publishers.

Part Three

Special Assignments

Chapter 9

The Essay Examination

The essay examination is one of the most practical of all composition assignments. By asking you to compose in one or more paragraphs an answer to a specific question, it calls on most of the skills the composition course tries to develop. It tests your ability to read accurately and to write purposefully within a rigidly limited time.

Instructors often complain that students write their worst on essay examinations. Of course the pressure of an examination is hardly conducive to stylistic finish. But the chief weakness of examination answers is not that they are ungrammatical or awkward, but that they are not composed at all. Many students do not first plan what they want to say and then develop their intention into an adequate answer. Too often they begin to write without clear purpose and assume that as long as they are writing they are somehow answering the question. The result is often an answer which is irrelevant, inadequate, unclear, and even self-contradictory.

This chapter attempts to improve the quality of essay examinations through applying the principles of purposeful writing which have been discussed in earlier chapters of this book. We can't, of course, teach subject matter, and a student who does not know his subject will not learn here how to conceal that fact. But many weaknesses in examination papers are caused by carelessness, haste, or panic, not by ignorance. The following recommendations should help you to avoid such weaknesses.

Read the Question Carefully

Before beginning to answer any part of an examination, read the question carefully to see what it asks you to do. If you misinterpret the question, your whole answer may be off the point, even if it shows detailed knowledge of the subject and is otherwise well written. So before you begin to write, ask yourself, "What does this question require me to do?" Notice especially whether it asks you to explain, summarize, discuss, evaluate, or compare. These are often key words in an essay question. If you are asked to *evaluate* a paragraph or a poem, a *summary* or an *explanation* of the paragraph or a *paraphrase* of the poem will not satisfy the requirement. If you are asked to *compare* two characters in a play, a *description* of each character may not develop a comparison. Presumably the wording of the question has been carefully thought out, and you will be expected to follow the directions it implies. Never begin to write until you have a clear idea what kind of answer is asked for.

To see how a competent student can drift into a bad answer by not reading the instructions carefully and seeing clearly what they require, study the following question and the two answers to it.

Illustrate the differences between early and late Renaissance painting by contrasting Fra Filippo Lippi's "Madonna and Child" with Raphael's "Sistine Madonna."

These directions clearly indicate that the answer must show how early and late Renaissance painting differed; evidence of the difference is to be drawn from two paintings, each of which is to be taken as typical of its period. Of the contrasted answers below, the first received a grade of *C*, the second a grade of *A*.

C-Answer

Filippo's picture is simply designed, and the figures are naturalistic. The Madonna is sweet, gracious, and human, dressed in the mode of the times. The Bambino is a natural, playful child. He is being lifted up by two older boys —undoubtedly Fra Filippo's family posed for the picture. The background is a stylized landscape of rocks and streams, bounded by a frame. The Madonna is seated in a chair with an elaborately carved arm which stands out in the foreground.

Raphael designed the Sistine Madonna in a pyramid with the Madonna herself at the apex. She carries the curly-haired Child, and although she is standing still, her garments swirl as in a strong wind. One's eye is first caught by the figure of Pope Sixtus at the lower left, and through the folds of his garment and his uplifted eyes, drawn toward the central figure of the Virgin. Her garments, billowing to the right, draw the eye downward again to the figure of St. Barbara, kneeling on a cloud. Her eyes are cast down, and the glance follows hers to discover two jaunty cherubs leaning on the lower frame. They look upward, thus deflecting the eyes of the beholder up again, completing the movement of the design. This painting is one of the high points of the development of Renaissance art.

A-Answer

Fra Filippo's picture is a good example of early Renaissance naturalism. The Madonna—his own wife—is wearing a stylish gown, which is painted in faithful detail. Her hair is dressed in the mode of the time. She is seated—as though in her own home—on an elaborately carved chair, with a framed painting of a landscape serving as the background. Her pose and expression are calm, perhaps devout, but neither exalted nor humble. She is an ordinary worldly mother with a chubby baby, who is being lifted to her rather ungracefully by a saucy angel. The entire scene is intimate, personal, and joyous, but hardly reverent. Filippo, pleased with the new-found technical mastery of his age, is content to paint what he sees.

Raphael was able to get above his technique and make it expressive of lofty emotion. The figures in the Sistine Madonna are monumental and stand out against a subdued background. The Madonna, her feet resting weightlessly on a cloud, wears an expression of sublime dignity. She holds with graceful ease the Child, whose sober eyes reveal the portent of His future. The figures wear classic robes, whose flowing lines give a wonderful, circling movement to the painting. A cloud of tiny cherubs' heads, peeping through the effulgence surrounding the Virgin, completes the heavenly setting. Where Filippo's work is mere copying, Raphael's is imaginative and spiritual. This loftiness of conception combined with grace of design and beauty of execution is the flower of the High Renaissance.

Why the difference in grades? Both answers are about the same length; both are well written; both show knowledge of the two pictures. What is the difference between them? The *C*-answer ignores a significant part of the question. It is a description of the "Madonna and Child" and another description of the "Sistine Madonna." The details describe the pictures, but they do nothing to show the differences between early and late Renaissance painting. Therefore the answer does not satisfy the question. The *A*-answer selects details which do illustrate the differences between the two periods, and thus gives purpose to the contrast between the pictures. This student is not merely describing two pictures; she is describing the characteristics which make them representative of two different periods. That is what the question asked.

Think Out Your Answer Before Writing

Think out your general answer before you begin to develop it. Since there is almost no chance of rewriting in an essay examination, your answer must be correctly planned the first time. If you have your thesis or topic sentence clearly in mind, explanatory and illustrative details will suggest themselves as you write. But a student who has not decided what he wants to say before he begins may veer away from the question or write a series of unrelated sentences which do not add up to a unified answer. On some questions, it may be wise to jot down on the back of your examination paper or blue book the information you want to work into your answer; on others, framing a topic sentence will be preparation enough. This advice repeats what was said in Chapters 1 and 3, but the advice becomes even more important in an examination because there is so little chance to revise.

The answer given below shows a carefully planned response to the following question:

Just before he dies, Laertes says to Hamlet, "Mine and my father's death come not on thee, nor thine on me." In view of the facts of the play, how do you interpret this statement?

The student thinks over the statement and the facts of the play and frames his general answer thus:

Laertes' statement fits some of the facts but not all of them and is best understood as a request to let bygones be bygones.

This is the topic sentence or thesis of his answer. It requires him to do three things: (1) to show that Laertes' statement fits some of the facts, (2) to show that it does not fit other facts, and (3) to explain what he means by interpreting the statement as a request to let bygones be bygones. Notice how he satisfies his own intention and the requirements of the question.

Laertes' statement fits some of the facts but not all of them and is best understood as a request to let bygones be bygones. True, Hamlet is not responsible for Laertes' death, because Hamlet thought he was engaging in a friendly bout with blunted swords. When he picked up Laertes' sword in the mix-up he did not know it was poisoned. Since Laertes deliberately put the poison there, he was responsible for both Hamlet's death and his own. Hamlet killed Polonius by mistake, thinking that the person behind the curtain was the king. To that extent it was an accidental killing, but a killing nevertheless. I think Laertes' statement is not intended as a literal description of the facts but as a reconciliation speech. I interpret the statement as meaning: "We have both been the victims of the king's treachery. Forgive me for your death, as I forgive you for mine and my father's."

This answer is an excellent example of purposeful writing in a paragraph: topic sentence, followed by supporting details, followed by a restatement of the topic idea in a concluding statement. The structure of the paragraph is implied in the topic sentence. Since the student thought out his whole answer before beginning to write, he has control of the paragraph's content. He knows that he must document his topic sentence from the facts of the play.

Contrast that answer with one by a student who has not thought out his general answer and plunges into a summary of the facts without considering how they relate to the question he is supposed to be answering.

Laertes returns from France and learns that his father has been killed by Hamlet. He is almost mad with grief and rage and in a stormy scene with the king he demands revenge. He and the king conspire to arrange a duel between Laertes and Hamlet in which Laertes will use a poisoned sword. The duel takes place after Ophelia's funeral, and Laertes cuts Hamlet with the poisoned sword. Then, in a scuffle, their swords are knocked from their hands and Hamlet picks up Laertes' sword and wounds him. Meanwhile the king has put poison in a goblet of wine he intended for Hamlet, but the queen drinks it instead. When Hamlet sees she is dying he kills the king; then both Hamlet and Laertes die.

This paragraph does not answer the question asked. It does not interpret Laertes' final speech, or even show its inconsistency with the facts. It simply summarizes the action of the play from the time of Laertes' return from France until his death in the duel. Since the question assumes that the facts of the play are known to everyone in the class, the answer contributes nothing.

Failure to read the question carefully enough to see what it asks, and failure to prewrite your answer, are related faults. If you know the subject, careful reading of the question suggests an answer, and prewriting the answer gives you a check against the wording of the question. A student who misses the first step will probably miss the second also. The sensible thing is to postpone the writing until you know what you are trying to say, and why. Hurrying into an unformed answer substitutes writing for thinking, a costly replacement always.

Support Your Answer with Details and Illustrations

Nothing so annoys a grader as a series of unsupported, unexplained generalizations. Next to irrelevance, vagueness is the chief fault of examination answers. Vagueness is understandable (though not excusable) when a student knows so little about the subject that anything he says is likely to be vague. Here we are concerned with the kind of vagueness that comes not from ignorance or poor preparation but from bad writing habits.

A common kind of vagueness is that which gives the answer at a general or abstract level and leaves it there without explanatory or illustrative detail. For example, the student who wrote the excellent paragraph on Laertes' speech might have written

Laertes' statement distorts the facts. It is not an accurate report of what happened. He is rationalizing away his own guilt and that of Hamlet by blaming Claudius.

If so, the grader would have had to guess what the student knew and thought. He would want to know: Why is Laertes' statement not an accurate report? In what sense is it a rationalization? For what, specifically, is he blaming Claudius? The answer scarcely goes beyond the topic sentence and remains so general that it does not make its meaning clear.

The amount of time you have for answering a question will, of course, affect the amount of detail you can give. But much can be done even in a very limited time if you appreciate the need to be specific. In the following example, students had ten minutes to answer the question: "Compare and contrast Wordsworth and Byron on their attitudes toward the French Revolution and Napoleon." The general answer is

Both poets at first welcomed the French Revolution and the rise of Napoleon; both later turned against them.

But a student who stops with this general answer makes three mistakes. First, he wrongly assumes that what is required is just a conclusion, not the facts and reasoning on which it is based. Had the instructor wanted short, unexplained answers, he could have designed the examination as a short-answer quiz and allowed about a minute for each answer. An essay examination requires at least a paragraph for an answer. That requirement is part of the context in which the student is being examined. Second, the student who gives such a general answer does not use the full time allotted to the question and therefore places himself at a disadvantage in competition with others who do use the full time. Third, he loses the chance to show the depth of his knowledge. If he can go beyond the general answer given above, he owes it to himself to do so. Even in a limited time, much more could have been done with the question, as the following answer shows:

Both poets at first welcomed the French Revolution and the rise of Napoleon; both later turned against them. Wordsworth changed first. He was ready at one time to throw in his lot with the revolutionists (*Prelude*), but their excesses and his own conservative inclinations made him increasingly unsympathetic. Byron seems to have been less shocked by the terror of the Revolution than by Napoleon's change from a liberator to a conqueror. His attack on Napoleon in *Childe Harold* is bitter, all the more bitter because of Byron's appreciation of what Napoleon might have done for Europe.

The difference between these two answers is not only the difference between an undeveloped topic sentence and a fully developed paragraph; it is also the difference between a grade of *D* and a grade of *A*. The second answer shows the ability to see what is needed, to select the information which meets that need, and to organize it into the comparison which the question requires.

**Do Not Pad
Your Answer**

Padding an answer is more likely to hurt than help. A student who pads his answer by wordiness, repetition, or irrelevant detail draws attention to the fact that he has little to say and is trying to conceal his ignorance. It is naive to think that a grader will accept obvious padding as a contribution to the answer. There is a relationship between length and content, because presenting content takes space. For example, the good answers in preceding pages could not have been reduced in length without losing significant content. But no experienced grader equates mere length with content. He is not easily persuaded that an answer is good just because it is long. He is more likely to be annoyed at having to spend time to separate a few kernels of wheat from a bushel of chaff. It is the student's responsibility to select and present what is relevant to the question.

A Padded Answer with the Grader's Comments

The French Revolution was one of the great events of the ~~nineteenth century~~. It brought to an end the government of the aristocrats and the king and their oppression of the common people. It was a New Deal for the French people, and liberals in Europe and America supported it, especially ~~since one of its heroes was Lafayette~~, who was also one of the heroes of the American Revolution, which also overthrew the government of a king and his aristocratic generals. Because of their interest in the common man, Wordsworth and Byron supported the Revolution which put an end to the tyranny of the aristocrats and the oppression of the common people.

It began in 1789

Declared a traitor by the National Assembly and forced to flee the country

Partly true but inadequate

Nothing to do with the question

sp!

useless repetition

Their attitude toward Napoleon was somewhat different. For years England lived in fear of a French invasion and Englishmen were united in their opposition to Napoleon and his wars of conquest. It was largely through their efforts that Napoleon was finally defeated at Waterloo by the Duke of Wellington. Wordsworth and Byron were against Napoleon's wars of conquest, and they were glad when he was finally defeated by Wellington at Waterloo.

Nothing to do with the question

Partly true but inadequate

useless repetition

There is nothing in this answer that suggests you have even read the assigned material. The crossed-out parts show irrelevant padding. The two sentences which deal with the question do not differentiate between Wordsworth and Byron, and distort the attitudes of both.

The answer on page 183 is a padded response to the question on the French Revolution and Napoleon given on page 181. The grader's marginal comments are included. When the padding in this answer is removed, the pertinent comment is reduced to two sentences. These sentences are not an adequate answer, but they are not made more adequate by the irrelevancies, which merely introduce new errors.

When the padding is not deliberate, it is a sign that the student is not thinking efficiently. He does not see what is needed, he is not controlled by a sense of purpose, and so writes one sentence at a time and drifts into repetitions and digressions. Given a knowledge of the subject, the best cure for inefficient thinking is purposeful prewriting.

EXERCISES

Each of the following lettered exercises consists of three answers to a given question. Since some of the questions may require information which you do not already have, the first essay is always an A-answer which can be used as a standard for judging the other two. For each set, write a specific criticism of the second and third answers by contrasting them with the first.

A. *Examination question:* Thoreau said, "A man is rich in proportion to the number of things which he can afford to let alone." In a paragraph, explain the meaning of this statement with reference to Thoreau's life at Walden.

(1)

This apparently paradoxical statement reflects Thoreau's values in his simple life at Lake Walden, uninvolved by the petty demands which harassed his neighbors. He deplored the fact that many men were not free, but were dominated by their acceptance of conventional needs. All around him in Concord he saw people distracted from a complete life by their efforts to pay off mortgages on their farms, by their wishes to travel, by trying to keep up appearances in dress, by a series of self-imposed duties to the community. Thoreau wished to be free to read, to observe nature, and to think. He obtained this freedom by restricting his material needs and reducing to a minimum the amount of time spent in maintaining a living. Judged by the norms of his society, his life at Walden was frugal, but by his own standards it was rich in time and tranquility.

(2)

During his time at Walden, Thoreau deliberately practiced letting things alone. He built himself a simple cabin with just enough space for his needs. Into this he put a minimum of furniture, and even abandoned some pieces of limestone on his desk because they needed to be dusted each day. He lived on a plain but nourishing diet. Whenever friends walked out to visit him, he entertained them simply and informally, not becoming trapped by the demands of conventional standards of hospitality. From this vantage point in the woods, he criticized the townsmen of Concord for their excesses in food, clothing, shelter, and social obligations.

(3)

At a time when people spend so much of their time in order to "keep up with the Joneses," one has to admire Thoreau for his willingness to be different. All of his life was marked by actions which seemed right to him. One example is his going to prison rather than paying taxes to support a system which he despised—slavery. He wanted to be let alone, to do as he pleased, without worrying about what his neighbors thought of him. Removing himself to Walden Pond was just another example of his originality. He wanted to be let alone, so for two years he maintained himself in a little cabin, enjoying the companionship of woodsmen and farmers who happened by and who shared his appreciation of the beauties of nature. Some people might think this is a dreary life. Most of us, if we were given an acre of country and our own company, would find ourselves bored because we have lost the habit of solitary thought. But it was what Thoreau wanted, and he did not care what other people thought about it.

B. *Examination question:* In Shakespearean tragedy, knowledge is the root of evil. Discuss this generalization briefly with reference to *King Lear* and *Macbeth.*

---

(1)

Ever since Eden, the Judaeo-Christian tradition has linked knowledge with evil. This linkage is sometimes suggested in Shakespeare's tragedies, but not in all plays and certainly not definitely enough to stand as a generalization. Perhaps *Macbeth* best illustrates the pairing of knowledge and evil. The Weird Sisters prophesy two increases in Macbeth's political power, the first of which is almost immediately verified when he is made Thane of Cawdor. One might say that his knowledge of the future impels him towards killing the king, that, if he had never heard the Weird Sisters, he might have remained a loyal, useful subject instead of becoming a tyrant and perpetrator of horrors. Yet the reader senses in Macbeth and his wife, even from the start, a latent ambition merely waiting to be touched off by some outside influence. The knowledge he receives is that influence and thus contributes to eventual evil. His knowledge, though, is neither complete nor solely responsible; given to a patient and gentle man like Banquo, it produces no evil at all.

King Lear presents a different relationship. Evil seems to spring from the absence of knowledge. The king, unable to evaluate his daughters accurately, lacking knowledge of their real qualities, divides his kingdom unfairly. Secondly, he lacks self-knowledge in his autocratic rashness. Even an evil daughter perceives, quite accurately, that he has "only slenderly known himself." Lear's humiliation, his suffering in the storm, and his temporary madness bring him to a more accurate understanding of himself and others. The final act of the play, though bleak indeed, is lightened by this better understanding. Knowledge is there associated with good, not with evil. One cannot, therefore, make the sweeping generalization that Shakespeare's tragedies present knowledge as the root of evil.

(2)

Knowledge is indeed the root of all evil. The reason for this is that one cannot imagine things without knowledge, but, once he knows a few things, he can combine them with others and imagine all sorts of possibilities, many of them evil. This is clearly shown in *Macbeth*. Macbeth is happy and successful until the Weird Sisters give him a vision of what his life might be. Then he becomes moody and dissatisfied, troubled to the point where he sees a dagger in empty air and sees the ghost of Banquo, whom he has unjustly murdered. The same knowledge works upon Lady Macbeth's personality and causes her to encourage the murder of the king. Later in the play, she too becomes psychologically disturbed and, while sleepwalking, re-lives the horrible, evil moments of her career.

King Lear provides additional evidence that knowledge is the root of evil. When the play begins, the king does not have a true knowledge of his daughters' characters and cannot see evil in Goneril and Regan when they make hypocritical protestations of their love for him. He is soon brought to realize how little these "dog-hearted daughters" love him, and this terrible realization brings him grief, suffering, and even insanity. Had he remained blind to their true characters, he might have lived out his remaining years in peace and happiness.

(3)

Like most generalizations, this one is false. *King Lear* includes some good characters who gain knowledge in the course of the play and some evil characters who make the good suffer. The evil characters seem to have more knowledge than the good at the opening of the first act, but, as the play goes on, the good characters acquire knowledge. This play seems to belie the generalization.

In *Macbeth*, the situation is somewhat different. Knowledge is more definitely at the root of evil. Macbeth gains more and more knowledge as the play develops, but his moral quality declines steadily, until he is finally like a vicious animal. An increase in knowledge seems to be closely related to an enlargement of evil in his character and the disintegration of his personality.

C. *Examination question:* Early in *Huckleberry Finn,* Huck contrives his own "murder." How does this episode illustrate the theme of the novel and the development of Huck's character?

(1)

A search for freedom, whether Huck's wish to be free of "sivilization" or Jim's wish to be free from slavery, is an important theme in *Huckleberry Finn.* Freedom involves a clean break with the past, an escape from the familiar and reappearance in a new environment. Huck tries to make this clean break by simulating his own "murder." The scene he contrives by scattering pig's blood on the ground and wrecking the cabin in which he has been held prisoner will prevent a search for him and will enable him to begin a new life. There is symbolic significance in this contrived "murder." Huck often seems to have a death wish, trying to cancel out the old Huck to be born again in some new place with some new family. Throughout the novel, though, these new identities are cut short by some violence or catastrophe on land, and Huck is lured back to the peacefulness of life on the river.

Besides its psychological significance, this contrived "murder" shows the reader something about Huck's character in contrast to Tom Sawyer. Tom's plans are always elaborate, influenced by the romantic books he has read. In operation, they become silly and usually ineffective, just as the "pirate" raid really becomes a raid on a Sunday School picnic. Huck, on the other hand, while admiring Tom's methods, contrives a plan that is orderly, practical, and successful. It is not surprising that, by the end of the novel, when Tom is master-minding Jim's escape in his typically silly fashion, Huck seems critical of his former idol. Although he still thinks of himself as a lesser person than Tom, he cannot but observe that he has succeeded in achieving an escape, something that Tom never quite manages.

(2)

Huck's contrivance of his own "murder" affirms Mark Twain's admiration for realism, as opposed to his contempt for romanticism. This preference is obvious throughout the novel. Huck's plotting is rather imaginative, but, more important, it is realistic. Huck has a definite purpose in his scheme—to escape from his drunken father. He is not inventing a murder just for the sake of adventure, as Tom Sawyer might do. This incident is one of several which are directed toward the support of realism. Another of Mark Twain's novels, *A Connecticut Yankee in King Arthur's Court,* also includes this theme. The practical hero succeeds because he is realistic, while those around him are infected with a romantic view of life. Mark Twain was always annoyed by romantic fiction, particularly the works of Sir Walter Scott and James Fenimore Cooper.

Realism is the key to Huck's character. When other boys are excited by forming a pirate band, Huck has doubts. He is down-to-earth and practical.

Huck always has a matter-of-fact view of life, which makes him a pleasant companion for the King and the Duke, two unsavory characters he meets on the river. Huck is not fooled by them, but acts congenial. He goes along with their schemes just to be agreeable. The ability to get along with people is part of Huck's realistic nature.

(3)

From the moment Huck sees those crossed nails in that heel print, he knows that evil is approaching. The evil is his father, who has always been jealous of his son. Huck has received beatings for doing nothing more than knowing how to read. This time when his father reclaims him, Huck firmly decides that he cannot put up with any more of Pap's cruel treatment. When the proper moment arrives and his father is away, Huck makes his escape. He contrives a "murder" scene which is realistic enough to be convincing. He kills a hog and scatters its blood at the scene of the "crime." He sets a scene of struggle and violence in Pap's cabin, thereby demonstrating his intelligence and attention to detail.

Huck desires freedom more than anything else in life. Jim, Huck's friend and companion, also desires freedom. Even Tom Sawyer, with his swashbuckling ideas, seems to desire freedom from the simple life of the small town in which he lives. But Huck needs freedom most because of his abusive father and his own innate dislike for the Widow Douglas's civilized way of life. Huck is always restless in town, but finds his true happiness and freedom on the river.

Chapter 10

The Critical Essay: Writing About Literature

One of the special assignments you will probably be given is to write one or several papers in which you respond to a piece of literature—a poem, a play, a novel, or a short story. Such papers may be called *literary criticism* or simply *critical essays*. The word "critical" in this context does not mean "fault-finding." The Greek root of the word meant to "separate," "discern," or "choose." Criticism is thus an exercise in interpretation and evaluation. A critical essay may be about anything worthy of study—a film or a television program, a building or a bridge, a statue or a painting, or a movement such as women's liberation or new trends in education. But because the critical essays written in an English class are usually on literary topics, this chapter will reflect that emphasis.

PREWRITING THE CRITICAL ESSAY

Most of the work for a critical essay is done before you begin to write. First, you have to read the work you are writing about. If the work is easy and your essay is to be short, a single careful reading may be enough. But usually you will have to read all or parts of it more than once. A poem may take several readings, as you saw on page 37, and so may any work that poses a difficult problem of interpretation. Only when you feel sure you know what a work says will you be ready to comment on it intelligently.

Students often have trouble with a critical essay because they try to respond to the work as a whole before they have examined it in detail. In Chapter 2 you were advised to delay making judgments about a subject until you had examined the observations on which any judgment must be based. Similar advice is pertinent to the prewriting of a critical paper. A student who tries to make a judgment of the whole work before he has carefully examined its individual parts may encounter two difficulties. He may lack detailed information to support his judgment and find that he has nothing to say after the first two or three paragraphs. Or his judgment may be inaccurate or superficial because he has not looked deeply enough into the work. The hasty judgment that the Emily Dickinson poem on page 37 "is just a poem about flowers and how soon they die" is such a judgment.

Significant Elements in Interpretation and Evaluation

Your reading of a literary work is likely to be more rewarding if you start with a knowledge of what to look for. Therefore the following pages will identify nine elements generally significant in interpretation and evaluation: *situation, character, action, theme, structure, symbol, irony, point of view,* and *voice.* All nine elements need not be present in a particular work, or, when present, equally important. You will have to decide which of them you wish to emphasize. To make this decision wisely you must have a working knowledge of all these elements. This knowledge will help you to read the work with more discrimination and to see things in it that you might otherwise miss.

Situation. The situation is the combination of circumstances out of which the action of the play, novel, short story, or poem emerges. We can illustrate it by taking a passage you probably studied in high school, Marc Antony's funeral oration in Shakespeare's *Julius Caesar.* Here is a summary of the situation in which Antony makes that speech.

Brutus and his fellow conspirators have killed Caesar because they thought he was about to establish a dictatorship. They also thought of killing Antony to prevent him from causing trouble for them after Caesar's murder. But Brutus persuaded them that one killing was enough. Antony requested permission to speak at Caesar's funeral, and permission was granted on the condition that Antony promise to speak no evil of the conspirators. Since he had no alternative, Antony made that promise. Brutus spoke first, defending the killing as an act of patriotism by high-minded men. Then Brutus left, and Antony began to speak.

In this situation Antony's conduct was governed by two motives: to preserve his own safety by following at least the letter of his promise, and to avenge Caesar by turning the Roman populace against the conspirators. A portion of his speech (Act III, scene ii), given below, shows how cleverly he satisfied these motives. Discuss it in class, noticing the means he uses to sway the citizens against the conspirators, while still pretending to speak no ill of them.

Friends, Romans, countrymen, lend me your ears!
I come to bury Caesar, not to praise him.
The evil that men do lives after them,
The good is oft interred with their bones;
So let it be with Caesar. The noble Brutus
Hath told you Caesar was ambitious;

If it were so, it was a grievous fault,
And grievously hath Caesar answer'd it.
Here, under leave of Brutus and the rest—
For Brutus is an honorable man;
So are they all, all honorable men—
Come I to speak in Caesar's funeral.
He was my friend, faithful and just to me;
But Brutus says he was ambitious,
And Brutus is an honorable man.
He hath brought many captives home to Rome,
Whose ransoms did the general coffers fill;
Did this in Caesar seem ambitious?
When that the poor have cried, Caesar hath wept;
Ambition should be made of sterner stuff:
Yet Brutus says he was ambitious,
And Brutus is an honorable man.
You all did see that on the Lupercal
I thrice presented him a kingly crown,
Which he did thrice refuse. Was this ambition?
Yet Brutus says he was ambitious,
And, sure, he is an honorable man.
I speak not to disprove what Brutus spoke,
But here I am to speak what I do know.
You all did love him once, not without cause;
What cause withholds you then to mourn for him?
O judgment! thou art fled to brutish beasts,
And men have lost their reason. Bear with me;
My heart is in the coffin there with Caesar,
And I must pause till it come back to me.

This illustration may persuade you that situation is not just introductory background, but something that influences the characters and their subsequent actions. All the rest of *Julius Caesar,* through the flight of the conspirators and the civil war that resulted in their defeat and death, is a working out of the conflict set in motion by the situation in which Antony spoke.

In thinking about situation in any work you are going to write about, the following questions may be helpful:

1. What precisely is the situation here? For example, what is the situation in *A Sum in Addition* (pages 42–44)?

2. How is it revealed? Through description or explanation by the author or narrator? By dialogue? By historical information which the reader already possesses?

3. How important is it in the total work? In some works it may be extremely important. For example, the prophecy of the witches in *Macbeth* motivates all the crimes that Macbeth and Lady Macbeth commit to seize

and keep the throne. In other works the situation may not be clearly defined or may be relatively unimportant.

4. Is the situation so dominant that the characters are trapped by it and have little choice but to act as they do? Or do they act out of some weakness or compulsion of their own? In dealing with a tragedy this question alone may suggest the subject of a critical essay; witness "Death of a Sad Man," page 226.

Characters. The major characters may be individuals who represent only themselves. They may be "universal" characters—that is, represent characteristics which everybody shares, like Walter Mitty and his daydreams. They may be stock characters—the despotic father, the hard-boiled sergeant, the spoiled brat—who represent conventional types of people.

The minor characters may be essential to the main action of the story, or they may be introduced for some special purpose—to provide comic relief, or romantic interest, to serve as the narrator who is telling the story, to act as a mouthpiece for the author, or as a "foil" to provide a contrast which emphasizes some quality in a major character.

In thinking about the characters, consider questions like the following:

1. Do you have a clear impression of the major characters? If so, how did you get it? Through what they do or say? Through what other characters say about them? Through the author's or narrator's comments?

2. Are the major characters to be considered as real people or as universal or stock characters? On what evidence do you make this judgment?

3. Do the major characters change as the story proceeds—that is, do their experiences make them stronger or weaker, nobler or more corrupt, than they were at the beginning? If so, do you feel that the change is justified by what happens within the story?

4. Does the dialogue ring true to you? Do characters speak in a way consistent with their regional, social, and economic backgrounds?

Action. Any play, novel, or short story usually depends on some kind of interaction among the characters. In a short story this interaction may be limited to a single incident, such as a lover's quarrel or a youth's response to a parental reprimand. But if the work may be said to have a plot, the action moves through a succession of episodes in which the characters are brought into a conflict which builds up to a climax and is then resolved. The plot may be described as "what happens" as the work proceeds. But of course what happens is closely related to both the situation and the characters. The plot, then, is the course of action through which the characters respond to the conflicts inherent in the situation.

In some works, such as adventure and mystery stories, plot will be dominant, and the satisfaction the reader gets will come from the suspense generated by its complications. In others, the appeal of the work may lie mainly in the characters, and such conflict as there is may be psychological and internal rather than physical and external.

In thinking about the action the following questions may be pertinent:

1. Is the action centered in a single incident or is it complex enough to form a plot?

2. If there is a plot, is it a single one, or are there subplots within the main one? How is the subplot related to the main plot?

3. Do events in the plot move forward in a straight time-line or is the time sequence broken by flashbacks or by having events which occurred at the same time reported successively by different characters?

4. Are the actions consistent with the characters and the situation?

5. What elements in the action create conflict and suspense?

6. What is the nature of the conflict? Is it a conflict between people for something they desire? Is it a conflict of values, or a psychological conflict within the mind of one character, or a conflict between man and his environment?

7. Does the conflict come to a climax in the story? If so, where? Is it resolved at the end, or is the reader left to guess what happened, as in *The Lady or the Tiger?*

8. Does the appeal of the work lie chiefly in the plot, in the characters, or in a combination of both?

9. What is your final judgment of the author's handling of the action?

Theme. In addition to showing characters in action a work may express or imply a general idea or theme which suggests the significance of the action. Usually a creative writer does not write a play or a piece of fiction or a poem merely to develop an idea. He is an artist, not a propagandist or a preacher. If he wanted to develop a thesis, he could do so more obviously by writing an essay. But in dealing with men and women in a society he is often concerned with the values revealed by his characters, so that the work, to some extent, is a criticism of these values. Thus, running through the *Adventures of Huckleberry Finn* is a contrast between Huck's sense of values and those which the adults in the story proclaim or reveal. Twain's criticism of society, as it is represented by Miss Watson, the Grangerfords, the Duke, and others is so clear that it can be said to be the theme of the book. If what these adults stand for is "civilization," Huck wants none of it. As he says at the end of the novel, "But I reckon I got to light out for the territory ahead of the rest, because Aunt Sally she's going to adopt me and sivilize me, and I can't stand it. I been there before."

Usually the theme of a literary work is implied, not explicitly stated. The reader infers it from the total work, so that the theme becomes part of his interpretation. Thus a reader who concludes that Emily Dickinson's poem on page 37 supports the idea that man's confidence in a moral order in the universe has no relation to what actually occurs in nature in inferring a theme from his reading of the poem. Another reader may find a different theme in that poem, but each determines a theme by detecting a unifying idea within the poem. That idea, whatever it is, is *part* of the meaning the reader finds in the poem, but only a part, since there is a great deal more to the poem than a statement of an idea.

There are no simple questions that will reveal the theme of a work, but the following questions may help direct your thinking about possible themes:

1. In addition to showing characters interacting in a situation, is the work also concerned with contrasting different attitudes or values so that there is an implied criticism of social, moral, or ethical values in the contrast?

2. Does the criticism, if any, run through most of the work so that it seems to be a major element in your interpretation?

3. Is there any sentence within the work that seems to sum up that criticism as a statement of the theme? For example, one of the characters in J. M. Barrie's play, *Dear Brutus*, quotes two lines from *Julius Caesar:*

> Our faults, dear Brutus, lie not in our stars,
> But in ourselves that we are underlings.

That quotation, along with the title, suggests the unifying idea of Barrie's play: the way we act in a situation is not a result of fate, but of our own defects.

4. If you feel that there is a dominant idea in the work but cannot state it in a single sentence, can you express it as an interpretive summary of the work, as one critic of William Golding's novel *Lord of the Flies* does in the following paragraph?

> The theme of the book is that the human condition is irrational. Man has no nature, but rather is an excrescence from chaotic, cruel and blind forces which are violent and yet meaningless. Man springs forth from these forces and regresses into them. The violence which develops on the island only reflects in microcosm the violence of the rest of the world: the boys appear on the island as a result of some atomic catastrophe, the sole intruder on the island is the dead pilot who is shot down from the firmament overhead, and the boys leave the island in the company of armed men traveling in a warship. When all is said and done, man's condition is represented as something hateful. Thus the novel is representative of much of modern thought and art.[1]

Structure. The structure of a literary work is the way the various parts fit together to produce a unified whole. It is useful to recognize two kinds of structures: the external form, imposed by the conventions of the *genre* or literary type (novel, play, poem, film); and the internal structure of a particular work. Generic or external structure is common to most works in the genre. Most detective stories begin with a crime to be solved, identify

[1] John M. Egan, "Golding's View of Man," *America*, January 26, 1963, p. 140.

possible suspects, begin to build a case against each major suspect, introduce new evidence that clears one, then another, of the suspects, and finally solve the crime by identifying the murderer. This is the generic pattern of the detective story, whether it is written by Agatha Christie or Erle Stanley Gardner. The internal structure is the way Hercule Poirot or Perry Mason solves a particular case. Each detective has his own characteristic way of getting at the truth, and the way he operates determines the internal structure of the story.

An analysis of the following poem will illustrate the relation of generic to internal structure. The rhyme scheme is indicated at the right.

Yet Do I Marvel

by Countee Cullen

1	I doubt not God is good, well-meaning, kind,	*a*
2	And did He stoop to quibble could tell why	*b*
3	The little buried mole continues blind,	*a*
4	Why flesh that mirrors Him must some day die;	*b*
5	Make plain the reason tortured Tantalus	*c*
6	Is baited by the fickle fruit, declare	*d*
7	If merely brute caprice dooms Sisyphus	*c*
8	To struggle up a never-ending stair.	*d*
9	Inscrutable His ways are, and immune	*e*
10	To catechism by a mind too strewn	*e*
11	With petty cares to slightly understand	*f*
12	What awful brain compels His awful hand.	*f*
13	Yet do I marvel at this curious thing:	*g*
14	To make a poet black and bid him sing.	*g*

From your experience with poetry in high school you may recognize this poem as belonging to the genre called a *sonnet*—a poem of fourteen lines in iambic pentameter, with a traditional rhyme scheme and a turn in the thought at the end of the first eight lines. You may even recognize it as an "English" rather than an "Italian" sonnet because of the rhyme scheme and the final couplet. These characteristics identify the generic structure of the poem. All English sonnets show a similar structure, except for possible variations in the rhyme scheme of the last six lines.

The internal construction of the poem is imbedded within that generic structure. It begins with four examples of creatures doomed to a hard fate, and the poet's assumption that God, if he wished, could explain why these hardships are necessary. Then at the beginning of line 9 the sonnet turns from these examples to a statement about the inability of the human mind to understand God's purposes. The last two lines present the most difficult of all things to understand—God's endowing a man with the gift of poetry yet making him black.

The two final lines, as is traditional in the English sonnet, express the theme of the poem. The implication is that the lot of the black man is worse than that of the mole, or Tantalus or Sisyphus, that a black poet has nothing to sing about, yet is compelled by his gift to sing. The contrast or contradiction in making a poet black seems so cruelly ironic that it is impossible to understand why a kind God would do such a thing.

The structural analysis of this sonnet shows that interpretation depends on understanding both the generic and the internal structure. That understanding comes from a careful reading which identifies and relates the different parts. In another work an analysis of the structure could be extended to take into account the situation, characters, action, symbols, and language. In this extended sense the structure becomes the whole internal context of the work, so that an analysis of structure may become an interpretation of the whole work. You will see such an analysis in the comments following "Barn Burning" on page 212.

Symbol. Literally, a symbol is something that conventionally represents something else, as the jerk of an umpire's thumb tells us that the runner is out. Such symbols can be considered "closed," since they are generally limited by the context to one interpretation. But a symbol may also suggest much more than its literal meaning. The nickname "Old Glory" is literally a symbol for the flag of the United States, but to many people it may suggest a whole cluster of associations about the nation and its history. Such a symbol may be called "open," since it does not limit the reader's or listener's response to one specific meaning.

Writers, especially poets, often use open symbols to invite the reader to make whatever associations the symbols reasonably suggest. Golding's *Lord of the Flies* is full of such symbols: the conch that Ralph blows to call the boys to a meeting is a symbol of democratic procedures, the fire is a traditional symbol of civilization in contrast to the barbarism of Jack and his hunters, the dead airman dangling from a parachute in a tree is a symbol both of the destructiveness of war and of the terror the boys associate with the "beast," and the sow's head covered with flies is a symbol of human corruption and of the devil.

Interpreting symbols requires both careful and imaginative reading. The reader must discover for himself the associations the symbol invites, and he cannot do that if he is hurrying through the work to find its plain meaning. But it also requires disciplined reading, since whatever associations he makes from the symbol must be appropriate to the whole context of the work. For example, Wordsworth's lines

> A primrose by a river's brim
> A yellow primrose was to him,
> And it was nothing more.

can be interpreted as referring not just to the "him" in the second line, but to all those unimaginative people who see only the obvious and thus miss much of beauty and significance in life. But if a reader associates the yellowness of the primrose with gold, and gold with wealth, and thus interprets the lines to mean that some people look on natural resources only as a source of commercial profit, he is making an eccentric interpretation. He is reading more into the lines than their context justifies. Interpreting symbols takes both freedom and restraint: freedom to explore the associations suggested by the symbol, and restraint in accepting those inconsistent with the thought or mood of the passage.

Irony.   Irony is a device of style in which the writer is understood to mean the opposite of what he says. Thus each time Marc Antony repeats that Brutus is an honorable man, the citizens gradually recognize that Antony means that Brutus and his fellow-conspirators are anything but honorable. You have seen an example of sustained irony in "Why We Need More Westerns on Television" (page 9) in which the narrator pretends to be praising westerns while the reader knows she is laughing at them.

In *dramatic irony,* often used in plays and novels, the words or actions of a character take on prophetic significance because the reader or listener knows something the speaker does not know which gives the words a different meaning. For example, in Sophocles' play *King Oedipus* the king is driven by a religious and legal obligation to find and punish the slayer of his father. What he does not know, though the audience does, is that he himself is the slayer. The more he pushes his search, the more he dooms himself. Much of the force of the play lies in the moves by which the well-intentioned king pursues his own ruin. In O. Henry's short story "The Gift of the Magi," the husband and wife each wants to give the other an expensive gift—a set of combs for the woman's beautiful hair, and a watch fob for the man's gold watch. The impact of the story lies in the ironic twist that in order to purchase these gifts the woman has to sell her hair and the man has to sell his watch.

Point of View.   Literally, a point of view is the position one occupies in viewing an object. Applied to literature, the phrase becomes a metaphor for the way an author views his subject or tells his story. Generally he can use either an omniscient or a limited point of view. With an omniscient view he can know everything about the characters. He can tell not only what they do and say, but also what they are thinking, and he can report what happened in the past or will happen in the future as well as what is happening at present. A limited point of view requires the author to tell the story as some one person knows it. That person may be one of the characters, or someone who witnessed the events but did not share in them, or the author himself, but without omniscience.

For example, the description of the young woman in "The Camera Eye" (page 25) is given from two limited points of view, first that of the unobservant husband, then that of the highly critical wife. Had it been told from an omniscient point of view, the author could have told us not only what the girl looked like, but where she came from, where she was going, and what she was thinking as she passed the husband and wife.

Voice.   The term "voice" is used in literature to identify the person or persona (see page 12) who is speaking in a story or a poem. The question "Who is speaking here?" is often important to the interpretation of a work, but the answer must be drawn from the whole context. It is not safe to assume that a story written in the first person must be about the author. An author can write in many voices, one of which may be his own. The "I" in "Yet Do I Marvel" clearly refers to the black poet, Countee Cullen, who is writing out of his personal experience with racial discrimination. But the "I" in T. S. Eliot's

> I grow old . . . I grow old . . .
> I shall wear the bottoms of my trousers rolled.

refers to the name character in "The Love Song of J. Alfred Prufrock." It may sometimes be difficult, especially in a poem, to decide whether the voice is that of the author himself or of a persona he is using. The decision has to be made as an inference from the whole context of the work.

A knowledge of the nine elements discussed in the preceding pages will not only help your reading but will also suggest a choice of subject for your paper. You may focus on any one of the elements, so that your paper is an analysis of situation, character, plot, theme, structure, or symbolism. Or you may deal with the interrelation of two or more elements —for example, the interrelation of situation, theme, and structure. Your choice of focus will be a major part of your decision about the purpose of your paper, and that decision will be easier to make if you know what your choices are.

The following story and the comments at the end of it demonstrate the prewriting of a critical paper.

Barn Burning

by William Faulkner

The store in which the Justice of the Peace's court was sitting smelled of cheese. The boy, crouched on his nail keg at the back of the crowded room, knew he smelled cheese, and more: from where he sat he could see the ranked shelves close-packed with the solid, squat, dynamic shapes of tin cans whose labels his stomach read, not from the lettering which meant nothing to his mind but from the scarlet devils and the silver curve of fish—this, the cheese which he knew he smelled and the hermetic meat which his intestines believed he smelled coming in intermittent gusts momentary and brief between the other constant one, the smell and sense just a little of fear because mostly of despair and grief, the old fierce pull of blood. He could not see the table where the Justice sat and before which his father and his father's enemy (*our enemy* he thought in that despair; *ourn! mine and hisn both! He's my father!*) stood, but he could hear them, the two of them that is, because his father had said no word yet:

"But what proof have you, Mr. Harris?"

"I told you. The hog got into my corn. I caught it up and sent it back to him. He had no fence that would hold it. I told him so, warned him. The next time I put the hog in my pen. When he came to get it I gave him enough wire to patch up his pen. The next time I put the hog up and kept it. I rode down to his house and saw the wire I gave him still rolled on to the spool in his yard. I told him he could have the hog when he paid me a dollar pound fee. That evening a nigger came with the dollar and got the hog. He was a strange nigger. He said, 'He say to tell you wood and hay kin burn.' I said, 'What?' 'That whut he say to tell you,' the nigger said. 'Wood and hay kin burn.' That night my barn burned. I got the stock out but I lost the barn."

"Where is the nigger? Have you got him?"

"He was a strange nigger, I tell you. I don't know what became of him."

"But that's not proof. Don't you see that's not proof?"

"Get that boy up here. He knows." For a moment the boy thought too that the man meant his older brother until Harris said, "Not him. The little one. The boy," and, crouching, small for his age, small and wiry like his father, in patched and faded jeans even too small for him, with straight, uncombed, brown hair and eyes gray and wild as a storm scud, he saw the men between himself and the table part and become a lane of grim faces, at the end of which he saw the Justice, a shabby, collarless, graying man in spectacles, beckoning him. He felt no floor under his bare feet; he seemed to walk beneath the palpable weight of the grim turning faces. His father, stiff in his black Sunday coat donned not for the trial but for the moving, did not even look at him. *He aims for me to lie,* he thought, again with that frantic grief and despair. *And I will have to do hit.*

"What's your name, boy?" the Justice said.

"Colonel Sartoris Snopes," the boy whispered.

"Hey?" the Justice said. "Talk louder. Colonel Sartoris? I reckon anybody named for Colonel Sartoris in this country can't help but tell the truth, can they?" The boy said nothing. *Enemy! Enemy!* he thought; for a moment he could not even see, could not see that the Justice's face was kindly nor discern that his voice was troubled when he spoke to the man named Harris: "Do you want me to question this boy?" But he could hear, and during those subsequent long seconds while there was absolutely no sound in the crowded little room save that of quiet and intent breathing it was as if he had swung outward at the end of a grape vine, over a ravine, and at the top of the swing had been caught in a prolonged instant of mesmerized gravity, weightless in time.

"No!" Harris said violently, explosively. "Damnation! Send him out of here!" Now time, the fluid world, rushed beneath him again, the voices coming to him again through the smell of cheese and sealed meat, the fear and despair and the old grief of blood:

"This case is closed. I can't find against you, Snopes, but I can give you advice. Leave this country and don't come back to it."

His father spoke for the first time, his voice cold and harsh, level, without emphasis: "I aim to. I don't figure to stay in a country among people who . . ." he said something unprintable and vile, addressed to no one.

"That'll do," the Justice said. "Take your wagon and get out of this country before dark. Case dismissed."

His father turned, and he followed the stiff black coat, the wiry figure walking a little stiffly from where a Confederate provost's man's musket ball had taken him in the heel on a stolen horse thirty years ago, followed the two backs now, since his older brother had appeared from somewhere in the crowd, no taller than the father but thicker, chewing tobacco steadily, between the two lines of grim-faced men and out of the store and across the worn gallery and down the sagging steps and among the dogs and half-grown boys in the mild May dust, where as he passed a voice hissed:

"Barn burner!"

Again he could not see, whirling; there was a face in a red haze, moonlike bigger than the full moon, the owner of it half again his size, he leaping in the red haze toward the face, feeling no blow, feeling no shock when his head struck the earth, scrabbling up and leaping again, feeling no blow this time either and tasting no blood, scrabbling up to see the other boy in full flight and himself already leaping into pursuit as his father's hand jerked him back, the harsh, cold voice speaking above him: "Go get in the wagon."

It stood in a grove of locusts in mulberries across the road. His two hulking sisters in their Sunday dresses and his mother and her sister in calico and sun-bonnets were already in it, sitting on and among the sorry residue of the dozen and more movings which even the boy could remember—the battered stove, the broken beds and chairs, the clock inlaid with mother-of-pearl, which would not run, stopped at some fourteen minutes past two o'clock of a dead and forgotten day and time, which had been his mother's dowry. She was crying, though when she saw him she drew her sleeve across her face and began to descend from the wagon. "Get back," the father said.

"He's hurt. I got to get some water and wash his . . ."

"Get back in the wagon," his father said. He got in too, over the tail-gate. His father mounted to the seat where the older brother already sat and struck the gaunt mules two savage blows with the peeled willow, but without heat. It was not even sadistic; it was exactly that same quality which in later years would cause his descendants to over-run the engine before putting a motor car into motion, striking and reining back in the same movement. The wagon went on, the store with its quiet crowd of grimly watching men dropped behind; a curve in the road hid it. *Forever* he thought. *Maybe he's done satisfied now, now that he has* . . . stopping himself, not to say it aloud even to himself. His mother's hand touched his shoulder.

"Does hit hurt?" she said.

"Naw," he said. "Hit don't hurt. Lemme be."

"Can't you wipe some of the blood off before hit dries?"

"I'll wash to-night," he said. "Lemme be, I tell you."

The wagon went on. He did not know where they were going. None of them ever did or ever asked, because it was always somewhere, always a house of sorts waiting for them a day or two days or even three days away. Likely his father had already arranged to make a crop on another farm before he . . . Again he had to stop himself. He (the father) always did. There was something about his wolflike independence and even courage when the advantage was at least neutral which impressed strangers, as if they got from his latent ravening ferocity not so much a sense of dependability as a feeling that his ferocious conviction in the rightness of his own actions would be of advantage to all whose interest lay with his.

That night they camped, in a grove of oaks and beeches where a spring ran. The nights were still cool and they had a fire against it, of a rail lifted from a nearby fence and cut into lengths—a small fire, neat, niggard almost, a shrewd fire, such fires were his father's habit and custom always, even to freezing weather. Older, the boy might have remarked this and wondered why not a big one; why should not a man who had not only seen the waste and extravagance of war, but who had in his blood an inherent voracious prodigality with material not his own, have burned everything in sight? Then he might have gone a step farther and thought that that was the reason: that niggard blaze was the living fruit of nights passed during those four years in the woods hiding from all men, blue or gray, with his strings of horses (captured horses, he called them). And older still, he might have divined the true reason: that the element of fire spoke to some deep mainspring of his father's being, as the element of steel or of powder spoke to other men, as the one weapon for the preservation of integrity, else breath were not worth the breathing, and hence to be regarded with respect and used with discretion.

But he did not think this now and he had seen those same niggard blazes all his life. He merely ate his supper beside it and was already half asleep over his iron plate when his father called him, and once more he followed the stiff back, the stiff and ruthless limp, up the slope and on to the starlit road where, turning, he could see his father against the stars but without face or depth—a shape black, flat, and bloodless as though cut from tin in the iron folds of the frockcoat which had not been made for him, the voice harsh like tin and without heat like tin:

"You were fixing to tell them. You would have told him." He didn't answer. His father struck him with the flat of his hand on the side of the head, hard but without heat, exactly as he had struck the two mules at the store, exactly as he would strike either of them with any stick in order to kill a horse fly, his voice still without heat or anger. "You're getting to be a man. You got to learn. You got to learn to stick to your own blood or you ain't going to have any blood to stick to you. Do you think either of them, any man there this morning, would? Don't you know all they wanted was a chance to get at me because they knew I had them beat? Eh?" Later, twenty years later, he was to tell himself, "If I had said they wanted only truth, justice, he would have hit me again." But now he said nothing. He was not crying. He just stood there. "Answer me," his father said.

"Yes," he whispered. His father turned.

"Get on to bed. We'll be there to-morrow."

To-morrow they were there. In the early afternoon the wagon stopped before a paintless, two-room house identical almost with the dozen others it had stopped before even in the boy's ten years, and again, as on the other dozen occasions, his mother and aunt got down and began to unload the wagon, although his two sisters and his father and brother had not moved.

"Likely hit ain't fitten for hawgs," one of the sisters said.

"Nevertheless, fit it will and you'll hog it and like it," his father said. "Get out of them chairs and help your Ma unload."

The two sisters got down, big, bovine, in a flutter of cheap ribbons; one of them drew from the jumbled wagon bed a battered lantern, the other a worn broom. His father handed the reins to the older son and began to climb stiffly over the wheel. "When they get unloaded, take the team to the farm and feed them." Then he said, and at first the boy thought he was still speaking to his brother: "Come with me."

"Me?" he said.

"Yes," his father said. "You."

"Abner," his mother said. His father paused and looked back—the harsh level stare beneath the shaggy, graying, irascible brows.

"I reckon I'll have a word with the man that aims to begin to-morrow owning me body and soul for the next eight months."

They went back up the road. A week ago—or before last night, that is—he would have asked where they were going, but not now. His father had struck him before last night but never before had he paused afterward to explain why; it was as if the blow and the following calm, outrageous voice still rang, repercussed, divulging nothing to him save the terrible handicap of being young, the light weight of his few years, just heavy enough to prevent his soaring free of the world as it seemed to be ordered but not heavy enough to keep him footed solid in it, to resist it and try to change the course of its events.

Presently he could see the grove of oaks and cedars and the other flowering trees and shrubs where the house would be, though not the house yet. They walked beside a fence massed with honeysuckle and Cherokee roses and came to a gate swinging open between two brick pillars, and now, beyond a sweep of drive, he saw the house for the first time and at that instant he forgot his father and the terror and despair both, and even when he remembered his father again (who had not stopped) the terror and despair did not return. Because, for all the twelve movings, they had sojourned until now in a poor country, a land of small farms and fields and houses, and he had never seen a house like this before. *Hit's big as a courthouse* he thought quietly, with a surge of peace and joy whose reason he could not have thought into words, being too young for that. *They are safe from him. People whose lives are a part of this peace and dignity are beyond his touch, he no more to them than a buzzing wasp: capable of stinging for a little moment but that's all; the spell of this peace and dignity rendering even the barns and stable and cribs which belong to it impervious to the puny flames he might contrive* . . . this, the peace and joy, ebbing for an instant as he looked again at the stiff black back, the stiff and implacable limp of the figure which was not dwarfed by the house, for the reason that it had never looked big anywhere and which now, against the serene columned backdrop, had more than ever that impervious quality of something cut ruthlessly from tin, depthless, as though, sidewise to the sun, it would cast no shadow. Watching him, the boy remarked the absolutely undeviating course which his father held and saw the stiff foot come squarely down in a pile of fresh droppings where a horse had stood in the drive and which his father could have avoided by a simple change of stride. But it ebbed only for a moment, though he could not have thought this into words either, walking on in the spell of the house, which he could even want but without envy, without sorrow, certainly never with that ravening and jealous rage which unknown to him walked in the ironlike black coat before him: *Maybe he will feel it too. Maybe it will even change him now from what maybe he couldn't help but be.*

They crossed the portico. Now he could hear his father's stiff foot as it came down on the boards with clocklike finality, a sound out of all proportion to the displacement of the body it bore and which was not dwarfed either by the white door before it, as though it had attained to a sort of vicious and ravening minimum not to be dwarfed by anything—the flat, wide, black hat, the formal coat of broadcloth which had once been black but which had now the friction-glazed greenish cast of the bodies of old house flies, the lifted sleeve which was too large, the lifted hand like a curled claw. The door oepned so promptly that the boy knew the Negro must have been watching them all the time, an old man with neat grizzled hair, in a linen jacket, who stood barring the door with his body, saying, "Wipe yo foots, white man, fo you come in here. Major ain't home nohow."

"Get out of my way, nigger," his father said, without heat too, flinging the door back and the Negro also and entering, his hat still on his head. And now the boy saw the prints of the stiff foot on the doorjamb and saw them appear on the pale rug behind the machinelike deliberation of the foot which seemed to bear (or transmit) twice the weight which the body compassed. The Negro was shouting "Miss Lula! Miss Lula" somewhere behind them, then the boy, deluged as though by a warm wave by a suave turn of carpeted stair and a pendant glitter of chandeliers and a mute gleam of gold frames, heard the swift feet and saw her too, a lady—perhaps he had never seen her like before either—in a gray, smooth gown with lace at the throat and an apron tied at the waist and the sleeves turned back, wiping cake or biscuit dough from her hands with a towel as she came up the hall, looking not at his father at all but at the tracks on the blond rug with an expression of incredulous amazement.

"I tried," the Negro cried. "I tole him to . . ."

"Will you please go away?" she said in a shaking voice. "Major de Spain is not at home. Will you please go away?"

His father had not spoken again. He did not speak again. He did not even look at her. He just stood stiff in the center of the rug, in his hat, the shaggy iron-gray brows twitching slightly above the pebble-colored eyes as he appeared to examine the house with brief deliberation. Then with the same deliberation he turned; the boy watched him pivot on the good leg and saw the stiff foot drag around the arc of the turning, leaving a final long and fading smear. His father never looked at it, he never once looked down at the rug. The Negro held the door. It closed behind them, upon the hysteric and indistinguishable woman-wail. His father stopped at the top of the steps and scraped his boot clean on the edge of it. At the gate he stopped again. He stood for a moment, planted stiffly on the stiff foot, looking back at the house. "Pretty and white, ain't it?" he said. "That's sweat. Nigger sweat. Maybe it ain't white enough yet to suit him. Maybe he wants to mix some white sweat with it."

Two hours later the boy was chopping wood behind the house within which his mother and aunt and the two sisters (the mother and aunt, not the two girls, he knew that; even at this distance and muffled by walls the flat loud voices of the two girls emanated an incorrigible idle inertia) were setting up the stove to prepare a meal, when he heard the hooves and saw the linen-clad man on a fine sorrel mare, whom he recognized even before he saw the rolled rug in front of the Negro youth following on a fat bay carriage horse—a suffused, angry face, vanishing, still at full gallop, beyond the corner of the house where his father and brother were sitting in the two tilted chairs; and a moment later, almost before he could have put the axe down, he heard the hooves again and watched the sorrel mare go back out of the yard, already galloping again. Then his father began to shout one of the sisters' names, who presently emerged backward from the kitchen door dragging the rolled rug along the ground by one end while the other sister walked behind it.

"If you ain't going to tote, go on and set up the wash pot," the first said.

"You, Sarty!" the second shouted. "Set up the wash pot!" His father appeared at the door, framed against that shabbiness, as he had been against that other bland perfection, impervious to either, the mother's anxious face at his shoulder.

"Go on," the father said. "Pick it up." The two sisters stooped, broad, lethargic; stooping, they presented an incredible expanse of pale cloth and a flutter of tawdry ribbons.

"If I thought enough of a rug to have to git hit all the way from France I wouldn't keep hit where folks coming in would have to tromp on hit," the first said. They raised the rug.

"Abner," the mother said. "Let me do it."

"You go back and git dinner," his father said. "I'll tend to this."

From the woodpile through the rest of the afternoon the boy watched them, the rug spread flat in the dust beside the bubbling wash-pot, the two sisters stooping over it with that profound and lethargic reluctance, while the father stood over them in turn, implacable and grim, driving them though never raising his voice again. He could smell the harsh homemade lye they were using; he saw his mother come to the door once and look toward them with an expression not anxious now but very like despair; he saw his father turn, and he fell to with the axe and saw from the corner of his eye his father raise from the ground a flattish fragment of field stone and examine it and return to the pot, and this time his mother actually spoke: "Abner, Abner. Please don't. Please Abner."

Then he was done too. It was dusk; the whippoorwills had already begun. He could smell coffee from the room where they would presently eat the cold food remaining from the mid-afternoon meal, though when he entered the house he realized they were having coffee again probably because there was a fire on the hearth, before which the rug now lay spread over the backs of the two chairs. The tracks of his father's foot were gone. Where they had been were now long, water-cloudy scorifications resembling the sporadic course of a lilliputian mowing machine.

It still hung there while they ate the cold food and then went to bed, scattered without order or claim up and down the two rooms, his mother in one bed, where his father would later lie, the older brother in the other, himself, the aunt, and the two sisters on pallets on the floor. But his father was not in bed yet. The last thing the boy remembered was the depthless, harsh silhouette of the hat and coat bending over the rug and it seemed to him that he had not even closed his eyes when the silhouette was standing over him, the fire almost dead behind it, the stiff foot prodding him awake. "Catch up the mule," his father said.

When he returned with the mule his father was standing in the black door, the rolled rug over his shoulder. "Ain't you going to ride?" he said.

"No. Give me your foot."

He bent his knee into his father's hand, the wiry, surprising power flowed smoothly, rising, he rising with it, on to the mule's bare back (they had owned a saddle once; the boy could remember it though not when or where) and with the same effortlessness his father swung the rug up in front of him. Now in the starlight they retraced the afternoon's path, up the dusty road rife with honeysuckle, through the gate and up the black tunnel of the drive to the lightless house, where he sat on the mule and felt the rough warp of the rug drag across his thighs and vanish.

"Don't you want me to help?" he whispered. His father did not answer and now he heard again that stiff foot striking the hollow portico with that wooden and clocklike deliberation, that outrageous overstatement of the weight it carried. The rug, hunched, not flung (the boy could tell that even in the darkness) from his father's shoulder struck the angle of wall and floor with a sound unbelievably loud, thunderous, then the floor again, unhurried and enormous; a light came on in the house and the boy sat, tense, breathing steadily and quietly and just a little fast, though the foot itself did not increase its beat at all, descending the steps now; now the boy could see him.

"Don't you want to ride now?" he whispered. "We kin both ride now," the light within the house altering now, flaring up and sinking. *He's coming down the stairs now,* he thought. He had already ridden the mule up beside the horse block; presently his father was up behind him and he doubled the reins over and slashed the mule across the neck, but before the animal could begin to trot the hard, thin arm came around him, the hard, knotted hand jerking the mule back to a walk.

In the first red rays of the sun they were in the lot, putting plow gear on the mules. This time the sorrel mare was in the lot before he heard it at all, the rider collarless and even bareheaded, trembling, speaking in a shaking voice as the woman in the house had done, his father merely looking up once before stooping again to the hame he was buckling, so that the man on the mare spoke to his stooping back:

"You must realize you have ruined that rug. Wasn't there anybody here, any of your women . . ." he ceased, shaking, the boy watching him, the older brother leaning now in the stable door, chewing, blinking slowly and steadily at nothing apparently. "It cost a hundred dollars. But you never had a hundred dollars. You never will. So I'm going to charge you twenty bushels of corn against your crop. I'll add it in your contract and when you come to the commissary you can sign it. That won't keep Mrs. de Spain quiet but maybe it will teach you to wipe your feet off before you enter her home again."

Then he was gone. The boy looked at his father, who still had not spoken or even looked up again, who was now adjusting the logger-head in the hame.

"Pap," he said. His father looked at him—the inscrutable face, the shaggy brows beneath which the gray eyes glinted coldly. Suddenly the boy went toward him, fast, stopping as suddenly. "You done the best you could!" he cried. "If he wanted hit done different why didn't he wait and tell you how? He won't git no twenty bushels! He won't git none! We'll gather hit and hide hit! I kin watch . . ."

"Did you put the cutter back in that straight stock like I told you?"

"No, sir," he said.

"Then go do it."

That was Wednesday. During the rest of that week he worked steadily, at what was within his scope and some which was beyond it, with an industry that did not need to be driven nor even commanded twice; he had this from his mother, with the difference that some at least of what he did he liked to do, such as splitting wood with the half-size axe which his mother and aunt had earned, or saved money somehow, to present him with at Christmas. In company with the two older women (and on one afternoon, even one of the sisters), he built pens for the shoat and the cow which were a part of his father's contract with the landlord, and one afternoon, his father being absent, gone somewhere on one of the mules, he went to the field.

They were running a middle buster now, his brother holding the plow straight while he handled the reins, and walking beside the straining mule, the rick black soil shearing cool and damp against his bare ankles, he thought *Maybe this is the end of it. Maybe even that twenty bushels that seems hard to have to pay for just a rug will be a cheap price for him to stop forever and always from being what he used to be;* thinking, dreaming now, so that his brother had to speak sharply to him to mind the mule: *Maybe he even won't collect the twenty bushels. Maybe it will all add up and balance and vanish—corn, rug, fire, the terror and grief, the being pulled two ways like between two teams of horses—gone, done with for ever and ever.*

Then it was Saturday; he looked up from beneath the mule he was harnessing and saw his father in the black coat and hat. "Not that," his father said. "The wagon gear." And then, two hours later, sitting in the wagon bed behind his father and brother on the seat, the wagon accomplished a final curve, and he saw the weathered paintless store with its tattered tobacco- and patent-medicine posters and the tethered wagons and saddle animals below the gallery. He mounted the gnawed steps behind his father and brother, and there again was the lane of quiet, watching faces for the three of them to walk through. He saw the man in spectacles sitting at the plank table and he did not need to be told this was a Justice of the Peace; he sent one glare of fierce, exultant, partisan defiance at the man in collar and cravat now, whom he had seen but twice before in his life, and that on a galloping horse, who now wore on his face an expression not of rage but of amazed unbelief which the boy could not have known was at the incredible circumstance of being sued by one of his own tenants, and came and stood against his father and cried at the Justice: "He ain't done it! He ain't burnt . . ."

"Go back to the wagon," his father said.

"Burnt?" the Justice said. "Do I understand this rug was burned too?"

"Does anybody here claim it was?" his father said. "Go back to the wagon." But he did not, he merely retreated to the rear of the room, crowded as that other had been, but not to sit down this time, instead, to stand pressing among the motionless bodies, listening to the voices:

"And you claim twenty bushels of corn is too high for the damage you did to the rug?"

"He brought the rug to me and said he wanted the tracks washed out of it. I washed the tracks out and took the rug back to him."

"But you didn't carry the rug back to him in the same condition it was in before you made the tracks on it."

His father did not answer, and now for perhaps half a minute there was no sound at all save that of breathing, the faint, steady suspiration of complete and intent listening.

"You decline to answer that, Mr. Snopes?" Again his father did not answer. "I'm going to find against you, Mr. Snopes. I'm going to find that you were responsible for the injury to Major de Spain's rug and hold you liable for it. But twenty bushels of corn seem a little high for a man in your circumstances to have to pay. Major de Spain claims it cost a hundred dollars. October corn will be worth about fifty cents. I figure that if Major de Spain can stand a ninety-five dollar loss on something he paid cash for, you can stand a five-dollar loss you haven't earned yet. I hold you in damages to Major de Spain to the amount of ten bushels of corn over and above your contract with him, to be paid to him out of your crop at gathering time. Court adjourned."

It had taken no time hardly, the morning was but half begun. He thought they would return home and perhaps back to the field, since they were late, far behind all other farmers. But instead his father passed on behind the wagon, merely indicating with his hand for the older brother to follow with it, and crossed the road toward the blacksmith shop opposite, pressing on after his father, overtaking him, speaking, whispering up at the harsh, calm face beneath the weathered hat: "He won't git no ten bushels, neither. He won't git one. We'll . . ." until his father glanced for an instant down at him, the face absolutely calm, the grizzled eyebrows tangled above the cold eyes, the voice almost pleasant, almost gentle.

"You think so? Well, we'll wait till October anyway."

The matter of the wagon—the setting of a spoke or two and the tightening of the tires—did not take long either, the business of the tires accomplished by driving the wagon into the spring branch behind the shop and letting it stand there, the mule nuzzling into the water from time to time, and the boy on the seat with the idle reins, looking up the slope and through the sooty tunnel of the shed where the slow hammer rang and where his father sat on an upended cypress bolt, easily, either talking or listening, still sitting there when the boy brought the dripping wagon up out of the branch and halted it before the door.

"Take them on to the shade and hitch," his father said. He did so and returned. His father and the smith and a third man squatting on his heels inside the door were talking, about crops and animals; the boy, squatting too in the ammoniac dust and hoof-parings and scales of rust, heard his father tell a long and unhurried story out of the time before the birth of the older brother even when he had been a professional horsetrader. And then his father came up beside him where he stood before a tattered last year's circus poster on the other side of the store, gazing rapt and quiet at the scarlet horses, the incredible poisings and convolutions of tulle and tights and the painted leers of comedians, and said, "It's time to eat."

But not at home. Squatting beside his brother against the front wall, he watched his father emerge from the store and produce from a paper sack a segment of cheese and divide it carefully and deliberately into three with his pocket knife and produce crackers from the same sack. They all three squatted on the gallery and ate, slowly, without talking; then in the store again, they drank from a tin dipper tepid water smelling of the cedar bucket and of living beech trees. And still they did not go home. It was a horse lot this time, a tall rail fence upon and along which men stood and sat and out of which one by one horses were led, to be walked and trotted and then cantered back and forth along the road while the slow swapping and buying went on and the sun began to slant westward, they—the three of them—watching and listening, the older brother with his muddy eyes and his steady, inevitable tobacco, the father commenting now and then on certain of the animals, to no one in particular.

It was after sundown when they reached home. They ate supper by lamplight, then, sitting on the doorstep, the boy watched the night fully accomplish, listening to the whippoorwills and the frogs, when he heard his mother's voice: "Abner! No! No! Oh, God. Oh, God. Abner!" and he rose, whirled, and saw the altered light through the door where a candle stub now burned in a bottleneck on the table and his father, still in the hat and coat, at once formal and burlesque as though dressed carefully for some shabby and ceremonial violence, emptying the reservoir of the lamp back into the five-gallon kerosene can from which it had been filled, while the mother tugged at his arm until he shifted the lamp to the other hand and flung her back, not savagely or viciously, just hard, into the wall, her hands flung out against the wall for balance, her mouth open and in her face the same quality of hopeless despair as had been in her voice. Then his father saw him standing in the door.

"Go to the barn and get that can of oil we were oiling the wagon with," he said. The boy did not move. Then he could speak.

"What . . ." he cried. "What are you . . ."

"Go get that oil," his father said. "Go."

Then he was moving, running, outside the house, toward the stable: this the old habit, the old blood which he had not been permitted to choose for himself, which had been bequeathed him willy nilly and which had run for so long (and who knew where, battening on what of outrage and savagery and lust) before it came to him. *I could keep on,* he thought. *I could run on and on and never look back, never need to see his face again. Only I can't. I can't,* the rusted can in his hand now, the liquid splashing in it as he ran back to the house and into it, into the sound of his mother's weeping in the next room, and handed the can to his father.

"Ain't you going to even send a nigger?" he cried. "At least you sent a nigger before!"

This time his father didn't strike him. The hand came even faster than the blow had, the same hand which had set the can on the table with almost excruciating care flashing from the can toward him too quick for him to follow it, gripping him by the back of his shirt and on to tiptoe before he had seen it quit the can, the face stooping at him in breathless and frozen ferocity, the cold, dead voice speaking over him to the older brother who leaned against the table, chewing with that steady, curious, sidewise motion of cows.

"Empty the can into the big one and go on. I'll catch up with you."

"Better tie him up to the bedpost," the brother said.

"Do like I told you," the father said. Then the boy was moving, his bunched shirt and the hard, bony hand between his shoulder-blades, his toes touching the floor, across the room and into the other one, past the sisters sitting with spread heavy thighs in the two chairs over the cold hearth, and to where his mother and aunt sat side by side on the bed, the aunt's arms about his mother's shoulders.

"Hold him," the father said. The aunt made a startled movement. "Not you," the father said. "Lennie. Take hold of him. I want to see you do it." His mother took him by the wrist. "You'll hold him better than that. If he gets loose don't you know what he is going to do? He will go up yonder?" He jerked his head toward the road. "Maybe I'd better tie him."

"I'll hold him," his mother whispered.

"See you do then." Then his father was gone, the stiff foot heavy and measured upon the boards, ceasing at last.

Then he began to struggle. His mother caught him in both arms, he jerking and wrenching at them. He would be stronger in the end, he knew that. But he had no time to wait for it. "Lemme go!" he cried. "I don't want to have to hit you!"

"Let him go!" the aunt said. "If he don't go, before God, I am going up there myself!"

"Don't you see I can't?" his mother cried. "Sarty! Sarty! No! No! Help me, Lizzie!"

Then he began to struggle. His mother caught him in both arms, he whirled, running, his mother stumbled forward onto her knees behind him, crying to the nearer sister: "Catch him, Net! Catch him!" But that was too late too, the sister (the sisters were twins, born at the same time, yet either of them now gave the impression of being, encompassing as much living meat and volume and weight as any other two of the family) not yet having begun to rise from the chair, her head, face, alone merely turned, presenting to him in the flying instant an astonishing expanse of young female features untroubled by any surprise even, wearing only an expression of bovine interest. Then he was out of the room, out of the house, in the mild dust of the starlit road and the heavy rifeness of honeysuckle, the pale ribbon unspooling with terrific slowness under his running feet, reaching the gate at last and turning in, running, his heart and lungs drumming, on up the drive toward the lighted house, the lighted door. He did not knock, he burst in, sobbing for breath, incapable for the moment of speech; he saw the astonished face of the Negro in the linen jacket without knowing when the Negro had appeared.

"De Spain!" he cried, panted. "Where's . . ." then he saw the white man too emerging from a white door down the hall. "Barn!" he cried. "Barn!"

"What?" the white man said. "Barn?"

"Yes!" the boy cried. "Barn!"

"Catch him!" the white man shouted.

But it was too late this time too. The Negro grasped his shirt, but the entire sleeve, rotten with washing, carried away, and he was out that door too and in the drive again, and had actually never ceased to run even while he was screaming into the white man's face.

Behind him the white man was shouting, "My horse! Fetch my horse!" and he thought for an instant of cutting across the park and climbing the fence into the road, but he did not know the park nor how high the vine-massed fence might be and he dared not risk it. So he ran on down the drive, blood and breath roaring; presently he was in the road again though he could not see it. He could not hear either: the galloping mare was almost upon him before he heard her, and even then he held his course, as if the very urgency of his wild grief and need must in a moment more find him wings, waiting until the ultimate instant to hurl himself aside and into the weed-choked roadside ditch as the horse thundered past and on, for an instant in furious silhouette against the stars, the tranquil early summer night sky which, even before the shape of the horse and rider vanished, stained abruptly and violently upward: a long, swirling roar incredible and soundless, blotting the stars, and he springing up and into the road again, running again, knowing it was too late yet still running even after he heard the shot and, an instant later, two shots, pausing now without knowing he had ceased to run, crying "Pap! Pap!", running again before he knew he had begun to run, stumbling, tripping over something and scrabbling up again without ceasing to run, looking backward over his shoulder at the glare as he got up, running on among the invisible trees, panting, sobbing, "Father! Father!"

At midnight he was sitting on the crest of a hill. He did not know it was midnight and he did not know how far he had come. But there was no glare behind him now and he sat now, his back toward what he had called home for four days anyhow, his face toward the dark woods which he would enter when breath was strong again, small, shaking steadily in the chill darkness, hugging himself into the remainder of his thin, rotten shirt, the grief and despair now no longer terror and fear but just grief and despair. *Father. My father,* he thought. "He was brave!" he cried suddenly, aloud but not loud, no more than a whisper: "He was! He was in the war! He was in Colonel Sartoris' cav'ry!" not knowing that his father had gone to that war a private in the fine old European sense, wearing no uniform, admitting the authority of and giving fidelity to no man or army or flag, going to war as Malbrouck himself did: for booty—it meant nothing and less than nothing to him if it were enemy booty or his own.

The slow constellations wheeled on. It would be dawn and then sun-up after a while and he would be hungry. But that would be tomorrow and now he was only cold, and walking would cure that. His breathing was easier now and he decided to get up and go on, and then he found that he had been asleep because he knew it was almost dawn, the night almost over. He could tell that from the whippoorwills. They were everywhere now among the dark trees below him, constant and inflectioned and ceaseless, so that, as the instant for giving over to the day birds drew nearer and nearer, there was no interval at all between them. He got up. He was a little stiff, but walking would cure that too as it would the cold, and soon there would be the sun. He went on down the hill, toward the dark woods within which the liquid silver voices of the birds called unceasing—the rapid and urgent beating of the urgent and quiring heart of the late spring night. He did not look back.

1. A great deal happens in this story, so much that you may have trouble sorting it all out at first reading, especially in the first few pages and at the end. But you have to understand the situations and events before you can fully appreciate the characters and themes and other significances of the story. In the opening trial scene, about the first two pages, we are given situation, background, and an introduction to character in swift, deft strokes. One man is being accused of burning another's barn because the first let his hog into the other's cornfield and refused to mend his fence even when given the wire to do it with. Because there is no positive evidence, the accused is freed but warned to leave the neighborhood. We also learn that he has moved a dozen other times in the past ten years, and get a clear premonition that his past locks him into an inescapable future. Describe the uses which are made of this situation in the remainder of the story. In what ways is the second episode an outgrowth of the first?

2. This story is thronged with people, most of them sharply described, but two are central to the action, the father and the boy. Indeed, the chief interest of the story is not so much what happens as why it happens, and much of this interest is a direct outgrowth of the interplay between these two characters. The father says little, even in court, or when he strikes his children or his wife. Yet he seems to be dominated by a cold rage against those better off than he—"the Enemy," to use the boy's word. He is described as having a "wolflike independence and even courage," and "latent ravening ferocity," and yet is like "something cut ruthlessly from tin, depthless." It was not indolence that kept him from fencing his hog from Harris's cornfield, nor accident that made him foul Major de Spain's rug. He goes to the house to speak to the man who "aims" to own him "body and soul" as a sharecropper. He deliberately steps in the horse manure and scrapes his boots *after* he leaves the house. His wife could have cleaned the rug, and wanted to. After the girls wash it he deliberately scars it with a stone. Do you see anything more than simple resentment in his attitude toward those above him? What do you make of his remarks on looking back at the house: "Pretty and white, ain't it? . . . That's sweat. Nigger sweat. . . . Maybe he wants to mix some white sweat with it."

Yet there is a contradictory strain in the man's character. He knew that the boy would try to warn Major de Spain, and he must have known that the means he chose to restrain him would fail. Why then did he reject the older son's advice to tie the boy to the bedpost? Does this action suggest some obscure willingness to have the boy escape and betray him? some self-destructive urge? Does it appear that he is motivated by something more than the wish to get even with people by burning their barns?

About the boy, we learn early, and again near the end of the story, that he is full of "despair and grief," that the "old fierce pull of blood" keeps him loyal to his father in spite of shame and disapproval, even to the point where he attacks someone half again his size who has called his father "barn burner." It is this terrible loyalty which makes such an agony of the final break with his father and his flight from home. Can you cite evidence from the story to indicate how well or how poorly the boy had resolved his own divided feelings at the end? How do you learn about the father's fate? What words tell you the boy's decision about whether or not he will go home again? Compared with the older brother and the sisters, the boy is the brightest, most courageous member of the family. He is in a sense the family's only hope, yet it is his acts that leave it finally hopeless.

Compared with the father and the boy, the other characters are simply and straightforwardly drawn, each with a few bold and vivid strokes but without the same depth and complexity. Support or deny this statement by specific references to the story.

3. Any story can be told in many different ways, and one of the great challenges to any writer is to decide which characters and incidents to stress and which to play down or pass over entirely. Basic to many of these choices is the choice of point of view. In this story we learn through the consciousness of the boy a great deal of what happens. In the opening scene he is so hungry he "smells" canned food, and feels weightless with anticipation as at the end of a long swing on a grapevine when he thinks he will be called to testify against his father. Whenever in the story something is going to happen, the father takes the boy with him, so that the boy is always where the action is. Why does the father do this? Until the end, the only time the boy ignores a direct command from his father is when he stays in the courtroom instead of going "to the wagon" as ordered. How is this act of disobedience necessary to sustain the point of view?

Yet the boy is not the narrator; the author is the narrator. This way the author can know and say things through the privilege of omniscience which could not be said in the boy's own voice. Thus the author is able to tell us things about the father's early life which the boy cannot know, and we can appreciate the irony of the boy's lament, "He was brave! . . . He was in Colonel Sartoris' cav'ry!" Equally interesting, the author can also make significant comments about the man's nature that we could not get through the boy's consciousness. Discuss, for instance, the traits revealed by the author's observations on Snopes's "voracious prodigality" with material not his own; his treating a mule as his descendants would treat an automobile, by whipping and reining in, or racing and braking, simultaneously;

his killing a fly with a stick with no thought of whose back bore the blow. By his choice of point of view in this story Faulkner gains the best of two techniques, the first-person character and the omniscient author.

4. The interaction of events and characters gives to the story its structure or shape—roughly comparable to that of an hourglass. The action proceeds from the first barn-burning episode to the second, although the narrative itself does not move in a straight line from one to the other but begins with the trial scene which is both review and preview. Compare and contrast the two parts of the story. Both barn burnings have similarities and differences. How, in each episode, was Snopes a provocateur? What injury did he receive? How did his victims react, first to the provocation, then to the barn burning? How is the ending a logical outgrowth of the situation presented in the opening scene? What is the significance of the father's desire to involve the boy in the second burning by forcing him to get the can of oil?

5. Beyond the events of the story and the interaction of characters which the events relate, the story deals with certain themes. One we readily discern is the clash between the rich and the poor, the haves and the have-nots, the conflict which is often called the class struggle, though in this story it is also the Southern landowner and the sharecropper. The relationship between father and son is also an embodiment of the perennial conflict between generations, which goes currently under the name of the generation gap. Here the conflict takes the extreme form of repudiation in violent circumstances which leads to the double outcome of death and liberation.

6. There also are symbolic elements in the story. Major de Spain's white house may be taken as a symbol of the Southern aristocratic ideal. Would you say that the fouling of the rug was a symbolic act? And what of Snopes himself? His black clothes, his limp, and his affinity with the element of fire suggest a certain Satanic quality. The fact that he was a horse thief in the Civil War, loyal to no one but himself, suggests an element of cold and selfish evil, a kind of original sin whose consequences are visited upon his family, other people he has dealings with, and the section of the country of which he is as much a part as is Colonel Sartoris—the heroic and legendary other side of the coin—for whom his son is named.

This kind of analysis has two aims: first, to achieve a detailed understanding of the story through careful reading and thinking; second, to discover ideas for writing and the material to develop these ideas. Do you feel, as a result of the analysis, that you could now write a paper on one of the following topics?

Father and Son in "Barn Burning": A Study in the Generation Gap
Snopes: A Character Analysis
Faulkner's Handling of Point of View in "Barn Burning"

Hourglass Structure in "Barn Burning": A Study in Technique
Thematic Elements in "Barn Burning"

EXERCISE

As an exercise in prewriting, study the following poem with the intent of writing about it. In reading it, ask yourself questions about the nine elements discussed on pages 190–98. For example, who is speaking? to whom? about what? in what voice? Does the phrase "The Unknown Citizen" remind you of anything else? Have you ever heard of "The Unknown Soldier"? What is the significance of the comparison? Would you describe the diction as poetic or prosaic? What do the rhymes contribute to the overall impression the poem gives? Are they in harmony with the diction, or in contrast with it? What does the author appear to think about the society he is describing? Do you sense any irony in the poem? Cite references in the poem to support your opinions on these and other questions that occur to you.

The Unknown Citizen

by W. H. Auden

     (To JS/07/M/378
     This Marble Monument
     Is Erected by the State

He was found by the Bureau of Statistics to be
One against whom there was no official complaint,
And all the reports on his conduct agree
That, in the modern sense of an old-fashioned word, he was a saint,
For in everything he did he served the Greater Community.
Except for the War till the day he retired
He worked in a factory and never got fired,
But satisfied his employers, Fudge Motors Inc.
Yet he wasn't a scab or odd in his views,
For his Union reports that he paid his dues,
(Our report on his Union shows it was sound)
And our Social Psychology workers found
That he was popular with his mates and liked a drink.
The Press are convinced that he bought a paper every day
And that his reactions to advertisements were normal in every way.
Policies taken out in his name prove that he was fully insured,
And his Health-card shows he was once in hospital but left it cured.
Both Producers Research and High-Grade Living declare
He was fully sensible to the advantages of the Instalment Plan
And had everything necessary to the Modern Man,
A phonograph, a radio, a car and a frigidaire.
Our researchers into Public Opinion are content
That he held the proper opinions for the time of year;
When there was peace, he was for peace; when there was war, he went.

He was married and added five children to the population,
Which our Eugenist says was the right number for a parent of his generation,
And our teachers report that he never interfered with their education.
Was he free? Was he happy? The question is absurd:
Had anything been wrong, we should certainly have heard.

QUESTIONS OF EMPHASIS

Your response to a work of literature will usually reveal a concern with finding an answer to one or more of the three following types of questions:

1. *Questions of interpretation.* What does the work say or mean? If the work is hard to understand, it may be enough for any one paper to find out and explain its principal meaning. Questions of interpretation are basic in the sense that they must be answered before anything else is done.

2. *Questions of technical analysis.* If the work is not hard to understand but uses skillful or interesting devices to get its effects, you may limit yourself to discussing these devices: for example, how the writer creates suspense or shock, contrasts one event or mood with another, develops character, or uses symbols or irony to enrich his work.

3. *Questions of judgment and evaluation.* How significant is the work as a whole? Does the author give the reader a new or deeper understanding of his subject, or of any aspect of it? Is the conception of the subject consistently developed? In answering such questions you will be trying to judge the contribution that the work makes or fails to make.

Any single paper may be limited to answering one of these types of questions, or it may combine two or three types. The three types of questions are not independent of each other, but you may prefer in your paper to put your emphasis on any one of them. Your decision about what to emphasize will be determined by what seems to you the most interesting or the most significant feature of the work. That decision will provide you with the real subject of your paper.

Interpretation

A writer who interprets a work is showing how he reads it, what it means to him. He may say, "This is what the work means" or "This is its meaning," but the interpretation does not lie in the work; it lies in the mind of the interpreter. This distinction is not a quibble. Here are eight interpretations of Shakespeare's *Hamlet,* each advanced and supported by a critic with considerable claim to being an authority on the subject:

1. *Hamlet* is a play about a man who could not make up his mind.

2. *Hamlet* is Shakespeare's refinement of a traditional revenge play.

3. *Hamlet* is the tragedy of a charming and accomplished prince who is a victim of melancholia.

4. *Hamlet* is the tragedy of a moral man corrupted by the evil standards and pressures of an evil environment.

5. *Hamlet* is a dramatic illustration of an Oedipus complex, of a young man who loves his mother and resents his father and stepfather as rivals.

6. *Hamlet* is the portrayal of an ambassador of death who brings ruin to all with whom he is intimately associated.

7. *Hamlet* is a study of the ruthlessness required of kings, and of the trouble that ensues in the state when the leader's sense of political responsibility is weakened by conscientious misgivings.

8. *Hamlet* is a spectacle play, the appeal of which lies in a series of spectacular scenes presented on the stage.

The fact that these eight interpretations exist does not mean that anything goes, or that any opinion is as good as any other. It means, rather, that like life itself, some works of literature and art are so rich and varied that they can be interpreted in a variety of ways. While it is generally true that one interpretation gives greater weight to some aspects of the evidence and less to others, it is by no means true that any opinion is therefore as good as any other. Indeed, no interpretation is worthy of expression unless it can be supported by detailed evidence from the text. There is a standard of reliability which requires that the interpretation contradict neither the text being examined, nor those facts about the author and his work which have been firmly established by scholarly research.

Interpretation is never mere summary. Telling the story of a play or a novel, or paraphrasing a poem, is almost never what is expected in a critical paper. The assignment requires that the student find meaning in the work, and this a summary cannot do. For example, a summary of John Barth's *Giles Goat-Boy* would simply tell what happened in the novel, incident by incident, as each occurs. The following paper does tell something of what happens, so that the reader gets some idea of the main lines of the story. But the focus is on interpreting the allegories in which the writer believes the author has cloaked his meaning. The main effort is thus focused on what the work means. For this writer, evaluation is therefore incidental.

Allegory in *Giles Goat-Boy* by John Barth

Allegory is a kind of narrative in which something concrete stands for something abstract. While in this book the things stood for are not always much more abstract than the things that stand for them, it is certainly true that everything stands for at least one thing, and sometimes two or three things, different from itself. While the book is interesting in many other ways, part of its fascination for me was in trying to untangle the allegorical threads out of which its complex plot is woven. This paper deals with a few of the main threads; there are a number of others.

First, the main setting of the book is the "West Campus" of a university which we soon see is the world. There is also an "East Campus," there have been "Campus Riots" I and II, a "Quiet Riot" is going on at the time of the story, and there is a deep fear of Campus Riot III. Read "War" for "Riot" and the allegory of our time is clear. Besides, in the last "Riot" the Siegfrieder Campus (Germany) was defeated, but only after the massacre of a great many Moishians (Jews). Moreover, there is a constant "boundary dispute" now going on between East and West Campuses, in which skirmishes are frequent but nobody ever wins.

We might call this "Allegory I." It merges into "Allegory II" early in the book when we realize that the machinery and administration of the West Campus is run by a computer called WESCAC, which has an eastern counterpart EASCAC, which is also powerful and efficient but not so much so. WESCAC came first, and is very important in the allegory of the book as a whole. Created by campus intellectuals, it was simple at first—did sums and performed simple calculations. Even as late as Campus Riot II it depended on a few scientists who fed it data and used its answers. But then they taught it to eat people (atomic radiation), and they made the fatal mistake of making it so complex that it developed a consciousness, a will and appetites of its own, and the ability to program its own work. It thus grew independent; it dominated the campus, and the university—the nation and the world.

Two of the scientists who helped create it, but from whom it became independent, were Eblis Eyerkopf and Maximilian Spielman. Eyerkopf is German for "egghead," and Eblis, according to the dictionary, is a devil or evil spirit in Islamic myth. Eyerkopf is the "pure" scientist to whom the problem is everything and its effects on human beings mean less than nothing. Spielman, whose name can be interpreted to mean "story-teller" is, in contrast, the humane scientist, and the one who has been banished from the campus because he wants no "supermind" computer. Penniless, he then gets the job of tending the goat barn that belongs to the Ag School. Ironically, it was he who pushed the button that "ate" the Amaterasus (the Japanese—at Hiroshima) because they knew the Germans were working on an atom bomb and it was a race to see who got it first. (Ironic allegorical sidelight: Eyerkopf is impotent and Spielman is sterile; a comment on scientists in general?)

Spielman leads to "Allegory III" and the heart of the story, the Goat-Boy, its central character and hero. He is fourteen when we meet him; he has been brought up as a goat in the goat barn, and he thinks he is a goat. At that age, an injury to his foot cripples him and brings him special attention. Spielman teaches him to be human and tutors him for seven years, and by then his head is so full of ambition and excitement that he sets off to make his way into the university, in order to correct the aim of the computer and make it more humane, and to become a Grand Tutor.

By this time, when he is twenty-one and leaves the goat barn to make his way onto the West Campus, the Goat-Boy has developed many of the marks of the typical hero. His parentage is unknown, he is embarked on a quest against almost insuperable odds, he is handsome and appealing beneath a comic and countryish appearance, and he is a cripple. He also thinks of himself as having a grand mission. His adventures from this point on make up the body of the book. Against great odds he gets into the campus by winning two contests that get him through two ordinarily impassable barriers. One of these is called the "scapegrate," suggesting that he is, among other things, a scapegoat figure. He wants to enter the university not for himself, but to save "studentdom" and to correct the "aim" of the computer. Another element is his search for his identity, and he learns that the computer is supposed to have given birth to a human child, after it discovered in an experiment on animal eugenics that it could enjoy sex! At almost the moment that our hero (now called George) gets onto the campus, he discovers he has a rival, a glib impostor called Harold Bray, who through most of the book convinces the campus that he and not George is the Grand Tutor, and only at the end is shown to be false.

George reminds us not only of a scapegoat, but of several other things also. In the book there is a crude satire of the Greek tragedy *Oedipus Rex,* and it is hard not to connect George with Oedipus—because of his crippled foot, first of all, but also because both were abandoned in infancy and in different ways are searching for a father.

Also, the computer gives George a series of tasks, somewhat like the labors of Hercules. After he performs these and passes all his trials, he is finally admitted to the belly of the computer and discovers that he is indeed the son of the computer, and also of a virgin—so there are elements of the Christ-Saviour theme too. Other suggestions of this are that in the last part of the book George is always in and out of "Main Detention," suffering in jail for the sins of the campus, trying to get the students to "Commencement" (salvation) and going mostly unheard.

The allegorical elements in the book remind me of a set of Chinese boxes: they go on almost endlessly, and seem to fit perfectly into each other. There are many more, but these are the main ones, set in a pessimistic theme which is very strongly stated at the beginning of the book and again at the end. At the beginning we read:

> Nothing "works," in the sense we commonly hope for; a certain goat-boy has taught me that; everything only gets worse, gets worse; our victories are never more than moral, and always pyrrhic; in fact we know only more or less ruinous defeats.

And at the end:

> Nay, rather, for worse, always for worse. Late or soon, we lose. Sudden or slow, we lose. The bank exacts its charge for each redistribution of our funds. There is an entropy to time, a tax on change; four nickels for two dimes; but always less silver; our books stay reconciled, but who in modern terms can tell heads from tails?

Thus, the book is fundamentally very pessimistic, though often the author forgets his pessimism, and is just plain funny and often dirty. But he almost never forgets some allegory, and sometimes it is possible to see two or three different but consistent allegories all going on at the same time. That is the main reason why the book fascinated me so much.

From start to finish this writer was trying to find out what the book means. Further, he limited his discussion to a few main allegorical threads, and simply indicated that there were other elements of meaning that he didn't plan to take up in this paper. His selection and arrangement of the strands of allegory which he discusses are essentially subjective. In the book the goat-boy's seven years' tutoring precedes the description of the warring campuses and the computer, but this writer changed the order, believing that these themes would be easier for his reader to grasp if he first described what he thought of as the setting. Other elements in the novel he scarcely mentioned, because his purpose, to show how Barth used allegory to express his meaning, was best served—or so at least he thought—by dwelling on the themes he chose to stress.

Technical Analysis

As already indicated, technical analysis comments on the means used to develop the situation, characters, action, theme, structure, or symbolism of the work. If we define "style" as the way a work is written, technical analysis deals with those stylistic features which most merit attention. Such an analysis emphasizes the *how* of the work, not the *what* or the *how well*.

The following extract from another critical paper focuses on technical analysis by showing how James Thurber handles contrasts and transitions in "The Secret Life of Walter Mitty."

What makes "The Secret Life of Walter Mitty" more than just another amusing short story is Thurber's unique and effective use of contrasts. Consider, for example, the first three paragraphs. Here the Walter Mitty of imagination is placed side by side with the Walter Mitty of reality. The contrast between the iron-hearted Naval Commander, bravely giving orders to his men, and the chicken-hearted Walter Mitty, timidly taking orders from his wife, is quite apparent. But the use of contrasts is by no means restricted to the beginning of the story. On the contrary, it is employed all the way through to the very last word. Compare the quick-thinking Doctor Mitty, famous surgeon, to the Walter Mitty who cannot park his car, remove his tire chains, or readily remember to buy a box of puppy biscuits. Compare also the "greatest shot in the world" or the daring Captain Mitty, or the "erect and motionless, proud and disdainful, Walter Mitty the Undefeated" with the Walter Mitty who seeks the quiet refuge of a big leather chair in a hotel lobby. Contrasts are effective tools for any writer, but the straightforward manner in which Thurber employs them enhances their effectiveness considerably.

After briefly skimming through the collection of contrasts that makes up "The Secret Life of Walter Mitty," one might feel that there is little connection between the paragraphs describing the imagined Walter Mitty and the Mitty of reality. However, closer observation reveals that Thurber does, by the use of suggestive words and phrases, cleverly establish links between the Mitty of fact and the Mitty of fancy. Examine the following lines taken from the end of paragraph one and the beginning of paragraph two of "The Secret Life of Walter Mitty":

> ". . . The Old Man'll get us through," they said to one another. "The Old Man ain't afraid of Hell!" . . .
> "Not so fast! You're driving too fast!" said Mrs. Mitty. "What are you driving so fast for?"

We shudder to think that there might be a connection between Hell and life with Mrs. Mitty, but, unfortunately, such could be the case. Consider how Mrs. Mitty's mention of Doctor Renshaw and the event of driving by a hospital lead to a daydream in which Walter Mitty, a distinguished surgeon, assists Doctor Renshaw in a difficult operation. Take note also of how a newsboy's shout about the Waterbury trial initiates the trial of Walter Mitty in the following paragraph. Such skillful employment of transitions, by which an event in reality triggers an event in the imagination, is sound not only from the literary standpoint, but also from the psychological point of view.

This writer has not concerned himself with interpretation, which is not a problem in the story. Instead, he has analyzed structural details. First he treats the repeated use of contrasts in moving back and forth between the "real" world of Walter Mitty and the more satisfying life of his daydreams, and gives illustrations of this movement. Next he demonstrates that the opposing elements in each of the contrasts have a subtle connection in language and thought. These connections provide swift transition from fantasy to fact, and create much of the humor as well as the pathos of the piece.

Judgment and Evaluation

In interpretation the writer discusses what the work means; in technical analysis he discusses how effects are achieved; in judgment he discusses the work's significance. At this stage, more clearly than at the others, he evaluates the work by expressing an opinion of it as a whole. Once more, to support his opinion he cites evidence from the text, and the evidence usually includes some technical analysis.

The following student essay makes judgments based on a contrast between two versions of the same work. The student has restricted her discussion to the portrayal of Dr. Zhivago's character in the motion picture and in the book. All she has to say bears on that contrast. She makes no attempt to interpret either this novel or this film as a whole, but she makes a strong point about the qualitative difference between the novel and the film as media. Read the essay and discuss your answers to the questions that follow it.

Two Faces of Zhivago

[1] I have become accustomed to the metamorphosis a novel undergoes before it is presented to the motion picture audience. Until recently, however,

it had not occurred to me to note particularly the types of changes that are effected, nor to ask why these changes are made. It was easy to shrug and say, "That's Hollywood for you." Several weeks ago, however, after seeing the movie adaptation of *Doctor Zhivago,* I decided to read the book. A very different title character emerges from the novel. So marked is the contrast between the two Dr. Zhivagos that I am *now* asking myself a far more specific and persistent *why?*

[2] What are the two faces of Zhivago, that of Zhivago-S (screen version) and that of Zhivago-N (novel)? Zhivago-S is patterned on the Shakespearean hero: he is a dashing, towering nobleman whose one tragic flaw, his adulterous affair with Lara, precipitates his downfall. The bloody Russian Revolution is merely the backdrop against which Zhivago's real drama is pitted: a love triangle composed of Yurii Zhivago, a sensitive and gifted doctor, his vibrant wife, Tonia, and his fiery mistress, Lara. This Zhivago faces the socialistic upheaval of his country with stoic acceptance and even optimism. Moved to love and serve all mankind, he generously offers his skill as a medical doctor and his talent as a poet. Zhivago-S is the embodiment of the ideals we hold dear in Western culture: truth, courage, compassion, and service. Despite his illicit love, this man is far more saint than sinner.

[3] How does Zhivago-N, the character actually created by Boris Pasternak, differ? Here, in contrast to the Shakespearean hero, is the common man as hero, a hero of a very different sort: a complex and morose man of many moods. The irrepressibly passionate love for Lara is only one of the many conflicts hammering at him. Perhaps the greatest torment he suffers is the sea of blood engulfing his native country, the condition he describes as a "senseless, murderous mess." Deeply troubled by the erosion of what he feels to be genuine character and originality, he finds that people of the new order have become dim, colorless, and even animalistic: "Man is a wolf to man." He is anything but optimistic, and he is not moved to love and serve all mankind. Even his own profession must be prostituted as he is forced to espouse political loyalty first, and practice medicine only incidentally. He comes to look upon his medical and diagnostic skill as "claptrap, not work" under this new regime. Zhivago-N is neither handsome nor saintly. Even his adoring wife, Tonia, realizes this. In the part of the letter omitted from the screen version that she writes to him, she cites his frailties:

> I love all that is unusual in you, the good with the bad, and all the ordinary traits of your character, whose extraordinary combination is so dear to me, your face ennobled by your thoughts, which otherwise might not seem handsome, your great gifts and intelligence, which, as it were, have taken the place of the will that is lacking.

[4] Those who have been confronted only by Zhivago-S may be left with a very sentimental portrait. I wonder, for instance, how many of those who have met only him realize that Tonia and Lara are not the only women in his life. After Lara, there is a Marina whom he is not free to marry but by whom he

also has two children; this family he also abandons, this time by his own choice, instead of by revolutionary circumstances, in order to devote his time to his writing. Somewhat disillusioning behavior for a saintly man. And they undoubtedly would be somewhat disappointed to learn that Zhivago's fatal heart attack is not at all triggered by his frenzied but tragically romantic chase of a woman he thinks is his long-lost Lara. Indeed, Lara is not even in his thoughts as he lunges painfully from the trolley to collapse on the Moscow streets. Whereas Zhivago-S faces every crisis to the end of his life with persevering courage, Zhivago-N, as developed by Pasternak, goes "more and more to seed, gradually losing his knowledge and skill as a doctor and a writer." His tragic life renders him indifferent: "Yurii . . . gave up medicine, neglected himself, stopped seeing his friends, and lived in great poverty."

[5] After viewing and experiencing these two divergent faces of Zhivago, I do indeed wonder why the screenwriters feel this distortion of the original character is necessary. If the adapting writer's first responsibility is to a producer who wants a box-office smash, then the changes that are made would probably serve to produce a hero of greater appeal to the American theater-going audience of the 1960's. There's little reason to doubt the wisdom of their efforts if this is the goal: "Doctor Zhivago" was and still is an enormously popular film. Could this popularity be a commentary on *our* values and taste? Are we, for example, unable to accept in our tragic hero his great strengths offset by a petty combination of human weaknesses bubbling intermittently to the surface: temper, profound depression, disloyalty even to dear ones, bitterness, stark indifference? Perhaps we sympathize with one adulterous love, but really must draw the line at two. Can we not identify with a hero who throws away his skills and talent because he is repeatedly lashed—finally beyond his endurance—by forces in his society and within himself that he cannot subdue? Are we too sophisticated or too cowardly to hear from Zhivago's lips the language of emotional force that is never emitted from the strong, taciturn Zhivago-S: the religious fervor, the political fury, the soul-searching lyric poetry, the heightened personal philosophy by which he is tragically unable to pattern his life? Perhaps the screenwriter's portrayal of Zhivago does indeed say something significant about us: apparently we prefer to leave the theater comfortably sighing, "Dear me, what a sad love story!" rather than weeping, "Dear God, what a tragic life!"

1. What is the function of the first paragraph of this paper? Which sentence in that paragraph gives the most specific clue to what the writer is going to do in this essay?

2. What are the functions of paragraphs 2 and 3? How are these paragraphs necessary to the writer's purpose?

3. What is the function of paragraph 4?

4. What is the function of paragraph 5 and what is the relation of that paragraph to the first one?

5. Is there any technical analysis of the means by which the screen version changes the character of Zhivago? Explain your answer.

6. What is the student's general conclusion about why these changes are made?

7. Admitting that there could be other judgments about the screen version, do you think the writer has effectively supported her judgment? Explain your answer.

EXERCISES

A. *The following paper discusses a television series based on a group of novels, John Galsworthy's* The Forsyte Saga. *Read it and answer the questions which follow.*

Forsytes Unlimited

The winter of *The Forsyte Saga* witnessed what had never happened before, an unlimited national love-affair with a story and a set of characters. You hear about popular plays and books like *Uncle Tom's Cabin* and *Pickwick Papers,* which had their fans and drew large audiences. But their "box office" was hardly anything compared to the number of people who could hardly wait for each new episode of *The Forsyte Saga.* It was shown on NET Sunday nights for a whole winter, and had replays on stations in various cities on just about every night in the week. People formed clubs and gave dinners to see it. While it is not possible to guess how many people saw it, the number must have run into the tens of millions, and it was seen and talked about by people all the way up and down the social ladder. You had to go a long way to find somebody who didn't like it.

Why? *The Forsyte Saga* was originally written by an author with a life-span which went from 1867 to 1933, and it includes six novels, the first of which was written in 1906 and the last in 1928. The first books take place in the middle of the Victorian period, and the last ones in the 1920's. That is, they closely agreed with the life-span of the author, so he knew his subject from experience, and in each book was near enough to its time to write about it first hand. I haven't read all the novels, but I read some of them all through and some part way. Thus I believe that I can back up the above statement, although I did feel that he created the characters and imagined the settings and happenings of the earlier books better than the later ones. Irene and Philip Bosinney and young Jolyon are more real and lifelike in the books than Fleur and Michael and Jon. I believe that is because the author was writing about the love affairs of the earlier people when he was a young man, and about the later group when he was older and did not have such a close perspective on such things. This difference shows up strongly in spite of the author's skill, and I think most readers of the books would agree with me.

However, in the television series, this was not true. I saw the whole set once, and quite a few of the installments, from both parts of the series, more than once. I would swear that they were produced and acted just as well all the way through from the beginning to the end. The first set of lovers in the Victorian period were very intense and their emotions and actions were very believable. The same thing was true for the second set. Likewise this quality of reality was the same for other things in the television series, in both parts. The early part was very full of carefully worked out details about the lives of the people in Victorian times, the way they dressed and decorated their houses, their ideas about wealth and family and property and morality. Also in the later part of the series, Fleur's unhappiness, and Michael's career, and the libel suit all seemed very real, and Fleur's parlor looked in every way just the way you imagine a drawing room in the 1920's would have looked; even if you never saw one before, now you suddenly "knew." The same is true of the clothes and the make-up, the morals and the conversation. Likewise there is enough happening in the later part of the series so that it does not seem to thin out the way the books do.

I believe the reason for this difference in the books but not in the TV series is that the series was written, produced, and acted in a short time by a single group of people, so that their enthusiasm, knowledge of the subject, and feeling about the story and characters would be the same all the way through. I don't think this was true of the author, but that he was "closer" to the earlier books than to the later ones. That is why I believe that while the early series is even with the early books, the later books fall behind the series. The series is unified in ways which the books are not, and that is one reason for its success.

I think, however, that there is also another reason why the series was so successful. All the way through it is easy for the viewer to identify with the characters, the events in their lives, and their love affairs and their sufferings. The characters are presented as mature people, so it is easy for a mature viewer to sympathize and feel for them. Besides, they are easy to understand as people, and so are the things which happen to them. Their motives are not hard to figure out, and yet we can take them and their problems seriously. Also there are no complicated allegories or symbols or any hidden meanings. Everything is about regular daily types of people, and the focus of the story is always on them and what happens to them. Yet the people and the events are grown up enough to be taken seriously even by people who think of themselves as very sophisticated. This is probably more true of the TV series than of the books, otherwise why would the books not have been more popular before the series? Perhaps even more important than this is what I think is the highest accomplishment of the TV production, that it does everything so well, makes it so real and so interesting, that you never see until afterwards how simple and easy yet how acceptable it all has been. It will be a long time before there is another *Forsyte Saga*.

1. Is this paper primarily an interpretation, a technical analysis, a judgment, or some combination of these?

2. How much of the paper is devoted to summary?
3. How much of it is devoted to a comparison or contrast between the television series and the novels on which it was based? In answering this question pay particular attention to how much of the paper is comparison and how much is contrast.
4. Does the paper have a thesis? Is it specifically stated? If so, where?
5. Is the author's final paragraph convincing?
6. Does the paper contain any surprises? Does the author seem to change his point of view, or say anything not anticipated from the beginning? How consistent is he?

B. *Following is a student paper about Arthur Miller's play* Death of a Salesman. *Read it and answer the questions which follow it.*

Death of a Sad Man

It may be difficult to determine whether or not *Death of a Salesman* fits the classical definition of tragedy, but there is no difficulty in seeing that it is one of the most moving and important contributions to the realm of modern theater. The problem which confronts Willy Loman is one which almost every human being must face at one time or another during his life. What do you do when you find that your dreams will never be anything more than dreams? What do you do when your self-image is tarnished and dented and finally destroyed by reality? What do you do when you fail?

Willy Loman suffers from his ineptness more than the average person because he has made success the basis for his whole life, and success is one thing which Willy has never achieved. Most people discover failure early in their lives and are able to make the necessary adjustments to keep their personal world and goals in perspective. Sooner or later we all realize that only a gifted few will ever conquer their environment and that the rest of us will have to be content with an uneasy compromise. Happiness can be found within the confines of a family. The bond of love can be the basis for any life. Unfortunately, Willy Loman has always frosted over his defeats and failures; he has never come to grips with himself and his problem. Because of this, he has never really been able to appreciate Linda, the wife who has loved him so faithfully despite all his faults. Through his constant deification of success, he has warped the values of his two sons until they hold the same views which have been Willy's downfall.

The strongest bond which Willy has been able to build between himself and another person is the one with his oldest son Biff. As Willy starts to grow older, he subconsciously begins to realize that the goals he has set for himself are unattainable. But, he tells himself, there is still one way open. Through Biff, Willy feels he can accomplish the things which up to now he has only dreamed of. Now the world will see what a Loman is made of. It almost seems possible, for Biff idolizes his father, but Willy's relationship with his son carries the seed of its own destruction. It is inevitable that Biff will realize that his father and everything his father believes in constitute nothing more than one lie piled on top of another. When Biff finds his father in a cheap hotel with a strange woman seeking the low and common pleasures which ill befit a man of success and character, he is lost and betrayed. The father whom he had idolized never really existed. His father's principles, in which he had believed, are nothing but lies and falsehoods. What can he do but reject his father and everything he stands for? Everything which had motivated him to love and admire his father before now fosters hatred and disgust.

And where does this leave Willy? It leaves him without any hope of making his mark upon the world. Now the failures, and defeats, and trivialities of a lifetime, which the intricacies of the human mind had so mercifully spared Willy, come back to him and he is forced to accept them for the realities which they are. It is a slow process, one which can last years. It is also a tragic process, especially for a man whose life has had a basis the like of Willy Loman's. Can any man look back on a life of failure when he knows that his failures have destroyed not only himself but the son for whom he had wanted so much? If there is such a man, it is not Willy Loman.

1. How much space does the author of this paper devote to (*a*) summary? (*b*) interpretation? (*c*) technical analysis? (*d*) evaluation?
2. Can you find an expressed thesis in the paper?
3. How well can you describe the action and story of the play from information given in this review?
4. Does the author leave you with a clear sense of the play's worth as a piece of literature? as a comment on life?
5. After reading this paper do you want to read or see the play? Explain your answer in detail.

C. *Below are a poem and two student papers about it. For each criticism, discuss its structure, content, and effectiveness; then write a short paper comparing the two.*

A Noiseless Patient Spider

by Walt Whitman

A noiseless patient spider,
I mark'd where on a little promontory it stood isolated,
Mark'd how to explore the vacant vast surrounding,
It launch'd forth filament, filament, filament, out of itself,
Ever unreeling them, ever tirelessly speeding them.

And you O my soul where you stand,
Surrounded, detached, in measureless oceans of space,
Ceaselessly musing, venturing, throwing, seeking the spheres to connect them,
Till the bridge you will need be form'd, till the ductile anchor hold,
Till the gossamer thread you fling catch somewhere, O my soul.

Student Paper 1

"A Noiseless Patient Spider" illustrates that what is avant-garde for one generation may become trite for another. In his own time, Whitman was an innovator, breaking loose from prescribed forms into free verse, substituting a passionate outpouring of responses for the more restrained observations of conventional poets. This poem provides a representative example of his achievement.

The whole poem rests on a comparison between the attempts of a spider to fasten the first thread for its web and the attempts of the human soul to find its security. In each action, the one real and specific, the other abstract and more vague, the process is one of continual trial and error. Within the poem, neither the spider nor the soul actually achieves success, but one feels that the process of trying will continue.

In order to express this continuity, Whitman uses appropriate devices of diction, syntax, and meter. The inclusion of several words ending in "ing" in both stanzas, the repetition of "filament" in the first stanza and "O my soul" in the second, and the long lines of the second stanza tend to elongate the action. All of the first stanza is a single sentence, which also conveys an impression of length. The second stanza suggests endlessness because it is an incomplete sentence.

Since the two stanzas compare such very different things as a spider and a soul, the poet has connected them with a common body of metaphor, using images of a boat in a vast ocean trying to get an anchor hold on some solid ground. The poem includes, then, three major images: the spider, the soul, and the boat unreeling its anchor rope.

If Whitman uses an accepted poetic device of comparing a specific item from nature with something more abstract, and follows the standard for good poetry by making his form appropriate to his meaning, why isn't this poem really interesting? I think it is because his idea is trite. Everyone knows the old story of Robert Bruce's watching the spider and making its patient aspiration the model for his own behavior. The poem seems to say almost the same thing, but in a more artificial way. Perhaps, too, poetry has progressed beyond Whitman to the point where we no longer appreciate such a simple comparison as this one. The reader can see the meaning easily, and will probably accept it with boredom and no argument. In our time, it is scarcely news to learn that each individual is isolated in a vast world and must try to establish lines of communication with someone or something outside himself. An excellent poem will outlast its own time, but this one, after the passage of a century, is very old-fashioned.

Student Paper 2

Walt Whitman is usually considered one of America's greatest poets. In my opinion, his reputation is unwarranted. "A Noiseless Patient Spider" offers evidence of some of the things which baffle the reader in Whitman's poems and raises a serious question whether this is really good poetry.

The poem is divided into two stanzas, each with five lines. The lines within stanzas are of unequal lengths and employ various metrical patterns, in the manner of free verse. The free-verse writer has poetic license to use this variety, but it is difficult to remember a poem when there is so little regularity in its pattern. I always feel that a poem like this isn't really finished, that the poet has stopped work before he was able to bring his idea into a more organized form.

The inadequate form in this poem conveys meaning that is also somewhat defective. The first stanza sets out to describe a spider's actions in beginning to make its web. Anyone who has ever watched a spider will immediately recognize that Whitman's description is inaccurate. The thread is actually extruded from a spider's body in a kind of slow, squeezing motion, which makes such words as "launch'd," "unreeling," and "speeding" seem inappropriate. The poet should have observed more carefully before setting out to write his descriptive verses.

In the second stanza, the poet turns to another idea and directly addresses his soul. Since the activities of a soul are not observable, one cannot complain of inaccuracy here. Yet it seems awkward to think of a human soul as throwing an anchor or flinging a gossamer thread. The poet has obviously tried to make the abstract idea of the soul more concrete, but, in my opinion, he has made it ridiculous.

One may well ask why Whitman wrote this poem. He ventures into the world of nature and comes out with a description which is neither accurate nor beautiful. He makes an impassioned plea to his soul, but it is impossible to discover what he is asking or what his final conclusion is about the soul. To be good, a poem, like any other communication, should have a purpose beyond the mere putting of words on paper.

D. *As an exercise in interpretation, critical analysis, and judgment, write a paper about one of the following poems.*

Tree at My Window

by Robert Frost

Tree at my window, window tree,
My sash is lowered when night comes on;
But let there never be curtain drawn
Between you and me.

Vague dream-head lifted out of the ground,
And thing next most diffuse to cloud,
Not all your light tongues talking aloud
Could be profound.

But tree, I have seen you taken and tossed,
And if you have seen me when I slept,
You have seen me when I was taken and swept
And all but lost.

That day she put our heads together,
Fate had her imagination about her,
Your head so much concerned with outer,
Mine with inner, weather.

beware   :   do not read this poem

by Ishmael Reed

tonite   ,   *thriller* was
abt an ol woman   , so vain she
surrounded herself w/
      many mirrors

it got so bad that finally she
locked herself indoors & her
whole life became the
      mirrors

one day the villagers broke
into her house   ,   but she was too
swift for them   .   she disappeared
      into a mirror

each tenant who bought the house
after that   ,   lost a loved one to
      the ol woman in the mirror   :
      first a little girl
      then a young woman
      then the young woman/s husband

the hunger of this poem is legendary
it has taken in many victims
back off from this poem
it has drawn in yr feet
back off from this poem
it has drawn in yr legs

back off from this poem
it is a greedy mirror
you are into this poem   .   from
    the waist down
nobody can hear you can they   ?
this poem has had you up to here
    belch
this poem aint got no manners
you cant call out frm this poem
relax now & go w/ this poem
move & roll on to this poem
do not resist this poem
this poem has yr eyes
this poem has his head
this poem has his arms
this poem has his fingers
this poem has his fingertips

this poem is the reader & the
reader this poem

statistic   :   the us bureau of missing persons reports
            that in 1968 over 100,000 people disappeared
            leaving no solid clues
                    nor trace   only
    a space   in the lives of their friends

___

WRITING THE PAPER

Writing a critical paper is not basically different from writing an expository one. Each requires that you know what you want to say and how you want to say it. If your prewriting has been efficient, you have at least a tentative answer to these two considerations. The job of the first draft is to develop the plan you have in mind; the job of the revision is to see in what respects the first draft can be improved. The advice that follows is simply an application of purposeful writing to a particular assignment.

1. *Determine your real subject.* Your real subject is what you really want to do in the paper. You cannot say everything about any subject; therefore you must decide what particular aspect of the subject you want to deal with. Usually that decision will be made in your prewriting. In a story like "Barn Burning" you almost have to devote considerable attention to technical analysis. In a contrast of the movie and book versions of a novel you are almost forced to explain differences and judge the relative merits of both. With some works you may feel that what you have to say requires a balanced treatment of technical analysis, interpretation, and judgment. There is no formula for deciding which approach is best. You do what seems best to you for a given work.

2. *Make clear to your reader what your real subject is.* One good way is to begin with a thesis. Notice how the theses of some of the essays we have read announce the idea that controls the development of the paper:

"A Noiseless Patient Spider" illustrates that what is avant-garde for one generation may become trite for another.

Walt Whitman is usually considered one of America's greatest poets. In my opinion, his reputation is unwarranted.

The winter of *The Forsyte Saga* witnessed what had never happened before, an unlimited national love-affair with a story and a set of characters.

What makes "The Secret Life of Walter Mitty" more than just another amusing story is Thurber's unique and effective use of contrasts.

If the paper you plan does not lend itself to beginning with a thesis, there are various other ways of introducing your real subject—by an appropriate anecdote or illustration or quotation that will suggest the main concerns of the paper, or with a statement of the problem to be considered. Notice that "Two Faces of Zhivago" has no expressed thesis but begins with a statement of the question which the author plans to answer.

3. *Select and evaluate your material.* Whether you are writing an interpretation, a technical analysis, or a judgment, you have to be persuasive. The best way to be persuasive is to base your comments on the facts of the text so that your reader sees why you say what you do. It is not enough to tell him that a character or an event is symbolic; you must show him the textual evidence for that opinion. In a sense, every piece of literary criticism is an argument that the author must prove. Mere assertion won't do; you have to build as strong a case as you can for your conclusions. To be persuasive the evidence must be both pertinent and adequate. To be pertinent it must clearly support the conclusion you are drawing. To be adequate there must be enough evidence so that it becomes cumulatively persuasive. The critic, therefore, must always be concerned with two questions: Does my evidence support my point, and is that evidence enough?

4. *Summarize purposefully.* One of the questions you will face is how much summary your reader will need. Any unnecessary summary is a waste of valuable space. But if a reader is not familiar with the work he will need some background to appreciate the pertinence and significance of your comment. The best procedure is to summarize only when necessary, and then only as much as is necessary. The paper on *Goat-Boy* tells enough about the three allegories and what they mean so that the reader can follow the reasoning with ease. And the writer gives enough information about the general content of the novel so that the reader has some grasp of it. At the same time, there are scores of characters, dozens of episodes, and whole story lines he doesn't mention at all, since these are not essential to his point. Likewise, the paper on Walter Mitty stresses Thurber's skillful use of contrast and transition, but there are many details it doesn't mention.

If your essay is a criticism of a poem, it will help the reader if you give him the text of the poem so that he can consult it while reading your comments. The first paper on "A Noiseless Patient Spider" (page 228) illustrates this practice.

5. *Use quotations when you need to, but do not overuse them.* All three of the papers we have just studied use quotations, and all use them with restraint. The paper on *Goat-Boy* quotes two brief passages on the same theme, one from the beginning of the novel, the other from the end. The paper on Walter Mitty makes excellent use of one brief quotation which illustrates Thurber's skill with contrast, and incidentally is a good sample of the story's tone and style. The Zhivago paper quotes twice, once from a letter, part of which is omitted from the film, and once quite briefly from the novel. Both quotations help to show how much more realistically the novel portrays the main character than the film does—a main point of the paper. But quotations which are not clearly needed to support the critic's purpose often result in padding. The student quotes to avoid writing. In general, quotations are best used to illustrate a point which the critic has already made.

It is customary to indent and single space quotations of five lines or more, and to incorporate shorter quotations in the text. Both forms are illustrated in "Two Faces of Zhivago." Notice how skillfully the short quotations in paragraphs 3 and 4 are worked into the structure of the writer's own sentences.

6. *Use footnotes if necessary.* Whether you need to identify the source of a quotation by a footnote depends on circumstances. If you are writing a short essay on a work printed in your textbook and so available to your reader, no footnotes are necessary. Notice that none of the criticisms presented in this chapter are footnoted. But if you are writing a term or a research paper drawn from several sources, you must use footnotes to identify the author, book, page number, and facts of publication for quotations and citations of material taken from specific sources. The conventions of footnoting are discussed in detail on pages 280–83 and are illustrated in the specimen research paper on pages 285–305.

7. *Always proofread your finished essay carefully, preferably more than once.* This is standard procedure for all essays.

EXERCISE   *First, read the following story; then discuss its major elements in class as a cooperative prewriting exercise. List possible topics for a paper, as we did with "Barn Burning." Finally, select one of the topics and develop it into an essay.*

The Conversion of the Jews

by Philip Roth

"You're a real one for opening your mouth in the first place," Itzie said. "What do you open your mouth all the time for?"

"I didn't bring it up, Itz, I didn't," Ozzie said.

"What do you care about Jesus Christ for anyway?"

"I didn't bring up Jesus Christ. He did. I didn't even know what he was talking about. Jesus is historical, he kept saying. Jesus is historical." Ozzie mimicked the monumental voice of Rabbi Binder.

"Jesus was a person that lived like you and me," Ozzie continued. "That's what Binder said—"

"Yeah? . . . So what! What do I give two cents whether he lived or not. And what do you gotta open your mouth!" Itzie Lieberman favored closed-mouthedness, especially when it came to Ozzie Freedman's questions. Mrs. Freedman had to see Rabbi Binder twice before about Ozzie's questions and this Wednesday at four-thirty would be the third time. Itzie preferred to keep *his* mother in the kitchen; he settled for behind-the-back subtleties such as gestures, faces, snarls and other less delicate barnyard noises.

"He was a real person, Jesus, but he wasn't like God, and we don't believe he is God." Slowly, Ozzie was explaining Rabbi Binder's position to Itzie, who had been absent from Hebrew School the previous afternoon.

"The Catholics," Itzie said helpfully, "they believe in Jesus Christ, that he's God." Itzie Lieberman used "the Catholics" in its broadest sense—to include the Protestants.

Ozzie received Itzie's remark with a tiny head bob, as though it were a foot-note, and went on. "His mother was Mary, and his father probably was Joseph," Ozzie said. "But the New Testament says his real father was God."

"His *real* father?"

"Yeah," Ozzie said, "that's the big thing, his father's supposed to be God."

"Bull."

"That's what Rabbi Binder says, that it's impossible—"

"Sure it's impossible. That stuff's all bull. To have a baby you gotta get laid," Itzie theologized. "Mary hadda get laid."

"That's what Binder says: 'The only way a woman can have a baby is to have intercourse with a man.' "

"He said *that*, Ozz?" For a moment it appeared that Itzie had put the theo-logical question aside. "He said that, intercourse?" A little curled smile shaped itself in the lower half of Itzie's face like a pink mustache. "What you guys do, Ozz, you laugh or something?"

"I raised my hand."

"Yeah? Whatja say?"

"That's when I asked the question."

Itzie's face lit up. "Whatja ask about—intercourse?"

"No, I asked the question about God, how if He could create the heaven and earth in six days, and make all the animals and the fish and the light in six days—the light especially, that's what always gets me, that He could make the light. Making fish and animals, that's pretty good—"

"That's damn good." Itzie's appreciation was honest but unimaginative: it was as though God had just pitched a one-hitter.

"But making light . . . I mean when you think about it, it's really something," Ozzie said. "Anyway, I asked Binder if He could make all that in six days, and He could *pick* the six days he wanted right out of nowhere, why couldn't He let a woman have a baby without having intercourse."

"You said intercourse, Ozz, to Binder?"

"Yeah."

"Right in class?"

"Yeah."

Itzie smacked the side of his head.

"I mean, no kidding around," Ozzie said, "that'd really be nothing. After all that other stuff, that'd practically be nothing."

Itzie considered a moment. "What'd Binder say?"

"He started all over again explaining how Jesus was historical and how he lived like you and me but he wasn't God. So I said I under*stood* that. What I wanted to know was different."

What Ozzie wanted to know was always different. The first time he had wanted to know how Rabbi Binder could call the Jews "The Chosen People" if the Declaration of Independence claimed all men to be created equal. Rabbi Binder tried to distinguish for him between political equality and spiritual legitimacy, but what Ozzie wanted to know, he insisted vehemently, was different. That was the first time his mother had to come.

Then there was the plane crash. Fifty-eight people had been killed in a plane crash at La Guardia. In studying a casualty list in the newspaper his mother had discovered among the list of those dead eight Jewish names (his grandmother had nine but she counted Miller as a Jewish name); because of the eight she said the plane crash was "a tragedy." During free-discussion time on Wednesday Ozzie had brought to Rabbi Binder's attention this matter of "some of his relations" always picking out the Jewish names. Rabbi Binder had begun to explain cultural unity and some other things when Ozzie stood up at his seat and said that what he wanted to know was different. Rabbi Binder insisted that he sit down and it was then that Ozzie shouted that he wished all fifty-eight were Jews. That was the second time his mother came.

"And he kept explaining about Jesus being historical, and so I kept asking him. No kidding, Itz, he was trying to make me look stupid."

"So what he finally do?"

"Finally he starts screaming that I was deliberately simple-minded and a wise guy, and that my mother had to come, and this was the last time. And that I'd never get bar-mitzvahed if he could help it. Then, Itz, then he starts talking in that voice like a statue, real slow and deep, and he says that I better think over what I said about the Lord. He told me to go to his office and think it over." Ozzie leaned his body towards Itzie. "Itz, I thought it over for a solid hour, and now I'm convinced God could do it."

Ozzie had planned to confess his latest transgression to his mother as soon as she came home from work. But it was a Friday night in November and already dark, and when Mrs. Freedman came through the door she tossed off her coat, kissed Ozzie quickly on the face, and went to the kitchen table to light the three yellow candles, two for the Sabbath and one for Ozzie's father.

When his mother lit the candles she would move her two arms slowly towards her, dragging them through the air, as though persuading people whose minds were half made up. And her eyes would get glassy with tears. Even when his father was alive Ozzie remembered that her eyes had gotten glassy, so it didn't have anything to do with his dying. It had something to do with lighting the candles.

As she touched the flaming match to the unlit wick of a Sabbath candle, the phone rang, and Ozzie, standing only a foot from it, plucked it off the receiver and held it muffled to his chest. When his mother lit candles Ozzie felt there should be no noise; even breathing, if you could manage it, should be softened. Ozzie pressed the phone to his breast and watched his mother dragging whatever she was dragging, and he felt his own eyes get glassy. His mother was a round, tired, gray-haired penguin of a woman whose gray skin had begun to feel the tug of gravity and the weight of her own history. Even when she was dressed up she didn't look like a chosen person. But when she lit candles she looked like something better; like a woman who knew momentarily that God could do anything.

After a few mysterious minutes she was finished. Ozzie hung up the phone and walked to the kitchen table where she was beginning to lay the two places for the four-course Sabbath meal. He told her that she would have to see Rabbi Binder next Wednesday at four-thirty, and then he told her why. For the first time in their life together she hit Ozzie across the face with her hand.

All through the chopped liver and chicken soup part of the dinner Ozzie cried; he didn't have any appetite for the rest.

On Wednesday, in the largest of the three basement classrooms of the synagogue, Rabbi Marvin Binder, a tall, handsome, broad-shouldered man of thirty with thick strong-fibered black hair, removed his watch from his pocket and saw that it was four o'clock. At the rear of the room Yakov Blotnik, the seventy-one-year-old custodian, slowly polished the large window, mumbling to himself, unaware that it was four o'clock or six o'clock, Monday or Wednesday. To most of the students Yakov Blotnik's mumbling, along with his brown curly beard, scythe nose, and two heel-trailing black cats, made of him an object of wonder, a foreigner, a relic, towards whom they were alternately fearful and disrespectful. To Ozzie the mumbling had always seemed a monotonous, curious prayer; what made it curious was that old Blotnik had been mumbling so steadily for so many years, Ozzie suspected he had memorized the prayers and forgotten all about God.

"It is now free-discussion time," Rabbi Binder said. "Feel free to talk about any Jewish matter at all—religion, family, politics, sports—"

There was silence. It was a gusty, clouded November afternoon and it did not seem as though there ever was or could be a thing called baseball. So nobody this week said a word about that hero from the past, Hank Greenberg —which limited free discussion considerably.

And the soul-battering Ozzie Freedman had just received from Rabbi Binder had imposed its limitation. When it was Ozzie's turn to read aloud from the Hebrew book the rabbi had asked him petulantly why he didn't read more rapidly. He was showing no progress. Ozzie said he could read faster but that if he did he was sure not to understand what he was reading. Nevertheless, at the rabbi's repeated suggestion Ozzie tried, and showed a great talent, but in the midst of a long passage he stopped short and said he didn't understand a word he was reading, and started in again at a drag-footed pace. Then came the soul-battering.

Consequently when free-discussion time rolled around none of the students felt too free. The rabbi's invitation was answered only by the mumbling of feeble old Blotnik.

"Isn't there anything at all you would like to discuss?" Rabbi Binder asked again, looking at his watch. "No questions or comments?"

There was a small grumble from the third row. The rabbi requested that Ozzie rise and give the rest of the class the advantage of his thought.

Ozzie rose. "I forget it now," he said, and sat down in his place.

Rabbi Binder advanced a seat towards Ozzie and poised himself on the edge of the desk. It was Itzie's desk and the rabbi's frame only a dagger's-length away from his face snapped him to sitting attention.

"Stand up again, Oscar," Rabbi Binder said calmly, "and try to assemble your thoughts."

Ozzie stood up. All his classmates turned in their seats and watched as he gave an unconvincing scratch to his forehead.

"I can't assemble any," he announced, and plunked himself down.

"Stand up!" Rabbi Binder advanced from Itzie's desk to the one directly in front of Ozzie; when the rabbinical back was turned Itzie gave it five-fingers off the tip of his nose, causing a small titter in the room. Rabbi Binder was too absorbed in squelching Ozzie's nonsense once and for all to bother with titters. "Stand up, Oscar. What's your question about?"

Ozzie pulled a word out of the air. It was the handiest word. "Religion."

"Oh, now you remember?"

"Yes."

"What is it?"

Trapped, Ozzie blurted the first thing that came to him. "Why can't He make anything He wants to make!"

As Rabbi Binder prepared an answer, a final answer, Itzie, ten feet behind him, raised one finger on his left hand, gestured it meaningfully towards the rabbi's back, and brought the house down.

Binder twisted quickly to see what had happened and in the midst of the commotion Ozzie shouted into the rabbi's back what he couldn't have shouted to his face. It was a loud, toneless sound that had the timbre of something stored inside for about six days.

"You don't know! You don't know anything about God!"

The rabbi spun back towards Ozzie. "What?"

"You don't know—you don't—"

"Apologize, Oscar, apologize!" It was a threat.

"You don't—"

Rabbi Binder's hand flicked out at Ozzie's cheek. Perhaps it had only been meant to clamp the boy's mouth shut, but Ozzie ducked and the palm caught him squarely on the nose.

The blood came in a short, red spurt on to Ozzie's shirt front.

The next moment was all confusion. Ozzie screamed, "You bastard, you bastard!" and broke for the classroom door. Rabbi Binder lurched a step backwards, as though his own blood had started flowing violently in the opposite direction, then gave a clumsy lurch forward and bolted out the door after Ozzie. The class followed after the rabbi's huge blue-suited back, and before old Blotnik could turn from his window, the room was empty and everyone was headed full speed up the three flights leading to the roof.

If one should compare the light of day to the life of man: sunrise to birth; sunset—the dropping down over the edge—to death; then as Ozzie Freedman wiggled through the trapdoor of the synagogue roof, his feet kicking backwards bronco-style at Rabbi Binder's outstretched arms—at that moment the day was fifty years old. As a rule, fifty or fifty-five reflects accurately the age of late afternoons in November, for it is in that month, during those hours, that one's awareness of light seems no longer a matter of seeing, but of hearing: light begins clicking away. In fact, as Ozzie locked shut the trapdoor in the rabbi's face, the sharp click of the bolt into the lock might momentarily have been mistaken for the sound of the heavier gray that had just throbbed through the sky.

With all his weight Ozzie kneeled on the locked door; any instant he was certain that Rabbi Binder's shoulder would fling it open, splintering the wood into shrapnel and catapulting his body into the sky. But the door did not move and below him he heard only the rumble of feet, first loud then dim, like thunder rolling away.

A question shot through his brain. "Can this be *me?*" For a thirteen-year-old who has just labeled his religious leader a bastard, twice, it was not an improper question. Louder and louder the question came to him—"Is it me? Is it me?"—until he discovered himself no longer kneeling, but racing crazily towards the edge of the roof, his eyes crying, his throat screaming, and his arms flying every-whichway as though not his own.

"Is it me? Is it me ME ME ME ME! It has to be me—but is it!"

It is the question a thief must ask himself the night he jimmies open his first window, and it is said to be the question with which bridegrooms quiz themselves before the altar.

In the few wild seconds it took Ozzie's body to propel him to the edge of the roof, his self-examination began to grow fuzzy. Gazing down at the street, he became confused as to the problem beneath the question: was it, is-it-me-who-called-Binder-a-bastard or, is-it-me-prancing-around-on-the-roof? However, the scene below settled all, for there is an instant in any action when whether it is you or somebody else is academic. The thief crams the money in his pockets and scoots out the window. The bridegroom signs the hotel register for two. And the boy on the roof finds a streetful of people gaping at him, necks stretched backwards, faces up, as though he were the ceiling of the Hayden Planetarium. Suddenly you know it's you.

"Oscar! Oscar Freedman!" A voice rose from the center of the crowd, a voice that, could it have been seen, would have looked like the writing on scroll. "Oscar Freedman, get down from there. Immediately!" Rabbi Binder was pointing one arm stiffly up at him; and at the end of that arm, one finger aimed menacingly. It was the attitude of a dictator, but one—the eyes confessed all—whose personal valet had spit neatly in his face.

Ozzie didn't answer. Only for a blink's length did he look towards Rabbi Binder. Instead his eyes began to fit together the world beneath him, to sort out people from places, friends from enemies, participants from spectators. In little jagged starlike clusters his friends stood around Rabbi Binder, who was still pointing. The topmost point on a star compounded not of angels but of five adolescent boys was Itzie. What a world it was, with those stars below, Rabbi Binder below . . . Ozzie, who a moment earlier hadn't been able to control his own body, started to feel the meaning of the word control: he felt Peace and he felt Power.

"Oscar Freedman, I'll give you three to come down."

Few dictators give their subjects three to do anything; but, as always, Rabbi Binder only looked dictatorial.

"Are you ready, Oscar?"

Ozzie nodded his head yes, although he had no intention in the world—the lower one or the celestial one he'd just entered—of coming down even if Rabbi Binder should give him a million.

"All right then," said Rabbi Binder. He ran a hand through his black Samson hair as though it were the gesture prescribed for uttering the first digit. Then, with his other hand cutting a circle out of the small piece of sky around him, he spoke. "One!"

There was no thunder. On the contrary, at that moment, as though "one" was the cue for which he had been waiting, the world's least thunderous person appeared on the synagogue steps. He did not so much come out the synagogue door as lean out, onto the darkening air. He clutched at the doorknob with one hand and looked up at the roof.

"Oy!"

Yakov Blotnik's old mind hobbled slowly, as if on crutches, and though he couldn't decide precisely what the boy was doing on the roof, he knew it wasn't good—that is, it wasn't-good-for-the-Jews. For Yakov Blotnik life had fractioned itself simply: things were either good-for-the-Jews or no-good-for-the-Jews.

He smacked his free hand to his in-sucked cheek, gently. "Oy, Gut!" And then quickly as he was able, he jacked down his head and surveyed the street. There was Rabbi Binder (like a man at an auction with only three dollars in his pocket, he had just delivered a shaky "Two!"); there were the students, and that was all. So far it-wasn't-so-bad-for-the-Jews. But the boy had to come down immediately, before anybody saw. The problem: how to get the boy off the roof?

Anybody who has ever had a cat on the roof knows how to get him down. You call the fire department. Or first you call the operator and you ask her for the fire department. And the next thing there is great jamming of brakes and clanging of bells and shouting of instructions. And then the cat is off the roof. You do the same thing to get a boy off the roof.

That is, you do the same thing if you are Yakov Blotnik and you once had a cat on the roof.

When the engines, all four of them, arrived, Rabbi Binder had four times given Ozzie the count of three. The big hook-and-ladder swung around the corner and one of the firemen leaped from it, plunging headlong towards the yellow fire hydrant in front of the synagogue. With a huge wrench he began to unscrew the top nozzle. Rabbi Binder raced over to him and pulled at his shoulder.

"There's no fire . . ."

The fireman mumbled back over his shoulder and, heatedly, continued working at the nozzle.

"But there's no fire, there's no fire . . ." Binder shouted. When the fireman mumbled again, the rabbi grasped his face with both his hands and pointed it up at the roof.

To Ozzie it looked as though Rabbi Binder was trying to tug the fireman's head out of his body, like a cork from a bottle. He had to giggle at the picture they made: it was a family portrait—rabbi in black skullcap, fireman in red fire hat, and the little yellow hydrant squatting beside like a kid brother, bareheaded. From the edge of the roof Ozzie waved at the portrait, a one-handed, flapping, mocking wave; in doing it his right foot slipped from under him. Rabbi Binder covered his eyes with his hands.

Firemen work fast. Before Ozzie had even regained his balance, a big, round, yellowed net was being held on the synagogue lawn. The firemen who held it looked up at Ozzie with stern, feelingless faces.

One of the firemen turned his head towards Rabbi Binder. "What, is the kid nuts or something?"

Rabbi Binder unpeeled his hands from his eyes, slowly, painfully, as if they were tape. Then he checked: nothing on the sidewalk, no dents in the net.

"Is he gonna jump, or what?" the fireman shouted.

In a voice not at all like a statue, Rabbi Binder finally answered. "Yes, yes, I think so . . . He's been threatening to . . ."

Threatening to? Why, the reason he was on the roof, Ozzie remembered, was to get away; he hadn't even thought about jumping. He had just run to get away, and the truth was that he hadn't really headed for the roof as much as he'd been chased there.

"What's his name, the kid?"

"Freedman," Rabbi Binder answered. "Oscar Freedman."

The fireman looked up at Ozzie. "What is it with you, Oscar? You gonna jump, or what?"

Ozzie did not answer. Frankly, the question had just arisen.

"Look, Oscar, if you're gonna jump, jump—and if you're not gonna jump, don't jump. But don't waste our time, willya?"

Ozzie looked at the fireman and then at Rabbi Binder. He wanted to see Rabbi Binder cover his eyes one more time.

"I'm going to jump."

And then he scampered around the edge of the roof to the corner, where there was no net below, and he flapped his arms at his sides, swishing the air and smacking his palms to his trousers on the downbeat. He began screaming like some kind of engine, "Wheeeee . . . wheeeeee," and leaning way out over the edge with the upper half of his body. The firemen whipped around to cover the ground with the net. Rabbi Binder mumbled a few words to Somebody and covered his eyes. Everything happened quickly, jerkily, as in a silent movie. The crowd, which had arrived with the fire engines, gave out a long, Fourth-of-July fireworks oooh-aahhh. In the excitement no one had paid the crowd much heed, except, of course, Yakov Blotnik, who swung from the doorknob counting heads. "Fier und tsvansik . . . finf und tsvantsik . . . Oy, Gut!" It wasn't like this with the cat.

Rabbi Binder peeked through his fingers, checked the sidewalk and net. Empty. But there was Ozzie racing to the other corner. The firemen raced with him but were unable to keep up. Whenever Ozzie wanted to he might jump and splatter himself upon the sidewalk, and by the time the firemen scooted to the spot all they could do with their net would be to cover the mess.

"Wheeeee . . . wheeeee . . . "

"Hey, Oscar," the winded fireman yelled, "What the hell is this, a game or something?"

"Wheeeee . . . wheeeee . . ."

"Hey, Oscar—"

But he was off now to the other corner, flapping his wings fiercely. Rabbi Binder couldn't take it any longer—the fire engines from nowhere, the screaming suicidal boy, the net. He fell to his knees, exhausted, and with his hands curled together in front of his chest like a little dome, he pleaded, "Oscar, stop it, Oscar. Don't jump, Oscar. Please come down . . . Please don't jump."

And further back in the crowd a single voice, a single young voice, shouted a lone word to the boy on the roof.

"Jump!"

It was Itzie. Ozzie momentarily stopped flapping.

"Go ahead, Ozz—jump!" Itzie broke off his point of the star and courageously, with the inspiration not of a wise-guy but of a disciple, stood alone. "Jump, Ozz, jump!"

Still on his knees, his hands still curled, Rabbi Binder twisted his body back. He looked at Itzie, then, agonizingly, back to Ozzie.

"Oscar, don't jump! Please, don't jump . . . please please . . ."

"Jump!" This time it wasn't Itzie but another point of the star. By the time Mrs. Freedman arrived to keep her four-thirty appointment with Rabbi Binder, the whole little upside down heaven was shouting and pleading for Ozzie to jump, and Rabbi Binder no longer was pleading with him not to jump, but was crying into the dome of his hands.

Understandably Mrs. Freedman couldn't figure out what her son was doing on the roof. So she asked.

"Ozzie, my Ozzie, what are you doing? My Ozzie, what is it?"

Ozzie stopped wheeeeeing and slowed his arms down to a cruising flap, the kind birds use in soft winds, but he did not answer. He stood against the low, clouded, darkening sky—light clicked down swiftly now, as on a small gear—flapping softly and gazing down at the small bundle of a woman who was his mother.

"What are you doing, Ozzie?" She turned towards the kneeling Rabbi Binder and rushed so close that only a paper-thickness of dusk lay between her stomach and his shoulders.

"What is my baby doing?"

Rabbi Binder gaped up at her but he too was mute. All that moved was the dome of his hands; it shook back and forth like a weak pulse.

"Rabbi, get him down! He'll kill himself. Get him down, my only baby . . ."

"I can't," Rabbi Binder said, "I can't . . ." and he turned his handsome head towards the crowd of boys behind him. "It's them. Listen to them."

And for the first time Mrs. Freedman saw the crowd of boys, and she heard what they were yelling.

"He's doing it for them. He won't listen to me. It's them." Rabbi Binder spoke like one in a trance.

"For them?"

"Yes."

"Why for them?"

"They want him to . . ."

Mrs. Freedman raised her two arms upward as though she were conducting the sky. "For them he's doing it!" And then in a gesture older than pyramids, older than prophets and floods, her arms came slapping down to her sides. "A martyr I have. Look!" She tilted her head to the roof. Ozzie was still flapping softly. "My martyr."

"Oscar, come down, *please*," Rabbi Binder groaned.

In a startlingly even voice Mrs. Freedman called to the boy on the roof. "Ozzie, come down, Ozzie. Don't be a martyr, my baby."

As though it were a litany, Rabbi Binder repeated her words. "Don't be a martyr, my baby. Don't be a martyr."

"Gawhead, Ozz—*be a Martin*!" It was Itzie. "Be a Martin, be a Martin," and all the voices joined in singing for Martindom, whatever *it* was. "Be a Martin, be a Martin . . . ."

Somehow when you're on a roof the darker it gets the less you can hear. All Ozzie knew was that two groups wanted two new things: his friends were spirited and musical about what they wanted; his mother and the rabbi were even-toned, chanting, about what they didn't want. The rabbi's voice was without tears now and so was his mother's.

The big net stared up at Ozzie like a sightless eye. The big, clouded sky pushed down. From beneath it looked like a gray corrugated board. Suddenly, looking up into that unsympathetic sky, Ozzie realized all the strangeness of what these people, his friends, were asking: they wanted him to jump, to kill himself; they were singing about it now—it made them that happy. And there was an even greater strangeness: Rabbi Binder was on his knees, trembling. If there was a question to be asked now it was not "Is it me?" but rather "Is it us? . . . Is it us?"

Being on the roof, it turned out, was a serious thing. If he jumped would the singing become dancing? Would it? What would jumping stop? Yearningly, Ozzie wished he could rip open the sky, plunge his hands through, and pull out the sun; and on the sun, like a coin, would be stamped Jump or Don't Jump.

Ozzie's knees rocked and sagged a little under him as though they were setting him for a dive. His arms tightened, stiffened, froze, from shoulders to fingernails. He felt as if each part of his body were going to vote as to whether he should kill himself or not—and each part as though it were independent of *him*.

The light took an unexpected click down and the new darkness, like a gag, hushed the friends singing for this and the mother and rabbi chanting for that.

Ozzie stopped counting votes, and in a curiously high voice, like one who wasn't prepared for speech, he spoke.

"Mamma?"

"Yes, Oscar."

"Mamma, get down on your knees, like Rabbi Binder."

"Oscar—"

"Get down on your knees," he said, "or I'll jump."

Ozzie heard a whimper, then a quick rustling, and when he looked down where his mother had stood he saw the top of a head and beneath that a circle of dress. She was kneeling beside Rabbi Binder.

He spoke again. "Everybody kneel." There was the sound of everybody kneeling.

Ozzie looked around. With one hand he pointed towards the synagogue entrance. "Make *him* kneel."

There was a noise, not of kneeling, but of body-and-cloth stretching. Ozzie could hear Rabbi Binder saying in a gruff whisper, ". . . or he'll *kill* himself," and when next he looked there was Yakov Blotnik off the doorknob and for the first time in his life upon his knees in the Gentile posture of prayer.

As for the firemen—it is not as difficult as one might imagine to hold a net taut while you are kneeling.

Ozzie looked around again; and then he called to Rabbi Binder.

"Rabbi?"

"Yes, Oscar."

"Rabbi Binder, do you believe in God?"

"Yes."

"Do you believe God can do Anything?" Ozzie leaned his head out into the darkness. "Anything?"

"Oscar, I think—"

"Tell me you believe God can do Anything."

There was a second's hesitation. Then: "God can do Anything."

"Tell me you believe God can make a child without intercourse."

"He can."

"Tell me!"

"God," Rabbi Binder admitted, "can make a child without intercourse."

"Mamma, you tell me."

"God can make a child without intercourse," his mother said.

"Make *him* tell me." There was no doubt who *him* was.

In a few moments Ozzie heard an old comical voice say something to the increasing darkness about God.

Next, Ozzie made everybody say it. And then he made them all say they believed in Jesus Christ—first one at a time, then all together.

When the catechizing was through it was the beginning of evening. From the street it sounded as if the boy on the roof might have sighed.

"Ozzie?" A woman's voice dared to speak. "You'll come down now?"

There was no answer, but the woman waited, and when a voice finally did speak it was thin and crying, and exhausted as that of an old man who has just finished pulling the bells.

"Mamma, don't you see—you shouldn't hit me. He shouldn't hit me. You shouldn't hit me about God, Mamma. You should never hit anybody about God—"

"Ozzie, please come down now."

"Promise me, promise me you'll never hit anybody about God."

He had asked only his mother, but for some reason everyone kneeling in the street promised he would never hit anybody about God.

Once again there was silence. ·

"I can come down now, Mamma," the boy on the roof finally said. He turned his head both ways as though checking the traffic lights. "Now I can come down . . ."

And he did, right into the center of the yellow net that glowed in the evening's edge like an overgrown halo.

Chapter 11

Using the Library

The library provides the literature of all areas of study and research. As you progress through college, your courses will require the use of an ever-wider variety of library materials. Many colleges offer a library orientation program to help incoming freshmen learn what kinds of resources are available, where they are located, and how they are used. This chapter is not a substitute for such a comprehensive and specific program; it is an introduction for those who are not familiar with the use of the library, a refresher for those who are, and a guide to the chief works of general reference and the standard specialized sources in various fields.[1]

THE CARD CATALOG

The card catalog is a register of all the books in the library. It consists of cases of trays in which 3-by-5-inch cards, marked with information, are filed alphabetically. Several types of cards are filed together according to the first significant word on the topmost line of the card: an "author card" has the author's surname first on the top line; a "title card" has the title on the top line; and a "subject card" has a subject heading at the top. There should be at least one of each kind of card for every book.

A typical author card is shown on page 246. This is a facsimile (reduced) of an author card manufactured by the Library of Congress for use in all libraries. It contains the basic and authentic information about the book.

---

[1] Although this chapter gives you an introduction to these resources, several full-length guides to reference work are available; for example, Robert B. Downs, *How to Do Library Research* (Urbana, Ill.: University of Illinois Press, 1966); Saul Galin and Peter Spielberg, *Reference Books: How to Select and Use Them* (New York: Random House, 1969).

The call number is added by the individual library. A duplicate of this card becomes a title card when *The heathens* is typed above the author's name. Another duplicate becomes a subject card when *Religion, Primitive* is typed across the top, usually in capitals and in red ink. There are then three cards in the catalog for this book, each filed in its alphabetical place—two under "H" and one under "R."

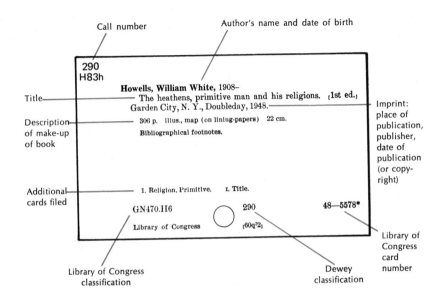

Call number

Author's name and date of birth

```
290
H83h
        Howells, William White, 1908–
              The heathens, primitive man and his religions.  ₁1st ed.₎
          Garden City, N. Y., Doubleday, 1948.

          306 p.  illus., map (on lining-papers)  22 cm.
          Bibliographical footnotes.



          1. Religion, Primitive.    I. Title.

        GN470.II6                    290              48—5578*
        Library of Congress       ₁60q²₂₎
```

Title

Description of make-up of book

Additional cards filed

Library of Congress classification

Dewey classification

Imprint: place of publication, publisher, date of publication (or copyright)

Library of Congress card number

In this subject heading, *religion* is the dominant word, so the normal word order is inverted. In the heading *Religious education,* however, the word *education* is not considered dominant, and so comes last. Subject headings can be confusing until you become familiar with library terminology. Remember that subject headings are made as specific as possible, and that you will save time by looking first for the precise topic you have in mind. For example, if you want to read about St. Paul's Cathedral in London, you would look for *S[ain]t Paul's Cathedral,* not for *Churches–England* or *Cathedrals–England* or *London–Churches.*

The card catalog will help you to find the proper headings by means of "cross-reference cards." A "see" reference gives a heading that is not used and tells which related term can be found in the catalog:

Farming	Humor
See	*See*
Agriculture	Wit and humor

"See also" cards refer to headings under which similar materials are placed, and come at the end of the filing sequence:

<table>
<tr><td>Cocoa</td><td>Pessimism</td></tr>
<tr><td>*See also*</td><td>*See also*</td></tr>
<tr><td>Chocolate</td><td>Optimism</td></tr>
</table>

Classification Systems

Most American academic libraries use either the Dewey Decimal System or the Library of Congress System for identifying and arranging materials on the shelves. Printed descriptions of these systems will be found at the main desk of the library, and brief versions may be posted in various places.

The main divisions of the Dewey subject classification are as follows:

000–099	General Works	600–699	Applied Sciences
100–199	Philosophy and Psychology	700–799	Fine Arts and Recreation
200–299	Religion	800–899	Literature
300–399	Social Sciences	F	Fiction in English
400–499	Languages	900–999	History, Travel, Collected Biography
500–599	Pure Sciences	B	Individual Biography

These numbers are expanded by adding decimal places, each with a meaning: 998.2—history of Greenland. You will need to know the numbers pertaining to your fields of special interest.

The main divisions of the Library of Congress classification are as follows:

A	General Works	L	Education
B	Philosophy, Psychology, Religion	M	Music
		N	Fine Arts
C–D	History and Topography (except America)	P	Language and Literature
		Q	Science
E–F	America	R	Medicine
G	Geography, Anthropology, Sports and Games	S	Agriculture, Forestry
		T	Engineering and Technology
H	Social Sciences	U	Military Science
J	Political Science	V	Naval Science
K	Law	Z	Bibliography

This system is expanded by adding letters (QA—mathematics) and numbers.

Each published item is given a "call number" (see the facsimile card, page 246) which consists of a subject designation from the classification scheme (290 for *The Heathens*) and a "book number" identifying the individual publication (H83h for the Howells book). A year may be added below for a later edition of a book or for the date of a serial publication. Taken as a whole, the call number is the only complete designation of a particular item in the library and therefore must be copied in full if you are to get the publication referred to by the card. The call number is always in the upper left-hand corner of the card.

Filing Rules

The following are widely accepted rules or conventions practiced by libraries in filing cards alphabetically, and a knowledge of them will help you to make thorough and efficient use of the card catalog.

1. Filing is done word-by-word, or short-before-long, rather than letter-by-letter.

> North America
> North Sea
> Northanger Abbey
> Northern Ireland
> Northern Rhodesia
> The Northerners

2. Abbreviations and numbers are filed as though they were spelled out —*Dr. Faustus* will be found under *doctor, St. Lawrence* under *saint, U.S. News* under *United States, 19th Century Authors* under *nineteenth.*

3. In personal names *Mac, Mc,* and *M'* are filed as though they were all *Mac.* The foreign prefixes *de, van,* and *von* are usually ignored—*Hindenburg, Paul von.*

4. Cards for books *by* an author are filed before those *about* him, and in between will be books of which he is a "joint author," that is, one whose name does not appear first on the title page.

5. For the same word or name, the filing order is person, place, title.

> Hudson, William Henry
> Hudson, New Jersey
> The Hudson and its Moods

6. Titles are filed according to the first significant word, ignoring *a, an,* and *the* and their foreign equivalents.

7. Subjects are usually subdivided in alphabetical order, but history is divided chronologically.

> Printing—Exhibitions   Italy—History—To 1559
> Printing—Specimens   Italy—History—1559–1789
> Printing—Style manuals   Italy—History—1789–1815

THE REFERENCE COLLECTION

When you need to get information for your themes and research papers, you will go first to the reference room. There you will find dictionaries, encyclopedias, indexes, directories, handbooks, yearbooks, guides, and atlases covering almost every area of human knowledge. You should know what kinds of reference works are available and should become acquainted with the most important works of each kind.

Printed Catalogs

Catalogs in book form supplement the card catalog of the library by showing what books are available elsewhere. Most academic libraries have the two great printed library catalogs, those of the British Museum and the Library of Congress. The latter is now called the *National Union Catalog,* and contains titles reported from other libraries in addition to those for which Library of Congress cards have been printed. It appears in monthly installments, in two sections, one arranged by author, the second by subject. Music, phonograph records, motion pictures, and filmstrips are cited as well as printed materials.

Lists of Books.   The main current-publication lists for the United States are these:

Cumulative Book Index. A monthly list of books published in the English language, except government documents. It is "cumulated" periodically, that is, several issues are combined into one volume.

Publishers' Trade List Annual. A collection of publishers' catalogs bound together.

Books in Print. The annual author-title index to the *Publishers' Trade List Annual.*

Subject Guide to Books in Print. Also published annually.

Lists of Periodicals and Newspapers.   The main lists of periodicals and newspapers are the following:

Union List of Serials in Libraries of the United States and Canada. New Serial Titles. A monthly supplement to the *Union List.*

Ayer Directory of Newspapers, Magazines and Trade Publications. The best source of information about newspapers of the United States and its territories, Canada, Bermuda, Panama, and the Philippines.

Ulrich's International Periodicals Directory. Biennial. A comprehensive list of periodicals, arranged by subject.

Indexes to Periodical Literature

Since much of your writing will be based on periodical articles, and since these articles are not included in the card catalog, you will need to make use of periodical indexes. The most widely used index of general periodicals is the *Readers' Guide to Periodical Literature,* which lists the articles in a selected group of American periodicals of a nontechnical nature. It is published semimonthly, except monthly in July and August, and is cumulated annually. At the front of each issue and of each bound volume is a list of the periodicals indexed, the abbreviations used for their titles, and a key to other abbreviations used. Articles are indexed mostly by subject, but some titles and authors are used as entries. Here are some sample entries.[2]

DAY, Thomas Fakery of guitar masses. il Cath World 211:270–2 S '70	*Author entry for an illustrated article in* Catholic World, *Volume 211, pages 270–72 of the issue for September 1970.*
DAY nurseries Communes and nurseries: are they as good for children as they are helpful to mothers? B. Spock. Redbook 135:28+ O '70	*Subject entry for an article by B. Spock in* Redbook *magazine, Volume 135, page 28 and continued on subsequent pages not following consecutively, in the issue of October 1970.*

DEBT
    See also
    Collecting of accounts
	Reference to a related subject heading under which articles on debt may be found.

DENTAL enamel. See Teeth	*Reference from a heading not used to the one used.*
DEVIL'S disciple; drama. See Shaw, G. B.	*Title entry referring the reader to the author entry for the citation.*
DRESSING rooms Husband-and-wife elbow room. Sunset 145:96 S '70	*Subject entry for an unsigned article in* Sunset *magazine.*

For research on a technical or highly specialized topic, you will need to consult a specialized periodical index, such as:

Applied Science and Technology Index	*Education Index*
Art Index	*Engineering Index*
Bibliographic Index	*Essay and General Literature Index*
Biography Index	*Index to Legal Periodicals*
Biological and Agricultural Index	*Public Affairs Information Service Bulletin*
Book Review Index	
Business Periodicals Index	*Social Sciences and Humanities Index*
Current Index to Journals in Education	*United Nations Documents Index*

The *Bibliographic Index* cites bibliographies appended to foreign and American books and periodical articles and also those published separately. The *Public Affairs Information Service Bulletin* is an index to American social science publications, including books and pamphlets.

[2] From *Readers' Guide to Periodical Literature,* November 10, 1970 (New York: H. W. Wilson Company, 1970).

The standard newspaper index for the United States is the *New York Times Index,* now available from 1851 on. This index will help you find the date of an event, so that you can consult the *Times,* or another newspaper of that date, for the comments of the press.

For quick reference and brief accounts of important news, the weekly world news digest, *Facts on File,* is useful. Published since 1940, it records events day by day, and has quarterly and annual indexes.

Government Documents

The bulk of government documents are neither cataloged nor indexed in periodical indexes; but two lists of documents are published by the United States government, and these lists are bound and kept in libraries—the *Monthly Catalog of United States Government Publications* and the *Monthly Checklist of State Publications.*

General Dictionaries (Unabridged)

Unabridged dictionaries, because of their completeness, are the best sources of information about words in the general vocabulary, and should be used as supplements to the student's own desk dictionary.[3] The best known are the following:

A Dictionary of American English, 4 vols., University of Chicago Press.

New Standard Dictionary of the English Language, Funk and Wagnalls.

The Oxford English Dictionary, 12 vols. and supplement, Clarendon Press, Oxford. (A corrected reissue, in 1933, of *A New English Dictionary on Historical Principles,* 10 vols. and supplement, 1888–1928.) This dictionary is a particularly valuable resource for tracing the history of words and their meanings.

The Random House Dictionary of the English Language.

Webster's Third New International Dictionary of the English Language, G. & C. Merriam Co. (The Second Edition of *Webster's New International Dictionary* is also still in general use.)

General Encyclopedias

The chief general encyclopedias for the college level are the *Encyclopaedia Britannica* and the *Encyclopedia Americana.* The *Britannica* is no longer published in England, but the influence of its distinguished British contributors since its beginning, in 1771, remains. The *Americana* is the second-oldest of the general encyclopedias. Both are continuously revised.

Collier's Encyclopedia is an attractive American work, more recently compiled; *Chambers's* is an old English encyclopedia last re-edited in 1966. The *Columbia Encyclopedia* is a good one-volume reference work. There are also, of course, encyclopedias for many nations in other languages.

Yearbooks

Yearbooks are devoted to the chief occurrences of the preceding year and are published as quickly as possible after its close. Each of the major encyclopedias publishes an annual supplement as a means of keeping its material up to date, and these you will find shelved with the parent sets.

[3] See page 367 for desk dictionaries.

The designation "yearbook" is used for various publications, some appearing every few years, and some, like the *Yearbook of Agriculture,* providing thorough coverage of one topic each year.

"Almanacs" are compilations of miscellaneous statistics, records, events, and information not otherwise gathered together. Any one of the four listed below would make a useful addition to a student's personal library; each contains some material not included in the others.

Information Please Almanac, Atlas and Yearbook. Named for a former radio program and first published in 1947.

New York Times Encyclopedic Almanac. First published in 1970.

Reader's Digest Almanac and Yearbook. First published in 1966.

World Almanac and Book of Facts. A source of data for nearly a century.

For information on governmental matters, there are several valuable annual or biennial publications.

Book of the States. Biennial. A compilation of data on state governments.

Congressional Directory. Annual. Gives detailed information about Congress.

Municipal Year Book. Annual. Gives statistical data for American cities.

Statesman's Year-book. Biennial. A British publication covering the nations of the world. Gives political and economic data.

Statistical Abstract of the United States. Annual. Published by the Bureau of the Census. Gives data on political, economic, and social institutions.

United States Government Organization Manual. Annual. Describes the departments of government, lists key personnel, and prints the Constitution of the United States.

Yearbook of the United Nations. Annual. Has resumes of the sessions of the General Assembly, and reports on the other activities of the UN.

SPECIALIZED REFERENCE WORKS

The multiplication of specialized reference books in recent years makes any brief list of them inadequate, but a selection indicating the broad scope of factual material available may be useful as a preliminary guide. For subject matter not indicated here, ask your librarian. For complete bibliographic details of the titles in the following list, check the standard source, *Winchell's Guide to Reference Books.*[3]

Arts

In the field of the arts some of the most famous reference works are of foreign origin, particularly French, German, and Italian. Numerous one-volume guides to individual arts complement the larger sets.

American Art Directory. A source for information on museums, art schools, art associations of the U.S. and Canada. One of several such guides.

[3] Constance M. Winchell, *Guide to Reference Books,* 8th ed. (Chicago: American Library Association, 1967). Biennial supplements beginning 1965–66.

Concise Encyclopedia of Antiques. Signed articles on furnishings, prints, drawings, crafts of all kinds, with many illustrations. In five volumes.

Dance Encyclopedia. All forms of dance are discussed in articles by specialists.

Dictionary of Architecture and Building. By Russell Sturgis. Although old, the standard dictionary in this field in English.

Encyclopedia of Jazz. One volume with definitions, history, biography, discography.

Encyclopedia of Painting. Covers the world from prehistoric times; includes appraisals of paintings.

Encyclopedia of World Art. A fifteen-volume set, published 1959–68, issued simultaneously in Italian and in English by the Istituto per la Collaborazione Culturale and McGraw-Hill. Authoritative monographic studies of topics including art by areas and individual artists of the world.

Focal Encyclopedia of Photography. One volume on a newly recognized art form.

Grove's Dictionary of Music and Musicians. A classic multivolume British work, kept up to date by supplements.

History of Architecture. By Sir Banister Fletcher. A standard work with a new edition in 1961.

History of Theatrical Art in Ancient and Modern Times. By Karl Mantzius. In six volumes; the pioneer work in the field, and still a useful source of information.

Oxford Companion to Music. An encyclopedic one-volume work covering all phases of music. Contains articles, biographies, definitions.

Oxford Companion to the Theatre. International in scope, covering all periods and emphasizing stage and actors rather than the drama as literature.

Variety Music Cavalcade. A chronology of popular music from 1620 to 1961.

Biography

Chambers's Biographical Dictionary. An English publication of general scope, with commentaries on people and events, and with an unusually good subject index.

Current Biography. Sketches and portraits of contemporary American celebrities.

Dictionary of American Biography. A multivolume set containing scholarly articles about important Americans no longer living.

Dictionary of National Biography. The British equivalent of the above. These two are the classic biographical works.

National Cyclopaedia of American Biography. More than fifty volumes to date, containing a broad coverage of American historical biography.

New Century Cyclopedia of Names. Includes literary characters, names from myths and legends, places, and events.

Webster's Biographical Dictionary. One volume of brief factual data and pronunciation of names of famous persons of history.

Who's Who. An annual listing of prominent living British persons, with abbreviated biographical data. *Who Was Who* (5 vols., 1897–1960) lists deceased biographees, with date of death.

Who's Who in America. A biennial equivalent of the British work, with the companion volumes *Who Was Who in America.*

Who's Who in ———. Besides those of other nations, there are many specialized publications using this general title, such as *Who's Who in Labor* and *Who's Who of American Women.* Other similar lists of living persons can be found under different titles, as *American Men of Medicine* and *Directory of American Scholars.*

Education

American Universities and Colleges. Published quadrennially by the American Council on Education. Gives detailed basic information on each institution.

Dictionary of Education. Definitions of educational and related terms.

Education Directory. A useful annual published by the U.S. Office of Education in four volumes. Lists institutions, educational officers, government officials, and educational associations at all levels, from city to federal.

Encyclopedia of Educational Research. A most important source, although only published about every ten years. Contains articles by educational leaders on developments in education.

Guide to Graduate Study: Programs Leading to the Ph.D. Degree. By the American Council on Education.

International Guide to Educational Documentation. By UNESCO. Arranged by countries, it gives sources, publications, reference works, research, statistics, biographies of leaders.

Mental Measurements Yearbook. Appears every four or five years. Reviews tests and refers to reviews published elsewhere.

Study Abroad. A biennial publication of UNESCO.

World of Learning. An annual list of educational, scientific, and cultural organizations of the world.

World Survey of Education. A four-volume publication of UNESCO. The volumes deal respectively with education in general, primary education, secondary education, and higher education; arranged by countries.

History

Atlas of African History. A British publication of 1958. Designed to show the historical development of Africa from the fourth century.

Cambridge Histories: Ancient, Medieval, and *Modern.* The greatest multivolume histories, published by the Cambridge University Press. The oldest of these, the *Cambridge Modern History,* has been replaced by an entirely new publication based on recent scholarship, called the *New Cambridge Modern History.*

Chronology of the Modern World. With its companion volume, *Chronology of the Expanding World,* comprehensively covers events since 1492.

Dictionary of American History. A multivolume work edited by James Truslow Adams, with short articles. A companion volume is the *Atlas of American History.*

Encyclopedia of American History. A one-volume compendium of events, facts, and biographies.

Encyclopedia of World History. One volume, chronologically arranged.

Guide to Historical Literature. A bibliography of selected works in history.

Guide to the Study of the United States of America. An annotated listing of works on various aspects of American civilization. Published by the Library of Congress.

Harvard Guide to American History. A valuable guide to research, with essays on methods and resources, and reading lists arranged by periods.

Shepherd's *Historical Atlas.* First published in 1911 and frequently reissued, this book of maps covers world history with emphasis on Europe.

Literature

Reference books in literature abound. There are indexes to various literary forms, encyclopedias, critical works, selected lists of good reading, and concordances to the works of great authors. A sample of other kinds of material is given here.

American Authors 1600–1900; British Authors Before 1800; British Authors of the Nineteenth Century; Junior Book of Authors; Twentieth Century Authors. Some of the titles in a series of biographical dictionaries edited by Stanley Kunitz and Howard Haycraft.

Annual Bibliography of the English Language and Literature. A source for studies of these topics, arranged by centuries of literature and types of language study.

Bartlett's Familiar Quotations. The most popular of several books of quotations from poetry and prose, identifying authors and works.

Bibliography of American Literature. The fifth volume of this work in progress was published in 1969. Valuable as a historical guide.

Cambridge Bibliography of English Literature. A major work in four volumes and supplement, currently being replaced by the *New Cambridge Bibliography of English Literature* (1969–   ).

Cambridge Histories of American and *English Literature.* Standard though now dated sets covering literature into the twenties.

Columbia Dictionary of Modern European Literature. Begins just before the turn of the century; gives critical comment.

Contemporary Authors. A "bio-bibliographical" guide to present-day writers and their works, in several volumes, 1962 to date.

History of English Drama, 1660–1900. By Allardyce Nicoll, a work of six volumes, with detailed articles, and also lists of theaters and plays.

History of the English Novel. By Ernest A. Baker, a ten-volume work covering the English novel from its beginnings to the early twentieth century.

Literary History of England. Edited by Albert C. Baugh. A four-volume work, also available in one volume.

Literary History of the United States. An evaluative two-volume work, sometimes identified by the name of one of its editors, R. E. Spiller. The second volume is a bibliography.

Masterplots. A multivolume cyclopedia of world authors, with critical biographies and plots of their literary works. Annual since 1957; two volumes indexing literary characters were published in 1963.

Oxford Companions to: *American Literature, English Literature, Canadian History and Literature, French Literature, the Theatre.* Useful volumes for quick reference.

Oxford History of English Literature. A compilation begun in 1945, with twelve volumes projected.

Reader's Encyclopedia. A second edition was published in 1965 of this favorite volume of brief reference to world literature from antiquity to the present.

Mythology and Classics

Dictionary of Greek and Roman Biography and Mythology. By Sir William Smith, a great nineteenth-century editor.

Encyclopedia of the Classical World. By J. H. Croon. A 1965 publication.

Everyman's Dictionary of Non-Classical Mythology. A source for material on non-Western cultures.

Funk and Wagnalls Standard Dictionary of Folklore, Mythology and Legend. A two-volume encyclopedia and dictionary covering all world cultures.

Gayley's *Classic Myths in English Literature and in Art.* A famous old multivolume work, known by its editor's name. Also in a one-volume edition.

The Golden Bough. By Sir James Fraser. A great exhaustive study of mythology in twelve volumes, also condensed into one volume.

Harper's Dictionary of Classical Literature and Antiquities. An older work of broad coverage.

Larousse World Mythology. One of a new series of lavishly illustrated encyclopedic volumes bearing the name of a great French encyclopedist.

Mythology of All Races. The standard multivolume set in the field.

New Century Classical Handbook. A compilation embodying recent archaeological research, with many photographs.

Oxford Classical Dictionary and *Oxford Companion to Classical Literature.*

Philosophy and Psychology

Concise Encyclopedia of Western Philosophy and Philosophers. Published in 1960. Articles by scholars on the main concepts.

Dictionary of Psychology. One volume, which includes foreign terms.

Encyclopedia of Philosophy. A recent eight-volume work embracing Eastern and Western philosophy.

Harvard List of Books in Psychology. Added to by supplements.

History of Psychology in Autobiography. A four-volume compilation of "intellectual histories" written by great psychologists about themselves.

History of Western Philosophy. By Bertrand Russell; one of several works on the history of philosophy.

Professional Problems in Psychology. A valuable guide for the literature of the field, as well as information on the profession.

Religion

Besides dictionaries, histories, concordances of the Bible, and other types of reference book in the area of religion, there are several encyclopedias of individual faiths. The chief of these are the multivolume Catholic and Jewish encyclopedias. Other one-volume encyclopedias of both of these faiths have more recently been published, and there are also encyclopedias of various Protestant sects. Among the more general works are the following:

Atlas of the Bible; Atlas of the Early Christian World. British publications.

Book of Saints. A dictionary of canonized saints with brief biographies and a calendar.

Cambridge History of the Bible: in the West from the Reformation to the Present Day. Long articles on the history of the Bible in Europe and the United States, with photographs of pages from famous Bibles.

Concise Encyclopedia of Living Faiths. Long, detailed articles on religions of the world make this British publication valuable.

Encyclopedia of Religion and Ethics. A multivolume standard work edited by James Hastings, who also edited a classic *Dictionary of the Bible.*

History of Religions. In two volumes, this work gives detailed accounts of the religions of the civilized peoples of Asia, the Near East, and Europe.

Interpreter's Bible. Twelve volumes containing the King James and Revised Standard texts in large print, accompanied by an exegesis.

New Schaff-Herzog Encyclopedia of Religious Knowledge. A standard work in thirteen volumes and two supplements.

Religions, Mythologies, Folklore: an Annotated Bibliography. Includes periodicals, and is arranged by subject areas and by type of book.

Sacred Books of the East. Translations of the most important works of seven non-Christian religions that have influenced the civilization of Asia. In 50 volumes.

Science and Technology

The constant multiplication of reference books in scientific and technological fields insures that information even on very new branches is available. There are handbooks and dictionaries of terms for nearly all fields. There are encyclopedias of the classic sciences and of specialties such as Electronics, X rays and Gamma Rays, Space Science, and Polymer Science and Technology. Multilingual glossaries of scientific terms are also growing in number. Some other samples:

Bibliography of North American Geology. An annual publication of the U.S. Geological Survey.

Dictionary of the Biological Sciences, 1967, and *Encyclopedia of the Biological Sciences,* 1961, both edited by Peter Gray, with bibliographies.

Famous First Facts. A record of first happenings, discoveries, and inventions in the United States, with dates and descriptions of patented devices.

Geography of Commodity Production. Treats commodities of the world by their derivations: agriculture, the forest, the sea, mining, and manufacturing.

Gray's *Anatomy of the Human Body.* A classic which is still re-edited.

Guide to the Literature of Mathematics and Physics. An excellent bibliographical aid.

Harper Encyclopedia of Science. A four-volume work of broad scope, issued in 1963; one-volume edition, 1967.

History of Magic and Experimental Science. By Lynn Thorndike. A well-documented eight-volume work.

Horus: A Guide to the History of Science. One of several works by George Sarton elucidating the early development of science. Has an extensive bibliography.

McGraw-Hill Encyclopedia of Science and Technology. A fifteen-volume set, supplemented by yearbooks.

Van Nostrand's Scientific Encyclopedia. A one-volume compendium on science in general.

Social Sciences

In addition to dictionaries of politics, economics, and the social sciences, and the classic *Palgrave's Dictionary of Political Economy,* there are a number of one-volume encyclopedias in this field. Some other references:

American Negro Reference Book. One volume giving history, statistics, economic and legal status of Negro people in the United States.

Biographical Directory of the American Congress, 1774–1961. Information not easy to find elsewhere.

Black's Law Dictionary. Defines terms and phrases in legal use in America and England, ancient and modern.

Cambridge Economic History of Europe. In six volumes; covers the time from the Middle Ages to the current era.

Commercial Atlas and Marketing Guide. One of Rand McNally's specialized atlases of the United States.

Encyclopaedia of the Social Sciences. In fifteen volumes, the main comprehensive reference work in the field.

Encyclopedia of Social Work. An extension of the former *Social Work Yearbook,* in its fifteenth issue in 1965.

International Bibliography of Economics; of Sociology. Annual publications of UNESCO.

International Encyclopedia of the Social Sciences. A sixteen-volume work issued in 1968 and designed to complement the *Encyclopaedia of the Social Sciences.*

The Negro in America: A Bibliography. A Harvard University Press publication; 2nd edition, 1970. Emphasis is on books and articles published since 1954.

Political Handbook and Atlas of the World. An annual publication of the Council on Foreign Relations.

Reference Encyclopedia of the American Indian. A guide to sources of information; includes a bibliography of books in print and a Who's Who.

Sources of Information in the Social Sciences: A Guide to the Literature. A good bibliography published in 1964.

Worldmark Encyclopedia of the Nations. A comprehensive five-volume work.

EXERCISES

A. *Suppose that you were going to write a paper on one of the following subjects. Choose the sources named in this chapter that you would consult for general preliminary information and the indexes you would search for periodical articles on the subject.*

Michelangelo	Charlotte Corday
American riots	Martin Luther King
Earthquakes	Ulysses
Zen Buddhism	Alchemy
The Moon	Transistors
Dolphins	*Catch-22*

B. *Compile a bibliography for an essay about one of the following persons. Consult all the possible sources suggested in this chapter, including your library's card catalog. Try to find at least twenty items: books, periodical articles, sources of biographical information.*

Winston Churchill	Bartolomeo Vanzetti
Mao Tse-tung	Jenny Lind
Henry David Thoreau	Sequoya
Gautama Buddha	Carry Nation
Hermann Hesse	Henri Christophe
Jack the Ripper	Margaret Fuller

Chapter 12

The Research Paper

The research paper goes under various names, but whether it is called a "research paper," a "documented paper," a "library paper," an "investigative paper," or a "reading report," it is based on a student's reading on a selected subject. The student chooses a topic, reads about it in books and periodicals, takes notes, and writes a long paper on his findings.

Depending on the time available for the project, the research paper may range in length from five to fifteen typewritten pages. The paper may be one of three types: a *report,* a *thesis,* or a *solution to a problem.*

The writer of a *report* wishes to find out the facts of his subject and present them in a clear, orderly, and detailed account; he is not required to make any judgment from the facts. For example, a student reporting the opinions of critics about one of Hemingway's novels must show what the criticism is; he need not evaluate it.

The writer of a *thesis* paper is studying the facts of his subject to draw a conclusion from them. This conclusion is the result of his study and becomes the thesis of his paper. His whole paper is an explanation or justification of that thesis. For example, a student who has studied the text and criticisms of *Adventures of Huckleberry Finn* and has decided that the final chapters weaken the novel begins with that thesis and devotes his paper to supporting it.

A student who is attempting to *solve a problem* in his research paper first states and explains the problem, then identifies and evaluates suggested solutions, and finally shows what solution he prefers and why. That solution is his judgment, but the judgment need not be stated as an introductory thesis; it may and probably will be withheld until the student has considered alternative solutions.

Which type of research paper you write will probably be decided by your instructor's directions for the assignment. Since both the thesis paper and the problem-solving paper necessarily include some reporting, the two latter types are emphasized in this chapter.

PREVIEW OF RESEARCH PROCEDURE

Before we consider the separate steps in preparing a research paper, let us first preview the whole procedure. This procedure may be summarized as follows:

1. Make a survey of the material available on your general subject.
2. Become familiar with the general subject through introductory sources, but postpone note-taking.
3. Restrict the general subject as quickly as you can. Remember that your reading does not become fully pertinent until you have decided the question you wish to answer or the specific phase of the subject that you wish to develop.
4. When you feel that your subject is becoming specialized, prepare a working bibliography and begin to take notes.
5. Continue to restrict your subject as soon as the results of your specialized reading suggest further restriction.
6. When you feel that restriction of the subject is complete, and that you have found your real subject, decide what precisely you intend to do with it.
7. Begin the preliminary outlining of your paper. You have probably already begun to plan the organization in your head or by means of scratch outlines, but you are now ready for more formal outlines.
8. Fill in by additional investigation the blank areas that remain.
9. When the research is complete, make a final outline and write the first draft of your paper.

Most of the steps summarized above are preparatory. The total process would be considerably shortened if you knew at the beginning what you know by the time you have reached step 6. The more quickly you arrive at step 7, therefore, the more profitable your investigations will be and the less time they will require. Under favorable conditions you may be able to skip some of the preliminary stages, but even if you cannot, a clear realization that you are looking for a phase of the subject that may be dealt with completely within the limits of your paper will help you to speed up the first steps.

THE INVESTIGATIVE PROCESS

The actual composition of a research paper is not basically different from the process you studied in earlier chapters of this book. Here, as in other essays, you first define your purpose, then gather, select, and organize material, and finally develop your material into a unified essay. Most of the new problems you will encounter in this assignment come from two sources: the extended scope of the investigation and the technical requirements of footnoting and bibliography. The following pages deal with these problems.

Choosing a Subject

The nature of the research paper rules out the following kinds of subjects:

1. One that could be developed solely from personal experience and therefore does not require research—for example, an autobiographical topic.
2. One that is so subjective that it cannot be significantly influenced by research. For example, no matter how much reading you do, you will not find any reliable answer to the question "Which is the greater poet—Yeats or Eliot?"
3. One that could be adequately developed from a single source, such as an explanation of a process.

If these subjects are avoided, any topic that a student could explore and come to a decision about may be suitable, *provided that the decision can be fully explained or supported within the time and space available for the assignment.* Ideally, your subject should arise out of your need or desire to find an answer to some question. If, as a result of previous experience, you want an answer to such questions as

Why is English spelling so illogical?

What do people mean by "the new grammars"?

Is Henry James's *The Turn of the Screw* a ghost story or a study of hysteria?—

you have a specific subject which poses the problem for investigation. If your reading provides you with an answer to the question, you then have a thesis for your paper. For example, on the first question you may decide that the invention of the printing press had the effect of standardizing English spelling while the sounds were still changing, so that the spellings of words today often reflect an earlier pronunciation. Even if you are not satisfied that any one answer is sufficient, you will have a specific problem that can be discussed and explained.

Make your subject as specific as possible. A general subject can be restricted when your reading suggests that it is too broad, and this kind of restriction is normal. But the longer it takes you to restrict a general subject, the less purposeful your reading will be. If you begin with "The Novels of Henry James" and then restrict that subject, first to *The Turn of the Screw,* and then to the question of how that novel should be interpreted, much of your early reading will have no bearing on the question you finally deal with.´

Introductory Reading

For most research studies the reading may be divided into three stages—introductory, intensive, and supplementary. The introductory reading gives the background needed in order to begin the investigation intelligently. The intensive reading provides the bulk of the information from which the paper will be written. The supplementary reading fills in gaps and provides added information needed to make the paper complete.

Once the function of the introductory reading is understood, it becomes clear that note-taking at this stage is not profitable. The information obtained from this reading is probably not going to appear in your paper, or if it does, it will probably be so general that notes are not needed. This reading should therefore be done quickly. Indeed, the early accumulation of miscellaneous notes may actually be confusing, since a student who has notes on every aspect of his subject is likely to have a harder time deciding which phase of it to concentrate on.

Usually the best sources for introductory reading are general works—articles in encyclopedias, chapters in textbooks, histories, biographical references, and specialized dictionaries. For example, a student setting out to answer the question, "How did English spelling become so illogical?" might begin with the article on the English language in a good unabridged dictionary, the *Encyclopaedia Britannica,* or textbooks such as Baugh's *History of the English Language* or Jespersen's *Growth and Structure of the English Language.* These works would not only refer him to more specialized studies but would also provide him with the background necessary to profit from such studies.

Preparing a Bibliography

In the sense in which you will use the term in your college work, a bibliography is a list of books, articles, and other publications. In this chapter it will be useful to distinguish between a *working* bibliography and a *final* one. A *working bibliography* is a set of cards identifying works you consult during your study. It is a tentative bibliography, from which you weed out cards for titles that prove on examination to have no value for your purpose, and to which you add cards for other titles that come to your attention as you read intensively in your subject. A *final bibliography* is a typewritten list placed at the end of your finished paper. It is a record, not of all the items you consulted, but of those you found valuable. It will naturally contain fewer titles than your working bibliography.

The Working Bibliography. In preparing a working bibliography, a few minutes' careful consideration of the problem may save hours of needless work. Many students rush uncritically to the card catalog. Before you begin your actual search for titles, ask yourself two questions: What kind of material do I want? What are the most likely places to find it?

Different subjects require different approaches to the preparation of a bibliography. If you are dealing with a subject recently developed, the card catalog will be of little use to you. It records only books, and the very latest material in a book is usually at least a year old. For a current topic you must get most of your information from newspapers and recent magazine articles. On the other hand, many subjects—the development of the alphabet, for example—have been thoroughly treated in books, and little of significance will be found about them in current periodicals. The best general sources of information are the card catalog and the *Readers' Guide to Periodical Literature*. For some subjects the best approach will be through an index to technical publications; for others, *The New York Times Index* may yield the required information most readily. Before beginning the bibliography, you should check the appropriate lists of reference works in Chapter 11.

Once you have started to prepare your bibliography, the following advice may be helpful:

1. Try to make your bibliography selective as you prepare it. There is no point in listing three titles which contain the same information, or books which have little to say on your subject. Develop the habit of guessing intelligently whether a book will be useful to you. In some subjects—space exploration, for example—an older book is likely to be out of date. Usually the best way to guess at a book's usefulness is to draw it out of the library and look at it quickly. Read the preface, or part of it; check the table of contents; see how much space it gives to your subject. With a little practice you will usually be able to tell within three minutes whether the book will be of use to you.

2. Watch for critical bibliographies, which evaluate the works they list and thus tell you what sources are best and for what topics. Many studies contain such bibliographies, at the ends of chapters or the end of the whole work, and so give you valuable leads to other sources.

3. Study the indexes of books on related subjects. A book on psychotherapy may contain a pertinent discussion of hypnotism. But do not begin to read it through merely in the hope that it *may* contain such information. Instead, turn to the index, see how many references are given under hypnotism or related headings, and sample the most likely of these references.

All this advice may be summed up in two words: *act purposefully*. You save time, and work with more confidence and enjoyment, if you are not just drifting around in a library hoping to pick up useful information but are following a calculated plan for discovering it.

The Form of the Working Bibliography. The working bibliography is made on 3-by-5-inch cards, with each title on a separate card. Each card should contain three essential pieces of information: (1) the name of the author, (2) the title of the work, (3) the facts of publication. In addition, a card may contain, for the convenience of the student, the library call number and a note concerning the contents of the work. The card on the opposite page is typical for a book.

The form of the entry varies with the kind of publication being cited, and the major variations are illustrated in the sample bibliographical entries shown on pages 265–69.

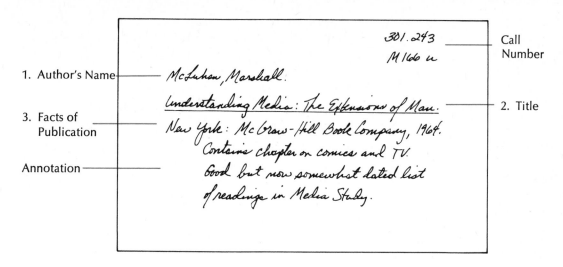

1. Author's Name

3. Facts of Publication

Annotation

301.243
M 166 u

Call Number

2. Title

McLuhan, Marshall.

Understanding Media: The Extensions of Man.
New York: McGraw-Hill Book Company, 1964.
Contains chapter on comics and TV.
Good but now somewhat dated list
of readings in Media Study.

Sample Bibliographical Entries

1. A Book by a Single Author or Agency

Gulley, Halbert E.   Essentials of Group Discussion.
    New York: Holt, Rinehart and Winston, Inc., 1969.

a. The author's surname comes before his given name or initials for ease in alphabetizing.

b. If the book is the work of an agency, committee, organization, or department, rather than of an individual, the name of the agency takes the place of the author's name.

c. If no author is given, the citation begins with the title.

d. The title of the book is italicized (represented in manuscript by underlining each word separately).

e. The facts of publication are the place of publication, the publisher, and the date of publication, in that order.

f. If more than one place is given on the title page, use only the first.

g. Give the publisher's name as it appears on the title page.

h. If no date of publication is given, use the latest copyright date, usually found on the reverse of the title page.

i. The punctuation in the sample above is the preferred form.

2. A Book by Two Authors

Ashby, Eric, and Mary Anderson.   The Rise of the Student Estate in Britain.   Cambridge, Mass.: Harvard University Press, 1970.

a. The name of the second author is not inverted; otherwise the form is the same as that of Example 1.

b. The order of the authors' names is the same as that on the title page; hence Ashby comes first, even though Anderson would be alphabetically earlier.

3. A Book by Several Authors

Murray, Elwood, and others. <u>Integrative Speech</u>. New York: The Dryden Press, 1953.

a. The Latin abbreviation *et al.* is a common variation of "and others" and is preferred by *The MLA Style Sheet*. Consult your instructor's preference. If *et al.* is used, the first part of this item would read:

Murray, Elwood, <u>et al</u>.

b. When there are three authors, but not more than three, it is a common practice to give all three names, as shown in Example 7, below.

4. An Edition Other Than the First

Bailey, Sydney D. <u>British Parliamentary Democracy</u>. 3rd ed. Boston: Houghton Mifflin Company, 1971.

a. If the work is a revised or later edition, the appropriate abbreviated designation (Rev. ed., 2nd ed., 3rd ed., 7th ed.) is placed immediately after the title and separated from it by a period.

b. Only the date of the edition being cited is given.

5. A Work of More Than One Volume

Johnson, Edgar. <u>Charles Dickens: His Tragedy and Triumph</u>. 2 vols. New York: Simon and Schuster, 1952.

a. The number of volumes follows the title, is separated from it by a period, and is always abbreviated as shown.

b. If the volumes of a multivolume work were published over a period of years, the inclusive dates are given, as shown in the next entry.

6. An Edition of an Author's Work

Haight, Gordon S., ed. <u>The George Eliot Letters</u>. 7 vols. New Haven: Yale University Press, 1954–55.

See also under item 8 below.

7. An Edited Collection or Anthology

Kinney, Arthur F., Kenneth W. Kuiper, and Lynn Z. Bloom, eds. <u>Symposium</u>. Boston: Houghton Mifflin Company, 1969.

8. A Translation or an Edited Work

Hesse, Hermann. Beneath the Wheel, trans. Michael
     Roloff. New York: Farrar, Straus and Giroux, 1968.

Arnold, Matthew. God and the Bible, ed. R. H. Super.
     Ann Arbor: The University of Michigan Press, 1970.

9. A Pamphlet

Because there is considerable variation in the bibliographical information
given in pamphlets, they are sometimes difficult to cite. Whenever possible,
treat them like books, with or without an author (Example 1). If the bibliographical information is so incomplete that you cannot confidently describe the pamphlet, show it to your instructor and get his advice. Following
are four variant forms:

Chafee, Zechariah, Jr. Freedom of Speech and Press.
     New York: Carrie Chapman Catt Memorial Fund, 1955.

League of Women Voters of the United States. Choosing
     the President. Publication No. 301. Washington,
     D.C., 1964.

U.S. Bureau of the Census. Historical Statistics of
     the United States, Colonial Times to 1957; Continua-
     tion to 1962 and Revisions. Washington, D.C.:
     U.S. Government Printing Office, 1965.

Your Library: A Guide for Undergraduate Students,
     University of Illinois [n.d.].

a. The last example is intended to show a difficult pamphlet, since the
only bibliographical information given is the title.

b. The symbol [n.d], meaning "no date," is used to show that no date of
publication or copyright is given and that the omission is not your over-
sight. If your typewriter does not have brackets, put them in by hand.

10. An Essay in an Edited Collection

Barnes, Robert J. "Junked Autos: An Embodiment of the
     Litter Philosophy." In Congress and the Environ-
     ment, ed. Richard A. Cooley and Geoffrey Wandesforde
     Smith. Seattle: University of Washington Press,
     1970.

a. This entry requires two titles and both an author and an editor.

b. The title of the essay (or story or poem) is in quotation marks.

c. The title of the book is italicized and is preceded by "In."

11. An Article in an Encyclopedia

Macaulay, Thomas Babington. "Samuel Johnson."
    Encyclopaedia Britannica, 11th ed., XV, 463–71.

"Navigation Acts." The Columbia Encyclopedia, 1950,
    pp. 1367–68.

a. Some encyclopedia articles are initialed, and the authors are identified in a list at the beginning of the volume. The article on Johnson is signed *M*, Macaulay's initial.

b. The British spelling *Encyclopaedia* is often bothersome to American students. Copy the title exactly as it is given on the title page.

c. Facts of publication are usually omitted.

d. Either the edition number *or* the date of publication may be used. Thus "1911" could have been used instead of "11th ed." in the first example, and "2nd ed." instead of "1950" in the second.

12. A Magazine Article

Rollin, Roger B. "Beowulf to Batman: The Epic Hero
    and Pop Culture." College English, 31 (February
    1970), 431–49.

Gilman, Richard. "The FemLib Case Against Sigmund
    Freud." The New York Times Magazine, January 31,
    1971, pp. 10–11, 42–47.

a. The first entry shows the standard form for a magazine article. No place of publication or publisher is given, but volume, date, and page numbers are shown. The volume number precedes the date, and the page numbers follow it. The words "volume" and "page" or "pages" (or their abbreviations "vol.," "p.," "pp.") are not used when, as here, both volume and page numbers are given.

b. The second entry shows the form for magazines published oftener than once a month and magazines issued as newspaper supplements. No volume number is given, and the abbreviation "p." (or "pp.") is used.

13. A Newspaper Article

Field, Roger Kenneth. "Automated Medicine." The New
    York Times, January 31, 1971, sec. 3, p. 8.

Editorial. The [Champaign, Ill.] News–Gazette,
    June 11, 1970, p. 12.

"Four–Day Workweek Gains More Converts." The Wall
    Street Journal, January 28, 1971, p. 5.

a. The examples successively illustrate a signed article, an untitled editorial, and a titled but unsigned story.

b. The name of the city is italicized if it appears on the newspaper as part of the title. If not, it is inserted without italics in square brackets, as shown in the second entry above. The definite article is included if part of the title.

EXERCISE

In order to get practice as quickly as possible with the various forms illustrated in this discussion, convert the following information into conventional bibliographical form. You can check your answers against the appropriate preceding illustrations, since the number of each exercise corresponds to the number of the appropriate illustration.

---

1. A book by John R. Reinhard called Medieval Pageant, copyrighted in 1939 and published by Harcourt, Brace and Company in New York.

2. A book called The Reader Over Your Shoulder, written by Robert Graves and Alan Hodge, and published in New York by The Macmillan Company in 1944.

3. A book published by the University of Illinois Press at Urbana, Illinois, in 1952. The book was written by Gordon N. Ray, Carl J. Weber, and John Carter and is called Nineteenth Century English Books.

4. The second edition of a book entitled A Browning Handbook, written by William Clyde DeVane and published by Appleton-Century-Crofts of New York. This second edition was published in 1955.

5. A two-volume edition of Selected Works of Stephen Vincent Benét, prepared by the author and published by Farrar and Rinehart of New York in 1942.

6. John M. Manley's edition of Canterbury Tales by Geoffrey Chaucer, copyrighted in 1928 and published in New York by Henry Holt and Company.

7. Masters of American Literature, a two-volume work edited by Leon Edel, Thomas H. Johnson, Sherman Paul, and Claude Simpson, and published in Boston by Houghton Mifflin Company in 1959.

8. A translation by Dorothy Bussy of a novel by André Gide. The translation, called Lafcadio's Adventures, was published by Alfred A. Knopf, Inc. of New York in 1928.

9. A pamphlet entitled Animal Books for Children, prepared by The American Humane Association and printed in Denver, Colorado, in 1969.

10. Edward Albee's essay entitled Which Theatre Is the Absurd One?, reprinted in Directions in Modern Theatre and Drama, which was edited by John Gassner and published by Holt, Rinehart and Winston, Inc., New York, with a copyright date of 1965.

11. An article on Printing, in the 1967 edition of Collier's Encyclopedia. The article appears on pages 380–92 of Volume 19 and is signed by Elbridge W. Palmer.

12. An article entitled The Relevance and Irrelevance of Romanticism, on pages 297–306 of Volume 9 of Studies in Romanticism, a quarterly journal. The article was written by Karl Kroeber and appeared in 1970 in the Fall issue.

13. An unsigned story headed "Pollution Spawned by Greed" in the Montreal newspaper The Gazette. The story appeared on page 5 on January 28, 1971.

The Final Bibliography. The final bibliography will be typed from the bibliographical cards and will follow the forms already discussed. It should contain a citation for each work mentioned in the footnotes. It may also contain a few works which you found to be useful background references, even though you neither cited nor quoted them in your paper. But padding a bibliography to make it look imposing is more likely to annoy than to impress an instructor.

In typing or writing your bibliography, observe the following conventions unless your instructor recommends modifications.

1. If the bibliography is long, group the publications according to type: books, magazine articles, newspaper articles, etc. When the bibliography consists of a single page, this grouping is less necessary. If in doubt whether grouping is desirable, consult your instructor.

2. Within each group, list items alphabetically by author's surname, or if the author is not given, by the first letter of the title (not counting "A," "An," or "The").

3. If more than one book by the same author is being listed, you may substitute a 7-space line for the author's name after you have once given it:

Baldwin, T. W. William Shakespeare's Five-Act
  Structure. . . .

————. William Shakespeare's Petty School. . . .

4. Single-space each item and double-space between items.
5. In each item, indent two spaces for all lines after the first.

Note-taking

When you begin intensive reading, you should also begin taking notes. The results of your preliminary reading may be carried in your head, but you are now beginning to collect the actual evidence from which your paper will be written, and it is important to the success of all the rest of your work that both the form and the content of your notes be satisfactory.

The Form of the Notes.   All notes should be written on cards[1] and should contain two kinds of information: (1) the fact or opinion being noted, and (2) the exact source from which you took it. This second item is absolutely necessary, since you will be required to identify the sources of your material in the footnotes to your paper. Here is a typical note made from a book:

> McLuhan; p. 166
>
> The depth involvement generated by TV encouraged people to take themselves more seriously, so that the distortions of the comics no longer seemed funny, and Dogpatch no more absurd than everyday life.

Your bibliographical card (page 265) would provide the author's full name, the title, and the facts of publication, so if you were using no other work by this author, and no work by another author having the same surname, "McLuhan, p. 166" would be identification enough for your note card; otherwise you should expand the identification to avoid confusion—for example, "McLuhan, Marshall, *Understanding Media,* p. 166." To avoid any possibility of a slip, *always write the identification before you begin the note.*

The practice of using note cards instead of notebooks has grown out of the experience of thousands of research workers. To be really useful your notes must be so flexible that you can shuffle them to suit whatever order you finally decide on and can discard useless notes easily. Notes written solid in a notebook cannot conveniently be arranged or edited. They are fixed in the order they had in the source from which they were taken, whereas the order that suits your final purpose may be entirely different. Recording information in a notebook is therefore inefficient, no matter how easy it may seem at first glance.

Only one note should be placed on a card. Two notes on one card are inseparably bound together. Since you must be free to shuffle your notes, to discard useless ones and add supplementary ones, the only satisfactory method is to use a separate card for each.

[1] Some instructors prefer 4-by-6-inch cards for notes, in contrast with the 3-by-5-inch bibliographical cards.

Leave enough space at the top of each card (see above) so that you may write in a subject heading when you group your cards and develop your outline. Because these subject headings may be changed as your organization develops, it is wise to enter them in pencil.

The Contents of Notes. Your notes may contain statements of fact or of opinion, in your own words or in the words of the author from whose work they came. The cards shown at the top of page 273 contrast a quoted opinion and the same opinion stated in the student's words. *If the wording as well as the content is taken from a source, be extremely careful to use quotation marks, both on your note card and, later, in your paper.* Failure to use quotation marks on the note card may later lead you to think that the information is expressed in your own words and thus may trap you into unintentional plagiarism.[2]

Whenever possible, your notes should be summaries of the source material, not direct quotations. Summarizing encourages you to *select* and *extract* the information most relevant to your purpose, and lessens the temptation to quote excessively when you write your paper. Too many quotations in a research paper give the impression that the student has merely strung together statements made by others without digesting these statements or doing any thinking about them. But in summarizing material, care must be taken to be sure that the summary accurately represents the content of the original source. You should therefore check your summary against the original before you consider the note card final. If you are then satisfied that you have not distorted the information in summarizing it, the economy

[2] Plagiarism is the presentation of another's writing or ideas as one's own.

Danzig, p. 35   zero

    "In the history of culture the discovery of zero will always stand as one of the greatest single achievements of the human race."

zero

Danzig, p. 35
· Discovery of zero one of greatest cultural accomplishments.

of the summary will be constructively carried over to your paper. A summary thus helps to make both the note-taking and the writing more efficient. The following note, for example, is an accurate summary of a five-paragraph passage containing about 500 words:

number sense

Danzig, pp. 1-3
    Says number sense not to be confused with counting. Counting confined to humans, but some animals, birds, insects — crows and "solitary wasps," for example — have remarkable sense of number.

Notice that such cards are identified just as carefully as if they contained direct quotations. The material is taken from the work of another and must be acknowledged in footnotes.

There are two exceptions to this advice to summarize content whenever possible. (1) If you are going to criticize a passage, you should quote it directly and you should be careful not to distort the meaning of even a direct quotation by presenting it out of context. If the context is so long that it cannot conveniently be given in full, you are under a special obligation to be sure that the quotation faithfully represents the author's meaning. (2) The second exception is statements that are so apt, dramatic, or forceful that they would lose some of their effect in a restatement or a summary.

What has been said about note-taking may be summarized as follows:

1. Put notes on cards, not in notebooks, with one note to a card.

2. On each card identify the exact source of the note, including the page number. Use abbreviations only when there is no danger of ambiguity.

3. Enclose in quotation marks the actual words of an author, whether the notes are statements of fact or of opinion.

4. Summarize extensive quotations if possible, but still identify the source.

5. Use direct quotation whenever the exact wording may be significant, especially if you are going to criticize a statement in the source.

6. Be careful that your notes—whether direct quotations or summaries—do not distort the meaning when taken out of their original context.

THE COMPOSING PROCEDURE

Stating the Problem or Thesis

If the paper is intended to solve a problem, it should begin with a clear statement of that problem. Such a statement not only serves as a natural introduction but also may indicate the purpose and organization of the paper. Notice how clearly the problem is stated in the following example.

While most critics agree that Henry James's novel *The Turn of the Screw* is one of the greatest horror stories ever written, they have disagreed vigorously for nearly fifty years about how it should be interpreted. The root of the quarrel is the character of the governess, from whose point of view and in whose words the story is told. Is she a courageous young woman fighting a losing battle to save two innocent children from evil spirits who are trying to corrupt them? Or is she a hysterical girl who destroys the children placed in her care by her efforts to save them from ghosts which are products of her neurotic imagination?

The purpose of this paper is to review the controversy and evaluate it. Specifically, the paper considers three questions: What are the key issues in the controversy? What was the author's intent? Is the controversy a result of the ambiguity of the work itself? Since those who believe that the ghosts are "real" and constitute a mortal threat to the children are in the majority, their judgment will be called the *majority interpretation*. The conviction that the governess imagines the ghosts will be called the *minority interpretation*. The problem is to decide, if possible, which interpretation is better supported by the evidence of the text and of James's own comments on the story.

If the paper is intended to develop a thesis, that thesis is the conclusion the student has reached as a result of his study of the subject. For example, any one of the following statements could be the thesis of an essay on the interpretation of *The Turn of the Screw:*

1. All things considered, the majority interpretation provides the most satisfactory reading of *The Turn of the Screw.*

2. The minority interpretation of *The Turn of the Screw* is consistent with the actions of the governess and her relations with the other characters in the story.

3. A study of *The Turn of the Screw* and of critical comments concerning it provides no definitive answer to the question of how it should be interpreted.

4. The controversy over the interpretation of *The Turn of the Screw* is inherent in the ambiguities which James, either consciously or unconsciously, built into the story.

Whichever thesis is chosen will be stated at or near the beginning of the paper, usually in the first paragraph, although it may be preceded by an introductory paragraph, as the following example shows. For ease of recognition the thesis has been italicized.

Distinguished critics have strongly disagreed about whether Henry James's *The Turn of the Screw* should be read as a ghost story or as a tale of hallucination. Both sides have presented documented arguments to support their case, and each insists that the other interpretation ignores significant evidence and weakens the artistry of the novel. After fifty years of such controversy, the question of interpretation is still unresolved.

A study of the novel and of the critical comments about it provides no definitive answer to the question of how it should be interpreted. On all key issues the text can be legitimately used to support either interpretation, and James's own comments are so ambiguous and inconsistent that each side can use them to support its case.

Outlining the Paper

Since the research paper is usually one of the longest and most complex papers written in a composition course, it nearly always requires a careful outline. Indeed, many instructors make the writing of a detailed outline a critical stage in the preparation of the paper and do not allow students to begin actual composition until the outline is approved.

The outline of a problem-solving paper may be either a sentence or a topic outline, although usually a topic outline is more convenient. On the problem of how *The Turn of the Screw* is to be interpreted, the outline suggested by the statement on page 274 would consist of five main headings: I. The statement of the problem; II. The key issues in the controversy; III. The author's intent; IV. The ambiguity of the text; and V. Conclusions. Except for the introductory and concluding headings, all headings would be subdivided as fully as necessary. For example, heading II might be subdivided as follows:

II. The key issues in the controversy
  A. The governess' relations with her employer
  B. The situations in which she sees the ghosts
  C. Her descriptions of the ghosts
  D. Her relations with the children
  E. The final scene

and these headings could be subdivided into smaller units.

A paper developing a thesis nearly always needs a sentence outline because it is working out a single idea through a sequence of sub-ideas and the rigor of the sentence outline helps to establish a logical relation among the parts. The best preparation for this kind of outline is a review of pages 67–77.

Writing the Paper

All that has been said about composition earlier in this book applies to the research paper. But in addition the research assignment has its special problem—the relationship between borrowed material and the use that is made of it. The research paper is admittedly and necessarily written from information derived from various sources. But that information has to be woven into an essay which is essentially the student's own work. A student who has worked purposefully will not have much difficulty reconciling these two conditions, for he will have selected his material with a view to using it in support of a purpose he has been forming as he reads. In a sense he is like a man who is building a house with bricks obtained from others. The bricks are not of his making, but the design and construction of the house are. *Writing a research paper, then, is not just stringing together statements from books and magazines. It is a complete reorganization and reworking of the source material into an original composition.*

Failure to recognize this sometimes results in a paper that is merely a transcription of the information in the note cards. The following excerpt from a student research paper reveals this weakness.

Article 123 of the Mexican Constitution has the sole purpose of solving the labor problem. It is

looked upon as the declaration of the rights of the
workmen.[10]

The workers' hours have a maximum limit of eight
hours for a day's work. At least one day's rest for
every six days' work is to be enjoyed by everyone.[11]

Children over twelve and under sixteen years of
age can work only six hours a day, and children under
twelve are not permitted to be made the subject of a
contract.[12]

The minimum wage that can be received by a workman should be considered sufficient according to the
conditions of life prevailing in the workman's particular region of the country. This same compensation
is to be paid without regard to the sex of the
worker.[13]

Wages are required to be paid in legal currency
rather than by any other representative token with
which it is sought to substitute money.[14]

---

[10]Tannenbaum, p. 529.
[11]Tannenbaum, p. 529.
[12]Tannenbaum, p. 529.
[13]Tannenbaum, p. 529.
[14]Tannenbaum, p. 530.

What this student is doing is simply copying his notes into his paper. If
that is all he is going to do, he might as well hand in his note cards. The
composition problem is to take the raw material of the notes and process it
into a unified paragraph, perhaps one like the following:

Article 123 of the Mexican Constitution attempts
to standardize labor conditions by setting up basic
principles governing hours and salaries. It provides
a maximum work-week of six eight-hour days, prohibits

the contractual hiring of children under twelve years
of age, and limits the employment of children between
twelve and sixteen to six hours a day. It requires
that all wages be paid in legal currency, thus elim-
inating company scrip and other cash substitutes. It
provides for a minimum wage scale which takes into account differences in the standard and cost of living
in various parts of the country. It abolishes discrimination against women by making the wage rate the
same for both sexes. In general, therefore, it seeks
to establish a uniform code which will provide the
general pattern of labor-management relations throughout the country.[10]

---

[10] Tannenbaum, pp. 529-30.

The first of these two versions is a series of raw notes; the second is a unified paragraph created by the student. Both contain exactly the same facts, but the revised version rearranges and rewords the facts to make them develop the idea stated in the opening sentence. It also avoids the over-documentation of the first version by acknowledging the two pages of Tannenbaum's book as the source for all the information in the paragraph. If an instructor were to compare the second version with the notes from which it was written, he would clearly see that the writer had mastered the information he was using and had shaped it to suit his own purpose.

Because of the scope of the research paper, the composition should usually be done in three stages: writing the rough draft, preparing the final revision, and proofreading the finished paper. No two of these stages should be completed at a single sitting; indeed, it is best to allow at least a day between the completion of one and the beginning of the next.

How a student should compose the rough draft will depend partly on his work habits and partly on the nature of his material. For the average student the best advice is to break the total job into the main units of the outline and to tackle these units in order. The first draft of a paper so developed is likely to be a bit stiff, to proceed rather mechanically from one step to the next, and to lack the qualities that make for an interesting or effective style. But these are not serious weaknesses if careful revision is to follow.

Footnotes and any graphic illustrations (or notations of them) should be written into the rough draft to insure that they are not overlooked in the revision and to avoid difficulties with spacing in the final version. Even though footnotes are finally placed at the foot of the page, some students find it convenient in the first draft to insert them between ruled lines within the text immediately after the line containing the footnote marker. Not all research papers need or are suited to graphic illustrations—tables, graphs, charts—but since these aids present complex or cumbersome data compactly and thus make the reader's task easier, they should be used when they are appropriate.

When the first draft has been revised, the final bibliography should be added. This will be a list of the sources actually used in preparing the paper. It should include all sources cited in the footnotes and may contain one or two works which were valuable as background material even though not actually cited in the paper. The form of this bibliography was discussed on page 270.

Finally, *the paper should be proofread at least twice* to detect any errors which survived the revision. These readings should be mainly concerned with mechanical matters—doubtful spellings, punctuation, usage, and typographical errors. The proofreadings should include both the footnotes and the bibliography, and it is wise at this stage to check these against the recommended forms. Proofreading should be done slowly—more slowly than reading for content. Some students find it helpful to read the paper aloud slowly so as to concentrate on the appearance of each word.

Documenting the Evidence

As we have said, all information taken from a specific source must be identified in a footnote.[3] That is, the evidence must be *documented*. The purpose of this convention is twofold: (1) to avoid the appearance of representing somebody else's work as yours; (2) to let the interested reader consult your sources and so check the accuracy of your investigation or carry on his own. This convention is so important in research writing that inaccurate documentation—or none at all—is regarded as a serious offense. For the research writer it is both good manners and good morals to acknowledge sources fairly and accurately.

When to Footnote.   In general you should cite the source of any statement for which you are indebted to the work of another. For most student research this general principle can be broken down into six conditions. You should provide a footnote whenever:

1. You use a direct quotation.
2. You copy a table, chart, or other diagram.
3. You summarize a discussion in your own words.

[3] The kind of footnote discussed here is called a "reference footnote." Footnotes may also qualify, explain, or comment on statements made in the text when it would be awkward to include such matters in the main discussion. Such footnotes may be called "explanatory footnotes." This footnote is explanatory. It provides an explanation which, though necessary, would be awkward to include in the body of the text.

4. You construct a diagram from data provided by others.

5. You paraphrase an opinion which you have read rather than reached independently.

6. You present specific evidence which cannot reasonably be considered common knowledge.

The first four of these conditions are sufficiently definite to require no discussion. Difficulties, if any, will come from the last two, and these difficulties are better resolved by experience than by definition. By the time you are well into any research project, you will have reached conclusions you did not have when you began your study. Unless these conclusions came specifically from one of your sources, they need not be documented. They are products of your total reading, not borrowings from any specific source.

The question of what can legitimately be considered common knowledge is difficult to answer in the abstract, except by the general advice, *When in doubt, footnote it.* Since one function of the research paper is to give experience in documentation, your instructor will probably prefer too many footnotes rather than too few.

How to Footnote. A footnote consists of two parts: the footnote marker, a number placed in the text at the end of the statement to be documented and slightly above the level of the typed or handwritten line; and the footnote proper, which usually comes at the foot of the page and is numbered to correspond with the marker. Footnotes are separated from the text by a triple space and from each other by a double space. The first line of a footnote is indented, and footnote numbers do not start afresh on each page but run consecutively throughout the paper. These conventions are illustrated in the specimen paper on pages 285–305.

The purpose of the footnote is to identify as precisely as possible the source to which the statement in the text is indebted. Although no one form is universally preferred, the minimum information required is a clear reference to the author, title, and page. The first reference to a source needs to give fuller information than do subsequent references to that source.

In general, a footnote reference is similar in form to a bibliographical citation, *but there are noteworthy differences.* The following summary presents the most important conventions of footnoting.

1. Author

a. In a footnote the author's name is given in its normal order—John Smith —not inverted as in a bibliography.

b. When more than one author is to be named, the form is the same as that used in a bibliography (page 265) except that the first author's name is not inverted.

c. When a book has an editor instead of an author (for example, an anthology or a book of readings), the editor's name in normal order goes in place of the author's name and is followed by "ed." (For a reference to an item *within* such a book, see specimen footnote 4, page 282.)

d. After the first reference to a work in a footnote, the author's or editor's name is usually shortened to surname only in subsequent footnotes.

e. If there is no author's or editor's name, the footnote begins with the title.

2. Title

All titles follow the forms used in bibliography, but in the second and subsequent footnote references, the author's surname and the page number are enough—for example: Gulley, p. 11—provided that only one author is being cited by that name and only one book or article by that author. Unless both these conditions are true, a short form of the title is commonly used—Gulley, *Essentials,* p. 11. After the first reference to a magazine or newspaper article, the title (or shortened title) of the magazine or newspaper may be used without the title of the article—*Life,* p. 17, or *New York Times,* p. 23. Obviously these short forms cannot be used if more than one issue is being cited.

3. Facts of Publication

a. The place, publisher, and date of publication are given in the first reference to a book. After that they are omitted. The facts of publication are enclosed in parentheses, and the style is as follows—(Boston: Houghton Mifflin Company, 1971). Sometimes the name of the publisher is omitted if there is a bibliography which gives this information. When only the place and date of publication are given in the first footnote reference, they are separated by a comma—(Boston, 1971).

b. The facts of publication for a magazine article do not include place and publisher, but do include the volume and page numbers (see heading 4 below) and the date of issue—month (not abbreviated) or season, and year.

c. The facts of publication for a newspaper article or an article in a magazine published oftener than once a month consist of the month, day, and year, *not in parentheses,* and the page.

4. Volume and Page Numbers

a. In reference to a one-volume work, the abbreviation "p." is used for *page* and "pp." for *pages.*

b. When the reference is to a work of more than one volume, both the volume number and the page number must be given.

c. When both volume and page numbers are given, the abbreviations "vol." and "p." (or "pp.") are *not* used. Instead, use Roman numerals for the volume number and Arabic numerals for the page number: X, 48. An exception to this Roman numeral form is a reference to a magazine article. Then the volume and page numbers are *both* given in Arabic numerals, the volume number before the date and the page number after it: 2 (February 1956), 289.

5. Punctuation

The punctuation of the footnote need present no problem, since, except for the colon between place of publication and publisher, commas may be used throughout. A period is used at the end and of course after any abbreviations.

The following footnotes illustrate and supplement the preceding discussion. They may be used as models against which to check your own footnotes.

First Reference to a Book

[1]Eric Ashby and Mary Anderson, <u>The Rise of the Student Estate in Britain</u> (Cambridge, Mass.: Harvard University Press, 1970), p. 25.

Subsequent reference: Ashby and Anderson, p. 30.

Reference to a Multivolume Work

[2]Edgar Johnson, <u>Charles Dickens: His Tragedy and Triumph</u> (New York: Simon and Schuster, 1952), I, 193.

Subsequent reference: Johnson, II, 82.

Reference to a Second or Later Edition

[3]John Hope Franklin, <u>From Slavery to Freedom: A History of Negro Americans</u>, 3rd ed. (New York: Alfred A. Knopf, 1967), p. 506.

Subsequent reference: Franklin, p. 620.

Reference to an Essay in an Edited Collection

[4]Robert J. Barnes, "Junked Autos: An Embodiment of the Litter Philosophy," in <u>Congress and the Environment</u>, ed. Richard A. Cooley and Geoffrey Wandesforde Smith (Seattle: University of Washington Press, 1970), p. 283.

Subsequent reference: Barnes, p. 292.

Reference to a Magazine Article

[5]Roger B. Rollin, "Beowulf to Batman: The Epic Hero and Pop Culture," <u>College English</u>, 31 (February 1970), 431.

Subsequent reference: Rollin, p. 435.

[6]Mario Pei, "Prospects for a Global Language," <u>Saturday Review</u>, May 2, 1970, p. 23.

Subsequent reference: Pei, p. 25.

Reference to a Newspaper Article

[7] Roger Kenneth Field, "Automated Medicine," <u>The New York Times</u>, January 31, 1971, sec. 3, p. 8.

Subsequent reference: Field, p. 8.

[8] "Four-Day Workweek Gains More Converts," <u>The Wall Street Journal</u>, January 28, 1971, p. 5.

Subsequent reference: *Wall Street Journal*, p. 5.

Reference to an Article in an Encyclopedia

[9] "Traquair, Sir John Stewart," <u>Encyclopaedia Britannica</u>, 11th ed., XXVII, 214.

This article is unsigned. In a signed article, the author's name would precede the title of the article.

Reference to a Play by Act, Scene, and Line

[10] <u>Hamlet</u> III.i.56.

PRESENTING THE FINISHED ASSIGNMENT

The assignment has not been fully met until the paper has been presented to the instructor in the form which he has stipulated. A typical student research paper consists of the following parts:

1. A title page containing at least the title of the paper and the student's name and section number.

2. A detailed outline of the paper.

3. The body of the paper, typed if possible, each page numbered and adequately footnoted. Only one side of the page is used, of course. If the paper is typed, the text should be double-spaced. Quotations of five or more lines should be indented and single-spaced without quotation marks.

4. Conventional footnotes with corresponding footnote markers at appropriate points in the text.

5. A bibliography of works used in preparing the paper.

6. The note cards used in writing the paper, arranged in the order in which they were used, labeled with outline symbols to show their relation to the outline, and tied together or sealed in an envelope. The purpose of handing in the notes is to allow the instructor to trace the development of your paper from outline and notes to finished composition.

If your instructor wishes to modify these requirements, he will notify you. Make sure that you understand clearly what is wanted. If you are uncertain, consult your instructor well in advance of the deadline.

EXERCISE   *Following is a specimen research paper, complete with outline, text, footnotes, and bibliography. For your convenience in studying the structure of the paper the appropriate outline symbols have been inserted in the margin, though they would not normally appear in your paper. First, read the text to become generally familiar with the content of the paper. Second, study the outline to see if it is a logical development of the thesis. Third, check the text against the outline symbols to see if the structure of the paper reflects the structure of the outline. Finally, check the forms of the footnotes and the bibliography.*

The format, or physical appearance, of this paper illustrates general principles of good usage.

The text is double spaced.

Paragraphs are indented 5 spaces.

Long quotations are single spaced and are indented 8 spaces from the left margin. Paragraphs within these block quotations are indented 3 additional spaces.

Footnotes are single spaced, but a double space (one blank line) is left between footnotes to allow for raising the footnote number. Each footnote begins on a new line, with regular paragraph indention.

Footnotes are separated from the text either (a) by a short ruled line starting at the left margin, a double space below the last line of text, as shown here, or (b) by a triple space with no rule, as preferred by *The MLA Style Sheet.* Your instructor's preference should be followed in this respect.

White typewriter paper of standard size (8½ by 11 inches) should be used, on one side only. Margins should be generous. Pages should be numbered in the upper right-hand corner, except for the opening page (page 1) for which the number may be omitted or centered at the bottom.

The Book That Refused to Die:
James Agee's Let Us Now Praise Famous Men

Thesis: The initial failure and ultimate success of Let Us Now Praise
Famous Men may be seen as the triumph of an unconventional
literary theory when the critical climate is ready for it.

I. The publishing history of the work shows a reversal of
critical standards.

   A. The book grew out of an article rejected by Fortune.

   B. In 1941 the book was rejected by both the critics and
the public.

   C. In 1960 a reissue of the book was favorably received.

II. The writing of the book was dominated by Agee's unconventional
literary theory.

   A. The book did not fit into any accepted category.

   B. Agee rejected realism as an adequate technique for describing real experience and preferred a subjective approach.

   C. He was seeking a breakthrough in literary form, one that
would bring prose closer to music and poetry.

   D. These unconventional aims dominated the content, structure,
and style of the book.

      1. His concern with a subjective approach to human
behavior determined his view of the sharecropper.

      2. His attitudes about literary form affected the
structure of the book.

      3. His style shows the influence of music and cinema.

III. The critical climate in 1960 made Agee's unconventional treatment of his material more acceptable than it had been in 1941.

   A. The relaxation of the emphases of a war economy allowed the
plight of the sharecropper to re-emerge as a significant
subject.

   B. A postwar generation of "anti-realistic" writers made critics
more receptive to subjectivity and literary experiment.

   C. Agee's other published works provided a context in which
Let Us Now Praise Famous Men could be re-examined, and his
untimely death encouraged a more sympathetic appraisal.

The question which posed the problem for investigation and the thesis which provides an answer are stated in the opening paragraph.

Thesis: The initial failure and ultimate success of <u>Let Us Now Praise Famous Men</u> may be seen as the triumph of an unconventional literary theory when the critical climate is ready for it.

I. The publishing history of the work shows a reversal of critical standards.

   A. The book grew out of an article rejected by <u>Fortune</u>.

The second paragraph begins with the development of subhead I A. The comprehensive Roman-numeral heading I is stated as a summary topic sentence at the end of Part I, under I C. Is this an effective position for the statement? Why or why not?

Footnote 1 is an example of an explanatory footnote which provides necessary or useful information that would be a digression in the text.

THE BOOK THAT REFUSED TO DIE:

JAMES AGEE'S LET US NOW PRAISE FAMOUS MEN

When James Agee's long prose work, Let Us Now Praise Famous Men,
was first published in 1941, it was condemned by the critics and
ignored by the public. When it was republished in 1960, it was both
a critical and a commercial success. Why so complete a reversal in
such a short time? The answer this paper will offer is that both
the initial failure and the later triumph resulted from Agee's unconventional treatment of his subject, a treatment that violated the
prevailing standards of the time but was more acceptable two decades
later.

Thesis

I A

The book had its beginnings in the summer of 1936 when Fortune
magazine sent Agee and Walker Evans, the photographer, into the deep
South to do a story on tenant farming.[1] The two men spent July and
August in Alabama getting to know and living with sharecroppers and
their problems. Then Agee wrote and submitted a story so unlike the
conventional documentary the editors of Fortune had in mind that they
refused to publish it. The material was released to Agee, who made it
into a book which was published by Houghton Mifflin Company in 1941.

---

[1]Evans was on loan for the assignment from the Department of Agriculture. As co-author of Let Us Now Praise Famous Men, he supplied the
magnificent photographs which complement Agee's text and which Agee
characterized in his preface as "not illustrative" but "coequal" and
"fully collaborative." Thirty-one of these (half the number Evans
intended to publish) appeared in the original edition; all 62 were
reproduced in the 1960 edition.

      [I] B. In 1941 the book was rejected by both the critics and
               the public.

Short quotations are enclosed in quotation marks and run into the text. If
material is omitted from the quotation, the omission is shown by three spaced
periods (ellipsis). Notice that a space is left before the first of these periods.

A footnote number in the text should come at the end of a sentence whenever
possible. It follows other marks of punctuation.

      [I] C. In 1960 a reissue of the book was favorably received.

      II. The writing of the book was dominated by Agee's unconventional
           literary theory.

      A. The book did not fit into any accepted category.

2

I B   <u>Let Us Now Praise Famous Men</u> was received with almost unanimous disfavor by the critics. Though it would be unfair to represent the whole tenor of criticism, or of any one review, by such phrases as the following, they do give some idea of the terms in which the book was condemned: "exhibitionism and verbosity" (<u>Time</u>); "too many aware-nesses on the subjective side" (<u>New Republic</u>); failure to "communicate . . . in objective terms" as demanded by "the specific nature of the subject" (<u>New York Herald Tribune Books</u>); "appalling inventory of the irrelevant" (<u>The Nation</u>); "repetitious . . . obsessed with irrelevant details . . . complete absence of discipline and form" (<u>Commonweal</u>); "a mass of unrelated, nonsensical matter" (<u>Library Journal</u>).[2] The book sold sluggishly--fewer than 600 copies in the first year--and by 1945 what was left of the first printing was being remaindered.[3]

I C   For most books, this would have been the end. Nevertheless, when it was reissued in 1960 it was taken up by the prestigious book clubs and given favorable reviews. This reception was such an obvious denial of the 1941 judgment that one reviewer wrote, "It begins to appear that we are present at the court's reversal and <u>Let Us Now Praise Famous Men</u> is to be widely acknowledged a great book."[4]

II A   <u>Let Us Now Praise Famous Men</u> was an unconventional work, in the sense that it did not fit into the established categories of contemporary

---

[2] Peter H. Ohlin, <u>Agee</u> (New York: Ivan Obolensky, Inc., 1966), pp. 51-52.

[3] James Agee, <u>Letters of James Agee to Father Flye</u> (New York: George Braziller, 1962), pp. 3-4.

[4] Erik Wensberg, "Celebration, Adoration and Wonder," <u>The Nation</u>, November 26, 1960, p. 417.

Kazin, p. 371

The most vigorous young novelists of the 30's were those "in whom the literal significance of the crisis had aroused a literature of literal realism."

Kazin, p. 368

The new prose writers in the 30's wrote to satisfy "the country's need to know what had happened to it, a demand that aroused interest in the oppressive facts of change," such as people on relief, migratory workers, miners and silicosis.

Says the documentary and sociological prose of the depression era often more interesting than the social novels dealing with same themes.

Summary, paraphrase, and direct quotation are combined in these note cards. In the paper, their content is further summarized and restated without direct quotation.

Footnote 6 shows that the statement in the text is based on two notes from the same source.

[II] B. Agee rejected realism as an adequate technique for describing real experience and preferred a subjective approach.

A quotation that is five or more lines long is set apart from the text as a block quotation; that is, by extra indention at the left and by single spacing. Block quotations are not enclosed in quotation marks, because the distinctive set-up shows that they are quotations. A block quotation is often introduced by a colon.

Three spaced periods are used at the opening of a block quotation only if the quotation begins in mid-sentence. For an omission at or after the end of a sentence, *four* periods are used: the period (or other terminal punctuation) for the sentence—with no space before this mark—followed by three spaced periods to show ellipsis. Any comments inserted by the writer are enclosed in square brackets.

writing or social thought.[5] The literary fashions of the thirties had decreed that a social-problem topic such as tenant farming be treated as a documentary or socio-economic study (if non-fiction) or as slice-of-life realism (if fiction).[6] For Agee, however, cotton tenantry was only the nominal subject; his real subject he defined as "an independent inquiry into certain normal predicaments of human divinity."[7] "My trouble is," he wrote, "that such a subject cannot be seriously looked at without intensifying itself toward a centre which is beyond what I, or anyone else, is capable of writing of: the whole problem and nature of existence."[8] To this enormous problem he brought, not the dogmas and techniques of the ideological thirties, but an unfashionably individual response.[9]

II B   Agee rejected both literal realism and scientific detachment as adequate techniques for describing the human condition:

> . . . it is important that your representation of "reality" does not sag into, or become one with, naturalism. . . .
> George Gudger [his sharecropper host] is a man, et cetera. But obviously, in the effort to tell of him . . . as truthfully as I can, I am limited. I know him only so far as I know him, and only in those terms in which I know him; and all of that depends as fully on who I am as on who he is.[10]

[not incl . in quotation]

---

[5]Ohlin, p. 1.

[6]Alfred Kazin, *On Native Grounds* (New York: Reynal & Hitchcock, 1942), pp. 368, 371.

[7]James Agee and Walker Evans, *Let Us Now Praise Famous Men* (Boston: Houghton Mifflin Company, 1960), p. xiv.

[8]Agee, *Letters to Father Flye*, pp. 104-5.

[9]Nash K. Burger, "A Story to Tell: Agee, Wolfe, Faulkner," *South Atlantic Quarterly*, 63 (Winter 1964), 36.

[10]*Let Us Now Praise Famous Men*, pp. 238-39.

```
[II]   C.  He was seeking a breakthrough in literary form, one that
           would bring prose closer to music and poetry.
```

Good transitions are essential to a coherent and orderly presentation. They need not be obtrusive to be effective. In the opening sentence of II C, for example, the phrase "equally unconventional" is a transitional device relating the discussion of Agee's experiments with form and style to the foregoing discussion of his subjectivity (II B) and repeating the word "unconventional" from the topic sentence of II A. How are transitions signaled in other paragraph-opening sentences in this paper?

The paragraph that develops II C shows how short quotations can be woven into sentences without formal introduction and without a break in the flow of the exposition. A paragraph that combines and assimilates material from several sources suggests adequate research and purposeful thinking.

4

Thus Agee himself becomes inescapably part of the picture; he cannot remove himself without falsifying it. His subjective approach, therefore, is not to be seen as an egotistic author's intrusion into his material, but as a necessary technique for dealing with the artistic problem of comprehending and communicating the "real" life-experiences of other human beings. As his friend Dwight Macdonald remarked, "In an age that was enthusiastic about social issues, Agee's whole style was individualistic and anti-scientific."[11]

II C   Agee was equally unconventional, by the literary standards of the day, in his search for a form and style that would represent "reality" on a plane closer to music and poetry. His letters to Father Flye show that even as an undergraduate at Harvard he was thinking of "writing symphonies" in words and of "inventing a sort of amphibious style--prose that would run into poetry when the occasion demanded."[12] This early intention was strengthened by his experience in Alabama: a vision "too intense to be expressed in conventional forms."[13] In his "Plans for Work: October 1937" submitted with his application for a Guggenheim Fellowship (which he did not get), he listed his "Alabama Record" as a work in progress, with the notation that it was likely "to involve the development of some more or less new forms of writing and of observation."[14]

---

[11]Dwight Macdonald, *Against the American Grain* (New York: Random House, 1962), p. 154.

[12]Agee, *Letters to Father Flye*, pp. 47-48.

[13]Granville Hicks, "Suffering Face of the Rural South," *Saturday Review*, September 10, 1960, p. 20.

[14]James Agee, *The Collected Short Prose of James Agee*, ed. Robert Fitzgerald (Boston: Houghton Mifflin Company, 1960), p. 133.

Although the footnote number is usually placed at the end of the sentence, it may come earlier if the reference is more appropriate to a part of the sentence than to the whole.

[II]   D.   These unconventional aims dominated the content, structure, and style of the book.

          1.   His concern with a subjective approach to human behavior determined his view of the sharecropper.

Again, notice the use of square brackets to enclose words within a quotation that do not appear in the original but are supplied by the writer. Sometimes a writer adds a few words to explain or comment; sometimes, as here, he substitutes words so that the quotation will fit grammatically into his own sentence. Care should of course be taken not to change the meaning. In the passage quoted, Agee writes as though addressing the sharecroppers directly, but the "you" would be confusing in the context of the paper.

> *Agee on "art" vs. life – reality*   II D 1
>
> Agee, <u>LUNPFM</u>, p. 366
>
> Repudiates idea of using sharecroppers' lives as materials for artistic shaping:
>
> "If I were going to use these lives of yours for 'art,' if I were going to dab at them here, cut them short here, make some trifling improvement over here, in order to make you worthy of The Saturday Review of Literature; I would just now for instance be careful of anticlimax...."

A block quotation begins with paragraph indention if the opening sentence begins a paragraph in the source. Otherwise it begins without indention.

5

But in 1941 the critics were not ready for these new forms. In an

appreciative review in 1960, Erik Wensberg identified Agee's dis-

regard for conventional practices in form and style as a major cause

of the rejection of the earlier publication.[15]

II D 1   Let Us Now Praise Famous Men, then, is as much an experiment in

new ways of seeing and writing as it is a record of the lives of

three representative white tenant families. Agee's conviction "that

human reality deserves above all a response in human and subjective

rather than critical and objective terms"[16] shaped his approach to

what he called the "unimagined existence" of the tenant farmer. He

refused to view the sharecropper families as "materials," whether for

documentary journalism, sociological study, or literary art ("to dab

at them here, cut them short here, make some trifling improvement over

here, in order to make [their lives] worthy of the Saturday Review of

Literature").[17] Walker Evans has testified to Agee's success in win-

ning the families' acceptance of himself and his work.[18] For Agee,

the relationship was a personal commitment that involved respect and

trust. It also involved an acute sensitivity that enabled Agee to

identify emotionally and physically with these people:

> Just a half-inch beyond the surface of this wall I face is
> another surface, one of the four walls which square and collab-
> orate against the air another room, and there lie sleeping on
> two iron beds and on pallets on the floor, a man and his wife
> and her sister, and four children. . . . Not even straining
> can I hear their breathing: rather, I have a not quite sensuous

---

[15]Wensberg, pp. 417-18.

[16]Ohlin, p. 9.

[17]Let Us Now Praise Famous Men, pp. 242, 366.

[18]Foreword, Let Us Now Praise Famous Men (1960), pp. xi-xii.

After a block quotation a new paragraph may or may not be required. Here the writer goes on to draw a conclusion from the quotation, the text is therefore closely related to what has gone before, and no new paragraph is necessary.

```
[II  D]  2.  His attitudes about literary form affected the
             structure of the book.
```

The note cards for references 22 and 23 are reproduced to show how material from different sources can be selectively used to develop a single sentence.

$$\text{II D2}$$
Structure of <u>LUNPFM</u>

Ohlin, p. 58
   The miscellaneous images and notes that precede and follow the three main parts "help define" the themes and attitudes of the work."

$$\text{II D2}$$
Structure of <u>LUNPFM</u>

Holder, p. 193
   Examining Agee's statement (in his preface) that <u>LUNPFM</u> was "a book only by necessity," Holder finds Agee consciously attempting to shock his readers out of a "middle-class talent for effortless consumption" of books. Sees Agee as trying "to keep the reader off-balance" by the proportioning and the miscellaneous character of his prefatory and appendix materials.

6

knowledge of a sort of suspiration, less breathing than that
indiscernible drawing-in of heaven by which plants live, and
thus I know they rest and the profundity of their tiredness,
as if I were in each one of those seven bodies whose sleeping
I can almost touch through this wall. . . .[19]

From this total commitment there emerges in Let Us Now Praise Famous

Men "a truth that includes and goes beyond the truth about poverty

and ignorance in sociological studies (and 'realistic' novels)."[20]

II D 2   To communicate these subjective awarenesses, Agee drew on his

unique ideas about literary form. The book is structured in three

main parts within a mosaic of smaller segments. Agee's record of his

summer with the tenant families is most directly communicated in the

three main parts, and most concretely in Part Two, which covers such

topics as Money, Shelter, Clothing, Education, and Work. Preceding

Part One, interrupting Part Two, and ending the book are three sections

called "On the Porch," which together form a continuous lyric meditation

and a framework for the whole, a center of consciousness "in relation to

which all other parts . . . are intended as flashbacks, foretastes, illu-

minations and contradictions."[21] Between the main parts, and grouped at

the beginning and the end of the book, are still other miscellaneous

materials which "help define the themes and attitudes of the work,"[22]

and which may also serve to "keep the reader off-balance," thereby

involving him in something more than the conventional experience of

reading a book.[23] One thematic fragment, for example, reprints the

---

[19]Let Us Now Praise Famous Men, p. 57.

[20]Macdonald, p. 157.

[21]Let Us Now Praise Famous Men, p. 245n.

[22]Ohlin, p. 58.

[23]Alan Holder, "Encounter in Alabama: Agee and the Tenant Farmer,"
Virginia Quarterly Review, 42 (Spring 1966), 193.

[II   D]   3.   His style shows the influence of music and cinema.

The three spaced periods indicating an ellipsis are used more often for omissions within a quotation than for omissions at the beginning or the end. The *Manual of Style* of the University of Chicago Press lists them as unnecessary before or after obvious fragments, before or after a run-in quotation of a complete sentence, before a block quotation beginning with a complete sentence, and after a block quotation ending with a complete sentence.

Footnote 24 shows the form for a Biblical reference. Notice that books of the Bible are not italicized (underlined). No bibliographical entry is required for a Biblical citation.

Footnote 26 shows how to cite a quotation from a footnote: the page number, followed (without a space) by the small letter *n*. When two or more quotations from the same source are cited in one footnote, the page citations should be listed in the order in which the quotations are used.

Biblical passage from which the book takes its title.[24] In these

interspersed bits and pieces, which both separate the main parts and

link them in a patterned whole, Agee returns again and again to his

central problem as a writer: how to actualize human experience. The

book is thus both the statement and the product of his literary theory.

II D 3   In style, Agee saw his problem as one of breaking through the lim-

itations of words as well as of literary forms:

> Words cannot embody; they can only describe. But a certain
> kind of artist, whom we will distinguish from others as a poet
> rather than a prose writer, despises this fact about . . . his
> medium, and continually brings words as near as he can to an
> illusion of embodiment.[25]

In his search for ways of making words embody rather than merely de-

scribe experience, he turned to the techniques of music and cinema:

statements of theme and mood, development, restatement, variation,

reprise and flashback, modulation and dissolve. His frequent use

of the colon, for example, both within his characteristically long

sentences and at the ends of paragraphs, may be seen as an attempt to

approximate the continuity of music or film, with a pause but not a

full stop between rhythmic units. In fact, the forms of Let Us Now

Praise Famous Men, as Agee saw them, were "chiefly those of music, of

motion picture, and of improvisation of states of emotion, and of

belief"; and he intended the book "to be read continuously, as music

is listened to or a film watched."[26] Dwight Macdonald finds in Agee's

best writing "a cinematic flow and immediacy,"[27] and Peter Ohlin argues

---

[24]Ecclesiasticus 44:1-14.

[25]Let Us Now Praise Famous Men, p. 238.

[26]Let Us Now Praise Famous Men, pp. 244n, xv.

[27]Macdonald, p. 153.

III. The critical climate in 1960 made Agee's unconventional treat-
      ment of his material more acceptable than it had been in 1941.

      A. The relaxation of the emphases of a war economy allowed the
          plight of the sharecropper to re-emerge as a significant
          subject.

The sparse documentation of this long paragraph is accounted for by the fact
that it is based almost entirely on common knowledge and the writer's total
reading, rather than on borrowings from specific sources.

[III] B. A postwar generation of "anti-realistic" writers made critics
           more receptive to subjectivity and literary experiment.

persuasively that the book, far from being formless, is carefully constructed, and that the structure closely resembles that of a symphony.[28]

III A
        The failure of the book in 1941 and its acceptance in 1960 suggest
how great was the shift in critical standards and reading tastes over
the nineteen-year interval. Looking back, we can now see that the original publication could hardly have been unluckier in its timing. The
year 1941, which ended in Pearl Harbor, was the watershed between the
depression of the thirties and the war effort of the forties. The
plight of the sharecroppers had been well worked over by this time, and
people were tired of a subject whose urgency had faded before the threat
of Hitlerism, the war in Europe, and the mobilization of American manpower and resources for the coming struggle.[29] By 1960, however, the
emphases of wartime and of the postwar readjustment had relaxed. After
a decade of affluence, Americans were beginning to re-examine their
society and its inequities. The plight of underprivileged minorities
became again a topical issue, especially among young people, who could
recognize in Let Us Now Praise Famous Men something of their own sense
of personal commitment to the common humanity of the deprived and the
alienated.

III B
        At the same time, a postwar generation of "anti-realistic" writers
had created, by the nineteen-sixties, a new literary climate in which
experimentation and subjectivity were prized, while the formal distinctions between poetry and prose--and between writing and other media of
communication--no longer seemed important or even valid.[30]

_____

[28]Ohlin, pp. 58-64.

[29]Ohlin, p. 51.

[30]Norman Foerster and others, eds., American Poetry and Prose, 5th ed.
(Boston: Houghton Mifflin Company, 1970), III, 146-52.

[III] C. Agee's other published works provided a context in which <u>Let</u> <u>Us</u> <u>Now</u> <u>Praise</u> <u>Famous</u> <u>Men</u> could be re-examined, and his untimely death encouraged a more sympathetic appraisal.

The note card for reference 31 combines summary and quotation. In composing the paper, the writer then selected from and restated the content of the note, weaving it into the paragraph that develops III C of the outline, and keeping only two words as a direct quotation.

Macdonald, p. 150   III C / An Agee cult

Macdonald speaks of the growth of an "Agee cult"—partly because of "the power of his writing and his lack of recognition – everyone likes to think he is on to a good thing the general public has not caught up with," but chiefly because his maimed career and untimely death seem symbolic, and appeal to "a resentment that intellectuals and teenagers alike feel about life in America, so smoothly prosperous, so deeply frustrating."

The next-to-last paragraph is transitional. It summarizes III, A, B, and C, which complete the development of the outline, and points ahead to the conclusion stated in the final paragraph.

The concluding paragraph represents the writer's own thinking. It sums up the significance of all that has gone before and brings the paper to a strong close. Since the conclusion of a research paper is presumably supported by the paper as a whole, specific documentation at this stage is usually inappropriate.

III C   Contributing significantly, also, to the revaluation of <u>Let Us Now</u> <u>Praise</u> <u>Famous</u> <u>Men</u> was the fact that by 1960 there existed a small body of work by Agee against which that book could be reassessed: notably, two short novels, <u>The</u> <u>Morning</u> <u>Watch</u> (1951) and the posthumous <u>A</u> <u>Death</u> <u>in</u> <u>the</u> <u>Family</u> (1957); and the motion-picture criticism done over the period of years when Agee was film critic first for <u>Time</u> and later for <u>The</u> <u>Nation</u>. After Agee's death at age 45, of a heart attack in a taxicab, there grew up a kind of "Agee cult," which made a virtue of his very failure to achieve widespread recognition, and saw a tragic symbolism in a life and talent so largely expended on Luce publications and Hollywood scripts.[31]

Summary of III A,B,C   All these things worked together to make a critical climate more sympathetic than that of 1941 to the literary theory of <u>Let Us Now Praise</u> <u>Famous Men</u>. At last it was possible for critics to explore what Agee was attempting to do, and how far he succeeded, instead of holding him to standards that he explicitly rejected.

Concluding paragraph   Most of the topically inspired writing of the thirties has long since receded into the past, but Agee's book survives because he lifted a topical issue out of its particular time and place and gave it universal significance through his individual way of experiencing and communicating it. In his insistence on working out his own original relationship to his age, and in his refusal to be confined by its social and literary dogmas, he forfeited contemporary acceptance, but he wrote a book that has spoken across the years to a later and more receptive generation of critics and readers.

---

[31]Macdonald, p. 150.

The bibliography begins a new page, with a centered heading in capital letters.

Entries are listed alphabetically by authors, surnames first. In works by two or more authors, only the first author's name is inverted; the other names are given in normal order.

The first line of an entry is not indented; all lines after the first are indented 2 spaces.

Entries are single spaced, but a double space (one blank line) is left between entries.

When more than one book by the same author is being listed, a 7-space line may be substituted for the author's name after the first entry.

Books by a single author are listed before those of which he is the first-listed collaborator, and his name is repeated for the co-authorship entry.

The three main parts of the bibliographical entry—author, title, and facts of publication—are separated by periods.

All sources cited in the footnotes should be listed in the bibliography. The bibliography shown here includes one title (Geismar) not mentioned in the footnotes, because the writer found that work valuable for general background and wished to credit its indirect contribution to the paper, even though it was not specifically cited or quoted. Some instructors prefer that *only* those works mentioned in the footnotes be listed in the bibliography. Consult and follow your instructor's preference.

BIBLIOGRAPHY

Agee, James. <u>The Collected Short Prose of James Agee</u>, ed. Robert
   Fitzgerald. Boston: Houghton Mifflin Company, 1968.

-------. <u>Letters of James Agee to Father Flye</u>. New York: George
   Braziller, 1962.

Agee, James, and Walker Evans. <u>Let Us Now Praise Famous Men</u>.
   Boston: Houghton Mifflin Company, 1941; reissued 1960 with
   additional photographs and a Foreword by Walker Evans.

Burger, Nash K. "A Story to Tell: Agee, Wolfe, Faulkner." <u>South
   Atlantic Quarterly</u>, 63 (Winter 1964), 32-43.

Foerster, Norman, and others, eds. <u>American Poetry and Prose</u>. 5th ed.
   3 vols. Boston: Houghton Mifflin Company, 1970.

Geismar, Maxwell. <u>Writers in Crisis: The American Novel, 1925-1940</u>.
   London: Secker & Warburg, 1947.

Hicks, Granville. "Suffering Face of the Rural South." <u>Saturday
   Review</u>, September 10, 1960, pp. 19-20.

Holder, Alan. "Encounter in Alabama: Agee and the Tenant Farmer."
   <u>Virginia Quarterly Review</u>, 42 (Spring 1966), 189-206.

Kazin, Alfred. <u>On Native Grounds</u>. New York: Reynal & Hitchcock,
   1962.

Macdonald, Dwight. <u>Against the American Grain</u>. New York: Random
   House, 1962.

Ohlin, Peter H. <u>Agee</u>. New York: Ivan Obolensky, Inc., 1966.

Wensberg, Erik. "Celebration, Adoration and Wonder." <u>The Nation</u>,
   November 26, 1960, pp. 417-18.

Chapter 13

Persuasion

So far in this book we have been dealing with expository writing—that is, with writing chiefly concerned with explaining a subject or a thesis through illustration, comparison, process, or causal relation. We now turn to persuasion, a more complex form of communication, and socially the most important form.

As we shall use the term, persuasion is "the use of language as a symbolic means of inducing cooperation. . . ."[1] The key words in this definition are the last two, "inducing cooperation." These words imply that the persuader and the persuaded become united in common action or, at least, are in agreement, are "of one mind." The persuader does not bully or threaten his reader; he tries to win him over or "convert" him. The first part of the definition limits the means of persuasion to words or symbols. Fists, nightsticks, bombs, blockades, and burnings are not "symbolic means" of inducing cooperation. They may or may not be effective in forcing one man to cooperate with another, but they lie outside the province of this chapter, and are not part of persuasion as it has been defined. Furthermore, in persuasion there are no "non-negotiable" demands. To say that certain demands are "non-negotiable" is to take them out of the realm of persuasion, since negotiation is the process of reaching agreement through discussion, and that is what persuasion is all about.

Throughout the discussion of exposition we emphasized the importance of keeping your reader in mind. This requirement is even more important in persuasion, because it is your readers you are trying to persuade and your whole effort is concentrated on bringing them into agreement with you. This task is easiest when they are already predisposed to agree with you, and most difficult when they have compelling reasons for not agreeing. For example, it would be relatively easy to persuade your class that students

[1] Kenneth Burke, *A Rhetoric of Motives* (New York: Prentice-Hall, Inc., 1950), p. 43.

should have a greater voice in deciding what courses they should take and how those courses should be conducted. It would probably be much harder to persuade them that the number of essays required in English should be doubled.

On many questions, however, the class will be divided. Those who already agree with you do not need to be persuaded, so the readers you have to worry about are those who are most likely to disagree. These are the people you must win over. The more sensitive you are to your whole audience, of which the instructor is a part, the better will be your chance of deciding correctly what means of persuasion are best. The one thing you must not do is to assume that any argument that pleases you should be equally persuasive to your classmates.

The prerequisite for any agreement of writer and reader is mutual identification. If persuasion is to be effective, the reader must identify with the writer by accepting the writer's position as his own. The responsibility for bringing about this identification rests with the writer. As Kenneth Burke puts it, "You persuade a man only insofar as you can talk his language by speech, gesture, tonality, order, image, attitude, idea, identifying your ways with his."[2] This advice does not mean that you tell your readers only what they want to hear. You tell them what you want to tell them, but in terms they can accept. For a writer, the ideal reader response is "How true! My sentiments exactly"—made in a situation in which the reader did not know these were his sentiments until he read the writer's work.

MODES OF PERSUASION

How does a writer provoke this ideal response? Often he does not, since the more his readers are motivated to disagree, the less chance he has to persuade them. But insofar as persuasion is possible, the writer has three general means of succeeding. First, he can appeal to his readers through the force of his character, that is, by being the kind of person they can trust. Second, he can appeal by the weight of his argument, by giving convincing reasons for his beliefs. Third, he can appeal to the emotions of his readers. If he can appeal by all three means at once, his persuasiveness is tripled.

Trustworthiness
Readers and listeners are likely to identify with someone they can trust. To be trustworthy, a writer or speaker must have three qualities: he must be knowledgeable, he must be fair, and he must be free of any suspicion of self-interest.

To be knowledgeable, he must know his subject. It helps if he has a reputation in that subject, but even without a reputation he can win the confidence of his readers if his whole treatment of the subject shows that he is well informed and that his statements are accurate. Thus a student

[2] *A Rhetoric of Motives*, p. 55.

who, because of his reading, shows a wide, specific, and accurate knowledge of a subject is likely to be considered trustworthy in contrast to one who has only a superficial knowledge and is often uncertain or wrong about details.

To be fair, he must demonstrate that he understands opposing positions and can state them without distorting them. If he misrepresents an opposing argument, if he ignores important evidence because it might weaken his case, or if he resorts to name-calling or ridicule to dismiss an argument that he cannot refute logically, he will give his readers the impression that he is too biased to be trusted. A trustworthy man does not need to misrepresent an opposing argument to refute it. He can state it in terms that everyone would accept and still show that it is faulty.

To be free of self-interest, a writer must give the impression that he has no personal interest that would encourage one judgment rather than another. If his record suggests that it is to his advantage to prefer one solution to another, that self-interest weakens his trustworthiness. Thus an official of the American Medical Association would be suspect on the question of national health insurance. He might lean over backward to be fair, but the fact that he was associated with an organization traditionally opposed to national health insurance would reduce his acceptability as an impartial informant.

Trustworthiness is so important that a writer who fails to convince his readers that he is knowledgeable, fair, *and* free of self-interest will be rejected or ignored. He does not have to fail in all three: the mere suspicion that he fails in one may be enough to discredit him. In 1970 the United States Senate refused to confirm two judges who had been nominated by the President to fill a vacancy in the Supreme Court. The first was rejected because of certain financial transactions which raised a question of his profiting from a legal decision. The second was rejected partly on the issue of legal competence (knowledge of the law) and partly on the issue of unfair treatment of blacks in his court. These issues did not have to be proved in court. Both men were rejected because a *majority* of the Senate *believed* them untrustworthy as members of the Supreme Court.

When a writer is not himself an expert on a subject, his trustworthiness often depends on the reliability of the sources he uses. He is held responsible for his choice of sources. If these are shown to be undependable, his own trustworthiness is weakened. For this reason, it is wise to evaluate your sources carefully and to satisfy your readers that they are reliable. If you are asking readers to accept a source as decisive, you ought to tell them why you think it can be trusted.

EXERCISE   *The following article raises a question about the motives of a paper company. After reading the article, evaluate its effect on your trust in the company. Then evaluate the trustworthiness of the article itself.*

Hammermill Paper Company is no piddling concern. It is No. 276 in *Fortune's* latest ranking of the 500 largest U.S. industrial corporations, with sales of more than $350 million, assets above $300 million, net income of $14 million, and more than 10,000 employees. Hammermill has been doing something very interesting, and it is probably a portent of more of the same to come. It has been running full-page ads, prepared by Batten, Barton, Durstine & Osborn, in such media as *Newsweek, Time, Business Week,* etc. The format is a question of public interest in big type at the top, then an illustrated explication of the issues involved (for instance, is it proper to hold prayers in public school classrooms?), and at the bottom, "Hammermill urges you to write your public officials." The only overt commercial angle is a sentence in the last paragraph of the body of the ad: "We hope you'll write your letters on Hammermill Bond—world's best-known letterhead paper," and a note to the effect that Hammermill manufactures thirty-three fine printing and business papers. But in any case: do write.

The pros and cons are in general fairly presented and the graphic material is effective. One of the best of the series shows a sick, discouraged-looking old man lying in an unheated slum bedroom—there are blankets on the bed but he seems to be fully dressed, and the question raised is: "Can we afford to explore the heavens when there's still a hell on earth?"

A good question, but a question may also be raised about Hammermill's (or any other corporation's) motives in advertising, other than its desire to sell its products. The astute public affairs people in all the big corporations know that the preservation of a healthy environment is a very live issue these days. Paper making can be a water-polluting process of the worst kind; on the other hand, its bad effects can be mitigated, although this may entail considerable expense.

The Committee on Economic Priorities found that Hammermill's record in this field was one of minimum initiative. It has two old mills in Pennsylvania, one mill in Wisconsin, and a new mill in Selma, Ala. The mill in Erie, Pa., has been the subject of stories in the press because of its contribution to the widespread pollution of Lake Erie. The mill in Lockhaven, Pa., was found, at the time of the CEP study two years ago, to be under orders to remedy its output of pollutants by the end of 1972; the investigators felt that the anti-pollution equipment could be installed sooner. The Selma mill, although of modern design, is said to spill a large volume of waste material into the waters of the state of Alabama. The company already has invested $36 million in anti-pollution equipment, and will have to spend, the investigators estimate, $6.5 million more. The record does not shape up as one of indifference, but if as much initiative were shown in preventing pollution as in advertising, the company image could be considerably brightened.[3]

---

[3] From *The Nation,* April 19, 1971.

Argument   As it is used here, "argument" is not synonymous with "persuasion." It is the second of the three modes of persuasion already identified. An argument is a reasoning process in which a conclusion is inferred from some evidence. Thus if a student says, "It is 7:50; I'll be late for my eight o'clock class," he is reasoning from an observation of the time to a conclusion that he will be late for class.

In this case the student is using argument to make up his own mind. But he could also use it to make up someone else's mind. Thus he could use exactly the same argument to persuade his roommate to hurry. Our chief concern here is with argument as a means of persuading others. But we should remember that it is a reasoning process which we use for ourselves as well as for others. Indeed, a writer who is trying to persuade readers to accept a conclusion is simply showing them the reasoning process by which he himself arrived at that conclusion.

The Structure of Argument.   In its simplest form, as in the example given above, an argument consists of two statements, one a conclusion from the other. The statement from which the conclusion is drawn is called a *premise*. Thus our introductory argument may be structured as follows:

Premise: It is 7:50.

Conclusion: I will be late for class.

The arrow shows the direction of the inference, from premise to conclusion.

In using argument as a means of persuasion, the writer's job is to give his readers the premises that will lead them to accept the desired conclusion. Sometimes a single premise will be enough, but usually not. Consider the following dialogue:

JOE: It's 7:50, Bill. You'll be late for class.
BILL: It can't be 7:50.
JOE: Well, look at the clock.
BILL: Oh, that clock has been running fast for weeks!
JOE: I reset it last night and checked it by the radio this morning.

In this argument Bill does not accept Joe's first premise, so Joe has to persuade him that the premise is true by offering corroborating evidence (a second premise) from the resetting and the radio report.

Because of the immediate feedback in a dialogue, Joe gets a quick check on the acceptability of his first premise and thus has an opportunity to provide additional premises. The writer has no such opportunity. He must provide all the necessary premises in the argument he presents to his readers. How much is necessary will depend on the amount of persuasion the readers need. That question has to be answered by the writer. He may err in either direction, but the consequences of giving too many premises are usually less serious than those of not giving enough.

In a complex argument not all the premises are of equal rank. Some are intended to get the readers to accept the conclusion. These refer directly to the conclusion and can be called *main premises*. They are similar to the main headings of an outline developing a thesis. Others are intended to support a premise already given and thus to support the conclusion indirectly. These are *sub-premises* and are similar to the subheadings of an outline.

We can best illustrate the relations between conclusion, main premises, and sub-premises by analyzing the structure of a long argument. In this argument two writers[4] are collaborating in trying to persuade their readers (students) that Joyce Kilmer's poem "Trees" is a bad poem, because it is technically bad and because it is trite in sentiment. These two reasons are the main premises of the argument. To persuade their readers that the poem is technically bad, the authors use two sub-premises: (1) that the imagery in the poem is confused, and (2) that the rhythm is monotonous. To support each of these sub-premises they present specific evidence from the text of the poem. Here is the structure of the argument through the first main premise:

Conclusion: Joyce Kilmer's "Trees" is a bad poem.

> *Main premise:* It is technically bad.
>
>> *Sub-premise:* The imagery is confused. (This sub-premise is supported by evidence that the basic comparison between a tree and a human being shifts four times in twelve lines and thus presents readers with an inconsistent set of images.)
>>
>> *Sub-premise:* The rhythm is monotonous. (This sub-premise is supported by evidence that each couplet in the poem has the same rhythm, with a full stop at the end of each couplet and no pauses within the lines.)

Translated into a conventional outline, the structure of this argument would be shown as follows. (Remember that we are dealing with only part of the whole argument. A complete outline would show II as well as I.)

Thesis: Joyce Kilmer's "Trees" is a bad poem.

    I. It is technically bad.

        A. The imagery is confused.

            1. The basic comparison changes four times.

            2. The resulting images are inconsistent.

        B. The rhythm is monotonous.

            1. The same rhythm is maintained in each couplet.

            2. The pauses always occur at the ends of the couplets.

[4] Cleanth Brooks and Robert Penn Warren, *Understanding Poetry* (New York: Henry Holt and Company, 1938).

The persuasiveness of this argument depends on the ability of the writers to get the readers to identify with them by seeing the poem through their eyes. If the readers do so, they will accept the final judgment about "Trees" and make it their own.

EXERCISE

For the following argument, outline the conclusion-premise structure by identifying the conclusion and the main premises; then evaluate the persuasiveness of the argument.

. . . Such basic rights of an American citizen as freedom of speech and assembly, protection from invasion of privacy, and the guarantee of due process of law do not exist for the overwhelming majority of American high school students.

After the first Earth Day, a student at Grady High School, Atlanta, Georgia, observes: "They let us have an assembly on Earth Day, but the principal warned me not to say anything about the war. He says the war is not relevant to high school education."

A student at Central High School, Muncie, Indiana: "They search the lockers anytime they want to. And we're not allowed to be present when they do. They took a bottle of aspirin out of my locker once and sent it down to Indianapolis to have it analyzed. It cost them a lot of money to find out it was really my aspirin. I get migraine headaches, and I really needed it."

In a high school in Sumter, South Carolina, a student running for school office is summarily removed from the ballot by the principal because the student has written in the school paper an article critical of the administration.

"But you can't do that!" the boy says. "It's un-Constitutional."

"The constitution of this school," the principal informs the student, "takes precedence over the United States Constitution."

In September 1970 in Roseville, Michigan, thirty students are refused entry to the high school because of a provision in the school's dress code that says male students' hair must not touch the ears or shirt collars or fall over the eyebrows.[5]

TYPES OF ARGUMENT

As we have seen, all arguments are reasoning processes in which a conclusion is inferred from one or more premises. In this section we will identify five main types of arguments and discuss their reliability. The five types are arguments from *examples, generalizations, causal relations, analogy,* and *deductions.*

[5] From Nat Hentoff, "Why Students Want Their Constitutional Rights," *Saturday Review,* May 22, 1971.

Examples   The passage on page 312 about violation of the constitutional rights of students is an argument in which the conclusion is based entirely on examples. The writer infers from the examples that students' rights are being violated. When he addresses his readers he presents the conclusion first and then supports it with the examples.

This is the simplest type of argument. It is especially effective when used to persuade readers that abuses exist and should be abolished. The examples dramatize the abuse and arouse the readers' indignation. They are therefore effective in getting the readers' attention and sympathy at the beginning of a complex series of arguments.

The chief weakness of argument from examples is that a reader may doubt that the examples are typical. In this imperfect world it is always easy to find some abuses, even in systems and institutions which are generally approved. A writer is entitled to point them out and urge that they be corrected. But few readers will be persuaded to change a whole system because of some specific abuses. Therefore if the writer thinks abuses are widespread or typical, he should take pains to show why he thinks so.

Examples are most effective when supplemented by other types of argument. The passage on violations of student rights was a small part of a long persuasive essay which began with examples and continued with other types of argument.

In the following passage Rachel Carson begins with two short paragraphs, the first an allusion to a Greek myth, and the second a series of short examples of the cause-to-effect process by which systemic insecticides work. After these two introductory paragraphs she settles down to a technical explanation of the process. Had she begun with the third paragraph, her readers might have been less willing to give her their attention.

In Greek mythology the sorceress Medea, enraged at being supplanted by a rival for the affections of her husband Jason, presented the new bride with a robe possessing magic properties. The wearer of the robe immediately suffered a violent death. This death-by-indirection now finds its counterpart in what is known as "systemic insecticides." These are chemicals with extraordinary properties which are used to convert plants or animals into a sort of Medea's robe by making them actually poisonous. This is done with the purpose of killing insects that may come in contact with them, especially by sucking their juices or blood.

The world of systemic insecticides is a weird world, surpassing the imaginings of the brothers Grimm—perhaps most closely akin to the cartoon world of Charles Addams. It is a world where the enchanted forest of the fairy tales has become the poisonous forest in which an insect that chews a leaf or sucks the sap of a plant is doomed. It is a world where a flea bites a dog, and dies because the dog's blood has been made poisonous, where an insect may die from vapors emanating from a plant it has never touched, where a bee may carry poisonous nectar back to its hive and presently produce poisonous honey.

The entomologists' dream of the built-in insecticide was born when workers in the field of applied entomology realized they could take a hint from nature: they found that wheat growing in soil containing sodium selenate was immune to attack by aphids or spider mites. Selenium, a naturally occurring element found sparingly in rocks and soils of many parts of the world, thus became the first systemic insecticide.

What makes an insecticide a systemic is the ability to permeate all the tissues of a plant or animal and make them toxic. This quality is possessed by some chemicals of the chlorinated hydrocarbon group and by others of the organophosphorus group, all synthetically produced, as well as by certain naturally occurring substances. In practice, however, most systemics are drawn from the organophosphorus group because the problem of residues is somewhat less acute.

Systemics act in other devious ways. Applied to seeds, either by soaking or in a coating combined with carbon, they extend their effects into the following plant generation and produce seedlings poisonous to aphids and other sucking insects. Vegetables such as peas, beans, and sugar beets are sometimes thus protected. Cotton seeds coated with a systemic insecticide have been in use for some time in California, where 25 farm laborers planting cotton in the San Joaquin Valley in 1959 were seized with sudden illness, caused by handling the bags of treated seeds.[6]

Generalization

A generalization is a conclusion about a whole class or group based on a study of some of its members. If we measured 2000 Americans and 2000 Englishmen and found that the average height of the Americans was greater, we might infer that Americans as a group are taller than Englishmen. We would be studying a sample of each group and, from the sample, drawing a conclusion about each class.

Obviously a generalization based on a few samples is riskier than one based on many samples. The measurements of twenty Americans and twenty Englishmen would be too few to warrant any conclusion. But the mere size of a sample is not by itself a trustworthy test of generalization. If we measured 10,000 Englishmen, all members of crack regiments with minimum height requirements of six feet, we could draw no reliable conclusions about the average height of the English, since we would have no reason to assume that the sample was representative. Indeed, we could conclude it was not: the members of the crack regiments are not typical in height.

It is important to understand this distinction, because hasty assumption that samples are typical is the chief cause of unsound generalization. It is often difficult—sometimes impossible—to be sure a sample is typical, and

[6] From Rachel Carson, *Silent Spring* (Boston: Houghton Mifflin Company, 1962).

much useful reasoning is based on samples which can only be presumed to be so. But for any serious generalization, care should be taken to see that the samples probably are typical. Any sample which tends to be "loaded"— that is, more likely true for part of a class than for all of it—should be rejected. The following samples are all loaded.

A study of college hospital records to determine how many days a semester a student is likely to be sick. (The sample will exaggerate because it ignores the healthiest part of the student population—those that did not need hospitalization.)

A contrast of unemployment figures in Michigan in June and January to determine whether unemployment is increasing. (A comparison between two Junes would be safer, since the January figures may be increased by seasonal unemployment.)

An analysis of all automobile accidents reported in a state during a year to determine whether men or women are the safer drivers. (If there are more men drivers than women drivers, or if men drive more frequently for longer distances or under adverse conditions, one would expect more men to be involved in accidents. The sample is likely to be loaded.)

Answers obtained by sampling express probability, not certainty. The better the sampling technique, the higher the probability of correct prediction. In the 1964 Presidential election, the Vote Profile Analysis used by one of the broadcasting companies predicted the results with 100 per cent accuracy from a sample of 2000 out of the nation's 175,000 precincts —a sample of little more than one per cent! In contrast to such accurate sampling is the hasty generalization, which draws a conclusion about a large group from a few samples, without regard to how typical the samples are. Many generalizations about ethnic or national groups, about men as contrasted with women, about teen-agers, about college students and faculty members, are the kind described as hasty.

One way to avoid hasty generalizations is to be suspicious of any statement that presumes to include *all* of a group or class—all women drivers, all teen-agers, all college professors. Such statements imply that your samples are typical and that therefore the judgment made about the class is true without exception. Your generalization may be true of *many* or of *some* members of the class. If so, say so. Do not use *all* unless you are ready to prove that there are no exceptions. Of course, a generalization that some women are poor drivers is not very persuasive, since nobody doubts that. But it is as persuasive as you have any right to be. If you overstate the generalization, you invite doubts about your own trustworthiness. Notice that even if a generalization does not include the word "all," it may still mean "all." To say that women are poor drivers implies *all women.*

EXERCISE	*Consider the following statements. For how many members of the class are they true—all, most, some, or only a few?*

1. All cats have bushy tails.
2. Don't trust anyone over thirty.
3. Women just can't keep a secret.
4. Men are so conceited.
5. Graduate assistants are inexperienced teachers.
6. Democrats are more liberal than Republicans.
7. One thing you can say about the younger generation—they're honest.
8. Parents just aren't with it.
9. He's an English teacher. I better watch my grammar.
10. All men are mortal.

Causal Relation   Another common type of reasoning is the search for causes and results. We want to know whether cigarettes really do cause lung cancer, why young people have rebelled against the establishment, what causes malnutrition, the decay of cities, or the decay of teeth. We are equally interested in effects: what is the effect of thalidomide on the formation of unborn infants, of sulphur or lead in the atmosphere, of mercury in tunafish, of oil spills and raw sewage in rivers and the sea, of LSD or marijuana, of staying up late on the night before an examination.

Causal reasoning may go from cause to effect or from effect to cause. Either way, we reason from what we know to what we want to find out. Sometimes we reason from an effect to a cause and then on to another effect. Thus, if we reason that because the lights have gone out the refrigerator won't work, we first relate the effect (lights out) to the cause (power off) and then relate that cause to another effect (refrigerator not working). This kind of reasoning is called, for short, *effect to effect*. It is quite common to reason through an extensive chain of causal relations. If when the lights go out we take the milk out of the refrigerator, we reason in the following causal chain: lights out—power off—refrigerator not working—temperature will rise—milk will sour. In other words, we diagnose a succession of effects from the power failure, each becoming the cause of the next.

Causes are classified as necessary, sufficient, or contributory. A *necessary* cause is one which must be present for the effect to occur, as combustion is necessary to drive a gasoline engine. A *sufficient* cause is one which can produce an effect unaided, though there may be more than one sufficient cause: a dead battery is enough to keep a car from starting, but faulty spark plugs or an empty tank will have the same effect. A contributory cause is one which helps to produce an effect but cannot do so by itself, as running through a red light may help cause an accident, though other factors—pedestrians or other cars in the intersection—must also be present.

In causal reasoning we usually go through one or more of the following stages of thinking:

1. *Whatever the cause, it must exist in the situation and it must be sufficient to produce the effect.* This assumption requires us (1) to check the situation carefully to identify possible causes, and (2) to consider which of the possible causes is sufficient to produce the effect. In making this analysis we are influenced by our past experience with similar situations. If we have often seen that event B follows event A, we incline to infer that A is the cause of B. But we should remember that one event can regularly precede another without being its cause. Eight o'clock classes always come before nine o'clock classes, but the first do not cause the second.

2. *If a sufficient cause is eliminated from the situation, the effect will be eliminated, unless there are other causes.* At this stage in our reasoning we are ready to test the possible causes to see if there is a connection between them and the effect. If the effect ceases when we remove a possible cause, this possible cause is the actual cause. If we suspect that a light failure is caused by a faulty bulb, we can substitute a new bulb and see whether the effect (no light) is removed. If it is, we need look no further. But if the new bulb does not give light, we cannot infer that the original bulb was all right, since the effect could have been produced by any of several sufficient causes —for example, a defect in the bulb, the wiring, the outlet, or in more than one of these.

3. *If the cause is introduced into a similar situation it will produce a similar effect.* This is an additional way to test possible causes. If we suspect that a light failure is due to a faulty bulb, we can predict that the bulb will not light when placed in a socket where another bulb has been burning. If the bulb does light, we must reject the hypothesis that it was faulty and caused the light failure. If the bulb does not light, we have additional support for our belief that it is the cause we are seeking.

Whether we go through all three of these stages to find a cause will probably depend on how important finding the cause is to us. To find our faulty bulb we need not go beyond the second stage, once we find that changing bulbs removes the difficulty; but a scientist seeking the cause of a disease would perform every experiment he could think of before reaching a final conclusion.

The most common errors in causal reasoning are:

1. Assuming that A causes B because A always precedes B, as in assuming that Labor Day causes the schools to reopen in the fall.

2. Mistaking an effect for a cause, as in blaming a car's inefficiency on the knocking in the engine.

3. Mistaking a contributory cause for a sufficient cause, as when a tailgating driver explains a crash by saying that the car ahead stopped suddenly.

4. Failing to recognize that the cause may be not a single event but a complex: for example, attributing racial strife to differences in color and ignoring the economic and social causes.

Two common ways to discover a probable cause are *the method of agreement* and *the method of difference*. The method of agreement assumes that if all possible causes of an effect are identified and only one of these always precedes the effect, then that possible cause is the probable cause. The method of difference assumes that if all possible causes of an effect are identified and only one of these is missing when the effect fails to occur, then that missing possible cause is the probable cause. Both methods are reliable only when all possible factors have been identified.

EXERCISE

Suppose you are running a series of experiments to discover under what conditions the effect E will appear. Your experiments yield the following data, in which each letter represents a possible cause of E. Use the methods of agreement and disagreement to discover the only conditions under which E will appear. Assume that all possible causes have been identified. If you find that no single letter is the cause of E, consider whether two letters acting in conjunction may be identified as the cause.

A	D	O	R	V	—— E
A	D	Q	S	T	—— No E
R	S	T	U	V	—— No E
M	O	R	T	V	—— E
O	K	L	M	N	—— No E
B	C	K	O	R	—— E
B	F	R	W	O	—— No E

Analogy

Analogy is the type of reasoning in which we infer that if two things are alike in several important respects they will also be alike in certain other respects. The following selection shows how this inference develops.

We often wonder whether or not Mars is inhabited. . . . Did you ever ask yourself why it is *Mars* that interests us so much in this connection? It is because Mars is so similar to the earth in major respects. It has a similar history, a comparable temperature, an atmosphere, is subject to similar solar seasons; it revolves around the sun, it gets light from the sun, it is subject to the laws of gravitation, etc. May it not also be similar in respect to harboring life? If Mars were without water, like the moon, or experienced great extremes of temperature, like Mercury, we should not be so much interested in it. But we entertain the idea because Mars is so similar in many respects to the earth *and life has evolved on the earth!*[7]

[7] From Roger W. Holmes, *The Rhyme of Reason* (New York: Appleton-Century-Crofts, Inc., 1939).

In Chapter 7 we saw the use of analogy to provide explanatory detail. An analogy can often make abstract ideas concrete or explain the unfamiliar by likening it to the familiar. In argument, however, analogy can be both useful and misleading. It is helpful in suggesting hypotheses for further investigation. For example, if we have found that the best protection against one virus disease is to isolate the virus and prepare an immunizing serum from it, we can predict that the same method will work with another virus disease. If the prediction proves true, the analogy has helped to solve our problem. If the prediction proves false, the suggested solution will be quickly rejected and no great harm will have been done.

Analogy is also useful when we have no other means of reaching a conclusion. For example, we cannot descend to the bottom of the ocean and collect evidence about the kinds of life, if any, existing there, but we can infer by analogy that the characteristics we observe in the depths we can penetrate will hold true in those we cannot reach. But such inferences are, at best, tentative, and we replace them by more reliable evidence where possible.

When analogy is used as the sole proof of a conclusion it is even less reliable. It may be more persuasive than it should be and lead us to a conclusion which is not valid. For a single difference can render a whole analogy false. The test of an analogy is the question, *Are the two things analogous for the purpose for which the analogy is being used?* They may have many differences which are unimportant to the inference based on the analogy. But they must not be different in any detail essential to that inference. Thus the analogy that a motherless baby ape could be reared by feeding it as if it were a human baby would be sound because, despite many differences, young apes and human babies have similar digestive systems. But to reason that because two varieties of mushrooms look alike, both will be good to eat, is a dangerous analogy, since the possibility that one is poisonous would be more important than all their similarities.

EXERCISE

Do you find the following analogy persuasive or not? Discuss your answers.

All great questions of the times are questions of the moment, and they represent only consequences of certain causes. Only one of them is of causal importance, that is, the question of the racial preservation of the nationality. In the blood alone there rests the strength as well as the weakness of man. As long as the people do not recognize and pay attention to the importance of their racial foundation, they resemble people who would like to teach the greyhound's qualities to poodles, without realizing that the greyhound's speed and the poodle's docility are qualities which are not taught, but are peculiar to the race. Peoples who renounce the preservation of their racial purity renounce also the unity of their soul in all its expressions. The torn condition of their nature is the natural, necessary consequence of the torn condition of their blood, and the change in their spiritual and creative force is only the effect of the change in their racial foundations.

He who wants to redeem the German people from the qualities and the vices which are alien to its original nature will have to redeem it first from the alien originators of these expressions.

Without the clearest recognition of the race problem and, with it, of the Jewish question, there will be no rise of the German nation.[8]

Deduction

Deduction is the kind of argument that starts with a general statement as a premise and draws conclusions from it. The conclusions are implied in the general statement. For example, the following conclusions are implied in the statement that "A square is a rectangle with equilateral sides":

1. A rectangle with the horizontal sides either larger or smaller than the vertical sides is not a square.
2. Squares are necessarily rectangles, but rectangles are not necessarily squares.
3. The sum of the angles within a square is 360 degrees.
4. If a square is divided into two triangles by a diagonal line, each of the triangles so formed is a right-angle triangle.
5. The triangles so formed are congruent.
6. The sum of the angles in each of these triangles is 180 degrees.
7. Each of the triangles has two acute angles.

In drawing these conclusions we do not need to measure lines or angles. We simply recognize that (1) above is another way of expressing the given general statement, that (2) above is another way of stating (1), and so on. In deduction we study statements and draw conclusions from what they imply. We are, in effect, saying "Given statement A, statement B follows." Deduction is "thinking out" the implications of statements. The following illustrates the process:

In College X, the English Department has a committee to advise the chairman on matters of policy. For this committee the first of the following statements is *permanently* true; the others are true *for the present year*:

1. All full professors in the department are members of the committee by virtue of their rank.
2. All members of this year's committee are married.
3. No woman is a member of this year's committee.
4. Every member of this year's committee has the Ph. D. degree.

[8] From Adolf Hitler, *Mein Kampf*, trans. Ralph Manheim (Boston: Houghton Mifflin Company, 1943).

It is possible to deduce conclusions by using some of these statements as premises (P1 and P2 below):

P1   All full professors in the department are members of the committee.
P2   All members of this year's committee are Ph. D.'s.
C   At present all full professors in the department are Ph. D.'s.

This conclusion necessarily follows from the premises. It is another way of saying what is implied in the premises. But these premises do not imply that it is necessary to have the Ph.D. degree to become a full professor, or to serve on the committee; nor do they imply that membership on the committee is restricted to full professors. In checking these implications, remember that statements 2, 3, and 4 refer to members of the current committee and that only statement 1 refers to any advisory committee appointed in this department.

A deduction is said to be *reliable* if it meets *both* of two conditions: first, that all its statements are *true;* second, that the inference it makes is *valid.* A statement is true if it is in accordance with the given facts; otherwise it is considered false. Thus a statement that all members of this year's committee are over forty has to be called false, because we have no information about the age of the members. A conclusion is valid when it necessarily follows from the premises. Thus in the deduction given above, the conclusion that at present all full professors in the department are Ph.D.'s is both true and valid. It is true because it is in accordance with the fourth of our given statements. It is valid because it necessarily follows from P1 and P2. But a conclusion that all members of this year's committee are men, while true, is not a valid deduction from P1 and P2, since it does not follow as a logical inference from P1 and P2. For the deduction to be reliable, the conclusion must be both true and valid.

EXERCISE

To test your ability to make reliable deductions, decide which of the following conclusions can be validly drawn from any combination of the four statements given above about the committee membership. Discuss your answers. An answer to one conclusion is given to illustrate the procedure.

Sample.   No woman in the department is a full professor.

This is a valid conclusion from statements 1 and 3 above:

P1   All full professors in the department are members of the committee by virtue of their rank.

P2   No woman is a member of this year's committee.

C   No woman in the department is a full professor.

If any woman were a full professor she would be on the committee by P1, but no woman is on this year's committee (P2); therefore no woman in the department is a full professor.

Now see which of the following conclusions can be validly drawn from the four statements on page 320.

1. No woman in the department has a Ph.D. degree.
2. The department discriminates against women.
3. All full professors in the department are married.
4. To be a full professor in the department, one must be married.
5. To become a full professor, one must be in the department for at least five years.
6. If a woman member of the department is promoted to a full professorship, she qualifies as a member of the committee.

The Syllogism

The form of deduction used above is called a *syllogism*. There are many kinds of syllogisms, but here we will consider only one, the *categorical syllogism*. A categorical syllogism is a three-sentence argument, consisting of a *major premise*, a *minor premise*, and a *conclusion*. Each sentence consists of two terms connected by a verb. There are three terms in all, each used twice. In the following examples the terms have been underlined and lettered to make each example more clearly reveal the structure of the model. (For convenient reference we shall abbreviate major premise, minor premise, and conclusion to *MP, mp,* and *c* respectively.)

Model	Example
	A ..... *B*
MP. All *A* are *B*.	All things created by men are subject to error.
	C ..... *A*
mp. *C* is *A*.	Books are created by men.
	C ..... *B*
c. *C* is *B*.	Books are subject to error.[9]

Model	Example
	A ... *B*
MP. All *A* are *B*.	All psychiatrists are M.D.'s.
	C ... *A*
mp. *C* is *A*.	John Doe is a psychiatrist.
	C ... *B*
c. *C* is *B*.	John Doe is an M.D.

[9] From W. Edgar Moore, *Creative and Critical Thinking* (Boston: Houghton Mifflin Company, 1967), p. 208.

A categorical syllogism begins with a statement about all members of a class, a statement which identifies some characteristic that all members of the class share. It then proceeds to identify one member of the class and to infer that this member has the class characteristic. Notice that, except for any necessary change from plural to singular in *A* and *B,* each term has precisely the same meaning each time it is used. This is important, because a term used in two meanings is actually two terms, and we then have more than three terms. As the model shows, the categorical syllogism cannot have more or less than three terms.

The following example illustrates a violation of this rule.

$$A \qquad\qquad B$$
MP. All <u>psychiatrists</u> are <u>M.D.'s</u>.

$$C \qquad\qquad\qquad\qquad D$$
mp. <u>John Doe</u> is an <u>amateur psychiatrist</u>.

"Psychiatrists" and "amateur psychiatrist" are not synonymous. The syllogism therefore has four terms and we can draw no conclusion from the premises.

Testing for Validity. Now let us gain some experience with validity in the categorical syllogism by taking a series of premises and seeing what conclusions may be validly derived from them. Remember that we are chiefly concerned with seeing what the premises imply. We cannot draw any conclusion which is not necessarily implied in the premises.

(1)

MP. All college professors are absent-minded.
mp. Father is absent-minded.

We can draw no conclusion from these premises. The major premise is a statement about college professors, not about absent-minded people; therefore we cannot infer that father is a college professor. But if the major premise read, "Only college professors are absent-minded," we could infer that father is a college professor. Or if the minor premise said, "Father is a college professor," we could conclude that he is absent-minded.

(2)

MP. All college professors are absent-minded.
mp. Father is not absent-minded.

We can conclude that father is not a college professor. If he is not absent-minded he does not qualify as a college professor according to the major premise. In this syllogism, saying that father is not absent-minded is another way of saying that he is not a college professor.

(3)

MP. No college professor is absent-minded.
mp. Father is absent-minded.

We conclude that father is not a college professor, since his absent-mindedness rules him out of the class according to the major premise. Notice that although this major premise does not start with "All," it is still a statement about all college professors, since to say that none of them has a certain characteristic is the same as to say that all of them lack that characteristic.

(4)

MP. No college professor is absent-minded.
mp. Father is not absent-minded.

We can draw no conclusion. The major premise does not say that *only* college professors are free of absent-mindedness. If it did, we could conclude that father is a college professor. But, as stated, the major premise does not imply that freedom from absent-mindedness is a sure sign of being a college professor.

The Enthymeme

Quite frequently a categorical syllogism lies half-concealed in a shortened form called an *enthymeme*, a form not easy to recognize without practice. Here are three enthymemes, each a shortened form of a syllogism:

(1) Father is a college professor; therefore he is absent-minded.
(2) Father must be absent-minded, because he is a college professor.
(3) Since all college professors are absent-minded, father must be absent-minded.

To test the validity of the shortened form, first rewrite the syllogism in its full form. In doing this, certain connectives can be important clues: *because, since,* and *for* introduce premises, and *therefore, so,* and *then* introduce conclusions. When these words appear it is not hard to reconstruct the syllogism. In (1) above, *therefore* identifies the second statement as the conclusion, and you can work backward from the conclusion to provide the missing major premise:

MP.
mp. Father is a college professor.
 c. Father is absent-minded.

By checking the clue words you should be able to identify the missing part of (2) also as the major premise, and the missing part of (3) as the minor premise.

When these clue words are not present, an enthymeme is more difficult to detect:

Father must be absent-minded! He's a college professor, isn't he?

Here, with major premise missing, is a classic example of "jumping to a conclusion"—from minor premise only. This is the danger that lurks in the unexamined enthymeme.

Common Errors in Syllogisms

The three most common errors with categorical syllogisms are hasty generalization in the major premise, ambiguous terms, and misinterpretation of the major premise.

Hasty Generalization in the Major Premise. In the categorical syllogism the major premise refers to all members of a class and is therefore a generalization. If that generalization is unacceptable, it cannot be used in a syllogism. Thus if not all college professors are absent-minded, the hasty generalization that they are cannot be used as a major premise of a syllogism, because it would be a false statement. Of course, a false minor premise would have to be rejected, too; but the more common error is a faulty major premise.

Ambiguous Terms. Unless the terms are precise, they cannot be used in a syllogism. What do "radicals" and "un-American" mean in the following premise?

All radicals are un-American.

We cannot make reliable deductions from such loose terms, so there is no point in proceeding with the syllogism.

Misinterpretation of the Major Premise. The major premise "All full professors are members of the advisory committee" does not mean the same as "All members of the advisory committee are full professors," since the first statement does not restrict membership to full professors, as the second statement does. Yet this kind of misinterpretation is frequent:

All Communists oppose U.S. policy in Vietnam.
He opposes U.S. policy in Vietnam.
He is a Communist.

This conclusion would be valid only if the major premise were reversed:

All who oppose U.S. policy in Vietnam are Communists.

But in its first form we must consider that the major premise is misinterpreted. "All Communists oppose U.S. policy in Vietnam" does not mean "All who oppose U.S. policy in Vietnam are Communists."

A helpful clue to a misinterpreted major premise of a categorical syllogism is the relative position of term A in the major and minor premises. In the major premise, term A occupies the subject position, but in the minor premise it occupies the complement position.

MP. All A are B.
mp. C is A.

But in the misinterpretation, A does not appear in the minor premise, and B is the complement in both premises:

MP. All A are B.
mp. C is B.

Remember that in the erroneous form both premises end with the B term.

EXERCISE

What valid conclusions, if any, can be drawn from the following premises?

---

1. All psychiatrists are M.D.'s.
   All surgeons are M.D.'s.

2. All widows have deceased husbands.
   Mrs. Jones is a widow.

3. No Canadian citizen may vote in the U.S. elections.
   Spiro Agnew is not a Canadian citizen.

4. Some football players are All-Americans.
   He is a football player.

5. Necessity is the mother of invention.
   Plumbers are a necessity.

6. Anyone with an IQ of 140 or more is classified as a genius.
   He has an IQ of 160.

7. All industrial cities have skyscrapers.
   All state capitals have skyscrapers

8. Boston is smaller than Chicago.
   Philadelphia is smaller than Chicago.

9. Wise men hate war.
   I hate war.

10. All X are Y.
    This is Y.

FALLACIES

A *fallacy* is an error which makes an argument unreliable. The following discussion will group fallacies in two general classes: those that distort an argument, and those that oversimplify it.

Fallacies of Distortion

Literally, the word *distort* means "to twist out of shape." Any error which misrepresents all or part of an argument by twisting its meaning is a fallacy of distortion. The following types are the most common.

Begging the Question. A question is "begged" when one or more of the premises by which it should be proved are assumed to be true without proof. The best defense against this fallacy is to show how the begging takes place. The following examples illustrate such arguments:

Examples

Dad, you don't need to worry about lending me the money for this business. Just as soon as the profits come in I can pay you back with interest.

Much of this talk about spending millions for slum clearance is based on the fallacy that if we provide fine homes for people who live in the slums they will suddenly become responsible and productive citizens. This argument puts the cart before the horse. The basic trouble is with the people who live in the slums. These people are thoroughly shiftless and irresponsible. The conditions under which they live prove this. If they had any initiative or industry they would not be living under slum conditions.

Analysis

This argument assumes that the profits will be sufficient to pay off the debt. That, however, is a major part of Dad's doubt, and needs to be proved.

This is an argument in a circle. The thesis that slum-dwellers are responsible for slum conditions is supported by asserting that if they were not responsible they would not be living in slums. The writer assumes that what he has to prove is true, and his argument goes round in the following circle: Slums are caused by shiftless tenants; this is true because shiftless tenants cause slums.

Examples	**Analysis**
"There is bound to be life on other planets." "Can you prove it?" "Well, can you prove there isn't?"	*This example shifts the burden of proof. In arguments both inside and outside law courts, "He who asserts must prove." We cannot prove an assertion by defying the opposition to disprove it.*

Ignoring Context   Words have specific meaning in context. If the context is changed, or—as more often happens—if part of it is ignored, the whole statement may be misrepresented. If an instructor says, "You will pass the course if your grades for the rest of the term are consistently above C," a student who ignores the conditional clause ignores a significant part of the instructor's statement. If such a student later complains that he ought to have received a passing grade ("But you told me I would pass!"), he should be prepared to prove that he met the condition which the instructor established in the context of the complete statement.

Distortion by ignoring context is not always deliberate. People sometimes read or hear what they want to be told, and through some emotional need misinterpret what is said. Whether distortion is deliberate or not, the way to correct it is to re-examine the whole context and show how omission misinterprets the original.

Extension.   This is the device of distorting an argument by extending or exaggerating it. Often it is a special case of ignoring context. Someone states that some high school graduates enter college inadequately prepared in English and mathematics. An opponent thereupon charges that the statement belittles high school teaching. This charge greatly extends and exaggerates the original remark. First, the original concerned only *some* students, not all; second, it concerned only *two* high school subjects, not all; third, it did not place the blame on the teachers of the deficient students. Again the best defense is to return to the original statement and show what it meant in its context. If the extension is not deliberate, the charge will be withdrawn. If the distortion is deliberate and is not withdrawn, it will be exposed and will damage the accuser more than the accused.

Red Herring.   The scent of a red herring dragged across a trail which hounds are following may be stronger than the original scent and so divert the hounds from their quarry. In rhetoric, a red herring is a false issue introduced to lead attention away from a real one. Usually the false issue arouses an emotional response which creates a digression. If in a discussion of the draft system someone asks, "Do those of you who want to change the draft believe that young men have no obligation to their country?" he has introduced a red herring. In the heat of emotional responses to that question, it may be hard to focus on the practical question whether specific changes in the draft would be wise or not. As this example shows, a red herring may be introduced by extension. The best defense is the defense against extension: a restatement of the issue originally under consideration, to show that the red herring is a false issue.

Name-Calling.   Name-calling presents an issue in loaded terms, thereby making it difficult for some persons to consider that issue objectively. They are, in effect, led into prejudging at a level of emotional associations. They are less willing to seek the evidence on which a rational judgment might be made when a proposal is branded, for example, as "communist-inspired" or "radicalization." If the charges implied in these names can be supported by evidence, the evidence should be presented. When that is done, the audience is given the facts before it is asked to make the judgment. There is nothing wrong with calling an event "communist-inspired" if the speaker proves the charge. The fallacy of name-calling is that the judgment is made without evidence.

Argumentum ad Hominem.   This is the fallacy of attacking the man instead of his argument. Such an attack is legitimate when the man presents no argument except his own unsupported testimony. The device is frequently used in law courts to discredit a witness who is testifying as an expert. If it can be shown that he is not expert, or that his testimony cannot be relied on because of his character, then his trustworthiness as a witness is seriously challenged. But if his argument rests on evidence and reasoning, it should be evaluated at these levels. The real fallacy in *argumentum ad hominem* is that it substitutes an attack on the man for an attack on his argument.

The fallacies so far mentioned are merely the most common types of distortion. The chief defense against any distortion is the ability to detect it and to explain how it works. The major risk a person runs in distorting an argument is that, if exposed, he forfeits confidence—and with it the chance of persuading others.

Fallacies of Over-simplification

Any argument that allows us to reach a conclusion without considering all pertinent factors tends to oversimplify. The most common fallacies of over-simplification are *hasty generalizations, stereotypes, inadequate causal relationships, either-or fallacies,* and *trivial analogies.*

Hasty Generalization.   A hasty generalization jumps to a conclusion from insufficient evidence. Unless the samples are clearly typical, a small number proves nothing, or at least much less than is claimed. Here is a representative case.

Example	**Analysis**
Girls just aren't any good at logic. Although there are twelve girls to ten men in our logic section, the four highest scores on the final exams were made by men and the four lowest by girls.	*In the first place, what would make us believe that what is true of twelve girls in one class will be true of all girls? In the second, are the top four and bottom four scores typical of the scores in the class? Even as a comparison for this class alone, the sample is faulty. It would be better to take the median score of the girls and compare it with the median score of the men. If the comparison favored the men, it would justify the conclusion that girls in this class do less well than men in this class on an examination in logic. That is a less impressive conclusion than the one offered in the original argument.*

Stereotype.   A stereotype is a description or standardized mental image which pays too much attention to characteristics supposedly common to a group and not enough to individual differences. We begin with a number of individuals who have one thing in common (let us say that they all have married children); we group them into a class (mothers-in-law); we develop an attitude towards that class (mothers-in-law are interfering) based on a hasty generalization; then we apply that attitude to individual mothers-in-law without waiting to see whether or not they actually are interfering. The reasoning behind the stereotype can be set up as a syllogism: *All mothers-in-law are interfering; she is a mother-in-law; she is interfering.* This syllogism is unreliable because the major premise is not universally true.

To help us avoid this fallacy some students of language advise us to use index numbers after the class names to remind us that each member of a group has his own personal characteristics—that $German_1$ is not $German_2$, that college $professor_A$ is not college $professor_B$, that $freshman_{1972}$ is not $freshman_{1962}$. Whether we write these index numbers or merely think them, they are useful reminders not to assume that individuals with a common class name will be alike in all respects.

Inadequate Causal Relations.   As superstitions illustrate, it is easy to find a cause, even for complex events, if we just pick a convenient item and call it the cause. Such a procedure, however, does not advance our understanding of the event. Two ways to oversimplify a causal relation are to accept a contributory cause as a sufficient cause and to accept another effect as the cause. An example of each type of oversimplification follows.

Examples	Analysis
I know my spelling is terrible. All the members of my family are poor spellers.	*Family environment may contribute to poor spelling, but it is not the sole cause. The student has oversimplified by failing to consider other causes, about which he could do something.*
I failed the course because the instructor had a prejudice against me.	*Even if we assume that the prejudice existed, it must be the effect of some cause. This reasoning mistakes a possible effect for a cause. A more probable reason is that the student's conduct caused both the alleged prejudice and the failure.*

The Either-Or Fallacy. In deciding on a course of action we often choose between alternatives. Sometimes there are only two alternatives, but if there are more than two, we oversimplify the choice by limiting it to two possibilities.

Example	Analysis
On the question whether the husband should be the boss in the household, there are only two alternatives: either the man will be the boss or the woman will. Any man who lets himself be dictated to by a woman is a sorry specimen and probably deserves what he will get. But most of us will not make that mistake. We will make it known at the start, gently but firmly, that we intend to be masters in our own homes. The sooner the little lady gets that idea through her head, the better for everybody.	*There are three possible positions to take on this question: the husband should be boss; the wife should be boss; nobody should be boss. This argument overlooks the third possibility; therefore it is not true that if the husband does not dominate, the wife will. Essentially the example oversimplifies the question by unnecessarily limiting the alternatives.*

Trivial Analogies. Although an analogy is always suspect when it is not supported by other kinds of reasoning, a carefully planned analogy is often persuasive. But, except possibly for hasty generalizations, there is no more common fallacy than the use of impromptu, ill-considered, and trivial analogies, based on a superficial resemblance between two events or conditions. Often these are mere clichés—*You can't teach an old dog new tricks.* In any controversy analogies come easily—usually too easily—to mind. It is wise not to accept them until they have been carefully examined to see if there is a significant difference between the things being compared.

Example	Analysis
A French Minister of Education is reported to have told a visitor that at that moment every fourth-grade pupil in all France was studying exactly the same lesson. In France the national government controls education. If we adopt the proposed federal aid to education bill, we will bring about federal control of our schools and get the same kind of regimentation that exists in France.	*A student using this analogy should first satisfy himself that there are no essential differences in the governmental structures of the two countries. When he tries to do so he will discover that France does not have a federal form of government and that the educational control in France more nearly resembles our state control. That discovery would make the student question the worth of the analogy in a question primarily concerned with federal control. If he still wants to use the analogy he will at least feel an obligation to show in detail that, despite this difference, the two countries are analogous where education is concerned.*

All these fallacies—*hasty generalizations, stereotypes, inadequate causal relations, either-or fallacies,* and *trivial analogies*—oversimplify the problem by allowing us to reach conclusions more easily and more quickly than is possible in disciplined deliberation.

EXERCISE

The following arguments contain various types of fallacies. Evaluate each and explain clearly what is wrong with it. Do not be content with naming the fallacy. The skill you are trying to develop is not identification but analysis; it is more important to explain the errors than to name them.

1. I don't know what the colleges are teaching nowadays. I have just had a letter of application from a young man who graduated from the state university last June. It was a wretched letter—badly written, with elementary errors in spelling, punctuation, and grammar. If that is the kind of product State is turning out, it does not deserve the tax support it is getting.

2. There are two kinds of rattlers, those whose bite is fatal, and those that cause swelling and discomfort but not death. That is why some people die from rattler bites and some don't. If we kept accurate records on snake bites we would find that people who recover were bitten by the non-fatal rattler; those who do not recover have been bitten by the fatal type.

3. It comes down to this: either NATO should require the European countries to finance and man the European part of the program or we should pull out of the organization.

4. We would not have all these strikes and riots and demonstrations if people would only practice the Golden Rule.

5. In taking the position that men accused of crimes cannot be interrogated without their lawyers being present, the Supreme Court is showing more concern for the protection of the criminal than for the protection of society. The laws were made to protect law-abiding citizens, not those who defy the law. A criminal loses his rights as a citizen when he commits a crime. It is the duty of the police to get at the truth, and they have a right to question him, as long as they don't use force.

6. College students, at least American, are different from all other people on this planet. They are the only people who try to get as little as possible for their money. They will spend the most valuable years of their lives and up to $20,000 in trying to get as little as possible out of their college courses, provided only that they get their coveted diplomas.

7. That's the kind of remark you'd expect from a college professor. They're all alike—a bunch of visionaries who never met a payroll.

8. The old Biblical injunction, "By their fruits ye shall know them," is still a pretty good test. The Communists are interested in stirring up trouble whenever they can; so if you find strikes and riots and demonstrations, you can be sure there's a Communist in the background.

9. Research shows that the most successful men have the largest vocabularies. This proves that the development of an extensive vocabulary is a cause of success.

10. The professor says that two negatives do not make an affirmative in English, but the facts are against him. Any high school freshman could tell him that when you multiply minus a by minus b, the result is a plus or positive quantity. That is not just opinion. It is a mathematical law. And it holds true whether it is written in English, Latin, Greek, or Hindustani.

11. The argument that football is a dangerous sport is disproved very simply by showing that the death rate—not total deaths, but deaths per thousand —among high school, college, and professional players combined is much less than the death rate of the total population.

12. No, I haven't read the bill. No, I haven't thought about it. I don't need to. It's being supported by Congressman Blank, and there isn't a worse scoundrel in the country. If Blank's in favor of something, I'm against it.

13. Korea produces so many good marathon runners because the Koreans have fewer automobiles than we do. They learn to use their legs instead of riding around in cars. That's why they win.

14. I don't think it's fair that teen-age drivers should have to pay an extra premium for car insurance. Most teen-agers I know drive better than their parents. Women don't have to pay a premium, and everybody knows what women drivers are like!

15. More people now die of cancer than ever before. That's what comes from living in cities and breathing polluted air. Fifty years ago there was much less cancer. The air was cleaner then.

EMOTIONAL APPEAL

The term "emotional appeal" has unfavorable connotations for some people because it is often associated with persuasion that appeals only to the emotions and ignores both trustworthiness and argument. But the abuse of emotional appeal should not discredit its legitimate use—to make the reader *feel* the force of a sound argument by arousing his indignation, sympathy, and sense of fair play, pride, shame, or fear. Emotional appeal is not a substitute for argument, but a supplement to it. Many readers can see the logic of an argument at the time they are reading it, but are not sufficiently motivated by it to overcome inertia or habit and do something about the problem. A writer therefore tries to reinforce the intellectual appeal of his argument by a supplementary appeal to the reader's emotions.

The arguments on the correlation between cigarette-smoking and cancer offer a good illustration. Many people who smoke cigarettes are intellectually persuaded that inhaling cigarette smoke can be injurious to health, but until they have been made to fear that *their* smoking will endanger *their* health, they are not sufficiently motivated to make a sustained effort to break a confirmed habit. In this situation both convincing arguments and emotional appeals are necessary if the persuasion is to be effective.

Emotional appeal is usually most important in that stage of the persuasion process when the writer is trying to make the reader feel that the situation is serious and something must be done about it. The most useful device is the example. Is LSD dangerous? Tell what happened to someone who used it, and then give the statistical, testimonial, and causal evidence that keeps the example from being dismissed as an exceptional case. This was the procedure used in the passage on the constitutional rights of high school students (page 312). The examples helped the reader to identify with the students (that is, to put himself in their place) and so made him sympathetic with them. Then the writer went on to show that the examples were typical and that the schools generally were denying students rights which are guaranteed by the Constitution and affirmed by the courts.

EXERCISE

Contrast the two following paragraphs written by Ralph Nader to persuade readers that something must be done to make automobile manufacturers give higher priority to safety in the design and construction of cars. Which paragraph has the greater emotional appeal, and why? What does that paragraph lack which the other provides? Would the argument be less persuasive if either paragraph were omitted?

(1)

Highway accidents were estimated to have cost this country in 1964, $8.3 billion in property damage, medical expenses, lost wages, and insurance overhead expenses. Add an equivalent sum to comprise roughly the indirect costs and the total amounts to over two per cent of the gross national product. But these are not the kind of costs which fall on the builders of motor vehicles (excepting a few successful law suits for negligent construction of the vehicle) and thus do not pinch the proper foot. Instead the costs fall to users of vehicles, who are in no position to dictate safer automobile designs.

(2)

As described by a California Highway Patrol officer, John Bortolozzo, who witnessed the flip-over while motoring in the opposite direction, the Pierini vehicle was traveling about thirty-five miles an hour in a thirty-five mph zone in the right lane headed towards Goleta. He saw the car move towards the right side of the road near the shoulder and then "all of a sudden the vehicle made a sharp cut to the left and swerved over." Bortolozzo testified at the trial that he rushed over to the wreck and saw an arm with a wedding band and wristwatch lying on the ground. Two other men came over quickly and began to help Mrs. Pierini out of the vehicle while trying to stop the torrent of blood gushing forth from the stub of her arm. She was very calm, observed Bortolozzo, only saying that "something went wrong with my steering."[10]

WRITING PERSUASIVE ESSAYS

Writing a persuasive essay is not basically different from writing an expository essay. Both kinds of composition require the writer to discover through prewriting what he wants to do for what kind of reader and how best to do it. So the best preparation for writing persuasion is the experience you have already had in writing purposeful exposition. The chief difference between the two is that persuasion requires greater sensitivity to the reader and more concern with the reliability of arguments. The following pages summarize as practical advice the main points to keep in mind in writing a persuasive essay.

1. *Address your essay to those readers who need to be persuaded.* In your classroom audience there are likely to be some students who already agree with the position you are going to take and some who disagree so strongly that your chances of changing their minds by a single essay are slight. Between these extremes there will be a number, perhaps a majority, who can be brought to agree, at least in part, with a sound and fair argument. These are the people to whom your essay should be mainly addressed.

[10] From Ralph Nader, *Unsafe at Any Speed* (New York: Grossman, 1965).

In the process of persuading them you may strengthen the convictions of your supporters and perhaps weaken those of your opponents. But if you cannot persuade those who have an open mind, your persuasion is not good enough.

2. *Make it easy for those readers to agree with you.* Usually you will encourage agreement by three means: first, by presenting your arguments clearly and in enough detail so that your readers can easily follow them; second, by identifying with your readers through the tone of your writing; third, by winning their confidence through your knowledge of the subject and your fairness in dealing with it. These are the basic requirements of persuasion. Let us look at each of them in more detail.

(*a*) *The clarity of your argument to the reader depends on its clarity in your own mind.* The best way to be sure it is clear is to outline and evaluate your arguments before you begin to write. What are the main premises which lead to the conclusion you want your readers to accept? What sub-premises are needed to make the main premises acceptable? Will these premises persuade the reader to accept your conclusion? In outlining the structure of your argument, you may have to decide whether it is too complex to be handled in a single paper. You may have to simplify it, but if you oversimplify it you will weaken it. The decision about complexity has to take into account two considerations: the amount of space you have available and the degree of complexity the reader can handle. When in doubt, the safest procedure is to restrict the scope of the argument by limiting it to one of the main premises. If you do that, the main premise becomes the conclusion or thesis of your essay. It will be your real subject, and you will have space enough to develop it thoroughly. Adequate development is important. Usually it is better to make one point thoroughly than to hurry over a number of points.

(*b*) *The tone of your paper establishes your relation with the reader.* You have seen in Chapter 8 on style that the distance between writer and reader increases as the style becomes more formal. Since you want mutual identification with your readers, anything that increases the distance between you and them is undesirable. The safest procedure is to treat your readers with respect, but with as much intimacy as the situation permits. Do not talk down to them; treat them as equals.

(*c*) *But tone by itself is not enough to ensure closeness of writer to reader.* Anything that repels a reader widens the distance. Therefore any statement that reveals ignorance, faulty reasoning, unfairness—untrustworthiness of any kind—will drive the reader off. Any obvious fallacy of distortion or oversimplification will repel him.

3. *Limit your real subject to what you can do thoroughly.* Inexperienced writers often try to prove too much in too little space. Such vast subjects as pollution, the war in Indochina, and civil rights cannot be effectively argued within the space of a single paper. They have to be drastically restricted

before a writer can deal with them in the necessary detail. For example, a recent magazine article on oil pollution runs to about 22,000 words—three or four times the length of even a long student essay. One-tenth of the article is devoted to the effects of oil pollution on birds. The following two paragraphs deal with the cost of cleaning just one oil-covered bird:

> Philip Stanton, a biologist at Massachusetts State College at Framingham, has been experimenting with different techniques for treating oiled birds at his Wildlife Rehabilitation Center in Upton, Massachusetts. The process is expensive. Oil-contaminated birds have to be collected, transported, and washed; pens, pools, food, heat, and caretakers are needed for six months or longer. "I wouldn't even want to think about the cost per bird," Stanton says.
>
> Others estimate it can cost $1,000 to *try* to save a single bird. With a success ratio of only 10 per cent, only 100 of every 1,000 oiled birds treated are likely to survive. Thus the cost could run to $10,000 per surviving bird.[11]

These figures are powerfully persuasive, but the writer would never have got down to them if he had been trying to cover the effects of oil pollution on birds in a single paragraph of a 600-word paper on oil pollution. Restriction permits the specific details which are the foundation of effective persuasion.

4. *Supplement statistics with examples.* Statistics can make effective generalizations, but they should be used with caution. A straight statistical argument is hard to read, and usually a reader presented with two conflicting sets of statistical figures has no way of deciding which to believe. Moreover, statistics are soon forgotten. For these reasons, they are not so persuasive as students sometimes think. They are best used in combination with concrete examples, as Ralph Nader used them in the two paragraphs on page 335. A well-chosen example will often be very persuasive emotionally. Once examples have been given, statistics can then be presented to show that the examples are typical. The two together can be highly effective, but if only one can be used, the example is likely to be the more moving for a general audience.

5. *Check the trustworthiness of your sources.* Most of the materials used in persuasive writing come from published sources. Your reader has a right to know not only the sources of the materials, but also the trustworthiness of these sources. Therefore you must be prepared to show that your sources are reliable. If you cannot do so, your own trustworthiness may suffer. It helps to identfy a source in a footnote, but a comment in the text on the authority of the source can add further weight to your argument. For example: "The endorsement of Linus Pauling, Nobel Prize winner in chemistry, adds weight to the claim that heavy doses of vitamin C will keep one free of colds."

[11] From Marvin Zeldin, "Audubon Black Paper No. 1," *Audubon*, May 1971.

6. Finally, remember that your reader has no obligation to agree with you. The burden of proof is on you as writer. You have no right to ask him to accept unsupported assertions as arguments. An argument consists of both premise and conclusion. An assertion is a conclusion without a supporting premise. Assertion, therefore, is not argument. It will be persuasive only to people who already agree with you and do not need to be persuaded. For all others you will be expected to show the evidence and the inferences on which your conclusion rests.

A. *Study the following selections as examples of persuasion. Then discuss each one with respect to the trustworthiness of the writer, the soundness of his arguments, his use of emotional appeal.*

Never, but Never!

One windy afternoon in March of 1968, a military jet sprayed 320 gallons of deadly nerve gas over a government testing ground at a site more than 45 miles away from the little town of Dugway, Utah. More than 6,000 of Dugway's sheep were dead by dawn of the following day. The Army was blamed for the mishap but protested complete innocence for more than fourteen months. As evidence backed up in opposition to their protests, officials were finally convinced that their testing was at fault. Their confession caused one of the hottest controversies ever to ensue in the months following the testing. The question to be decided upon: should nations resort to chemical and biological weapons as a form of warfare? Several arguments strongly disfavor any such action on the part of any civilized country.

In the first place, no one can predict how enduring the effects of chemical and biological warfare (CBW) will be and how the structure of the environment may possibly be affected. Many United Nations experts agree that it would be impossible even to attempt to determine the outcome of such a drastic method of warfare.

Secondly, biological warfare undoes the work of medical science and research. Billions of the taxpayers' dollars are spent annually in a never-ending effort to find panaceas for many of the diseases which plague mankind and threaten its welfare. At the same time, billions of the taxpayers' dollars are also being spent for the development of CBW projects, the purpose of which will be to create and spread new diseases as a means of disposing of the enemy. It makes little sense to search for cures for natural diseases if mass-produced man-made diseases are to replace them. Wouldn't it be much easier (and less expensive) to simply discontinue medical research altogether and allow nature to get rid of our enemies for us? But, we could never do that. After all, we do have a speck of decency left.

Next, gases cannot easily be kept under control. A shift in the wind may blow the gases into the faces of friendly troops rather than the enemy. Also, the numbers of innocent victims which the deadly gases and diseases will no doubt reach must be kept in mind.

In spite of what CBW advocates say about using such methods of warfare only if the enemy uses it first, CBW is in direct violation of the Geneva Protocol of 1925 (which 45 nations have signed) and general standards of international law.

Finally, it hardly seems plausible to think that any nation could have an escape plan worked out in case of a CBW attack. It is next to impossible to protect any great number of people in case of an attack, seemingly because no one is quite certain of what kind of precautions to take against such an unpredictable situation as the use of CBW could possibly engender.

To the advocates of chemical and biological warfare, then, we should offer no "ifs," "buts," or "maybes," but a flat uncompromising "Never!" and let it go at that. Their cries of "They used it; why can't we?" or "That's one quick way of getting rid of the enemy!" can easily be put down by a sense of humanity even in the tiniest proportion. A country which must resort to such protective methods as the creation of fatal diseases and gases is not worth protecting in the first place because it has already lapsed into a state far beyond the limits which human decency can allow.

from **Silent Spring**[12]

Where do pesticides fit into the picture of environmental disease? We have seen that they now contaminate soil, water, and food, that they have the power to make our streams fishless and our gardens and woodlands silent and bird-less. Man, however much he may like to pretend the contrary, is part of nature. Can he escape a pollution that is now so thoroughly distributed throughout our world?

We know that even single exposures to these chemicals, if the amount is large enough, can precipitate acute poisoning. But this is not the major problem. The sudden illness or death of farmers, spraymen, pilots, and others exposed to appreciable quantities of pesticides are tragic and should not occur. For the population as a whole, we must be more concerned with the delayed effects of absorbing small amounts of the pesticides that invisibly contaminate our world.

Responsible public health officials have pointed out that the biological effects of chemicals are cumulative over long periods of time, and that the

[12] Rachel Carson, *Silent Spring* (Boston: Houghton Mifflin Company, 1962).

hazard to the individual may depend on the sum of the exposures received throughout his lifetime. For these very reasons the danger is easily ignored. It is human nature to shrug off what may seem to us a vague threat of future disaster. "Men are naturally most impressed by diseases which have obvious manifestations," says a wise physician, Dr. René Dubos, "yet some of their worst enemies creep on them unobtrusively."

For each of us, as for the robin in Michigan or the salmon in the Miramichi, this is a problem of ecology, of interrelationships, of interdependence. We poison the caddis flies in a stream and the salmon runs dwindle and die. We poison the gnats in a lake and the poison travels from link to link of the food chain and soon the birds of the lake margins become its victims. We spray our elms and the following springs are silent of robin song, not because we sprayed the robins directly but because the poison traveled, step by step, through the now familiar elm leaf-earthworm-robin cycle. These are matters of record, observable, part of the visible world around us. They reflect the web of life—or death—that scientists know as ecology.

Today's Campus: The Eerie Calm[13]

The great issue that dominated so much social and political thought in the early sixties—the threat of widespread unemployment among young people who were entering the labor market just when the jobs usually available to them were disappearing—seems to be on the verge of reawakening with a roar. It is true that we missed that crisis, to some extent, but now the problem has reappeared in a more complex guise. We are perhaps approaching a time when the educational system and the occupational structure will be seriously out of step in this country.

In the first place, unemployment rates are beginning to shoot up for the younger age groups in the labor force—and particularly for Negro youths in the ghetto, where unemployment rates are horrendous. This apparently is more than a matter of the current recession and is not likely to go away. It is due in part to inadequate education and a lack of vocational skills that trap large masses of young people at the bottom of the socio-economic ladder where they drift into a mood of violent alienation. Continually dazzled by a vision of the affluent society dangled before them by the mass media, they must finally face the squalor of their own lives. To make matters worse, as Ivan Berg points out in his recent *Education and Jobs: The Great Training Robbery*, we have elevated educational prerequisites for jobs out of all proportion to the realistic requirements, so that even when people at the bottom of the heap do manage to get some degree of schooling, they still find much of the occupational structure closed to them. And the problem is also hitting the college student, who suddenly finds that the diploma held out in front of him

[13] Gresham M. Sykes, in *The Nation*, April 19, 1971.

for so long is neither a ticket of entry into the world of work nor a true symbol of an education received.

In the second place, jobs and education are progressively diverging because schooling turns large numbers of students away from the whole concept of work, even when their education is relevant to jobs and careers. It is not just that a "counter-culture" absorbs the interests and commitments of a new generation, nor simply that the politics of protest is in ascendancy. What seems to be happening, rather, is that an increasing number of students take what goes on in the school as a model of what will happen in the adult workaday world; and they then say, "If that's what it's like, we don't want it." The tyranny of grading that is often badly done or based on whims, so that it breeds anxiety rather than a sense of being objectively evaluated; the standardized mush that is compressed into textbooks and passed off as scholarship; the prison routines, particularly in the secondary schools, that make obvious that the educational system places a higher priority on order than on learning; the inability of students to gain more than a token vote in the administration of a system where they may spend as much as a quarter of their lives—all these help to create a resentment that is likely to spawn a rejection of the world to which the school is supposed to lead. It is quite possible that some of the student dissatisfaction is not justified and that the students dismiss too lightly the discipline of deferred gratification. The resentment is nonetheless there and must somehow be confronted. . . .

"But What About My Children?"[14]

Recently we met an extremely intelligent and dedicated so-called Hippie who had braces on her teeth. Whether this was a result of communal orthodontia or of desperate parental love we do not know, but we are inclined to take the latter view.

We say this because nearly every day we hear statements such as the following:

"I didn't really want to move out of the inner city into the suburbs. Felt like a deserter. I knew I should have stayed there and worked to improve the wretched conditions. On the other hand, as my wife said to me, *'What about your children?'* "

"Of course there is no one religion that is superior to the rest. I would be the first to admit that. And I can easily understand how a Protestant boy and a Catholic girl might fall in love. But when young people ask me how I feel about intermarriage, I always answer: 'It may be all right for you to marry, but think about the hardships faced by the children of mixed marriages. *What about your children?'* "

[14] Daniel Roselle, in *Social Education*, December 1970.

"I have always believed in the value of a public school education. I always will. *But what about my children?* For the sake of their education, I had to reject the chaotic public schools for a good private school."

"Grades? Of course they are absurd. So is the competition for marks in school and the tensions they build in students. *But what about my children?* The only way they are going to get into a decent college is to demonstrate that they have ability—and good grades show that. So I want my children to be graded."

"Blacks are as good as whites any day. I've always said that. And the idea of 'black depravity' is vicious nonsense. *But what about my children?* I don't want them to be innocently injured in some racial brawl. That's why I keep them away from interracial activities of any kind."

Thus, despite the admonitions of Kahlil Gibran and others ("your children are not your children; they are the sons and daughters of Life's longing for itself"), children have become a nationwide escape hatch for adults who refuse to face issues. Through no choice of their own, children have emerged as the immaculate reason-why, the haloed excuse-me-but-it-is-necessary buffers to justify adult inaction, lethargy, bigotry, and deceit. If this is not the best of all possible worlds, some of us have at least developed the best of all possible reasons for not changing it—our children—and the coat of parental love is worn with pride to cover the shameful nakedness of our callousness.

It was not always thus. There have always been courageous Abrahams who refused to permit love for a beloved Isaac to come between them and their principles. The significance of their actions was not their willingness to sacrifice their children, but their refusal to use their love for them as a means of evading responsibility. "When I was a child, I spake as a child, I understood as a child, I thought as a child; but when I became a man, I put away childish things," says *Corinthians*. Yet that was long ago, and many of us neither remember nor even know that there are such lines worth remembering.

What had to happen then—and what is happening—is a Revolt against Good Intentions. A revolt against those adults who say: "Let the whole world go mad. I don't care just so long as my own children are safe." A revolt against what Dr. Malvina Kremer of the Bellevue Medical School called the desire of some parents "to put their children on an escalator," instead of letting them walk up the steps themselves.

What is more, the significance of this revolt is clearly understood by the rebels. As author Kay Hurley points out: "The double standard is a form of hypocrisy so widespread that most adults are scarcely aware of it even when they are indulging in it personally. Yet it has been obvious to most young people since they were toddlers. Children learn early that rules are to be broken —especially if it suits a parent's convenience—just as they learn that adults will lie to avoid unpleasant obligations or to defend their own actions." Many children more easily accept the benign indifference of the universe than they do the benign indifference of their parents to that universe.

Then what is to be done about parental obsession with one's own rather than with everyone's all? Our children themselves are answering this question, in our homes, in our schools, and in our streets. And yet, ironically, they too will soon face the same problem. Thus, Lucia Perry, 18, a student at Kent State University who described her reactions to the killings there, declared:

> I want to have children. It's a fantastic thing, you know, especially for a woman. But partly because of the population problem and partly because of what happened at Kent, I wouldn't want to have children who would have to go to school and go through what I went through. *I really couldn't stand the thought of my children having to go through that,* and God knows what it will be like by the time they get here.

Will Lucia Perry and other members of her generation have the strength to refuse to use love of child as a means of circumventing principle? For no rational, logical, scientific, sensible, or provable reason, we believe that many of them will.

Inflation and Wages[15]

I have seldom met a businessman who was not persuaded that inflation is produced by rising wages—and rising wages, in turn, by strong labor unions—and many a nonbusinessman is of the same mind. This belief is false yet entirely understandable. To each businessman separately, inflation comes in the form of higher costs, mostly wages; yet for all businessmen combined, higher prices produce the higher costs. What is involved is a fallacy of composition. Any one person may be able to leave a crowded theater in two minutes without difficulty. Let everyone try to leave in two minutes and there may be utter chaos. What is true for each separately need not be true for all together.

It is easy to show that the widely held union-wage-push theory of inflation is not correct. If A is *the* cause of B, then whenever A occurs, B will also occur, and whenever B occurs, so will A. *Trade unions* (A) were as strong in the U.S. in 1961–64, when there was no *inflation* (B), as in 1965–69, when there was inflation. Prices in the U.S. more than doubled in the Civil War, when unions were almost nonexistent, in World War I, when unions were weak, and in World War II, when unions were strong. Prices in the U.S. rose more than 30 per cent from 1849 to 1857, and again from 1895 to 1914, both periods when unions were extremely weak. Inflation has plagued countries with negligible trade unions and with strong trade unions; and both kinds of countries have had periods of price stability. Communist countries, like capitalist countries, have experienced both inflation and price stability.

[15] Milton Friedman, in *Newsweek*, September 28, 1970.

Why Appearances Deceive. In light of these historical examples, why do businessmen believe so firmly in a wage-push theory of inflation? A simple hypothetical example may explain the puzzle.

Suppose that there was a sudden fad in the U.S. for male footwear. Despite a rush of customers, the shoe stores would not immediately raise the prices they charge. They would, with pleasure and profit, sell more shoes, depleting their inventories. Orders would pour in to wholesalers, who similarly would fill them at list prices, depleting their inventories in turn, and sending on larger orders to manufacturers. The manufacturers, delighted with the flood of business, would try to step up production. To produce more shoes requires more leather. But at any time, there is only a limited stock of leather. To get more leather for themselves, the shoe manufacturers will have to offer higher prices at auctions, in order to bid the leather away from other uses. To produce more shoes, they will also have to hire more labor. How? One way is surely by offering higher wages.

At this point, manufacturers discover that their costs have risen—because of rising wages and the higher cost of leather. They reluctantly raise their prices. Wholesalers discover that their costs have risen and reluctantly raise their prices. Retailers discover that their costs have risen and reluctantly raise their prices.

The Real Culprit. At each step, prices rise because costs rise—yet the whole process was initiated by a rise in demand.

This example describes accurately a period of inflation. An increase in aggregate money demand leads businessmen to try to increase output. Beyond some limited point, when manpower, equipment and other resources are fully occupied, they cannot all do so, but the *attempt* to increase output raises costs and makes it look to each businessman as if he must raise his prices because his costs have risen.

The only exception is for a brief period after the turning of the tide. Let an inflationary increase in demand subside. For a time, wages and other costs will continue to rise, reflecting the unspent impetus from the earlier rise in demand. That is what we have been experiencing this past year. But it is a temporary phase that cannot be sustained.

The common element in inflation is not strong unions but an increase in money demand accompanying a rapid increase in the quantity of money. In 1848–1857, the increased quantity of money was produced by gold discoveries in California; in 1896–1913, by the perfection of the cyanide process for extracting gold from low-grade ore; in the Civil War and the two world wars by the creation of money to finance military expenditures; in 1964–1969 by the Federal Reserve System, partly to help finance large government deficits.

Inflation is always and everywhere a monetary phenomenon.

B. *Select any one of the above pieces which you have discussed and write a critical essay in which you evaluate its effectiveness as persuasion for you as a reader.*

C. *Select any campus problem or any subject of interest to your class and write a three- or four-page essay in which you try to persuade the class that something ought to be done about the problem. If you can advocate a solution, so much the better. But be sure that your essay treats the subject with thoroughness and fairness.*

Part Four

Handbook of Grammar and Usage

A Point of View
Toward Grammar

English, like all languages, has developed a great many conventions popularly and generally known as "the rules of grammar." The nature of these rules is widely misunderstood, and because of this misunderstanding, the study of usage is often less profitable than it might be. The first step toward using your native language with confidence is to acquire a sensible attitude toward these rules. We shall attempt to foster such an attitude by showing you what is meant when we talk about rules of grammar, how these rules have grown up and are still growing, and how you can apply this knowledge to your own use of language. A point of view from which you can see particular questions of usage in perspective will help you to judge for yourself which usages to follow, and when.

THE EVOLUTION OF ENGLISH

The language that Americans speak and write is descended from the language spoken by the English, Scottish, and Irish immigrants who founded the British colonies in America. Their language, in turn, was descended from the dialects of Germanic tribes which, during the fifth and sixth centuries, invaded Britain and settled there. One of these tribes, the Angles, later became known as the Englisc (English) and gave their name to a country and a language, both of which they shared with other peoples—the Saxons, the Jutes, and later, the Danes and the Normans.

These ethnic groups were the Founding Fathers of the English language, but other peoples too have made their contribution to its development. As England grew in political, economic, and cultural importance, the language borrowed from various sources the words it needed to name the things and ideas that Englishmen were acquiring. Today the vocabulary of the English language is international in origin, and to talk, as some people do, of "pure" English is to use a word as mistaken as it is misleading.

The language which has come down to us through some fifteen centuries has undergone great changes. Modern college students find Chaucer's four-teenth-century English something of a puzzle. And before Chaucer—well, judge for yourself. Here are the opening lines of the Lord's Prayer in the English of nearly a thousand years ago:

> Fæder ūre,
> þu þe eart on heofonum,
> sī þīn nama gehālgod.
> Tōbecume þīn rīce.
> Gewurþe ðīn willa on eorðan swā swā on heofonum.

A contrast of this form of the Lord's Prayer with the modern version offers a brief but revealing impression of the changes that have occurred in the language during its development from an insignificant Germanic dialect to one of the most widely spoken languages the world has known. These changes were the product of evolution rather than of revolution. True, there were times when so many basic changes occurred so rapidly that they seem revolutionary in retrospect. But by and large, the language changed slowly as it reflected gradual shifts in the speech habits of those who spoke English.

This evolutionary process is still going on. Any one of us can notice hundreds of examples of it in our own experience. We can hear the older pronunciations of *penalize* (peenalize), *status* (staytus) and *detour* (detoor) being challenged by pronunciations which were at first labeled "uneducated" but which have gradually become more common, even in the speech of educated people. We can observe words acquiring new meanings. And we can watch grammatical distinctions which once were generally observed falling more and more into disuse as substitutes take over their work.

THE RULES OF GRAMMAR

Contrary to popular belief, the rules of grammar do not determine how the language should be spoken and written. Grammar is a science, and it follows the general scientific method of reporting not what *ought to be* but what *is*. Except for differences of subject matter, the rules of grammar are much like the laws of physics and chemistry: they are scientific generaliza-tions about the facts. In grammar, as in physics, these generalizations must be verifiable. If the rule does not fit the facts, or if it ceases to fit them, it must be revised or discarded.

Ideally, the grammar of a language is a description of the speaking and writing habits of the people who use it. Since there are more than 300,-000,000 users of English, widely separated geographically, politically, eco-nomically, and socially, the task of drawing a picture of their common linguistic habits is not easy. The grammarian simplifies his task by confining himself to the basic patterns of speech intonation (pitch, pause, and stress), morphology (the forms of words), and syntax (the relations of words within a sentence). He collects samples, analyzes them, finds patterns in them, and generalizes the patterns into a system. By these means he describes the very elaborate set of signals by which English conveys grammatical meaning. But he is describing how the language works, not how he thinks it ought to work. The only "rules of grammar" he recognizes are those statements which most accurately describe the system.

What most people mean by "rules of grammar" are statements about preferred usage. In addition to studies of grammar, we have numerous studies of how people speak and write English. The schools are committed to informing students on these matters, and they do what they can to help students learn and employ existing patterns and usages in their speech and writing. For this reason teachers insist that, in spelling, punctuation, sentence structure, grammatical agreement, and diction, students know the conventions of standard usage. Some of these conventions include grammatical details, but others are not part of grammar as it has been described above.

Decisions about usage are sometimes difficult for two reasons. First, in an ever-changing language, usage is not constant. Spellings, pronunciations, styles of punctuation, meanings, and grammatical constructions which were not recognized by one generation may be accepted by another, and there is likely to be a "usage gap" between what people think standard usage is and what it has in fact become. Second, many people have strong opinions about usage and approve or condemn certain uses no matter what the facts are. These two conditions make it difficult in particular constructions to get an authoritative description of usage which is acceptable to everyone. Fortunately, such constructions are relatively few. For the most part, the facts of usage are clearly established and can be accurately described. If we want to call these descriptive statements "rules of grammar," we may do so, but it would be wise to remember in what sense we are using "rules" and "grammar."

The rules of grammar, then, are not "Thou-shalt-not's"; they say, "This is how it is done." They are explanations of conventions that have grown up between writers and readers. Learning to use one's language is learning to use these conventions. A writer who ignores them may find his work rejected or discredited.

ON BEING YOUR OWN AUTHORITY

In human affairs, a sophisticated person is one who is familiar with social conventions and observes them naturally and successfully. In linguistic matters also, a sophisticated person is one who observes language conventions naturally and successfully. One aim of the composition course is to encourage the student to develop linguistic sophistication, to make him aware how things are done in English, and to help him do them habitually without having to stop and puzzle over them.

There are two reasons why this aim cannot be met by viewing grammar as a set of arbitrary rules which must be learned and practiced. First, this view distorts the relationship between purpose and technique. Just as the Sabbath was made for man, not man for the Sabbath, so the conventions of usage should serve, not be served by, the writer's purpose. A student whose main thought is to get his spelling, punctuation, and grammatical forms "correct" is in no condition to communicate. For him, writing will be a frustrating exercise, to be done only under compulsion and to be avoided whenever the compulsion is removed. This is why some students believe that all their linguistic worries will be over as soon as they pass the composition course.

Second, memorizing the conventions of usage is at best a poor substitute for working with them. All we know about learning tells us that memorized facts are soon forgotten unless they are clearly related to life goals and put to use outside the classroom. A student who conscientiously learns the rules of spelling or punctuation *in order to please or pacify his instructor* will soon forget them, and the progress that he and his instructor worked so hard to achieve will largely be lost. This is one reason why student writing so often deteriorates after completion of the composition course.

To accomplish the purpose of the course, at least with respect to the conventions of usage, a student must realize two things: he must recognize that following the conventions of language may help him communicate better and so make him a more powerful person; and he must understand that, while dictionaries and handbooks are helpful reference works, he must often make his own decisions about usage when these books are not available or are not decisive.

This second requirement may seem like a tall order, since, in effect, it asks the student to become his own authority on language. But there is no alternative. To use a language well, one must use it confidently. No one can speak or write with confidence if he continually depends on the crutch of a handbook. It is only a temporary aid, useful for those linguistic questions which cannot yet be answered from experience, but to be dispensed with as soon as possible.

How is this confidence to be won? In the long run, it is gained, as are so many other things, by observation. That is how the grammarian learns grammar and how the editors of dictionaries learn the meanings of words— by observing how people use their language. An intelligent curiosity about language is therefore the first requirement for using it well. A student who has or develops that curiosity will seldom be seriously bothered about the "rules," because he has discovered them through his own observation of language practices.

The handbook that follows is a temporary substitute for your own experience. It presumes to tell you what the conventions are. If you know what they are, you do not need the advice. If you do not know, the advice will provide you with information to solve some of your immediate writing problems. It is assumed that your instructor will decide from your writing which conventions you need to study and will refer you to the section or sections dealing with them. It is hoped that you yourself will care enough about your own writing to make a special point of mastering, by observation as well as by handbook exercises, whatever conventions are now conspicuously ignored in your writing.

The material of the handbook is organized under seven main headings, the first five of which are marked by an identifying letter: *sentence structure* **(S),** *diction* **(D),** *word order* **(WO),** *grammatical forms* **(F),** *punctuation* **(P),** *mechanics* (spelling, capitalization, italics, etc.), and a *glossary* of grammatical terms and usage. Under each lettered heading, the numbered sections deal with specific parts of the subject. Thus **S1–S4** deal with the distinction between sentences and non-sentences; **S5–S8** deal with inconsistencies in sentence patterns. If you have occasion to use the handbook, it might be wise to familiarize yourself with at least its over-all organization.

S   Sentence Structure

S 1   Period Fault and Sentence Fragment

Use complete sentences, not sentence fragments, in expository writing. Especially avoid separating a subordinate clause or phrase from its main clause by a period.

Sentence Fragment	Explanation	Full Sentence
He is always complaining about his social position. *Although he does nothing to improve it.*	*The italicized element is a modifying clause, not a sentence.*	He is always complaining about his social position, although he does nothing to improve it.
It was difficult to decide which choice to make. *To return to school or to stay out and be drafted.*	*The italicized infinitives modify* choice; *therefore they do not act as independent finite verbs.*	It was difficult to decide whether to return to school or to stay out and be drafted.
The procedure was quite new to me. *Reading and discussing every week and debating once a month.*	*The italicized words are gerunds, verbals used as nouns. They are changed to verbs at the right.*	The procedure was quite new to me. We read and discussed every week and debated once a month.

The use of a period between a main clause and a subordinate clause or phrase, as in the sentences above, is a **period fault.** As the revisions indicate, period faults may be corrected either by changing the period to a comma, thus incorporating the separated phrase or clause into the sentence to which it belongs, or by expanding the fragment into a main clause so it can stand as an independent sentence.

In dialogue and in colloquial writing, which imitates conversation, fragmentary sentences are more common than they are in more formal exposition. A fragment may simply be an exclamation: *Oh! Wonderful! Watch out!* It may serve as a question: *Ready? Lemon or sugar? Anything else?*

It may be a phrase or a clause uttered in response to a question: *Not right now. If you wish. Whatever is convenient.* Or it may be a stereotyped expression, such as: *The more, the merrier. First come, first served. Easy come, easy go.* A fragment so used is sometimes called a **minor sentence.**

EXERCISE *In the following sentences correct the period faults.*

1. This being the third time the child had run away. The social worker decided that a new foster home might be more suitable for her.
2. I slammed the door as if I meant it. Although deep in my heart I felt that I might never see her again.
3. Joe ate an enormous meal. Two hamburgers. A banana split. A bowl of chili. And topped it off with a stomach ache.
4. Whenever I hear a fife and drum. I remember the Fourth of July parades we used to have at home.
5. A small group of students lined up just inside the campus gate. Spoiling for a fight and yelling that they would take on all comers.
6. The authors of most popular books and magazine articles write for the general public. Not just for a small audience of scholars and critics.
7. The Communists publicize every act of oppression and intolerance in the lands of their enemies. Thus exaggerating the failures of Democracy and implying that Communism is a philosophy of brotherly love.
8. After swearing the oath and signing my name. I was formally inducted into the Army of the United States.
9. We were lectured for an hour on our sins and shortcomings. Without having a single moment in which to answer our accusers.
10. Once acclaimed as the chief literary spokesman of the Beat generation. Jack Kerouac was alone and almost forgotten when he died.

S 2 Fused Sentences

Do not fuse two sentences by omitting necessary terminal punctuation between them.

Fused Sentences

I knocked on the door when the lady came I gave her my most ingratiating smile.

Why should I apologize when he insulted me he did not apologize.

Separated Sentences

I knocked on the door. When the lady came I gave her my most ingratiating smile.

Why should I apologize? When he insulted me he did not apologize.

Fused Sentences

It is hard to believe he said that what could he have been thinking about?

Why do you ask what business is it of yours?

Separated Sentences

It is hard to believe he said that. What could he have been thinking about?

Why do you ask? What business is it of yours?

EXERCISE

Separate the following fused sentences.

1. For most students it takes a long time to absorb the ideas and procedures involved in learning the calculus that is why most calculus courses take two years.
2. The individual concepts seem easy to grasp at first the more you read the more difficult it is to keep them clearly in mind they all tend to blur into one incomprehensible mass.
3. I am willing to contribute on the other hand I will not join the movement.
4. At Kennedy's death Johnson succeeded to the Presidency without exactly creating national enthusiasm he was called on to fill the most demanding job in the world.
5. I wrote to Mother when she answered I knew that the story had been exaggerated since then I have learned that the newspaper printed a retraction.
6. There is no way of reaching a compromise in situations like this unless both sides are willing to make concessions the dispute will become a stalemate.
7. The food-vending machines are a great convenience at noon we can eat without leaving the building.
8. Some people are very inconsiderate about trash disposal even though they attend ecology rallies and sign petitions they still expect others to pick up after them.
9. I sent a telegram to my Congressman when he acknowledged it I felt that he really wanted to hear from his constituents.
10. The first few weeks will be agony gradually you will begin to see light finally much of the work will be routine.

S 3   Run-on Sentence

Do not string together a number of main clauses with *but, and, for, so,* **or** *and so.*

Sentences so formed are called **run-on sentences.** They can be improved by subordinating part of the material to the rest.

Run-on Sentence	**Revision**
I did not know how Mother would feel about my accepting the invitation, *so* I called her on the phone *and* she said it was all right, *so* I accepted.	Because I did not know how Mother would feel about the invitation, I called her on the phone. When she said it was all right, I accepted.

EXERCISE   *Remove the run-on effect in the following examples.*

1. The boys ranged in age from 7 to 14 and we had to find an activity that would interest all of them or we would spend the afternoon chasing stragglers, and so we planned a trip to a candy factory.

2. Cigarette advertising was taken off TV but more advertising than ever went into some newspapers and the same was true for magazines and so the end effect was no very great change.

3. The little girl dashed out into the street and an oncoming truck swerved abruptly to avoid hitting her and as a result it sideswiped a utility pole but fortunately nobody was hurt.

4. The early morning is the most beautiful time of day so I always like to get up at the crack of dawn and one day last week I got up as usual and had my first cup of coffee and I walked down to the stream and there I saw an alligator and it was the first one I had ever seen.

5. It would be a good thing to abolish the grading system, for students get anxious and tense over examinations, and they study unwisely so what they learn does not stay with them, and I am not the only one who feels this way, for many professors do too but they won't say so.

S 4   Comma Splice

Do not join main clauses by only a comma unless they are in series.

The use of a comma instead of a period or a semicolon between main clauses not linked by a coordinating conjunction is a **comma splice**. A comma by itself is a purely internal mark of punctuation, and a reader may read through it and be confused:

He preaches sermons in stones, proposals in rock gardens are more to her liking.

In the following constructions, the italicized element could attach to either clause:

Jackson has never before been suspected of theft, *to the best of my knowledge,* he has been employed by his present firm since he graduated from high school.

Which statement is the writer qualifying? The reader is free to guess, but he will get no help from the sentence. It could mean

Jackson has never before been suspected of theft, to the best of my knowledge. He has been employed by his present firm since he graduated from high school.

or

Jackson has never before been suspected of theft. To the best of my knowledge, he has been employed by his present firm since he graduated from high school.

Comma splices can be corrected in any one of three ways.

1. The simplest way is to change the faulty comma to a period or a semicolon, whichever gives the more desirable degree of separation.

Comma Splice	Revision
His chances of election are not good, because the independents do not like him, it would be safer to nominate another candidate.	His chances of election are not good, because the independents do not like him. It would be safer to nominate another candidate.
	His chances of election are not good, because the independents do not like him; it would be safer to nominate another candidate.

2. A second way is to provide a coordinating conjunction between the two main clauses, thus making the comma acceptable.

Comma Splice	Revision
She says she does not like football, I doubt that she has seen two games in her whole life.	She says that she does not like football, *but* I doubt that she has seen two games in her whole life.
It will cost a great deal of money, there is no guarantee that the plan will succeed.	It will cost a great deal of money, *and* there is no guarantee that the plan will succeed.

3. The third way is to subordinate one main clause to the other.

Comma Splice	Revision
He is discouraged about doing the work, I think he will drop out of school.	He is *so* discouraged about doing the work *that* I think he will drop out of school.

When two main clauses are joined by a transitional connective—*consequently, however, moreover, nevertheless, therefore*—the usual punctuation between them is a semicolon, though a period is not uncommon.

I admit that he is honest and conscientious; nevertheless, I will not vote for him.

When two short independent clauses are closely related, informal usage permits a comma by itself.

I passed, Mary doubled.
The women like him, the men don't.

EXERCISE   *Using whatever method seems best, correct the comma splices in the following sentences.*

---

1. In all these bills there is a free choice of doctors, dentists, and hospitals, the only requirement is that they be participants in the plan.

2. As my eyes grew accustomed to the light I saw two small faces at the back of the nest, they gazed at me steadily and without surprise.

3. The week before Mardi Gras is filled with festivities and excitement, all the carnival organizations have parades and lavish parties.

4. The lectures are dull and the reading is burdensome, moreover the course offers little to stimulate the imagination.

5. I had to fight nightly temptations which led me away from study, much to my ultimate dismay, the temptations often won.

6. There is still opportunity for new industry in our state, if a company wants to make a new home for itself, an attractive location is not hard to find.

7. I spent my evenings in a world of intrigue and swordplay, following the fortunes of rebels and loyal courtiers, some of them were men of superhuman virtue, some were villains of the blackest kind.

8. The problems were hard, but they could be solved, although the answers did not come easily, they could be reached by hard work.

9. The factory had four hundred employees, this count included both the day and the night shifts.

10. Many parents today are too permissive, not believing that children should be punished, this theory is responsible for much of our trouble, I firmly believe.

S 5   Faulty Parallelism

Sentence elements which are parallel in thought should be parallel in grammatical form.

For a detailed discussion of parallel and balanced sentences, see pages 112–16.

Faulty Parallelism	Explanation	Acceptable Structures
Few people understood the full extent of his disappointment or *how angry* he really was.	*Compound object of* understood. *The first object is a phrase, the second a subordinate clause. The two should be in parallel form.*	Few people understood the full extent of his disappointment or *the degree of his* anger.
Because he has always been wealthy *and with indulgent parents,* he has never been forced to accept responsibility.	*Compound modifier consists of a subordinate clause and a phrase. Should be two clauses or two phrases.*	Because he has always been wealthy and *has been protected by indulgent parents,* . . .
		Because of *his wealth* and *his indulgent parents,* . . .

Sentence elements in a series should have the same form: a phrase should be followed by a phrase, a clause by a clause, a noun by a noun, and a verb by a verb. The following sentence contains a series which enumerates the powers of a commission:

The Commission has the power *to investigate, to conciliate, to hold* hearings, *to subpoena* witnesses, *to issue* cease-and-desist commands, *to order* reinstatement of a discharged employee, and *to direct* the hiring of a qualified applicant.

Most of this sentence consists of a series of infinitive phrases, each identifying one of the powers of the commission and modifying the noun *power*. Since all elements in the series have the same function, they all have the same form. They could have been put in a form other than the infinitive: "The Commission has the power *of investigating, of conciliating, of holding,* etc." But the forms should not shift, as they do in the following sentence:

The Commission has the power of *investigation, conciliation, holding* hearings, *subpoena* witnesses, *issue* cease-and-desist commands, *order* the reinstatement of a discharged employee, and *directing* the hiring of a qualified applicant.

EXERCISE

Rewrite the following sentences to correct faulty parallelism.

1. Jody pleased both young and old with "Happy Days," "Betty Coed," and singing other songs of the thirties.
2. Does anyone believe that it is the function of college to teach a girl to be a lady, courteous, and provide her with culture?
3. He arrived in a sports car and wearing a straw hat.
4. He went to college because of the hopes of his mother, his teachers urged him to, and to prepare for a better job.
5. She is inclined to be giggly and frequently embarrassing her date.

6. Joe's chief faults are that he expects too much, being unwilling to make the necessary effort, and not accepting criticism.

7. Speak softly and you should carry a big stick.

8. A decision must be made whether the wetlands are more important for the conservation of wild life or to be filled in and converted into low-income housing developments.

9. Mr. Barry gave an informative talk on the new community youth center and how volunteers are needed.

10. Rock music began in the counterculture but became Big Business with long hair and playing a guitar.

S 6   Dangling Modifiers

Avoid dangling modifiers.

A modifier is said to dangle when it has nothing in the main clause to modify. Most danglers are participial phrases at the beginning of a sentence.

Dangling Modifier	Explanation	Revised Version
Walking downtown, a streetcar jumped the tracks.	*In the absence of anything else to modify,* walking *seems to modify* streetcar. *The revised version contains a subject which the participle can logically modify.*	Walking downtown, I saw a streetcar jump the tracks.
Impressed by the newspaper stories, war seemed inevitable.	*Who was impressed? The opening phrase needs something to modify. The revised version gets rid of this difficulty by making* we *the subject of the main clause.*	Impressed by the newspaper stories, we felt that war was inevitable.

Errors such as these are the result of making a shift in the subject of the main clause while the sentence is being written. Presumably the writer meant to make *I* the subject of the main clause in the first sentence and *we* the subject in the second, but he inadvertently switched subjects to *streetcar* and *war*, and thus left the modifiers dangling. Often the best way to correct a dangler is to revise the main clause so that it has a subject which can be modified by the introductory phrase, as shown in the revised versions. Another way is to recast the opening phrase as a subordinate clause:

When I was walking downtown, a streetcar jumped the tracks.

Because we were impressed by the newspaper stories we felt that war was inevitable. (This revision combines both methods suggested above.)

Sometimes a dangling modifier is an **elliptical clause,** that is, a subordinate clause some elements of which are not expressed. The simplest way to revise a dangling elliptical clause is to supply the necessary elements and complete the clause:

Dangling Modifier

When only five years old, my mother died.

While still in grade school, my father began teaching me about business.

Although working full time on an outside job, my grades remained good.

Revised Version

When *I was* only five years old, my mother died.

While *I was* still in grade school, my father began teaching me about business.

Although *I was* working full time on an outside job, my grades remained good.

As all these examples suggest, the most troublesome dangling modifiers are those beginning with an introductory verbal phrase or elliptical clause. A dangling modifier at the end of a sentence is more likely to be awkward or unemphatic than ambiguous:

Dangling Modifier

He took a full program of studies during each summer session, *thus graduating in three years.*

Revised Version

By taking a full program of studies during each summer session he was able to graduate in three years.

The main idea in this sentence is that the student graduated in three years. The revision expresses that idea as a main clause at the end of the sentence and thus gives it greater emphasis.

EXERCISE

Correct the dangling modifiers in the following sentences.

---

1. Working in the bookstore, many professors chat with me every day.
2. Hearing a sharp click, the trap door opened and a masked face appeared before my eyes.
3. After viewing the suspects, the police should be told whether you recognize any of them.
4. When in high school, most classes were dull and monotonous.
5. By getting your purpose clearly in mind at the beginning, the actual writing will be easier.
6. Being very tired, the walk home took much too long.
7. Completely unaware that the landing gear had been damaged and that a crash landing was inevitable, the plane, with its carefree passengers, flew on through the night.

8. After rushing to get to the station on time, the information clerk said that the train would be more than an hour late.

9. The car failed to observe the curve sign, thus losing control and going over the embankment.

10. I believe that, by delaying marriage until after graduation, the chances of happiness are much better.

S 7 Shifts in Subjects and Verbs

Unintentional shifts from one sentence pattern to another create awkward, inconsistent structures. Such inconsistencies may arise from shifts in the form of the subject or verb.

a. Avoid unnecessary shifts of subject within a sentence or a paragraph, especially shifts between personal and impersonal pronouns.

In the examples below, the grammatical subjects are italicized.

Shifted Subjects	Explanation	Revised Version
When *one* gets through with a three-hour examination *you* are exhausted.	*The subject shifts from the impersonal pronoun* one *to the second person pronoun* you. *A shift from* one *to* he *is conventional but the shift to* you *is not. Any of the three revisions at the right would be an improvement.*	When *one* gets through . . . *one* is exhausted. When one gets through . . . *he* is exhausted. When *you* get through . . . *you* are exhausted.
The *worries* about entrance examinations leave the minds of the students before *they* leave for college. The last *days* are spent shopping for clothes during the day and visiting with friends at night. Their *families* receive little attention, and entrance *examinations* are no longer thought of.	*Although these three sentences all deal with the same logical subject (the students' activities before leaving for college), the paragraph has five grammatical subjects. This unnecessary shifting of the subject weakens the unity of the paragraph. The revision at the right reduces the subjects to two forms: the noun* students *and the pronoun* they.	During the last week before leaving for college, *students* spend their days shopping for clothes and their nights attending farewell parties with their friends. *They* have little time to spend with their families and no longer worry about entrance examinations.
I did not like to refuse his invitation, but a *person* can't spend all their time going to shows.	*Although the writer is the logical subject of both clauses, the grammatical subject shifts from* I *to* person. *Then this shift leads to the plural pronoun* their *in the second clause. It would be better to use the first person pronoun throughout.*	I did not like to refuse his invitation, but *I* can't spend all my time going to shows.

b. Avoid unnecessary shifts in the forms of the verbs. Keep tenses consistent and avoid shifts from active to passive voice.

In the following examples the verb forms are in italics.

Shifted Verb Forms	Explanation	Consistent Verb Forms
The older girls *had* a party to get us acquainted and it *was* deeply *appreciated* by me.	*The shift from active voice in the first clause to passive in the second is unnecessary and awkward. The revision subordinates one clause and keeps both verbs in the active voice.*	I *appreciated* the party which the older girls *gave* to get us acquainted.
As centuries *passed,* the dress patterns *become* more and more complicated.	*The tense changes from past to present. Since both actions are past, both verbs should be in the past tense.*	As centuries *passed,* the dress patterns *became* more and more complicated.
He *said* he *will* call for me at eight.	*The writer is confusing the tenses for direct and indirect discourse. Either form at the right will serve.*	He *said* he *would call* for me at eight. He *said,* "I *will call* for you at eight."

EXERCISE   *Revise the following sentences to remove awkward shifts in subjects or verbs.*

1. He said we would be late for class anyway, so let's finish our coke and not worry.

2. To me dependability means just what the word says—that you can depend on a person, whether they are to do a simple errand, or to provide a home and love for your children.

3. In choosing a mate for the rest of one's life, certain qualities are searched for according to your individual preferences.

4. We argued for an hour, but no conclusion was reached.

5. It's funny how a person can have such different feelings about something they want to do.

6. I was told to go to University Hall first or I may not get the courses I wanted.

7. A good way to judge a person's character is to play bridge with them.

8. These children had known misery, for to them war was a firsthand experience.

9. It often makes one wonder about humanity, the things you hear.

10. I have had the experience of losing one's wallet. When something like this happens, you don't know what to do.

S 8 Incomplete Constructions

Do not omit words necessary to the structure of a sentence.

Careless omissions often occur in making a clean copy of a paper, since copying is a mechanical task which takes little attention. The final copy should be carefully reread before it is turned in.

Other omissions result from confusion about the structure of a sentence. The constructions most likely to be left incomplete are illustrated below.

Incomplete	Explanation	Complete
We searched through all our pockets, but no money.	*Incomplete main clause. The conjunction* but *requires a main clause to balance the sentence. The verb* found *cannot be omitted.*	We searched through all our pockets, but *found* no money.
I don't like the crowd which he associates.	*Omitted preposition. With a choice of two forms for the subordinate clause—*with which he associates *or* he associates with—*the writer has failed to supply* with *in either position.*	I don't like the crowd *with* which he associates. (or) I don't like the crowd he associates *with*.
Statistics show that college men like their studies better than women.	*Omitted verb causing a possible ambiguity. The comparison is not* studies *and* women, *but* men *and* women. *The clause with* women *as subject needs a verb.*	Statistics show that college men like their studies better than women *do*.
Their hope is the child has wandered off with some older companions who will take care of him.	*Omission of the subordinating conjunction* that *allows the subject of the subordinate clause,* child, *to be misread as the complement of the verb in the main clause.*	Their hope is *that* the child has wandered off with some older companions who will take care of him.
Today is as hot, if not hotter, than any day this summer.	*This construction confuses two idioms—*as hot as *and* hotter than. *Since these take different connectives,* than *will not serve for both. The best solution is to avoid this construction by using one of the alternatives shown at the right.*	Today is one of the hottest days of the summer. Today is at least as hot as any day we have had this summer. Today may be the hottest day of the summer.

EXERCISE   *Revise the following sentences to complete the incomplete constructions.*

1. It gets much colder in Maine than Massachusetts.
2. He handles the transmitter better than his teacher.
3. Betty weighs as much if not more than her mother.
4. I looked all over for a room, but no luck.
5. I always have and always will try to do the right thing.
6. The trouble was the fuel pipe was clogged.
7. Glasses often add rather than detract from a person's appearance.
8. She would rather live on campus than home.
9. The state he wants to live in his old age is California.
10. He made her from a girl to an old woman in twelve short years.

D   Diction

D 1 Using a Dictionary

Become familiar with at least one good college-level desk dictionary.

Since a good dictionary may well contain more useful information on more subjects than any other one book you are likely to use, it is a good idea to own one. Useful dictionaries are of two sizes, the so-called unabridged, and the collegiate or desk size. Unabridged dictionaries are listed on page 251. The following desk dictionaries are those most commonly recommended for student use:

The American Heritage Dictionary of the English Language, 1969.

Funk and Wagnalls Standard College Dictionary, 1963.

The Random House Dictionary of the English Language, College Edition, 1968.

Webster's Seventh New Collegiate Dictionary, 1963.

Webster's New World Dictionary of the American Language, Second College Edition, 1970.

All these dictionaries are equipped with useful study aids which are supplied by their publishers on request.

When you look up a word in a dictionary, try to find out as much as you can about it. A good desk dictionary records many kinds of information about a word, as the entry on page 368 shows.

While dictionaries vary in detail, they all give the following kinds of information. Check your dictionary against this list and make notes of any variations.

1. *Spelling and syllabication.* The entry word is spelled and is divided into syllables, usually by dots: *con·tract.* When a word has several correct spellings, the preferred spelling is given first.

2. *Pronunciation.* Immediately after the entry word is the pronunciation, usually in parentheses. Each dictionary has its own pronunciation key, usually printed at the foot of the page. Words of more than one syllable also include one or more accent marks (′ ′) placed before or after syllables to indicate secondary or primary stress. Note that *contract* has alternative pronunciations when used as a verb.

3. *Part of speech.* The abbreviation is given for the part of speech in which the word is used (*n., v., adj.,* and so on). If a word is used in several parts of speech, all meanings for the first are grouped together, then all meanings for the next.

4. *Abbreviations.* Most dictionaries list common abbreviations, though not always near the beginning of the entry.

5. *Grammatical features.* Irregular plurals are given for nouns (*mice, oxen*), principal parts for verbs, and comparative forms for adjectives and adverbs that do not take *more* and *most.*

6. *Meanings.* Within part-of-speech groupings, meanings are given in historical order, in order of frequency of use, or from primary or basic to secondary or extended. Check the front matter of your dictionary to see which order it uses.

1. Spelling and Syllabication   2. Pronunciations   5. Grammatical Features:
                                                             Principal Parts
                                3. Part of Speech
                                         4. Abbreviations   6. Meaning Within
                                                                    Part of Speech Groupings

con·tract (kŏn′trăkt′) *n. Abbr.* **contr., cont. 1.** An agreement between two or more parties, especially one that is written and enforceable by law. **2.** The writing or document containing such an agreement. **3.** The branch of law dealing with contracts. **4.** Marriage as a formal agreement; betrothal. **5.** In the game of bridge: **a.** The last and highest bid of one hand. **b.** The number of tricks thus bid. **c. Contract bridge** *(see).* —*v.* (kən-trăkt′, kŏn′trăkt′) **contracted, -tracting, -tracts. —***tr.* **1.** To enter into by contract; establish or settle by formal agreement. **2.** To acquire or incur. **3.** To reduce in size by drawing together; shrink. **4.** To pull together; wrinkle. **5.** To shorten (a word or words) by omitting or combining some of the letters or sounds; for example, *I'm* for *I am.* —*intr.* **1.** To enter into or make a contract. **2.** To become reduced in size by or as if by being drawn together. [Middle English, from Old French, from Latin *contractus,* from the past participle of *contrahere,* to draw together, bring about, enter into an agreement : *com-* together + *trahere,* to draw (see *tragh-* in Appendix*).] —**con·tract′i·bil′i·ty, con·tract′i·ble·ness** *n.* —**con·tract′i·ble** *adj.*

8. Synonyms

7. Etymology

Synonyms: *contract, condense, compress, constrict, shrink.* These verbs refer to decrease in size or content of a thing and sometimes to a resultant change in its form. *Contract* applies to internal drawing together that reduces the volume of a thing. *Condense* refers to an increase in compactness produced by the removal or reduction of parts or by a change in physical form of the thing involved, such as a change from gas to liquid or from liquid to solid. *Compress* applies to increased compactness brought about by external force; the term implies reduction of volume and change of form or shape. *Constrict* refers to decreasing the extent of a thing, usually by external pressure. *Shrink* refers to contraction that produces reduction in physical extent.

From *The American Heritage Dictionary of the English Language,* reproduced courtesy of the American Heritage Publishing Co., Inc., N.Y.

7. *Etymology.* When it is known, the origin of the word is given, and is one of the most valuable things you can learn about it. Thus *contract* is one of a large class of words which came into English from Latin via Old French, and is made up of the prefix *con-* and the root *-tract*.

8. *Labels.* Labels are used to indicate usage (*Nonstandard, Slang, Informal*), dialect (*Dial.*), region (*Brit., Southern*), and specialization (*Law, Med.*). A word not labeled (*contract,* for example) is in standard general use.

9. *Synonyms and antonyms.* Dictionaries vary in the position of these elements and in the space given to them. Check the front matter of your dictionary if in doubt.

EXERCISE

The following quiz will test your knowledge of your own dictionary. Check your answers by the introductory pages and by reference to particular entries.

1. Does your dictionary record variant spellings of the same word in one entry or in different entries? Is the preferred spelling necessarily "more correct" than an alternate spelling?

2. How is pronunciation indicated in your dictionary? Is there a key to the symbols at the bottom of the page, or only in the introductory matter?

3. Where are the etymologies shown: after the inflectional forms, or at the end of the entry? In many dictionaries, *L* is the symbol for Latin. Other common origins are *Gr* (Greek), *F* (French), *N* (Norse), *O* for *Old,* as in *Old English, Old French,* etc. If you are not sure how to interpret these symbols, where in your dictionary can you find out?

4. In what order are the definitions given? If you are not sure, where can you find out?

5. How are foreign words identified—that is, words that are still considered foreign rather than English, and so have to be underlined in manuscript or italicized in print? If you are not sure, how can you find out? (Hint: Check *Gestalt, bon voyage, in absentia.*)

6. For which of the following entries are synonyms or antonyms given: *ambition, deface, fiendish, luster, restive, voracious?*

7. How are the following words pronounced: *acclimate, alias, banal, data, ennui, impious, impotent, joust, schism, Wagnerian?*

The things you most need to know about a new word are its pronunciation, etymology, and meanings. The pronunciation not only helps you to pronounce it correctly in reading aloud or in speech, but also helps you fix the word in your memory. Since the appearance of a word is often no safe clue to its sound, we have all had the embarrassing experience of making a very obvious mispronunciation when called upon to read an unfamiliar word aloud. Even such fairly common words as *abyss, blatant, caprice, decade, echelon, façade, gauge,* and *ribald* can be troublesome for a person who has met them only in reading and has never heard them spoken.

The etymology of a word gives you its family history and thus makes your knowledge of it more complete. When you learn that *crucial* comes from the Latin word for *cross,* you can see that in a crucial decision, we figuratively stand at a crossroads and decide which way we will go, and you may discover an unsuspected relationship among *crucial, crucify, crusade,* and *crux.*

Apart from its usefulness in making you a more discerning or more critical user of words, the study of etymology gives valuable insights. For example, what do their etymologies tell you about the relation of *calculus* and pebble, about *sinister* and left-handed, about *jail* and coop?

D 2   Word Analysis

Learn to recognize common Latin prefixes and roots, and common Greek combining forms, and to use this knowledge in analyzing the meanings of words.

Because many Latin and Greek words have been borrowed and assimilated by English, a knowledge of the most common Latin and Greek combining forms helps us to recognize, at least in a general way, the meanings of many words. For example, the ability to recognize *-cede* (*-ceed*) and *-cess* as forms of the Latin *cedere,* "to yield" or "go," gives us a partial clue to the meanings of the English words *cede, cessation, cession, accede, access, accession, accessory, antecedent, ancestor, concede, concession, concessionaire, exceed, excess, incessant, intercede, intercessor, precede, precedence, predecessor, procedure, proceed, process, procession, recede, recess, recessive, secede, succeed, succession,* and their inflectional forms. One writer has estimated that a knowledge of fourteen Latin and Greek roots will help us to recognize over 14,000 words.[1]

Common Latin prefixes and roots, their original meanings, and illustrative English words derived from them are given in the following lists.

Latin Prefixes

ab (away from, down): abase, abate, abdicate, abhor, abnormal
ad (to, toward): adapt, addict, adduce, adequate, adhere, admit
ante (before): ante-bellum, antecedent, antedate, anterior
bi (two): biannual, biaxial, biceps, bicuspid, bigamist, bilabial
circum (around): circumference, circumlocution, circumspect
com, con (with): command, commence, commission, compare, convention
de (off, down): debase, decapitate, decay, decline, deduce

[1] James I. Brown, *Efficient Reading* (Boston: D. C. Heath and Company, 1952), p. 117.

ex (beyond, from, out): examine, exceed, except, excite, extend
extra (outside): extracurricular, extradite, extraneous, extrapolate
in (on, in, toward): inaugurate, incipient, incline, include
in (not): inactive, inane, incest, infamous, insensible
inter (among, between): interaction, intercept, interfere
mal (bad): malady, malcontent, malefactor, malice, malpractice
post (after): postdate, posterity, posthumous, postmortem
pre (before): preamble, precaution, precede, predict, prefer
pro (forward): proceed, produce, profane, profess, proficient
re (again, back): react, rearm, recall, recede, recreate, return
sub (under): subaltern, subconscious, subject, submerge, subside
super (above): superb, supercilious, superfluous, superior, supersede
trans (across, over): transcend, transcribe, transfer, transgress

Latin Roots

bellum (war): bellicose, belligerent, rebel, rebellion
cap, cept (take): capable, capture, concept, deception, intercept
cide, cis (cut, kill): decide, suicide, concise, incision
cogni (know): cognition, cognizance, connoisseur, recognize
cor (heart): cardiac, core, courage, discord, encourage, record
cult (care for): cult, cultivate, culture, horticulture
curr, curs (run): currency, current, curriculum, courier, course
dent (tooth): dental, dentifrice, dentoid, denture, incident
dict (say): dictate, diction, edict, indicate, predict, verdict
duc, duct (lead): conduct, deduce, duct, duke, educate, induct
fac, fect (make): facile, fact, factory, faculty, manufacture, affect
fin (end): confine, define, final, finish, infinite, refine
ject (throw): abject, dejected, eject, interject, reject, trajectory
loqui, locut (talk): colloquial, loquacious, ventriloquist, elocution
luc (light): elucidate, illustrate, lucid, pellucid, translucent
mit, miss (send): admit, commit, remit, transmit, missile
mor (dead): morbid, moribund, mortal, mortify, mortuary
ped (foot): biped, impediment, pedal, pedestrian, pedometer
pel, puls (drive): compel, dispel, expel, propel, repel, pulse
pon, posit (place): component, exponent, preposition, transpose
port (carry): deport, import, portable, report, support, transport
rupt (break): abrupt, bankrupt, disrupt, erupt, rupture
scrib, script (write): circumscribe, script, scripture, transcription
spect (look): aspect, inspect, perspective, spectator, spectrum
tain, ten (hold): abstain, contain, detain, tenable, tenacious, tenet
tang, tact (touch): tangent, tangible, tact, tactical, tactual
uni (one): unicorn, uniform, unify, union, Unitarian, unity
vene, vent (come): convene, intervene, revenue, adventure, invent
vers, vert (turn): verse, version, avert, extrovert, invert, vertical
vid, vis (see): evident, provident, revise, vision, visor, vista
voc (call): advocate, avocation, evoke, provoke, vocabulary

EXERCISE   *Using the above lists, or your knowledge of Latin prefixes and roots, relate the etymologies of the following words to their present meanings.*

abduct, convene, export, inscribe, postpone, prevent, project, prospect, remit, subvert

Greek Forms

anthropo (man): anthropoid, anthropology, anthropomorphic, misanthrope
auto (self): autism, autobiography, automation, automobile, autotoxin
bio (life): biochemistry, biogenesis, biology, biometry, biotic
chrono (time): anachronism, chronic, chronicle, chronological
gen (birth, race): eugenics, genealogy, genesis, genetics
gram, graph (write): diagram, epigram, graphic, phonograph
homo (same): homocentric, homogenize, homograph, homonym
hydr (water): dehydrate, hydrant, hydraulic, hydrophobia
log (science, speech): biology, cosmology, etymology, eulogy
micro (small): microfilm, micrometer, microphone, microscope
mono (one): monocle, monogamy, monograph, monologue
morph (form): amorphous, metamorphosis, morphology
pan (all): panacea, Pan-American, pancreas, pandemonium, panorama
phil (friend): Anglophile, bibliophile, Philadelphia, philharmonic
phon (sound): euphony, gramophone, phoneme, symphony
poly (many): polyandry, polygamy, polyglot, polysyllabic
syn (together): synonym, synthesis, sympathy, symposium
tele (far): telegraph, telepathic, telescope, television

EXERCISE   *Identify the Greek forms in the following words and explain the modern meanings of the words.*

biography, hydrogen, philanthropy, polymorphous, synchronize, telephone

WO   Word Order

WO 1   Normal Order and Accepted Inversions

Normal Order   The normal order of words in English sentences may be summarized as follows:

1. Except in questions and expletive-type sentences (*Why do you despair? There is a ray of hope*) the standard order of the main sentence elements is subject-verb-object or complement. An indirect object precedes the direct object (*He sent her flowers*).

2. Single adjectives or series of adjectives precede, and adjective phrases follow, their headword—the word they modify (a *trusted* man *of the people*).

3. Adverbs usually follow the verbs they modify, but may come elsewhere. Adverbs modifying adjectives or other adverbs precede the headword (He is *very* old. They dance *remarkably* well).

4. Main clauses usually precede subordinate clauses, but the following exceptions are common:

    a. Adjective clauses immediately follow their headwords (The man *who did it* should be punished).

    b. Adverbial clauses, especially conditional clauses, often precede the main clause (*If you do that,* you'll be sorry).

    c. Noun clauses acting as subjects or objects occupy the subject or object position (*That he will accept* is taken for granted. He says *that you are afraid*).

5. Closely related elements are kept as close together as possible. Thus a preposition precedes the object and its modifiers (the top *of the highest mountain*); modifiers remain close to their headwords; and subject-verb,

verb-object, and pronoun-antecedent combinations are not separated more than the special needs of the sentence require. In short, the order of elements in a sentence should do everything possible to reveal relationships, not to obscure them.

Accepted Inversions

Any inversion of normal word order tends to attract attention and to emphasize the inverted expression. If this emphasis is desirable and if the departure from normal order is not outlandish or unidiomatic, a writer may gain interesting variety in sentence structure by moderate use of inversion. The commonest inversions for emphasis are as follows:

a. If it does not create misinterpretation or awkwardness, an element may be transposed from its normal order for emphasis.

Normal Order	Emphatic Inversion
The skies cleared *slowly*.	*Slowly* the skies cleared.
No leaf stirred *in all the forest*.	*In all the forest* no leaf stirred.
He threw *out* the runner.	He threw the runner *out*.
That is a good country *from* which to come.	That is a good country to come *from*.
There is no excuse *for him*.	*For him* there is no excuse.
Think only this of me *if I should die*.	*If I should die,* think only this of me.
I broke the window *in order to unlock the car door*.	*In order to unlock the car door,* I broke the window.

b. If no vagueness or awkwardness results, related elements, which normally would not be separated, may be interrupted by absolute or modifying constructions.

Interruption	Explanation
These, *I am told,* were his last words.	*Absolute between subject and verb.*
Their conduct *in this situation* was heroic.	*Modifying phrase between subject and verb.*
Related elements, *which normally would not be separated,* may be interrupted.	*Nonrestrictive modifying clause between subject and verb. This particular interruption is normal order.*
He answered, *with obvious annoyance,* that the story was false.	*Modifying phrase between verb and complement.*
Don't *under any conditions* make such a promise.	*Modifying phrase between parts of a verb.*
I was ready, *when he appeared,* to tell him what I thought.	*Adverbial clause interrupting main clause.*

WO 2　Ambiguous Order

Be sure that the relationship between modifying words, phrases, or clauses and the elements they modify is clear.

If a modifier is so placed that it could modify either of two elements, its reference will be ambiguous. If the ambiguity is complete, the reader will be unable to tell which meaning was intended. More frequently he will be able to make the correct interpretation but will be conscious of the writer's carelessness.

Ambiguous Order	Explanation	Revised Order
The car is in the garage *which he smashed.*	*Since adjective clauses follow the nouns they modify, a reader is tempted to take* garage *as the antecedent of* which. *Putting the modifying clause immediately after* car *removes this possibility.*	The car *which he smashed* is in the garage.
There is a panel discussion tonight about drug addiction *in the student lounge.*	*The italicized phrase modifies the main clause, but its position suggests that it locates the scene of the addiction rather than of the discussion.*	Tonight there is a panel discussion *in the student lounge* about drug addiction.

Because they can occupy so many positions, adverbial elements are particularly troublesome.

Ambiguous Order	Explanation	Revised Order
They talked about going on a second honeymoon *frequently,* but they never did.	Frequently *is closer to* going *than to* talked *and could modify either. Placing it immediately before or after* talked *removes the ambiguity.*	They talked *frequently* about going on a second honeymoon, but they never did.
The list of expenses tells the story of the man who wrote it *swiftly and clearly.*	*The italicized adverbs modify* tells, *not* wrote.	The list of expenses *swiftly and clearly* tells the story of the man who wrote it.

EXERCISE　　*Remove possible ambiguities in the following sentences by changing the position of faulty modifiers.*

1. Fortunately, the fire was put out before any serious damage was done by the volunteer firemen.
2. A car came down the street decked with ribbons.

  3. I listened while he talked attentively.

  4. Who is the girl dancing with the dean in the low-cut gown?

  5. There was a noisy disturbance when the speaker said that at the back of the hall.

  6. Richard Burton played the part of the man who was corrupted by power superbly.

  7. He looked at the boy with sad eyes.

  8. My roommate brought me the book from the library that I wanted.

  9. At one time his neighbors said he had been in jail.

 10. No one would treat his father like that unless he was irresponsible.

WO 3   Awkward Separation of Elements

Avoid unnecessary separation of a subject and its verb, a verb and its object or complement, a modifier and its headword, or a preposition and its object.

Unnecessary separation of closely related elements can distort the sentence pattern and interfere with ease of reading.

Awkward Separation	Explanation	Revised Order
My *father,* after considering what the trip would cost and how long it would take, *refused* to go.	*Awkward separation of subject and verb. The unnecessary interruption of the main clause by a phrase and two subordinate clauses distorts the structure of the main clause.*	After considering what the trip would cost and how long it would take, my father refused to go.
The evidence *shows,* if you examine it carefully and impartially, *that the best baseball is played in the National League.*	*Awkward separation of verb and object. The reader has to leap over the if-clause to find the object of shows.*	A careful and impartial examination of the evidence shows that the best baseball is played in the National League.
He gave the *sweater* to his girl *that he had won in track.*	*Awkward separation of noun and modifying clause. (See the ambiguous modifiers on page 337.)*	He gave the sweater that he had won in track to his girl. (or) He gave his girl the sweater that he had won in track.
We *have* since then *had* no more trouble.	*Awkward separation of verb parts by modifying phrase.*	Since then, we have had no more trouble.
I am neither in support *of* nor opposed to *the bill.*	*Awkward separation of preposition of and its object. The revision at the right is the best way of expressing the idea.*	I neither support nor oppose the bill.

EXERCISE	*Revise the following sentences to eliminate unnecessary separations.*

1. The contractor insisted before he would give us an estimate on rebuilding the wall that we promise to pay when we accepted the estimate for half the work.

2. I was so surprised that I forgot what I intended to say to her when she smiled.

3. Our scouts reported that although they had found no evidence of enemy activity in the wooded sector we should for the greater safety of our troops retreat.

4. He said while he did not object to our going that he would prefer to stay home all things considered.

5. Her mother, even, admits that she is extravagant.

6. My political science teacher I firmly believe thinks he knows everything.

7. He promised that he would in plenty of time give us some specimen questions for the exam to study.

8. I until yesterday thought that too.

9. Give him something to eat if he asks for it when he comes.

10. While Mother entertained her guests by playing marbles we amused ourselves.

WO 4 Unemphatic Order

The emphasis on any sentence element often depends on its position. The following precautions should help you to avoid the most frequent faults of emphasis. (See also *Emphasis*, pages 120–23.)

a. Do not place minor ideas at the ends of sentences.

The most emphatic positions in an English sentence are the end and the beginning; the least emphatic is the middle. An unimportant idea at the end of a sentence will be unduly conspicuous, and the sentence will seem to run down hill.

Unemphatic Order	Emphatic Order
Someone stole our car while we were at the theater last night.	Last night, while we were at the theater, someone stole our car.
She is innocent in my opinion.	In my opinion she is innocent.
Nothing can be done, however.	Nothing, however, can be done.
He is going to propose, I think.	I think he is going to propose.

b. Do not weaken an important concluding statement by reducing it to a participial phrase.

Many a good sentence ends with a participial phrase, but to use such a phrase for an idea which is important enough to deserve a main clause often creates a lame ending. For example, in

He fell from the roof, *thus breaking his neck.*—

the italicized phrase is at least as important as the main clause, yet it is grammatically subordinate and trails off weakly. The idea in the phrase is important enough to come at the end, but it deserves the dignity of a stronger grammatical form:

He fell from the roof and *broke his neck.*

c. Do not place a conjunctive adverb at the beginning of a sentence unless you deliberately wish to emphasize it.

Conjunctive adverbs—*however, moreover, nevertheless, therefore*—serve in a double capacity. As conjunctions they connect; as adverbs they modify. But they are relatively weak modifiers, and the opening of the sentence gives them too much emphasis. When they really deserve emphasis, as the third example below may do, they may be used to start the sentence; but they are usually better near, not at, the beginning.

I am willing to advise you. I will not, *however,* accept responsibility for what you do.

He thinks she deceived him deliberately; he is *therefore* in no mood for a reconciliation.

We have repeatedly tried to make friends with them and have been consistently repulsed; *nevertheless,* I shall try again.

d. Do not confuse meaning by putting a modifier in the wrong position.

A modifier usually attaches to the nearest possible referent. The following sentence can mean quite different things depending on the position of the adverb.

They *secretly* intend to be married.

They intend to be married *secretly.*

In the first sentence the position of the modifier emphasizes the intention; in the second, the nature of the ceremony. Either meaning is possible, but the position of the modifier determines which it will be.

The following sentences further illustrate how the position of a modifier can affect meaning.

John *just* made it.

Just John made it.

Mary knows *only* the date.
Only Mary knows the date.

Until today they promised to stay.
They promised to stay *until today*.

e. Do not overuse inverted word order as a short cut to a "literary" style.

Inexperienced writers sometimes try to be literary by using self-conscious inversions. While unusual word order is arresting, strained or distorted inversion is more a vice than a virtue. Inverted order is exceptional order. It should be used deliberately and with restraint.

Affected

Pleasant were those days.

Little cared I what my parents said.

Learn he must to appreciate his own deficiencies.

Natural

Those were pleasant days.

I cared little what my parents said.

He must learn to appreciate his own deficiencies.

EXERCISE

Revise the following sentences to improve the emphasis.

---

1. Neither army planned to attack, as far as we could tell, or so it looked.
2. Putting on a tremendous burst of speed the favorite forged ahead, thus finishing in first place by a full length.
3. I think he might propose tonight, if he comes over.
4. I almost read the whole book last night. I could have finished it if I had started an hour earlier, I think.
5. I would have liked to take her to a show and I almost asked her, but I didn't have the money and I had a final the next day anyway.
6. Time for my assignments I never seem to find, thus being always behind.
7. The murder was committed on this very spot, as I was told by my maternal grandfather when I was only five years old.
8. She got her degree in three years, *magna cum laude*, in English from the college of liberal arts, humanities division.
9. He said I could come over and listen to his new tape of Beethoven's Fifth if I wanted to and got through dinner by seven o'clock.
10. The chairman said that if it took all night the committee would stay in session until all business had been completed, if there was no objection.

F   Forms of Words

F 1   Principal Parts of Verbs

Use the accepted principal parts of verbs. Especially distinguish between the forms for the past tense and the past participle.

If you are not sure what these forms are, check under **Verb** on page 468 of the Glossary.

Wrong Form

These tires are *wore* out.

He has *began* all over again.

The river is *froze* solid.

Everybody has *went* home.

Have you *wrote* to him?

Have you *took* your vacation?

Right Form

These tires are *worn* out.

He has *begun* all over again.

The river is *frozen* solid.

Everybody has *gone* home.

Have you *written* to him?

Have you *taken* your vacation?

F 2   Tense Forms

a. Avoid illogical sequence of tenses.

1. Keep the tenses of main clauses consistent.

Do not shift needlessly from present to past or from historical present to simple past.

Inconsistent	Explanation	Consistent
She laughed, and I asked her what she knew about him. She *laughs* again, this time much louder.	*In the first sentence all verbs are in the past tense; in the second,* laughs *is in the present tense. There is no reason for the shift.*	She laughed, and I asked her what she knew about him. She *laughed* again, this time much louder.

Inconsistent	Explanation	Consistent
For five rounds the young challenger danced and ducked and jabbed and piled up points. Then the champion found an opening —and Bam! The fight *is* over.	*All the verbs except the last one are in the past tense. The last shifts to historical present. Either that tense or the simple past should be used throughout.*	For five rounds the young challenger danced and ducked and jabbed and piled up points. Then the champion found an opening —and Bam! The fight *was* over.

2. Keep the tense of a subordinate clause in logical sequence with that of the main clause.

Illogical	Explanation	Logical
They *have made* so much money last year that they *bought* a second store.	*The present perfect* (have made) *suggests action more recent than the simple past* (bought); *it is illogical to use the present perfect for the earlier action.*	They *made* so much money last year that they *have bought* a second store.
Before I was introduced to her I *heard* rumors about her reputation.	*Since the rumors came before the introduction, the past perfect tense should be used in the main clause.*	Before I was introduced to her I *had heard* rumors about her reputation.

b. In converting direct discourse to indirect discourse observe the normal change in tense.

Direct discourse repeats the actual words of the speaker, and verbs should be in the tense the speaker used. When direct discourse is converted to indirect, the tenses of the original are, when possible, pushed one stage further into the past. Thus present becomes past, and past becomes past perfect. Since there is no tense more past than past perfect, an original verb in that tense does not change.

Direct Discourse	Explanation	Indirect Discourse
He said, "I *want* to read that novel."	*Change simple present to simple past.*	He said that he *wanted* to read that novel.
He said, "I *wanted* to read that novel yesterday."	*Change simple past to past perfect.*	He said that he *had wanted* to read that novel yesterday.
He said, "I *had wanted* to read that novel until I *saw* the movie."	*Leave the verbs as they are. There is no way to make* had wanted *more past than it is, and to change* saw *to* had seen *would destroy the sequence of tenses.*	He said that he *had wanted* to read that novel until he *saw* the movie.

The following examples contrast faulty and correct conversion from direct to indirect discourse.

Direct Discourse	Faulty Conversion	Correct Conversion
I said, "He *is* a good risk."	I said he *is* a good risk.	I said he *was* a good risk.
I asked, *"Have you consulted your physician?"*	I asked if he *consulted* his physician.	I asked if he *had consulted* his physician.

c. Observe the tense relationships between verbs and verbals.

The tense of a verbal is not determined by the tense of the verb in the main clause. Regardless of the tense of the verb, a present participle expresses an action occurring at the same time as that of the verb. A perfect participle expresses time before that of the verb. A present infinitive indicates the same time or a later time than that of the verb. A perfect infinitive suggests time before that of the verb.

Rounding the last turn he *was* ahead by two yards.	The present participle *(rounding)* and the past tense verb refer to simultaneous actions.
Having finished housecleaning she *washed* her hair.	The perfect participle *(having finished)* refers to an action before that of the verb *(washed)*.
I *tried to telephone* you.	The verb *(tried)* and the present infinitive *(to telephone)* refer to actions occurring at the same time.
I *expect to hear* from him tomorrow.	The expectation is now; the hearing has yet to occur. Therefore the present infinitive refers to a time later than that of the verb.
They *are reported to have adopted* a child.	The perfect infinitive points to a time before the reporting.

Faulty Sequence	Explanation	Correct Sequence
Asking the blessing, we began to eat.	*Since the blessing was asked before the eating began, the perfect participle is required.*	*Having asked* the blessing, we began to eat.
Having faced the spectators, the referee signaled a holding penalty.	*Since both actions took place at the same time, the present participle is required.*	*Facing* the spectators, the referee signaled a holding penalty.
We meant to *have told* you earlier.	*The perfect infinitive suggests that the telling occurred before the intention. The present infinitive is the required form.*	We meant to *tell* you earlier.
I am sorry *to overlook* that fact.	*Since the overlooking occurred before the regret, the perfect infinitive should be used.*	I am sorry *to have overlooked* that fact.

EXERCISE

Revise the following sentences where necessary to correct illogical or faulty sequence of tenses.

1. I have always wanted to have read Gibbon's *The Decline and Fall of the Roman Empire.*
2. She said that he had been coming to dinner next Saturday.
3. It was obvious that just before I arrived they had a serious quarrel.
4. Joan asked if I consider Dr. Bald a good teacher.
5. I replied that I have not taken his course.
6. "Oh, you don't know what you're missing," she said.
7. When I ask whether she really meant that, she repeated that I don't know what I am missing.
8. For years now she had been his great admirer, but they disagree more and more frequently.
9. We wondered what they think of it all.
10. They said that they are more and more concerned with the direction of things.

F 3 Case

Case is a system of inflection which shows the relation of nouns and pronouns to other words in the sentence. English has three cases: **subjective** (or nominative), **possessive** (or genitive), and **objective** (or accusative). In general, a noun or pronoun is in the subjective case when it acts as a subject, in the objective case when it acts as an object, and in the possessive case when it modifies a noun (*his* bicycle, the *boy's* dog, the *girl's* future).

English nouns, pronouns, and adjectives were once fully inflected to show case, but word order and idiomatic constructions have largely replaced case endings in modern English. Adjectives are no longer inflected for case; nouns are inflected only in the possessive case (the *fireman's* hat); only pronouns (and chiefly the personal pronouns) still make any considerable use of case forms. The study of case in modern English, therefore, is pretty much restricted to pronouns.

a. The case of a pronoun is determined by its function in its own clause.

If a pronoun is the subject of its clause, it takes the subjective case; if it is an object, it takes the objective case; if it is a modifier, it takes the possessive case. There are two exceptions to this practice: (1) a pronoun subject of an infinitive takes the objective case (I want *him to see* it); and (2) the complement of the verb *to be* takes the subjective case in formal usage (It was not *I* who said that).

Pronouns take the subjective case when:

1. They are subjects of verbs (*I* think that *he* missed).
2. They are in apposition with subjects (Three men—Fred, Roy, and *I* —were elected delegates).
3. They are complements of the verb *to be* (I am sure it was *he*).

Pronouns take the objective case when:

1. They are objects of verbs (Mother likes *her*).
2. They are objects of prepositions (They pointed at *me*).
3. They are in apposition with objects (They gave *us*—Dave and *me*—the money).
4. They are subjects or objects (or complements) of infinitives (I want *her* to go. We didn't expect to see *him*. Wouldn't you like to be *me?*).

Pronouns take the possessive case when:

1. They modify a noun or a pronoun (Those are *my* six children, this is *his* one).
2. They precede and modify a gerund (What's wrong with *his* swimming? *His* winning was a surprise).

b. Most errors in case occur in a few constructions.

In general, errors in case occur for two reasons: (1) because the function of a pronoun is obscured; and (2) because a case form inappropriate in writing is so often used in speech that the colloquial form seems more natural than the more formal one. Often these two reasons merge. That is, the construction requires more deliberate analysis than speakers have time to give it and so begets a colloquial usage which competes with the formal one.

The following constructions create most of the irregularities in the use of case forms.

1. Parenthetical constructions. Any construction which interrupts the normal pattern of a clause is likely to obscure the function of a pronoun in the clause. In the following sentence it is quite clear that *who* is the subject of *won* and takes the subjective case:

That is the man *who* won the prize.

But if we introduce a parenthetical clause—*they say*—into the sentence, the function of *who* becomes less clear:

That is the man who they say won the prize.

There is now a tendency to assume that *who* is the object of *say* and to put it in the objective case. But its function has not changed. *They say* is an absolute and has no grammatical relationship to any element in the sentence.

Yet the faulty analysis suggested by the interrupting construction often leads to the use of the wrong case.

Wrong Case	Explanation	Correct Case
The man **whom** *they think did it* has been arrested.	*Pronoun is subject of* did, *not object of* think.	The man **who** *they think did it* has been arrested.
She introduced me to a man **whom** *she said* was her employer.	*Pronoun is subject of* was, *not object of* said.	She introduced me to a man **who** *she said* was her employer.
He is the general **whom** *the reporters agree* was most popular with the troops.	*Pronoun is subject of* was, *not object of* agree.	He is the general **who** *the reporters agree* was most popular with the troops.

2. Complement of "to be." **(See page 447 in Glossary.)**

3. "Whoever" and "whomever." These two relative pronouns follow the rule that the case of a pronoun is determined by its function in its own clause. But because they often follow a transitive verb or the preposition *to*, they are often mistaken as objects when they are not.

Faulty	Explanation	Correct
Invite *whomever* will come.	*Pronoun is subject of* will come; *object of* invite *is clause,* whoever will come.	Invite *whoever* will come.
Send it to *whomever* you think would like it.	*Relative pronoun is subject of* would like. *The preposition* to *and the clause* you think *do not affect its case.*	Send it to *whoever* you think would like it.

4. Comparative with "than" or "as." The case of a pronoun following *than* or *as* in a comparison often causes difficulty. In such comparisons as the following, *than* and *as* are connectives between a full clause and an elliptical (incompletely expressed) one:

He is at least as old **as** *she* (is).
I am about twenty pounds lighter **than** *he* (is).
The judge liked us better **than** *them* (**than** he liked them).

In the expanded form it is clear that *than* and *as* are connectives joining two clauses. Pronouns in contracted comparisons take the same case they would take if the comparisons were fully expanded. That is, a pronoun takes the subjective case if it is the subject of an unexpressed verb, and the objective case if it is the object of such a verb.

5. Possessive with a gerund. A pronoun preceding and modifying a gerund takes the possessive case (I am opposed to *his going*). In formal writing, a noun modifying a gerund also takes the possessive case (Imagine *John's saying* that!) Both colloquial and informal usage usually ignore this latter convention and put the noun modifier in the objective case (Imagine *John saying* that!).

The following sentences further illustrate the use of the possessive case when a noun or a pronoun modifies a gerund:

There is really no excuse for *his failing* the course.
We are embarrassed by *their* continual *begging*.
They object to *my having signed* the petition.
Mary's interrupting annoys him.
Their believing that doesn't surprise me.
We could not sleep because of the *baby's crying*.

EXERCISE

In the following sentences some of the italicized case forms are acceptable and some are not. Place a check (√) opposite the number of any sentence in which the preferred case has been used. Where a wrong form has been used, write the acceptable form opposite the number of the sentence.

1. There is a man *whom* I respect.
2. All the time I had expected *her* to be my partner.
3. *His* refusing to run was a serious blow to the party.
4. Jones, *who* I dislike, is coming to lunch with us.
5. He means *us two*, you and *I*.
6. He was the kind of man *whom* everybody thought would make a wonderful father.
7. They all went on strike, *him* along with the others.
8. I don't sing as well as *her*.
9. Between you and *I*, she is smarter than *him*.
10. Speak to *whoever* will listen.

F 4   Agreement (Subject-Verb)

In grammar the term **agreement** is used to describe the relationship between the inflectional forms of different elements within a sentence. When two related elements (subject and verb, pronoun and antecedent) show the same kind of inflection, they are said to agree. Thus a verb agrees with its subject if its form shows the same number and person as the subject. A pronoun agrees with its antecedent if both show the same gender, number, and person. *The fundamental convention of agreement is that the inflectional endings of two related elements should agree as far as possible.*

Verbs agree with their subjects in number and person.

A singular subject requires a singular verb, a plural subject a plural verb. If the subject is a personal pronoun, inflected for person, the verb agrees in person. If the subject is a noun it is always considered to be in the third person, and takes the third person form of the verb.

I am late. (subject first person singular; verb first person singular)
He is sorry. (subject third person singular; verb third person singular)
The *man works* slowly. (*works* third person singular to agree with *man*)

Troublesome Constructions

The following constructions cause most of the difficulties in subject-verb agreement:

1. When two or more singular subjects are connected by *and,* **a plural form of the verb is required.**

He and his brother *are* identical twins.
Tom, Joe, Griff, and I *make* a good foursome.
A fool and his money *are* soon *parted.*

There are three exceptions to this rule:
First, when each of the singular subjects is considered individually, the verb is singular. This usage is most frequent after *each* or *every*.

Here, every man and woman *works* for the good of the organization.
Each boy and girl *makes* a separate report.

Second, when the two singular subjects refer to the same person or thing, the singular verb is used.

My wife and boss *has* something to say about that.
Grape juice and ginger ale *is* a good drink.

Third, mathematical computations may take either a singular or a plural verb.

Five and five *is* ten.
Five and five *are* ten.

Two times three *is* six.
Two times three *are* six.

2. When two or more singular subjects are connected by *or, nor,* **or** *but,* **a singular form of the verb is required.**

Mason or Dixon *is* to be elected.
Neither Bill nor Hugh *has* a chance.
Not Sue but Betty *was invited.*
Neither the Giants nor the Dodgers *is going* to win.
Not only his wife but even his mother *finds* him selfish.

3. When one of two subjects connected by *or, nor,* **or** *but* **is singular and the other is plural, the verb agrees in number with the nearer one.**

Neither Lewis nor his lawyers *were* there.
Not only the boys but also their father *encourages* it.

4. When two subjects connected by *or* **or** *nor* **differ in person, the verb agrees with the nearer.**

Jean or you *are* to go.
Either Red or I *have won*.

When following this rule creates an awkward sentence, restate the idea in a form which is both correct and natural. For example, rather than write

Neither Mary nor I am to blame.
You or he is the leading contender.—

restate these sentences as follows:

Mary is not to blame; neither am I.
You and he are the leading contenders.

5. A singular subject followed immediately by *as well as, in addition to, including, no less than, with, together with,* **or a similar prepositional construction, requires a singular verb.**

The husband as well as the wife *needs* advice.
The senator together with his assistants *was praised*.
The president no less than the secretary *is* responsible.
The store in addition to the farm *was sold*.

Because this rule sometimes creates some strained and far-fetched sentences, it is sometimes best to avoid the construction altogether and to write:

Both the husband and the wife *need* advice.
The senator and his assistants *were praised*.
The president *is* just as responsible as the secretary.
The store and the farm *were sold*.

6. A singular subject followed by a plural modifier requires a singular verb.

The *attitude* of these men *is* definitely hostile.
The *leader* of the rebel forces *has* been captured.
One of the women in the back row *looks* sick.
A *list* of the names of all survivors *is* on file.

In conversation, a plural modifier immediately before a verb often leads to a plural verb. This is most likely to happen in sentences like the fourth above, in which the subject is followed by a long modifier containing two plural nouns. This colloquial usage has less justification in writing, since the more deliberate nature of writing and revision makes it easier to use the correct form.

7. Indefinite pronouns such as *anybody, anyone, each, either, everybody, neither, nobody, no one,* **and** *somebody* **generally require a singular verb.**

Anybody who does that *is* just reckless.
Does anyone want to split this with me?
Each of them *makes* fifty dollars a week.
Somebody has been using my bicycle.
Nobody in town *admits* seeing him.
Everybody does as he pleases.

8. The pronouns *any* **and** *none* **take either singular or plural verbs.**

Are any of you *going* to the show?
Any of these times *is* satisfactory.
None works so faithfully as he.
None are expected from that district.

9. When the subject is a relative pronoun, the verb agrees with the antecedent of that pronoun.

He is one of the *men who act* as advisers.
This is one of those *problems which have* two solutions.

10. When a sentence is introduced by the expletive *There* **or the adverb** *Here,* **the verb agrees with the subject which follows the verb.**

Here *is* your *money.*
Here *are* the *receipts.*
There *are* no second *chances.*
There *are* a *man* and a *boy* in that boat.
Is there a *chance* of his winning?
Were there many *people* present?

This usage is not strictly observed in speech, because we often begin a sentence with an expletive followed by a single subject and then add more subjects before we finish the sentence. For example:

Did you see anyone there that I know?
Well, there was Joe Botts, and Ray Carroll, and Dan Snyder.

In speech, we cannot conveniently revise the verb to take care of these additional subjects. But we do have such an opportunity in writing, and hence a plural verb is expected in such sentences.

11. When a sentence is introduced by the expletive *It,* the verb is always singular, regardless of the number of the subject.

It *is* the *Johnsons.*
It *is we* whom they want.

12. The complement of the verb *to be* does not affect the number of the verb.

Books are her chief source of enjoyment.
The one *thing* you must be ready for *is* their attempts to break up the meeting.
What annoys me about them *is* their constant complaints.

If this rule produces an awkward sentence, the wisest thing to do is to recast it.

Awkward	Revised
The amusing *thing* about campaign speeches *is* the attempts that both sides make to represent themselves as the only friends of the people.	In campaign speeches, it is amusing to see how both sides attempt to represent themselves as the only friends of the people.

13. A collective noun takes a singular verb when the class it names is considered as a unit, a plural verb when the members of the class are considered individually.

Singular	Plural
The jury *is* finally complete.	The jury *were* divided in their opinions.
The family *holds* an annual reunion.	My family *have* never been able to agree.
The clergy *is* wretchedly underpaid.	The clergy *are* supporting this proposal from their pulpits.

This rule also applies to such nouns as *number, part,* and *rest.*

A large number *is* expected.	A number of errors *have* been found.
Only part of the order *was* delivered.	A great part of the people *have* no opinion on the question.
The rest of the page *is* illegible.	The rest of the votes *are* about equally divided among the three candidates.

14. Titles of books, magazines, movies, newspapers, plays, and the like take a singular verb.

The Immoralists is a fine novel.
The Outcasts was not a success at the box office.
The New York Times is his bible.

15. Plural numbers take a singular verb when they are used in a phrase to indicate a sum or a unit.

A million dollars *is* a great deal of money.
Ten years *is* too long to wait.
Five per cent *is* good interest.
Forty hours *is* the regular work week.

16. Certain nouns which are plural in form but singular in meaning generally take a singular verb. Some of these are *dynamics, economics, electronics, ethics, mathematics, news, physics, semantics, statics, whereabouts.*

Economics *has* been called the dismal science.
No news *is* good news.
Semantics *is* the study of meanings.

EXERCISE

Indicate which of the forms in parentheses is the preferred form.

1. Bacon and eggs (are, is) my favorite breakfast.
2. The defendant, together with all his "family," (was, were) arrested.
3. There (is, are) two things you simply have to learn.
4. Neither one of my favorite uncles (has, have) any children of (his, their) own.
5. Every member of the committee together with his research assistants (is, are) present or accounted for.
6. Two hundred dollars (was, were) more than any of us thought we should pay.
7. The leader no less than his followers (is, are) to blame.
8. There (is, are) one pair for each couple.
9. It (is, are) the Reynoldses who are knocking on the door.
10. (Is, Are) there two girls in the world like that?

F 5   Agreement (Pronoun–Antecedent)

Pronouns agree with their antecedents in gender, number, and person.

If the antecedent is a masculine singular noun, the pronoun should be the masculine singular third person pronoun (*he, his,* or *him*). A pronoun does not necessarily agree with its antecedent in case, since its case is determined by its function in its own clause (see page 383).

Examples	**Explanation**
The *men* got *their* wages.	*Their* is third person plural to agree with *men*. The plural form of the pronoun is the same for all genders.
The *girl* found *her* watch.	*Her* is third person feminine singular to agree with *girl*.
The *boy* misses *his* dog.	*His* is third person masculine singular to agree with *boy*.
The *plane* changed *its* course.	*Its* is third person neuter singular to agree with *plane*.

Troublesome Constructions

Most troubles with agreement of pronouns occur in a half-dozen constructions, and arise because of conflict between formal and colloquial usage. Generally, in formal usage the *form* of the antecedent, not its *meaning*, determines the number of the pronoun; whereas in colloquial usage number tends to be governed by *meaning*. For example, *everybody* is singular in form but plural in meaning, since it refers to more than one person. Formally, *everybody* requires the singular *his;* colloquially, *everybody* is often followed by the plural *their.*

1. Two or more antecedents connected by *and* take a plural pronoun.

Bill and *Ted* are looking for *their* girls.
Helen and *I* are buying *our* tickets today.
That *man* and his *partner* have ruined *themselves.*

2. *Each, either,* or *neither,* followed by a plural modifier, takes a singular pronoun.

Each of the girls is sure *she* is going to win.
Neither of the men would admit *his* mistake.
Either of these women may lose *her* temper.

3. *Everybody, each, either, everyone, neither, nobody,* or *a person,* takes a singular pronoun.

Each has *his* own group of supporters.
Everybody had *his* work in good shape.

Nobody had *his* speech ready today.
Everyone was keeping *his* fingers crossed.
A *person* finds *himself* in trouble if he begins to cut classes.

Notice that the masculine form of the pronoun is generally used when the sex of the antecedent is unknown or when the antecedent refers to both sexes:

Everyone should vote for the candidate of *his* choice.
The boys and girls have been told that *everybody* must do *his* share of the work.

But if the context clearly shows that the antecedent is feminine, the feminine pronoun is used:

When the girls have a picnic *everyone* brings *her* own utensils.

4. The impersonal *one* takes the third person pronoun unless the style is very formal.

One must watch *his* step with that girl.
One can't really blame *himself* for that.
If *one* had a second chance, how much wiser *he* might be.

In a very formal style the impersonal pronoun is sometimes used throughout.

Under such conditions *one* laments *one's* utter incapacity to be of any genuine service.
One finds *oneself* wishing that the evidence were more convincing.

5. A collective noun takes either a singular or a plural pronoun, depending on whether the group is considered as a unit or as a number of individuals.

Singular	Plural
The *family* keeps pretty much to *itself*.	The *family* may have *their* private quarrels but *they* always agree in public.
The judge reprimanded the *jury* for *its* disregard of the evidence.	At the request of the defense attorney, the *jury* were polled and *their* individual verdicts recorded.
The *team* had *its* back to the wall.	The *team* are electing *their* captain.

6. The relative pronoun *who* is used when the antecedent is a person; *which* is used when the antecedent is a thing; *that* is used to refer to persons, animals, or things.

This is the *man who* drove the car.
The *girl who* found it is here.

The *woman that* I mean had brown hair.
Here is the *parcel which* (or *that*) she left.
This is the *cow that* jumped over the moon.

The possessive form *whose* is theoretically confined to persons, but in practice is often used when the more formal *of which* seems awkward.

The *nation whose* conscience is clear on that score is exceptional.
The newspaper *whose* reporters are most alert gets the most scoops.

EXERCISE   *Choose the preferred form of the pronoun in parentheses.*

1. One is obliged to do (one's, his, their) best.
2. Everybody has to decide for (himself, themselves).
3. There is the man (which, that, who) lost the campaign.
4. Every man and woman on the committee (was, were) officially thanked for (their, his, her) part in compiling the report.
5. Give this book to the young lady (which, who, that) left it here.
6. Neither one of them will promise (his, their) support.
7. Nobody in the room (was, were) willing to give up (his, their) (seat, seats).
8. One must work twenty-five years to be eligible for (his, their, one's, your) pension.
9. Has everyone got (his, their) own coat?
10. The elder generation in our town (has, have) always acted according to (its, their) convictions.

F 6   Vague Pronoun Reference

A pronoun which refers to a whole clause rather than to a specific antecedent can be vague or misleading. The following examples contain vague pronoun references.

Vague Reference	Explanation	Revision
They have agreed to have a formal church wedding, *which* pleases their parents.	*The pronoun* which *has no explicit antecedent but refers to the whole idea expressed in the main clause. The vague reference may be improved by supplying an antecedent as in the first revision or, better, by recasting the sentence as in the second revision.*	They have agreed to have a formal church wedding, *a decision* which pleases their parents. (or better) Their decision to have a formal church wedding pleases their parents.

Vague Reference	Explanation	Revision
The bigger plane will be expensive to operate. Not only will its maintenance cost more but its fuel consumption will be greater. We should take *this* into account.	*The demonstrative pronoun* this *has no explicit antecedent, is singular in form, and refers to two different costs. In the revised version, the phrase* these added costs *removes the difficulties.*	The bigger plane will be expensive to operate. Not only will its maintenance cost more but its fuel consumption will be greater. We should take *these added costs* into account.
The crash is being investigated. At present *they* think that the planes must have collided.	*The antecedent of* they *is not identified. The writer, of course, is thinking of the investigators. The statement would be improved by dropping the pronoun.*	At present the investigators think that the planes must have collided.
If he does not get to work on his research assignment pretty soon *it* is going to be difficult for him to get *it* finished on time.	*The first* it *is impersonal but seems at first glance to refer to* research assignment—*particularly unfortunate because the second* it *does have this reference. The sentence would be improved by keeping* he *the subject of both clauses.*	If he does not get to work on his research assignment pretty soon he may not get it finished on time.

EXERCISE   *Revise the following sentences to make the pronoun references clear.*

1. In many slum apartment buildings a whole family has only one room, which makes life nearly intolerable.

2. Plastic doesn't rot, bottles are not bio-degradable, and tin cans rust away but ever so slowly. This makes our problem very hard to solve.

3. I usually read a novel and part of a non-fiction book every week, which on top of my assignments keeps me pretty busy.

4. In the service they tell you exactly what to do and when to do it. That's the worst thing about it.

5. My dictionary says that word usage is determined by how people use them, which surprised me.

6. In college they treat you as an adult and call you Mister or Miss. This is a change for the better from the way it was in high school.

7. He liked electronics, which was good because it got him a better job.

8. It's lucky I like to eat out, because what they give you at my dorm they don't eat themselves.

9. At our school all the professors know the students, and they call them by name.

10. John married right after graduation, which changed his life entirely.

F 7   Faulty Complement

a. Avoid an illogical or awkward construction as the complement of the verb *to be*.

The verb *to be* is most frequently used either as an auxiliary verb (I *am* learning) or as a linking verb (Honesty *is* the best policy). When used as a linking verb, it links its complement to its subject and thus acts as a kind of equals sign (Honesty = best policy). A reader expects two things of this linking verb: (1) that it will be followed by a complement, (2) that the complement can be logically equated with the subject. If either of these expectations is denied him, he will be bothered. Thus if he encounters the sentence, "Honesty is in the little details of everyday life," he will feel that the promised linking relationship has not been provided. He will want to revise the sentence to read, "Honesty is best expressed in the little details of everyday life," thus changing *is* from a linking to an auxiliary verb (*is expressed*).

Similarly, a reader who meets the sentence, "Honesty is what you do in such a situation," will feel that the complement throws the equation out of balance, since it equates the abstract noun "Honesty" with a statement of action. He will want to revise the sentence to read, "What to do in such a situation is to tell the truth," so that each side of the equation refers to an action (*to do* and *to tell*).

To avoid such annoying constructions, make sure that the complement of *to be* can be logically equated with the subject. If it cannot, or if the equation results in a wordy or awkward sentence, either revise the form of the complement or rewrite the sentence to get rid of the linking verb.

Illogical or Awkward Complement	Explanation	Revised Sentence
Before I built the house all I had learned about carpentry was *watching my dad.*	*The equation requires some statement of knowledge, not a statement of how the knowledge was obtained. Of the various possible revisions, perhaps the best is to substitute a more active verb which does not promise an equation.*	Before I built the house all that I knew about carpentry *I had learned from* watching my dad.
The chief disadvantage of weeping willows is the branches are brittle and break easily.	*The sentence has two faults. Logically, it is the brittleness that constitutes the disadvantage, not the branches; grammatically, the plural noun* branches *following* is *sounds like a subject-verb disagreement. The sentence may be saved very simply, by providing a subordinating conjunction so that the final clause is revealed as a complement.*	The chief disadvantage of weeping willows is *that* the branches are brittle and break easily.

The most unusual food I ever had was when I ate a serving of boiled snails.	*The reader expects the food to be identified immediately after the linking verb. Instead the adverbial clause stresses time.*	The most unusual food I ever ate was a serving of boiled snails.

b. Avoid the use of *is when, is where,* **and** *is if* **when the complement of** *to be* **is intended to describe or define the subject.**

This advice is a special application of the more general statement given in **a.** The use of an adverbial clause instead of a noun or noun phrase is one kind of illogical complement which occurs frequently in student definitions. This error and its revision are illustrated by the following examples.

Faulty Complement	Explanation	Revision
Plagiarism is *when you represent another person's writing as your own.*	*The reader expects to find what plagiarism is, not when it is. The construction calls for a noun phrase similar to the italicized phrase at the right.*	Plagiarism is *the representation of another's writing as one's own.*
Manslaughter is *where a person is killed deliberately but without premeditation.*	*Again, the construction requires a statement of what manslaughter is, not where it is.*	Manslaughter is *the deliberate but unpremeditated killing of a person.*
A comma splice is *if a comma is used to separate two independent sentences which are not connected by a coordinating conjunction.*	*The complement should tell what a comma splice is, not how a comma splice is made. Use a noun such as* use *at the right.*	A comma splice is *the use of a comma to separate two independent sentences which are not connected by a coordinating conjunction.*

c. Use the adjective form as the complement of a sensory verb.

A **sensory verb** is one which identifies some action of the senses—seeing, hearing, feeling, tasting, smelling. Since the complements of these verbs usually describe the subject rather than the action of the verb, they should be adjectives, not adverbs. Their adjectival function can be illustrated by turning the construction around and expressing the complement as an attributive adjective, as in the parenthetical phrases below:

The table feels smooth. (smooth-feeling table)
The barrel looks clean. (clean-looking barrel)
That note sounded flat. (flat-sounding note)
The syrup tasted sweet. (sweet-tasting syrup)

To use an adverb after these verbs would suggest that the writer was describing the manner in which the feeling, looking, sounding, and tasting were performed. Unless the modifier completing a sensory verb is clearly intended to describe the action suggested by the verb, an adjective is the correct form.

EXERCISE *Revise the following sentences to correct faulty complements.*

1. The cause of my confusion was from not hearing very well.
2. The reason I earned so little was I picked only a third of the cherries.
3. A mongrel is when two kinds of dogs are crossed.
4. By the look of it, that dish should taste marvelously.
5. Being a duffer is when you shoot over 100.
6. I saw in today's paper where unemployment is on the increase.
7. Technically a star is being in two hit movies.
8. What pleases the crowd most is he always drives for the goal.
9. Shortly after class he began to feel very sickly.
10. The only antiques I own are my grandmother gave me a dozen old spoons.

F 8   Confusion of Adjective–Adverb

Modifiers which are faulty because of word order are discussed in **WO 2.** This section is limited to errors in the forms of modifiers.

a. Do not use an adjective to modify a verb.

Adjective for Adverb	Correct
The old car still runs *good*.	The old car still runs *well*.
Do it as *careful* as you can.	Do it as *carefully* as you can.
Listen *close* to what I tell you.	Listen *closely* to what I tell you.

b. Do not use an adjective to modify an adverb or another adjective.

Adjective for Adverb	Correct
He is *considerable* better today.	He is *considerably* better today.
It will *sure* be a difficult decision.	It will *surely* be a difficult decision.

c. Do not use an adverb as the complement of a sensory verb unless you clearly intend to modify the verb, not the subject. (See F7)

d. When a modifier could modify either a noun or a verb, indicate by the form which you intend.

Adverb	Adjective
Tie the knot *tightly* and *securely*.	Tie the boat *tight* to the dock.
Her husband held her *firmly*.	He kept his resolutions *firm*.
John spoke out *forthrightly*.	His answers seemed *forthright*.

EXERCISE   *Rewrite the following sentences to revise or delete faulty modifiers.*

1. They divided the loot equal among them.
2. Kate slipped on the ice and near sprained her ankle.
3. Stretch pants look terribly on some girls.
4. On my new record player everything sounds well.
5. She held the handle tight as he swung around the curve.
6. I passed the exam easy; the questions were easy.
7. It sure was a heartening experience.
8. I spoke real sharp to the contractor.
9. The work had been done so sloppy that we had to do most of it over ourselves.
10. Jon handled the part of Hamlet real good, but Jenifer was hopelessly miscast as Ophelia.

Punctuation

The common marks of punctuation are the *period* [.], *comma* [,], *semicolon* [;], *colon* [:], *question mark* [?], *exclamation mark* [!], *quotation marks* [" " or ' '], *apostrophe* ['], *dash* [—], *parentheses* [( )], and *square brackets* [ ]. Most of these marks have highly specialized functions, and once these are understood, it is easy enough to use them conventionally. The chief exception, perhaps, is the comma, which is at once the most common mark of punctuation and the one with the most complex uses.

P 1 Uses of the Comma

The comma is used to make the internal structure of the sentence clear. It does so in three general ways: (1) by separating elements which might otherwise be confused, (2) by setting off interrupting constructions, and (3) by marking words out of normal order.

a. Use commas to separate elements which might otherwise seem to run together.

1. To prevent a confused, ambiguous, or awkward reading.

The most important use of the comma is to prevent a confused, ambiguous, or awkward reading. All other uses are subordinate to this one. Notice how the confused sentences at the left are made clear at the right by the use of commas.

Ambiguous	Explanation	Clear
Mr. Smith our milkman has been hurt.	*Is this a statement to or about Mr. Smith?*	Mr. Smith, our milkman has been hurt. (or) Mr. Smith, our milkman, has been hurt.

Ambiguous	Explanation	Clear
I do not care for money isn't everything.	*So that* money *will not seem to complete* care for, *a comma should be inserted after* care.	I do not care, for (*or* because) money isn't everything.
A hundred yards below the bridge was flooded.	*Comma necessary to avoid misreading of* bridge *as the object of* below.	A hundred yards below, the bridge was flooded.
When we had finished eating the cigarettes were passed around.	*Comma necessary to show that* cigarettes *is not the object of* eating.	When we had finished eating, the cigarettes were passed around.

2. To separate two main clauses joined by a coordinating conjunction (*and, or, nor, but, for*).

The comma prevents possible misinterpretation on first reading; specifically it keeps the subject of the second main clause from being misread as a second complement in the first clause.

He sprained his ankle and his temper was ruined.
He traded his car and his wife was angry.

In both these sentences the noun following the conjunction appears at first glance to be part of a compound object of the first verb. A comma before the conjunction shows clearly that the two nouns are in different clauses:

He sprained his ankle, and his temper was ruined.
He traded his car, and his wife was angry.

When there is no danger of a confused reading, the comma becomes less necessary and may be omitted. But even when it is not necessary, careful writers use it if the subject of the second clause is different from that of the first:

I tried to sleep, but my neighbor's dog made that impossible.

The huge elm had been cut down, and a garage now covered the spot where it once stood.

But notice that a comma is generally not used when the subject of the first clause is understood as the subject of the second:

I discussed the question with the family and then made my decision.

3. To separate elements in a series.

Churchill promised the English only *blood, sweat, toil,* and *tears.*

Reading, swimming, and *dancing* are my favorite recreations.

It was said of Washington that he was *first in war, first in peace,* and *first in the hearts of his countrymen.*

North passed, East bid two spades, South bid three hearts, and *West doubled.*
We were *tired, hungry,* and *disconsolate.*

As these illustrations show, the series may consist of single words, phrases, or clauses. The items in the series may be nouns, pronouns, verbs, verbals, adverbs, or adjectives, though within a single series they must not shift from one part of speech to another. The comma before the conjunction joining the last two items is optional. Its use is largely a matter of personal preference, though it is more likely to be omitted in an informal style than in a formal one.

She is small, dark, and vivacious.
                    (or)
She is small, dark and vivacious.

4. To separate contrasted elements in a *this, not that,* construction.

He is sick, not drunk.
We are disgusted, not angry.
This is a problem which must be handled with sympathy, not harshness.

5. To separate directly quoted material from such speech tags as *He said, She answered, We replied,* etc.

She said, "You are only half right."
"This," I said, "is the last straw."
"Nobody asked you, sir," she said.
"But," he asked, "what if they do?"

Since the quotation marks themselves set off the quoted material, no confusion would result if the comma were omitted; but convention requires the comma. Whether the punctuation should come *inside* or *outside* the quotation marks is discussed in **P 9.**

6. To separate elements in dates, addresses, and place names.

January 1, 1970; Dec. 25, 1972. (comma between day and year)

875 Main Street, Galesburg, Illinois. (comma between street and city and between city and state)

Chicago, Illinois, is the third-largest city in this country. (Notice the comma before and after the state.)

He was born in London, England. (comma between city and country)

7. In the following miscellaneous constructions:

In figures—22,745; 1,000,000; 150,743,290.
In names followed by titles—R. W. Leeds, M.D.
At the end of the salutation in informal letters—Dear Joe,
After an introductory *Yes* or *No*—Yes, I'll do it.

EXERCISE

In the following sentences insert commas where they are needed for ease of reading or are conventionally required. Some of the sentences may be satisfactory as they are.

1. Mail your application to R. B. Jonas Ph.D School of Graduate Study University of Minnesota Minneapolis Minnesota.
2. Mark quarreled with his wife and her sister tried to intercede.
3. The runners crouched tensely till the gun went off then sprang forward as one man.
4. "Is there any reason" Joe asked "why we should keep Grandfather's old bonds any longer?"
5. "I doubt it" I said "the Confederacy has been out of business for some time now."
6. I cannot wait any longer for the newly appointed Dean of Women has asked me to tea.
7. Throughout the house was as quiet as the grave.
8. His room was a clutter of discarded clothing strewn books and newspapers overflowing ashtrays and dirty dishes.
9. When we looked in we saw little for someone had masked the windows on the inside.
10. After all he wanted too much.
11. Below the city glittered with a million lights.
12. He criticized the embroidery and the girl started to cry.
13. When he finished polishing the table was shining.
14. My father taught arithmetic to my brother and my mother gave me piano lessons.
15. I'll have orange juice ham and eggs and coffee.

b. Use commas to set off an interrupting construction.

Any element which comes between a subject and its verb, a verb and its object or complement, or any two elements not normally separated, may be called an interrupting construction. If the interruption is awkward, it should be avoided; but many interrupters are necessary. These should be set off by commas, so that a reader can recognize the basic pattern of the sentence.

But we must distinguish between constructions which actually interrupt and those which come between related elements without interrupting them. For example, in

The girl, *you say,* has gone.—

the italicized clause comes between subject (*girl*) and verb (*has gone*). The interrupter need not occupy this position. The sentence could have been written:

You say that the girl has gone.
The girl has gone, you say.

But in the sentence

The girl *you want* has gone.—

the italicized clause identifies the particular girl and cannot be moved without weakening the sentence. Although the clause modifies the subject, it so closely identifies it that we may consider *The girl you want* as the "whole subject" of *has gone*. A modifying phrase or clause which is so closely related to another element that it is felt to be a part of it should not be set off with commas, since the commas would distort the relationship, not clarify it. The italicized modifiers in the following sentences are so necessary that they are not considered interrupting constructions:

The man *with him* is his brother.
The girl *at the piano* is his wife.
The leader *of the revolt* has been captured.

As you study the following uses of commas to set off interrupting constructions, notice this about them: *an interrupting construction between subject and verb or verb and complement requires two commas to enclose it.* These commas act like mild parentheses and *are always used in pairs.*

1. To set off an appositive.

An **appositive** is an identifying word or phrase (a noun or pronoun and its modifiers) which is considered grammatically equivalent to the noun or pronoun it identifies:

His father, *the president of the company,* will be responsible.
They want us, *you and me,* to go.
I want to see Dr. Roberts, *the guidance counselor.*

The first two examples show that the appositive is often a particular kind of interrupter. The third appositive does not interrupt the main clause, but is conventionally separated from the rest of the sentence by a comma.

2. To set off nouns of address.

A **noun of address** is a common or proper noun used to name the listener when we are speaking to him directly (I wish, *Dad,* you would reconsider your decision. I understand, *Mrs. Ellison,* that you are now a grandmother). Such nouns may occupy the beginning, middle, or end of a sentence, so that strictly speaking they are not always interrupters. But they are always set off from the rest of the sentence by commas.

I would like to ask you, *Mr. Jones,* for your opinion.
Sir, I'd like to ask a question.
Listen, *chum,* I've had enough of you!
I wish I were going with you, *Ted.*

3. To set off conjunctive adverbs and other transitional markers.

Conjunctive adverbs (*however, moreover, therefore,* etc.), sometimes called **transitional connectives,** are adverbs which serve as connectives between main clauses or sentences. Usually they provide a transition between two such statements, and they come *near,* and occasionally *at,* the beginning of the second one.

We planned our demonstration for noon sharp. We thought, moreover, that we could bring it off.

Most students seemed excited enough. On the other hand, there was a chance that some would have doubts at the last minute.

Commas around *therefore* are sometimes omitted:

I am therefore canceling the order.

4. To set off a nonrestrictive modifier.

A modifier is said to be **restrictive** when it specifies a particular member or members of a group. Thus in "The President *who said that* was Lincoln," the italicized modifier restricts the whole class of Presidents to a particular one. When a modifier does not limit a class to a particular group or individual but modifies the whole class, it is said to be **nonrestrictive.** Thus in "The President of the United States, *who is both the chief of state and the leader of his party,* holds one of the most powerful offices in the world," the italicized modifier refers to all Presidents of the United States and does not restrict the statement to any particular one. It is nonrestrictive.

The following sentences illustrate restrictive and nonrestrictive modifiers. Context often determines how a modifier is to be interpreted. Thus it may be possible to place the sentences at the right in contexts which would make the modifiers restrictive.

Restrictive	Nonrestrictive
All students *who were absent* will be required to do an additional assignment.	College students, *who represent a superior intellectual group,* must be asked to accept the responsibility of leadership.
Soldiers *who have flat feet* are not assigned to the infantry.	Soldiers, *who are selected by physical fitness tests,* should show a lower sickness rate than that of the total population.

Restrictive modifiers cannot be omitted without changing the basic meaning of the sentence. Nonrestrictive modifiers can be omitted without significant change in basic meaning. Compare the following revisions with the originals above.

All students . . . will be required to do an additional assignment. (This is not what the original statement meant.)

College students . . . must be asked to accept the responsibility of leadership. (This is substantially what the original statement meant.)

Soldiers . . . are not assigned to the infantry. (Not the original meaning.)

Soldiers . . . should show a lower sickness rate than that of the total population. (The original meaning has not been substantially changed.)

Nonrestrictive modifiers are set off by commas; restrictive modifiers are not.

EXERCISE

In the following sentences, provide commas to set off appositives, nouns of address, conjunctive adverbs, and nonrestrictive modifiers. Some sentences may require no additional punctuation.

1. Mrs. Schwarz our next-door neighbor has a daughter who placed in a national beauty contest. There is some talk that she may be given a movie contract. That however may be just a rumor which has no foundation.

2. Mr. Alexander the new math teacher who has flaming red hair comes from Australia.

3. A great thinker who was named Galileo helped formulate the concept of the universe which prevails today.

4. Nonetheless the man wearing blue jeans is the mayor John Ogilvie.

5. The paper says that Ed Thorpe the director of admissions will resign when his replacement is found.

6. I wonder Bill why indeed you didn't ask the man who runs the pro shop.

7. Water which is not pure enough to drink should first be boiled.

8. The Senator who happened to be wearing Texas boots said he had never been near an oil well.

9. I got permission from the sergeant who is not so tough as you made me think.

10. Joe the radio says it is going to rain.

11. The doctor looking very grave shook our hands.

12. He promised moreover that there would be enough to eat for all who came hungry.

13. The woman nearly in hysterics could hardly talk.
14. No I mean Mrs. Trilby who is my mother-in-law.
15. The wig which she bought in the bargain basement however looked better than the one she bought in that shop which has such high prices.

---

c. Use commas to mark an inversion.

1. To emphasize an inverted element.

Any word, phrase, or clause transposed from its normal position is said to be inverted.

Myself, I will vote in favor of it.
Except for physics, my courses are not difficult.

But if the inversion is so common as to seem normal, the comma is usually omitted. No commas would be used in the following inversions:

Yesterday I had a bad time of it.
In 1913 the concept of total war was unknown.
In the following sentences the verbs are underlined.

2. To set off a long introductory phrase or an adverbial clause preceding the main clause.

When a sentence opens with a long phrase or adverbial clause, use a comma between this element and the main clause:

Pulling over to the curb at the first opportunity, I waited for the fire engines to pass.
If there is going to be any difficulty about this request, I would rather withdraw it.
Being ignorant of the facts of the situation, I could say nothing.
If I go, you'll be sorry.
To be sure of getting up in time to catch the train, I left a call with the switchboard operator.
When you say that, smile.

This usage is not universal. The comma is generally used when, as in the last example, the introductory construction is clearly an inversion, when an introductory phrase contains a verbal (examples 1, 3, 5), and when the subordinate and main clauses have different subjects (example 4). The comma should always be used if it makes the sentence clearer and reading easier.

EXERCISE

In the following sentences insert commas to set off inversions and introductory constructions where desirable.

1. For all I know this is the only road to Jericho.
2. Livid with rage and hurt she threw his ring in his face.
3. In a last desperate plea for sympathy he made a clean breast of the whole affair.
4. Knowing that he had a tendency to take a five-minute walk in ten minutes my uncle always used to carry his watch on his strolls.
5. If you want it take it.
6. Just last week I had lunch with him.
7. Whoever did it should be prosecuted to the full extent of the law.
8. They also serve who only stand and wait.
9. On being told that we had never formally been introduced the Ambassador took me at once to the Viceroy.
10. When the judge enters the courtroom be sure to stand up.

P 2 Misuse of the Comma

Too many commas can be more annoying than too few. Observe the following "don't's."

a. Do not use a comma instead of a period between sentences.

A comma instead of a period between sentences may cause serious misinterpretation. (See "Comma Splice," **S 4;** see also **P 3a.**)

Comma Splice	Clear
He spoke very quietly, as I listened, I had the impression that he was speaking to himself.	He spoke very quietly. As I listened, I had the impression that he was speaking to himself.
There was nothing more to be said, when they took that attitude, further negotiation was impossible.	There was nothing more to be said. When they took that attitude, further negotiation was impossible.

b. Do not use a comma between closely related elements except to mark an interrupting construction.

The comma should reveal the structure of a sentence, not disguise it. Closely related elements (subject-verb, verb-object, verb or noun and modifier) should not normally be separated. If these elements are interrupted, a pair of commas to enclose the interrupting construction helps to bridge the interruption.

Faulty Comma	**Correct**
My car, is at the service station.	My car, which is at the service station, needs a thorough overhauling.
He said, that he would try.	He said, when I asked him, that he would try.
The student who lost this money, may need it badly.	The student, who had lost money on other occasions, was reprimanded for his carelessness.

The last pair of illustrations contrasts a restrictive and a nonrestrictive clause (see page 405). There should be no comma in the sentence at the left because the subordinate *who-* clause is a necessary part of the whole subject. It is a restrictive modifier.

c. Do not use commas excessively.

It is not necessary to use a comma in any particular sentence simply because convention recommends it in sentences of the type. The conventions describe general practice. There are times when slavishly following the rules will chop a sentence to pieces by commas. In such cases, either revise the sentence or ignore the strict letter of the law. The following examples illustrate excessive and adequate punctuation:

Excessive	**Adequate**
However, it is not, in my opinion, desirable.	However, it is not in my opinion desirable.
Yesterday, a little, old lady, in a dilapidated, old Ford, picked me up and brought me home.	Yesterday a little old lady in a dilapidated old Ford picked me up and brought me home.
Sometimes, she would appear in an elaborate beach outfit, sometimes, she wore a simple, white suit, and, occasionally, she put on a red, white, and blue bathing suit, with a detachable skirt.	Sometimes she would appear in an elaborate beach outfit, sometimes she wore a simple white suit, and occasionally she put on a red white and blue bathing suit with a detachable skirt.

P 3   Uses of the Semicolon

a. Use a semicolon to separate closely related independent clauses not connected by a conjunction.

Try this one; it looks like your color.
His mother won't let him; she is afraid he might get hurt.
Your car is new; mine is eight years old.

In each of these sentences a period could be used instead of the semicolon. But the clauses, even though grammatically independent, are felt to be so closely related that a period makes too sharp a separation.

The semicolon provides a more emphatic separation than the comma; it affords an easier transition than the period; it is therefore the most suitable mark to balance two contrasted ideas parallel in form:

Take care of the children; the adults can take care of themselves.

It was not the hours or the pay that discouraged me; it was the constant monotony of the work.

b. Use a semicolon between independent clauses joined by a transitional connective (conjunctive adverb).

Transitional connectives are words like *also, besides, consequently, furthermore, hence, however, likewise, moreover, nevertheless, in addition, then, therefore.* Since these connectives are not subordinating conjunctions, they require a stronger mark of punctuation than a comma.

His argument has some merit; *however,* he goes too far.

His eyes went bad; *consequently,* he had to resign his position as a proofreader.

He argued brilliantly; his opponent, *nevertheless,* had the stronger case.

c. Use a semicolon to separate elements in a series which contains internal commas.

Among those present were Dr. Holmes, pastor of the First Methodist Church; A. C. Levitt, superintendent of schools; B. L. Rainey, manager of the Benson Hotel; and M. T. Cord, vice president of Miller and Sons.

Commas between the elements in this series would be confused with the commas which set off the appositives.

P 4   Misuse of the Semicolon

a. Do not use a semicolon as the equivalent of a colon.

Although the names suggest a close relationship, the semicolon and the colon have quite different uses and are not interchangeable. The colon (see **P 7**) is used chiefly to indicate that something is to follow, usually a series of items; the semicolon separates parallel elements and is never used to introduce a series. In the following examples the faulty semicolon is followed by the correct colon in parentheses.

My records show that the following students have not handed in the assignment; (:) Mr. Andrews, Mr. Richardson, Mr. Smith, and Miss Wallace.

Dear Sir; (:) May I call your attention to an error. . . .

b. Do not use a semicolon as the equivalent of a comma.

Except in the special usage illustrated in **P 3c,** a semicolon cannot be substituted for a comma between a main clause and a subordinate construction. In the following examples the faulty semicolon is followed by the correct comma in parentheses.

Although I seldom have trouble with grammar or spelling; (,) I never seem to use the right punctuation.

We stayed up until two o'clock in the morning; (,) hoping that they would arrive.

P 5   The Period

a. A period is used to mark the end of a declarative sentence.

Unless a sentence is intended as a question, a command, or an exclamation, it is declarative and is closed by a period.

Today is Tuesday.
We have three days to go.

b. A period is used to mark an accepted abbreviation.

Titles: Col., Dr., Hon., Mrs., Rev.
Degrees: B.A., B.S., M.D., Ph.D.
Names: John A. Jones; Chas. W. Brown
Months: Jan., Feb., Aug., Nov.
States: Ala., Ga., Me., Ill., Wash.
Miscellaneous: Ave., St., vol., p., U.S.A., B.C., A.D.

Notice, however, that periods are not used in such shortened forms as *exam, gym, prom, per cent, 1st, 2nd, 3rd.* Periods are usually omitted in abbreviations of government agencies—*USNR, TVA, AEC, FBI, CIA.*

c. A period is used before a decimal and between dollars and cents.

The error is less than .01 inch.
The correct answer is 57.39.
The price tag read $11.98.

P 6   Question and Exclamation Marks

a. The main use of the question mark is to indicate that a sentence is to be understood as a question.

Whose is this?
You mean he's ill?

But if the question is a courteous way of stating a request, the end punctuation is a period, not a question mark:

Will you please hand in your papers now.

The question mark is sometimes used in parentheses to query the accuracy of the preceding word:

These amateurs (?) make a comfortable living out of sports.

As a device for irony, however, it is generally weak. Avoid:

Those funny (?) remarks are uncalled for.

Notice that a question reported in indirect discourse does not take a question mark:

They asked where we were going.

b. The exclamation mark is used to show that a statement is imperative or that it is spoken with strong emotion.

Be quiet!
Fasten your seat-belts!
Don't just stand there! Do something!
Oh, what a mess!
God help us!

P 7 The Colon

The main uses of the colon are:

a. To indicate that something is to follow, especially a formal statement or series.

Here are the facts: The money was there five minutes before he entered the room; it was missing immediately after he left; the next day he bought a new record player, though he had already spent all this month's allowance.

The slogan goes like this: Look sharp! Feel sharp! Be sharp!

b. In place of a comma before long or formal direct quotations.

In his most famous speech Bryan said: "You shall not press down upon the brow of labor a crown of thorns; you shall not crucify mankind upon a cross of gold."

This is his statement reported in the papers: "I have never advocated such ideas; I do not advocate them now; I do not approve of them; and I have no reason to believe that I ever will approve of them."

c. Before a clause which restates the idea of the preceding clause in different words.

Romeo and Juliet is one of the great experiences in film. It is not, to be sure, the greatest: the creation of new dramatic poetry is more important than the re-creation of old.

Except for differences of subject matter, the rules of grammar are in essence like the laws of physics and chemistry: they are scientific generalizations about the facts.

In such uses the clause after the colon says, in another way, what was said in the clause before the colon. But the restatement is not needless repetition: it illustrates or amplifies the content of the preceding clause.

P 8   Quotation Marks

This section is limited to the use of quotation marks. The position of other punctuation in relation to quotation marks is treated separately in the next section.

Quotation marks may be double (" ") or single (' ').

Double Quotation Marks

Double quotation marks have the following uses:

a. To enclose the actual words of a speaker (direct discourse).

I said, "That's your worry."
"Bob," he said, "you can't do that!"
"What is the matter?" she asked.

Since all the words of a speaker are enclosed in quotation marks an interrupting *he said, she replied,* etc., requires two sets of quotation marks in the sentence. Notice also that when direct discourse is reported as indirect discourse, quotation marks are not used.

She asked what was the matter.

b. To identify words which are being discussed as words.

The word "garage" comes from French; the word "piano" comes from Italian. "Buxom" originally came from the Old English verb meaning "to bend."

This use is sometimes extended to include technical terms (*A "field" in mathematics is not what it is in agriculture*) and slang terms (*Her brother "socked" her in the eye and "beaned" her with a ruler*). Though occasionally acceptable, this usage is often overdone. Quotation marks do not make a term appropriate. If a word is appropriate in context, it can usually stand without quotation marks; if it is not appropriate, it should not be used.

Another method, preferred by some writers, is to underline or italicize the word being cited (see page 434).

To be is the trickiest verb in the language.

c. To enclose the titles of short stories, poems, paintings, songs, etc. (but not books).

I think Kipling's best short story is "Without Benefit of Clergy."

It was Cole Porter who wrote "Begin the Beguine."

Tennyson asked to have "Crossing the Bar" placed at the end of every edition of his poems.

He says that Da Vinci's "Mona Lisa" is a portrait of an Italian noblewoman.

d. In bibliography, to distinguish the title of a selection from that of the book from which it is taken.

Faulkner, William. "Two Soldiers," *Collected Stories of William Faulkner.* New York: Random House, 1950.

For additional examples of this use, see pages 267–68. Notice that titles of books are set in italics, not enclosed in quotation marks.

Single Quotation Marks

Single quotation marks are used:

a. To mark quotations within quotations.

When it is necessary to include one set of quotation marks within another, the internal quotation is placed in single marks, the longer quotation in double marks:

Here is an excerpt from my brother's letter: "Today in class Mr. Blair quoted Wordsworth's line 'A three-months darling of a pigmy size,' and said it appeared in one edition as 'A three-months darling of a pig my size.'"

When the director said, "Let's try that passage again, beginning with 'Once more into the breach,' and remember that this is a battle, not a declamation contest," there was an audible bronx cheer from one of the veterans.

b. In type, as a substitute for double quotation marks to improve the appearance of the page.

When in a printed work it is necessary to place quotation marks around a great many single words, an editor will sometimes attempt to improve the appearance of the page by substituting single marks for double. The need for this substitution almost never exists in student writing.

P 9   Punctuation with Quotation Marks

It is often a question whether punctuation should be placed *inside* or *outside* quotation marks. Practice is not uniform, but the following excerpt from *The MLA Style Sheet*—widely used by English instructors—states the prevailing procedure:

For the sake of appearance put all commas or periods *inside* quotation marks. . . . Other punctuation goes inside quotation marks only when it is actually part of the matter quoted.[1]

This convention may be stated in detail as follows:

a. When the quoted words are followed by a comma, put the comma inside the quotation marks.

"If you insist," I said, "I'll do it."
The word "skirt," for example, has both standard and slang meanings.

A comma after *he said*, *she replied*, and similar tags should be placed immediately after these phrases, not after the quotation marks which follow.

b. A period, like a comma, always goes inside the quotation marks.

That is not the way to spell "eclectic."
He said, "You can always count on Tom to muddy the issue."

c. If the quotation is a question, the question mark goes inside the quotation marks; if the whole sentence is a question but the quotation is not, the question mark goes outside.

Somebody yelled, "Why don't you go home?" (What was yelled was a question.)

Did he actually say, "Let Williams do it"? (The quotation is not a question, but the whole sentence is. The question mark goes outside the quotation marks, and no other end punctuation is used.)

Well, how *do* you spell "eclectic"? (The whole sentence is a question, not the word "eclectic.")

d. The exclamation mark, like the question mark, goes inside if the quotation itself is an exclamation; otherwise it goes outside.

"Get out of my sight!" he yelled. (The quoted portion is an exclamation.)

I did, too, say "Friday"! (The whole sentence is an exclamation; "Friday" is not.)

His only answer was "Nonsense!" (Only the quoted word is an exclamation.)

---

[1] From *The MLA Style Sheet*, Second Edition, 1970. The omitted material indicated by the ellipsis refers to exceptions which almost never occur in student writing.

e. Since the semicolon and the colon almost never occur at the end of a quotation, they are always placed outside the quotation marks.

He said, "You can be confident that I'll do it"; but I was by no means confident.

If the sentence ended with the quotation, the period would come inside the quotation marks. The semicolon is used to provide contrast between the two main clauses, not to end the first one.

"There are three parts," she said; "we have two of them."

Although the semicolon would be included in the quotation if it were written —She said, "There are three parts; we have two of them."—the semicolon is always placed after *she said*, *he said*, etc., when the speech tag interrupts such a quotation.

f. When the dash is used to stand for an omitted part of a quotation, it is included within the quotation marks.

Occasionally a speaker is interrupted or for some reason fails to finish what he has begun to say. When this happens, a dash is used to show that the quotation is not finished.

"But Mary said—" she began, then stopped suddenly.

Nicholson said loudly, "In my opinion, our instructor is—" Just then the instructor walked into the room.

Notice that a concluding period is not used after the dash.

P 10   The Apostrophe

The apostrophe (') has three general uses:

a. To indicate the possessive case of nouns and some pronouns.

An apostrophe followed by *s* is added to the regular form of the following types of nouns:

Both singular and plural nouns which do not end in s:

boy's, girl's, ox's, mouse's, tooth's, antenna's
men's, women's, oxen's, mice's, teeth's, antennae's

Singular nouns ending in s:

James's, Charles's, Keats's, Burns's, Dickens's

Usage for this group varies. Some writers omit the final *s* (James', Charles', etc.). When a noun already contains two *s* sounds, there is a greater reluctance to add a third (Massachusetts', mistress', Jesus'), but since most written communications are not read aloud the repetition of *s* sounds is usually not so objectionable as it might seem to be. With such nouns, follow your own preference. Notice that an apostrophe without *s* is added to plural nouns already ending in *s*—*babies' clothing.*

Indefinite pronouns:

anybody's, anyone's, everybody's, one's, nobody's, someone's

b. To indicate the omission of letters or figures.

I've, can't, hasn't, isn't, '48 (1948), the class of '39

c. To indicate the plural of letters or figures.

Let's begin with the A's; look under the K's; the S's look like 8's.

P 11   Ellipsis and Dash

Ellipsis (. . .)

The basic use of the ellipsis (three periods) is to mark an omission.

Usually the ellipsis indicates that one or more words have been omitted from a quotation. It is also used to indicate that a progression of numbers continues beyond the last figure given (1,4,7,10,13,16 . . .). When an ellipsis occurs at the end of a sentence, a fourth period is used.

Original Quotation	Elliptical Quotation
Death is at all times solemn, but never so much as at sea. A man dies on shore, his body remains with his friends, and "the mourners go about the streets," but when a man falls overboard at sea and is lost, there is a sadness in the event, and a difficulty in realizing it, which gives it an air of awful mystery.	Death is at all times solemn, but never so much as at sea. A man dies on shore, his body remains with his friends, . . . but when a man falls overboard at sea and is lost, there is a sadness in the event, and a difficulty in realizing it. . . .

Dash

The dash should not be used as a general utility mark in place of a comma, period, semicolon, or colon. It is a specialized punctuation mark which serves the following purposes:

a. To stress a word or phrase at the end of a sentence.

In the whole world there is only one person he really admires—himself.

And now it is my pleasure to present a man whom we all know and admire and to whom we are all deeply indebted—the Reverend Dr. Mason.

Absence makes the heart grow fonder—of somebody else.

b. To set off a summary or conclusion to an involved sentence.

To live as free men in a free country; to enjoy, even to abuse, the right to think and speak as we like; to feel that the state is the servant of its people; to be, even in a literal sense, a trustee and a partner in the conduct of a nation —all this is what democracy means to us.

c. To mark an interrupted or unfinished construction.

"I'd like to," he said, "but I'm—"
"You're what?" I asked.
"Well, I'm—I—you see, I've never done anything like that before."

d. Used in pairs, dashes set off a pronounced interruption.

There will never again be—you may be sure of this—so glorious an opportunity.

This answer—if we can call it an answer—is completely meaningless.

P 12   Parentheses and Brackets

Parentheses

The three most common uses of parentheses are:

a. To enclose an explanation, qualification, or example.

His wife (he married about a year ago) is a member of a fine New England family.
I have never (except for that one time) expressed the fear of death.
Foreign words (*data*, for example) slowly become naturalized and lose their foreign characteristics.

b. To enclose cross-references.

(See Appendix A), (See page 271)

(Consult *Webster's Biographical Dictionary*.)

George Bellows transcribed the world of sports in vivid oil paintings like "Dempsey and Firpo" (see Plate VI).

c. In formal business transactions, to repeat a sum previously stated in words.

I enclose three hundred dollars ($300.00) to cover my share of the costs.

Brackets

Square brackets are used chiefly to enclose an editorial explanation or comment within a passage being edited or reported. The words within the brackets are supplied by the editor or reporter.

According to the Associated Press, Mrs. Henry Thall [the former June Wexler of this city] was a passenger on the missing plane.

I have written to [name of correspondent illegible] that I will not be a party to that transaction.

Brackets are occasionally used to enclose symbols which cannot conventionally be left without some enclosing device. The identification of the various punctuation marks on page 400 is an example of this use.

REVIEW
EXERCISES

A. *Rewrite the following sentences, inserting any needed punctuation. If no additional punctuation is necessary, do not copy the sentence. To make your insertions obvious, use red ink or red pencil for the punctuation which you add.*

1. White meat or dark she asked.
2. He studied it carefully. It should fly he finally said.
3. That he won't want to may very well be true.
4. He said he would go to the university next year.
5. He said I intend to go to the university next year.
6. I intend he said to go to the university next year.
7. This meaning see *The American Heritage Dictionary* is no longer questioned.
8. Dr. Koch a German scientist discovered the tuberculosis bacillus.
9. I am enclosing eighty-five dollars $85.00 for the first year's premium.
10. The cars in that series were as follows Nova Vega and Impala.
11. The manuscript was dirty blotched and unevenly typed.
12. She said When I asked his opinion he answered I don't give free advice.
13. See the revolutionary new car of the year the Ford.
14. I have not seen him since his wife left he has been keeping to himself.
15. Mr. Reynolds the insurance man called.

B. *Distinguish between restrictive and nonrestrictive modifiers by inserting commas around the nonrestrictive modifiers in the following sentences. Use red ink or red pencil for inserted commas.*

1. The girl who made the best record refused the prize.
2. The man in the back row was asked to leave.
3. The man obviously quite badly hurt was taken to the infirmary.
4. The Senator who was clearly temporizing would not admit that he had no solution.
5. The boy who was obviously hungry continued to shake his head.
6. Girls who want careers deserve all the encouragement they can get.
7. Helicopters which are less maneuverable than airplanes are less satisfactory for certain tactical assignments.

8. The man driving the Alfa Romeo is Clark.
9. Clark driving an Alfa Romeo won easily.
10. The cutter rapidly shipping water radioed for help.
11. The cutter which radioed for help no longer answers our signal.
12. Oliver still hungry after his porridge asked for more.
13. The Arabs satisfied with their gains fell silent.
14. Salesmen who don't argue with customers make more money.
15. Salesmen most of whom are young men lead unsettled lives.

C. *The best way to develop a confident knowledge of the conventions of punctuation is to observe how punctuation marks are actually used in modern writing. In the following selection particular punctuation marks have been numbered. Write down each number and describe the purpose for which the punctuation is being used.*

Turning to the more modern theories,[1] which agree at least that language is of human rather than divine origin,[1] we encounter first what is best known by its nickname,[2] the "bow-wow" theory. This asserts that primitive language was exclusively "echoic"; that is,[3] that its words were directly imitative of the sounds of nature or of animals. All the wordstock is thought to have originated in a way parallel to the child's calling a dog "bow-wow"[4] or a duck "quack-quack."[4] The great objection to this theory is that it has not been demonstrated that early or primitive languages are composed exclusively or in great part of onomatopoetic words; on the contrary,[5] it is clear that the primitive languages of savage tribes are largely made up of words that are quite as conventional as those of civilized peoples. At best,[6] the "bow-wow" theory can explain the origin of but a part,[7] and not the largest part,[7] of language. Yet it seems fair to add that the theory has in the past been somewhat unjustly derided. Words that are imitative or at least partly so—[8] for there are many gradations between the purely imitative and the purely conventional—[8] do form an appreciable part of the vocabulary of most languages. There are many words that we instinctively feel to be symbolic, or semi-echoic. Thus,[9] such English words as *battle*,[10] *roar*,[10] and *thunder* have not perhaps a completely imitative quality, certainly not as compared with *hiss*,[11] *whistle*,[11] *bang*,[11] and *crash*; yet they approach echoism in a way that the conventional words of language do not. If,[12] then,[12] the "bow-wow" theory does not solve the riddle of the origin of language, [13] it does at least help to account for the sounds of many words.*

   * From Stuart Robertson and Frederic G. Cassidy, *The Development of Modern English*, Second Edition. © 1954 by Prentice-Hall, Inc.

D. *In the following selection all punctuation has been omitted, except the periods at the ends of the sentences. Copy the selection, adding all necessary punctuation in red.*

The Bible is written in very poor English isnt it remarked a grade school child to his father as they walked home from church.

What makes you say that inquired the astonished parent for whose ears the musical dignity of the King James Version approached the perfection of English prose.

Well our teacher said it was bad English to begin sentences with and. But almost every sentence the minister read this morning began with and replied the child.

The father smiled as he recognized the accuracy of the childs observation. The reading had been from the eighth chapter of the Gospel according to St Matthew it was true enough that almost every sentence began with and. He thought a moment longer before he spoke. Your teacher has made a natural mistake he began. In trying to give good advice to boys and girls just learning to write she has made a rule about and. The rule is too big. People who know how to write well use and correctly and effectively at the beginning of sentences. On the other hand boys and girls in schools use and too much. Your teachers purpose in trying to help you was good but the rule she stated is untrue.

In this trifling episode may be found the epitome of the problem of correctness in English. It lies in the recurrent conflict between rule and practice. Rules of usage are usually made to cover specific situations to govern the use of language at a certain time for a certain purpose. Gradually as the rule is taught and applied the specific purpose for which it was created is forgotten and the rule is applied universally often in defiance of a language custom centuries old. Take for example the much taught but erroneous rule that a sentence must not end with a preposition. Or as one grammar is supposed to have stated it A preposition is a bad thing to end a sentence with. In certain types of formal literary English the terminal preposition is considered undesirable because of the rhetorical looseness it gives to the style. Because certain formalists disliked the construction the rule was created. It was repeated copied placed in school books. Teachers unaware of the reason behind the origin of the rule taught that a sentence must never end with a preposition. Teachers are still teaching this rule. Yet English for centuries has been idiomatically and correctly expressed in such sentences as Where are you from I didnt know whom to give it to. John will go but I dont expect to. What city has he lived in To apply the rule to such sentences as these which are characteristic of informal or colloquial English is to make an absurdity of a caution. Many such absurdities have been created and are being perpetuated through honest but misguided zeal.*

* From Robert C. Pooley, *Teaching English Usage.* Copyright, 1946, by the National Council of Teachers of English. Reprinted by permission of Appleton-Century-Crofts, Inc.

Mechanics

sp Spelling

If you have trouble with spelling, the first step toward improvement is to take an inventory of your errors. Keep a written record in a notebook of the words *which you actually misspell in your writing*. This is your basic list. It should be reviewed periodically and kept up to date by crossing out those words you have mastered and by adding new ones which you have misspelled.

When you study your list, concentrate on the *part* of the word which you have misspelled. Generally we do not misspell words but syllables. For example, most students who misspell *secretary* interchange the second and third vowels; most misspellings of *tragedy* come from placing an extra *d* before the *g;* and misspellings of such words as *receive, belief,* and *friend* come from reversing the *i* and *e*. Identifying your specific errors allows you to concentrate on the syllable in which the error occurs.

For words which prove unusually troublesome it often helps to learn or invent some memorizing device: a rule, a slogan, a jingle—anything, no matter how absurd, which will remind you of the correct spelling of a particular syllable. The rule of *i* before *e* except after *c,* which is stated as a jingle on page 425, and the rules for prefixes and suffixes, are generally useful memorizing devices. Unfortunately some rules have so many exceptions that they are hardly worth learning. It is therefore often wise to invent your own memorizing device. Some students find it helpful to remember statements like *A good secretary keeps a secret, Remember the gum in argument,* and *Every cemetery has a "meter" in the middle*. Other students are helped by capitalizing the danger spots when they practice—tRAGedy, mainTENance, desPERate. If these devices help you, use them; if not, invent your own.

Finally, so far as possible, don't worry about spelling while writing the first drafts of your papers. Wait until revision. If you break off writing a paragraph to use the dictionary, you may lose a thought you cannot recapture. If you keep a record of your misspellings, you will remember your troublesome words, so that when you are unsure of a spelling, you can put a check in the margin and go on. Then, when the first draft is finished, you can look up the spellings of all the words you have checked. Indeed, a student with severe spelling troubles should proofread his whole paper at least once for spelling alone.

In short, then: (1) Keep a spelling record, (2) study it at regular intervals, (3) identify the trouble spot in the word, (4) figure out a way to remember the correct spelling, and (5) check your spelling when you proofread. If you follow this procedure conscientiously, spelling will soon cease to be a major problem.

The Most Common Traps in Spelling

Although any word which is not spelled the way it sounds may give trouble, six types of words are especially likely to cause errors. These are:

1. Words containing a "colorless" vowel. A vowel in an unstressed position (*a*go, ag*e*nt, awkw*a*rd, maint*e*nance, incred*i*ble, bachel*o*r) is likely to be pronounced as a very weak *uh*. This sound is called the colorless or neutral vowel.[1] Because it is quite common in English and because its sound gives no indication of its spelling, the colorless vowel is responsible for many spelling errors. There is nothing to guide you in spelling this sound. The only solution is to memorize the vowel in any word which repeatedly causes trouble. The best help is a memorizing device, such as magnifying the syllable in question—*baLANCE, indepenDENT, eligIBLE, sponSOR, foREIGN, chauffEUR.*

2. Words with ie *or* ei. Words like *niece, receive,* and *friend* are frequently misspelled through the interchanging of the *e* and the *i.* Most of these errors may be easily removed by following Rule 4 on page 425 and memorizing the eleven exceptions.

3. Words with similar sounds but different meanings. Such words as *altar, alter; peace, piece; weak, week; weather, whether* are easily confused. A list of troublesome contrasted pairs is given on page 427. You should study that list and copy into your personal spelling record any pairs which you tend to confuse.

4. Words with irregular plural forms. Since most English nouns take *s* plurals, all plurals formed in any other way may be considered irregular.

---

[1] Most dictionaries represent the colorless vowel by the phonetic symbol called the *schwa,* and written ə, like an inverted e.

The most troublesome plurals to spell are those of nouns ending in *o* or *y*. Such nouns have regular *s* plurals when the *o* or *y* immediately follows a vowel (*cameo, cameos; key, keys; studio, studios*), but are generally irregular when the *o* or *y* follows a consonant (*cargo, veto, lady, torpedo*). See Rules 6 and 7 on pages 425–26.

5. Words which double the final consonant before a suffix beginning with a vowel.   Some words double a final consonant before adding a suffix beginning with a vowel (*refer, referred*), while others (*benefit, benefited*) do not. This inconsistency causes many spelling errors, and the "rule" is so cumbersome and has so many exceptions that students often prefer to study the individual words which cause them trouble. The more useful part of the rule concerning doubled consonants is given as Rule 9 on page 426.

6. Common exceptions to general rules.   Any exceptional spelling is likely to be difficult because of the tendency to make it conform to the regular pattern. For example, a student who is not sure how to spell *seize* is likely to interchange the *e* and *i* because of the *i*-before-*e* rule. Similarly the rule that a silent *e* at the end of a word is retained in adding a suffix beginning with a consonant leads many students to misspell *argument*. Words like these are exceptions to general rules and cause many spelling errors. The only safe procedure is to *memorize the exceptions along with the rule.* Whenever a rule is given in the following pages, the common exceptions are also noted. Study these as carefully as you study the rule itself.

Rules of Spelling   The rules given here are those which are most generally useful.

1. The prefixes *un-, dis-, mis-* **do not affect the spelling of the root.**

Thus, *unafraid* but *unnecessary; disappoint* but *dissatisfy; misrepresent* but *misspell.*

unable	disable	misbehave
unknown	disorder	misconduct
unopened	disregard	misguided
but	*but*	*but*
unnatural	disservice	misshapen
unnerved	dissimilar	misspent
unnoticed	dissolve	misstatement

2. When a suffix beginning with a consonant is added to a word ending in silent e**, the** e **is retained.**

Examples: *absolutely, achievement, extremely, indefinitely, sincerely.*

Exceptions: *argument, awful, duly, ninth, probably, truly, wholly.*

Three common words have alternative spellings: *abridgment, abridgement; acknowledgment, acknowledgement; judgment, judgement.*

3. When a suffix beginning with a vowel is added to a word ending in silent *e*, the *e* is dropped unless it is required to indicate pronunciation or to avoid confusion with a similar word.

Examples: *accumulating, achieving, boring, coming, grievance, icy*

Exceptions:

To Keep a c or g Soft	To Prevent Mispronunciation
advantageous	canoeist
changeable	eyeing
courageous	hoeing
manageable	mileage
noticeable	shoeing
outrageous	
peaceable	
serviceable	*To Prevent Confusion with Other Words*
singeing	
tingeing	dyeing
vengeance	

4. The order of the vowels in the *ie* combination (*ceiling, niece*) is explained in the jingle:

Write *i* before *e*
Except after *c*
Or when sounded like *ay*
As in *neighbor* and *weigh.*

Exceptions: *counterfeit, either, foreign, forfeit, height, leisure, neither, seize, seizure, sovereign, weird.*

5. Words ending with the sound *seed* are usually spelled -cede.

Examples: *accede, concede, intercede, precede, recede, secede.*

Exceptions: There are only four exceptions. Three of them end in -*ceed* (*exceed, proceed, succeed*); the fourth is the only word that ends in -*sede* (*supersede*).

6. Singular nouns ending in a consonant plus *y* form their plurals by changing the *y* to *i* before adding -*es*.

This rule also applies to the third person singular of verbs.

Examples: *ally, allies; baby, babies; city, cities; cry, cries; try, tries.*

Exceptions: The plurals of proper names often add *s* immediately after the *y:* *the Kellys, the Marys, the Sallys.*

Notice that singular nouns ending in a vowel plus *y* are regular and simply add *-s* to form the plural: *attorneys, donkeys, valleys.*

7. Singular nouns ending in a consonant plus o generally form their plurals by adding -es.

There are, however, so many exceptions that it may be safer to dispense with the rule and learn troublesome words individually.

Examples: *buffaloes, cargoes, echoes, heroes, potatoes, torpedoes, vetoes.*

Exceptions: The chief exceptions are musical terms: *altos, bassos, oratorios, pianos, solos, sopranos.* Others are *autos, cantos, dynamos, Eskimos, halos, mementos, provisos, quartos.*

Notice that singular nouns ending in a vowel plus *o* are regular and simply add *-s* to form the plural: *cameos, folios, radios, studios.*

8. Most singular nouns ending in -s, -ss, -sh, -ch, -x, or -z, form their plurals by adding -es.

Examples: *Jameses, Joneses, ashes, bushes, matches, pitches, foxes, taxes, buzzes.*

Exceptions: *bass, fish, perch, Swiss,* and borrowed Greek nouns ending in *-is* (*ellipsis—ellipses, thesis—theses,* etc.).

9. Words of one syllable double the final consonant before adding a suffix beginning with a vowel if (1) they end in a single consonant, and (2) they contain a single vowel.

Notice that the rule holds only if both conditions are satisfied. Thus a word of one syllable ending in two consonants does not double the final consonant before a suffix beginning with a vowel (*acting, asked, parting, sifted,* etc.). And a one-syllable word containing two vowels does not double the final consonant (*bearing, creeping, dealing, reeling, soaring,* etc.).

This rule is extended to words of more than one syllable, provided that the accent falls on the last syllable (thus prefér—preferred, but bénefit—benefited; confér—conferring, but cónference). This part of the rule, however, has so many exceptions that the rule may be more confusing than helpful.

**REVIEW
EXERCISES**

A. *Errors in the following words may be classified as errors in spelling or errors in diction, since both meaning and spelling are involved in their correct use. Study these words carefully. Check those which you have confused in the past, or which you are uncertain of, and look them up in your dictionary.*

accept, except	its, it's
access, excess	knew, new
adapt, adopt	know, no
adaptation, adoption	later, latter
affect, effect	lead, led
all together, altogether	loath, loathe
altar, alter	loose, lose
angel, angle	luxuriant, luxurious
berth, birth	moral, morale
born, borne	past, passed
canvas, canvass	peace, piece
capital, capitol	plain, plane
censor, censure	precede, proceed
cite, sight, site	presence, presents
coarse, course	principal, principle
complement, compliment	prophecy, prophesy
conscience, conscious	quiet, quite
council, counsel	respectively, respectfully
dairy, diary	right, rite
decent, descend, descent	shone, shown
desert, dessert	sleight, slight
dining, dinning	speak, speech
dying, dyeing	staid, stayed
elicit, illicit	stationary, stationery
emigrant, immigrant	straight, strait
euphemism, euphuism	suit, suite
fare, fair	threw, through
formally, formerly	to, too, two
forth, fourth	troop, troupe
hear, here	vain, vein, vane
holy, wholly	weak, week
instance, instants	weather, whether
irrelevant, irreverent	who's, whose

B. *Some of the following words form their plurals by adding -s to the singular form, some by adding -es. Write out the plurals which take -es:*

alto, analysis, auto, ditch, dynamo, echo, Eskimo, fox, hero, piano, radio, solo, synopsis, tobacco, tomato, veto

C. *Write the plural forms of the following nouns:*

alley, alumna, alumnus, attorney, axis, baby, basis, belief, category, crisis, half, key, lady, loaf, ox, quantity, study, tax, taxi, try, 5, 7, A

D. *Write the simple past tense form of the following verbs:*

act, annul, benefit, confer, crop, defer, develop, drip, drop, equip, excel, gas, kidnap, occur, propel, quiz, reap, rebel, refer, regret, rip, rob, scar, slip, stop, strap, worship, wrap

abr Abbreviations

In general, abbreviations should satisfy two conditions: they must be standard abbreviations recognized by dictionaries, and they must be appropriate to the context. The first condition rules out such slang abbreviations as *b.f.* (boy friend) and *n.g.* (no good). The second implies that many standard abbreviations (*advt., Ave., Feb., Xmas*) are inappropriate in most student essays and that abbreviations of certain titles (*Col., Dr., Mr., Rev.*) are used only when followed by the name of the person to whom the title applies.

The following is a summary of the most common standard abbreviations. For the correct form of abbreviations not included in this list, consult your dictionary.

Bibliographical terms: *cf., ibid., vol., pp.*

Names of days: *Sun., Mon., Tues., Wed., Thurs., Fri., Sat.* (Used only in dates.)

Names of months: *Jan., Feb., Aug., Sept., Oct., Nov., Dec.* (Used only in dates.)

Names of organizations: *A.F.L., D.A.R., U.S. Steel, A.A.A.S.;* but *SDS*

Names of government agencies: *AAA, CIA, FBI, SEC, TVA.* (Notice that abbreviations of government agencies generally do not require periods.)

Names of states: *Calif., Del., Mass., N.Y., Ill.* (Used chiefly in addresses.)

Signs: When the context permits, the following signs are used as abbreviations: & (ampersand: see Glossary), $ (dollar), £ (British pound sterling), % (per cent), " " (ditto marks, used in tabulations to repeat the item immediately above the marks).

caps Use of Capital Letters

a. Capitalize the first word of each sentence and of each line of regular poetry.

Ask for Mr. Lane. He is in charge of services.
Too bad! Better luck next time.

> Earth has not anything to show more fair;
> Dull would he be of soul who could pass by
> A sight so touching in its majesty: . . .
> —Wordsworth, "Composed Upon Westminster Bridge"

b. Capitalize the first word of a direct quotation.

The President's answer was, "No comment."
"If you will give me a receipt," I said, "you can have the money now."

c. Capitalize proper nouns.

Sergeant York was one of the great heroes of World War I.
She works for the National Broadcasting Company.
Laurence Olivier was knighted after his production of *Henry V.*
I find French easier than German.
The battleship *Texas* is on display at Houston.
The Amazon is longer than the Mississippi.

NOTE: Words which were originally proper nouns but have taken on more general meanings are regarded as common nouns and are not capitalized: *boycott, calico, china* (dishes), *port* (wine), *tweed.*

d. Capitalize adjectives formed from proper nouns.

They seem to be ignorant of the *American* point of view.
There is a *Miltonic* quality in this verse.
The *Renaissance* period was Italy's second hour of glory.
The inductive method has been called the *Baconian* method.
He is studying the *Pauline* doctrines.

NOTE: Words originally derived from proper nouns cease to be capitalized when they are used as allusions rather than as direct references to the original noun. For example, *colossus, draconian, herculean, meandering,* and *panic* do not take capitals. *Philippic* is capitalized when it refers directly to the orations made by Demosthenes, but not when it is used to describe some other denunciatory speech.

e. Capitalize nouns or pronouns referring to the deity:

God, Lord, our Father, Saviour, Messiah, Trinity, Holy Ghost, He, His, Him.

f. Capitalize names of offices only when they are used as titles.[1]

Capitalized	Not Capitalized
District Attorney Johnson	Tell it to the district attorney.
Prime Minister Heath	Wilson is a former prime minister.
Dr. A. L. Street, Chairman of the Civic Betterment Committee	He was made chairman of the committee.
Professor Swanson	He is a college professor.

NOTE: *President, Presidential,* and *Presidency* are capitalized when they refer to the office of President of the United States: *One of these men will be our next President; the Presidency is at stake.*

g. Capitalize *north, south, east,* and *west* and their derivatives only when they refer to geographical areas.

Capitalized	Not Capitalized
We found the South charming.	Next year we are going south.
Her parents live in the East.	New York is east of Chicago.
They live on the West Side.	The west side of the field is wet.
The Southern armies fought gallantly.	The house has a fine southern exposure.

h. Capitalize titles of books, magazines, plays and the headings of chapters or sections of a work.

The general practice is to capitalize all significant words in a title, including the first word:

A Child's History of the United States
The Return of the Native
Mourning Becomes Electra

Some publishers capitalize every word in the title:

A Child's History Of The United States

Either form is acceptable, but be consistent.

---

[1] The convention stated here is a simplification of actual practice. The usage of newspapers varies: some capitalize important offices when they are not used as titles; others omit capitals even in titles.

i. Capitalize the names of days of the week, months, and holidays.

New Year's Day will fall on Tuesday.
Next Sunday is Mother's Day.
The favorite vacation months are July and August.

j. Avoid unnecessary capitalization.

In general, do not use capitals unless they are required by one of the conventions stated above. The modern tendency is to use capitals sparingly. Especially avoid unnecessary capitalization of the names of the seasons, of family relationships (*father, mother, sister, uncle*), and of such words as *army, college, freshman, navy, sophomore, university,* unless they are being considered as proper nouns.

Capitalized	Not Capitalized
He is a captain in the Army of the United States.	In foreign affairs an army is a political instrument.
Whom do you pick in the Army-Navy game, General?	The general said we must have an army and a navy second to none.
Uncle Bill and Aunt Martha are here.	All the uncles and aunts were present.
Where is Sanford Community College?	He wants a college education.
The University will have a strong team next year.	He is a university professor.
Are you going to the Freshman Mixer?	Are you a freshman or a sophomore?
The Summer Festival starts next week.	I like summer best and winter least.
He belonged to The Society for the Prevention of Cruelty to Animals.	He belonged to a society for the prevention of cruelty to animals.

hyph   Hyphenation

Hyphens are used for two purposes: to divide a word at the end of a line, and to join two or more words of a compound which is not written solid.

a. Use a hyphen to break a word at the end of a line.

This use of the hyphen is less frequently necessary in typed or handwritten copy than it is in print. In student writing, words should be broken at the ends of lines only when failure to hyphenate would result in noticeably awkward spacing. If hyphenation seems necessary, the following conditions should be observed.

1. Do not break words of one syllable.

If there is not room at the end of a line for a word such as *burst, change, drink, through,* carry the whole word over to the next line.

2. Do not separate a suffix of less than three letters from the rest of the word, or break on a one-letter prefix.

An *-ing* may be separated, but single letters or *-al, -le, -ly,* and *-ed* endings should not. Words like *about, against,* and *open* should not be broken.

3. Break words only between syllables.

When in doubt about syllabication, consult your dictionary.

4. Break compound words between the elements of the compound.

Compound Word	Hyphenation
armchair	arm-chair
blackbird	black-bird
sailboat	sail-boat

5. Subject to the limitations stated in (2), hyphenate between prefix and root or between root and suffix.

Between Prefix and Root	Between Root and Suffix
ante-cedent	adapt-able
be-loved	back-ward
com-mit	depend-ent
con-tagious	ego-ism
dis-appear	kitchen-ette
inter-rupt	lemon-ade
intro-duce	mile-age
per-suade	racket-eer
trans-late	trouble-some

b. Use a hyphen between elements of a compound when usage calls for it.

Hyphenation of compounds varies so much that (1) for any particular word, the only safe authority is a reliable, up-to-date dictionary, and (2) whenever usage is uncertain, a writer is allowed a choice between competing usages.

Some compounds (*applesauce, blackboard, steamship*) are written solid; others (*dirt cheap, place kick, wedding ring*) are nearly always written as separate words; still others (*father-in-law, ready-made, up-to-date*) are hyphenated. A hyphen is required in the following types.

1. Hyphenate a compound modifier preceding a noun.

A self-made man   An off-the-cuff judgment
A well-dressed woman   A tear-jerking film
A pay-as-you-go tax   A Sunday-morning golf game
A round-by-round report   A dog-in-the-manger attitude

Compound numerical modifiers fall into this class: *Twenty-seven dollars, one hundred and twenty-five pounds, a two-thirds majority.* However, whole numbers below twenty-one, because they are single words, are not hyphenated: *Their nineteenth anniversary; the sixteenth of May.* Notice also that a compound modifier following a noun is usually not hyphenated: *The woman was well dressed; the machine is worn out.*

2. Hyphenate a compound consisting of a prefix and a proper noun.

pro-Russian, un-American, anti-Castro.

3. Hyphenate compounds of ex **("former") and a noun.**

ex-wife, ex-sweetheart, ex-President.

4. Hyphenate to avoid confusion with another word.

re-cover to prevent confusion with *recover*.
re-creation to prevent confusion with *recreation*.

5. Hyphenate most compounds beginning with *self.*

self-satisfied, self-government, self-conceit. (But *selfless* and *selfsame* are written solid.)

ital   Use of Italics

Words in print are made to stand out by using a special kind of slanting type called *italic;* they are similarly set off in manuscript by underlining. Italics or underlining is used for the following purposes:

a. To indicate that a word is still considered a foreign element in the language.

en rapport, in absentia.

b. To mark titles of publications, movie and stage productions, musical compositions, etc., and the names of airplanes, ships, and trains.

Mencken's *The American Language*
the *Saturday Review*
Beethoven's *Eroica*
Da Vinci's *Last Supper*
Lindbergh's *Spirit of Saint Louis*
the French liner, the *France*

c. To call attention to a word being named. (See also page 414.)

The word *judgment* has two spellings.
What does *discriminate* mean?
A good example is the phrase *to go scot free.*

d. To emphasize a word.

Not *Angles* but *angels.*
That is *precisely* the point.

This last device should be used sparingly. Overused, it becomes a poor substitute for emphatic diction.

no   Forms of Numbers

Whether numbers should be written in words or figures depends partly on the nature of the writing. In scientific, statistical, and technical writing, figures are used whenever possible. In essays and literary publications, numbers are more frequently written out, and the more formal the style, the less figures are used.

a. Figures are used in writing dates, hours, and street numbers.

January 22, 1967	5:00 A.M.	17 Main Street
January 1	6:15 P.M.	417 Fifth Avenue
the year 1860	0430 (military style)	1021 Third Street

Notice that figures are used for street numbers but that street names, even when they are numbers, are usually written out and capitalized to avoid confusion with other numbers.

b. Figures are used in recording sums of money other than round sums.

$2.75; 98 cents; *but* a hundred dollars; thirty cents.

If the style is informal, even round sums may be expressed as figures.

$40 million; 100 dollars; 30 cents; 40,000 spectators.

c. Use figures for large numbers that would be awkward to write out.

365 days; 1760 yards; 14,320 students.

d. Use figures in citing volume, chapter, and page references.

This whole question is discussed in Volume 2 of Brand's work.
Our topic is discussed in Chapter 5; turn to page 37.

e. Do not use figures at the beginning of a sentence.

Sixty per cent is a passing grade. *Not:* 60% is a passing grade.

f. Generally avoid figures when a number can be conveniently expressed in one word.

one, five, third, quarter, twelve.

But in an informal style and in scientific writing, numbers over ten are frequently expressed in figures.

g. Do not use figures in a formal invitation or reply.

on Saturday the twenty-third of June
at seven o'clock in the evening

This most formal usage is an exception to the practice recommended in **a** above.

h. Roman numerals are used chiefly as volume and chapter numbers in some books and as page numbers in the front matter of books.

Because Roman numerals are so little used, they can be confusing. Most of this confusion can be eliminated if you recognize the key numerals and understand the principle by which they are combined.

The key numerals are i (1), v (5), x (10), l (50), c (100), d (500), m (1000), which may be written in capitals: I, V, X, L, C, D, M. The basic principle is that the higher number is created by adding another unit to a lower number—i, ii, iii, vi, xi—or by subtracting a unit from a higher number— iv, ix, xl, xc.

	Units	Tens	Hundreds
1	i	x	c
2	ii	xx	cc
3	iii	xxx	ccc
4	iv	xl	cd
5	v	l	d
6	vi	lx	dc
7	vii	lxx	dcc
8	viii	lxxx	dccc
9	ix	xc	cm

A. *Rewrite the following sentences to substitute abbreviations and figures where permissible in college composition.*

1. Have you seen the new professor? He has a Doctor of Philosophy degree from Cornell.
2. Mister Thompson is not here, but you can telephone him at three-nine-seven-five-seven-five-two.
3. My sister graduated from the University of Illinois with a Bachelor of Arts degree in June nineteen hundred and sixty-eight.
4. She was married on the twentieth of January, nineteen hundred and sixty-nine.
5. Her husband is Doctor Robert Reid, a consulting psychologist with the Society for the Prevention of Cruelty to Children.
6. Look on page one thousand four hundred and seventy.
7. He was born on January thirty-one at five minutes after eleven post meridiem.
8. The date of the battle of Hastings is anno Domini 1066.
9. Send this letter to Colonel Donald Andrews, care of the Thirty-third Division at Fort Sam Houston.
10. Fifty-four people were hurt in the wreck, including three top executives of the Columbia Broadcasting System.

B. *Rewrite the following sentences to remove any abbreviations or figures which would be undesirable in college composition.*

1. The speaker was a prof. from the U. of Michigan.
2. I saw her downtown this A.M.
3. 10 days later, the man died.
4. The candidate spoke as often as 8 times in a single day.
5. Somebody said to me, "Mr., this man needs a Dr."
6. The party consisted of Brig. Gen. T. A. Smith, a Col., and two Lt. Cols.
7. The math exam will be held in Rm. 511 at 2:00 P.M.
8. He paid $20; he could have bought a good second-hand one for $5.
9. I saw the Rev. just yesterday.
10. Miss Walsh requests the pleasure of your company on Sat., Sept. 23, at 7:30 P.M.

C. *In the following sentences, change lower case letters to capitals wherever the conventions require such a change.*

1. She asked, "what makes it spin?"
2. it is one of the best of the swedish films.

3. Some of his activities are alleged to be unamerican.
4. The words are, "our father which art in heaven, hallowed be thy name."
5. The greeks called their chief god *zeus;* the romans called him *jupiter.*
6. The king James bible is called the authorized version. It was translated by a committee of biblical scholars.
7. The title is *20,000 leagues under the sea.*
8. F. D. Roosevelt is the only president who won the presidency four times.
9. What did you get your mother for mother's day?
10. The bowl games are played chiefly in the west and south. The winter weather in the north and east is not suitable for post-season football.

D. *In the following sentences remove unnecessary capitalization.*

---

1. He is a Four-Star General in the U.S. Army.
2. If you are not in a hurry, leave the State highways and explore the byways.
3. This course is required for all Freshmen. Sophomores who are transfers from another University may also be required to take it.
4. My Father wants me to be a University Professor, but I prefer a better-paying Profession.
5. Spring may be the most beautiful Season, but I prefer Fall.
6. Go East for three blocks and then turn North.
7. It will soon be time for the birds to start their Southern migrations.
8. Her Uncle is a Rear Admiral in the Navy and an authority on Naval strategy.
9. He studied for the Ministry before going to Law School.
10. "I will do it," She said, "If you will help me."

Glossary

This is a reference section. Its main purpose is to list those words and constructions which frequently cause trouble in composition and to advise you whether particular usages are acceptable in college writing and, if they are, under what conditions. A secondary purpose is to explain some grammatical and rhetorical terms not discussed elsewhere in the text. Since this book has a separate index giving page references for all subjects discussed in the text, the Glossary usually does not duplicate these references.

The judgments about usage recorded here have been made after consulting the following sources: *The American Heritage Dictionary of the English Language, The Shorter Oxford English Dictionary, Webster's Third New International Dictionary, Webster's New World Dictionary* (Second College Edition), Theodore M. Bernstein's *The Careful Writer,* Margaret M. Bryant's *Current American Usage,* Bergen and Cornelia Evans's *A Dictionary of Contemporary American Usage,* and H. W. Fowler's *A Dictionary of Modern English* (Second Edition); but because these sources do not always agree, the judgments made here are the author's conclusions.

Since dictionaries do not always distinguish between formal and informal standard usage,[1] it has seemed wise to indicate whether particular usages would be more appropriate to a formal than to an informal style, and whether certain expressions would be generally acceptable in college writing. The usefulness of this advice, however, depends on your understanding its limitations. In any choice of usage, the decision depends less on what dictionaries or textbooks say than on what is consistent with the purpose and style of the writing. The student and his instructor are the best judges of that question. All that this Glossary can do is report what is generally acceptable. You yourself must decide whether a specific usage is appropriate in the particular paper which you are writing. The general

---

[1] *Webster's Third New International Dictionary* and a number of other dictionaries have dropped the usage label "Colloquial" and no longer so identify usages which are more appropriate in conversation than in writing. The label "Informal," however, is in general use.

assumption in the Glossary is that college writing is predominantly informal rather than either colloquial or formal. That assumption implies that the classification of a usage as *informal* in no way suggests that it is less desirable than a *formal* usage.

absolute   An element in a sentence which has no specific grammatical relationship to any other, yet clearly belongs.

Nonsense, it is all a hoax!
Good heavens, is it that late?
Mr. Hughes, may I talk to you for a moment?
No, I won't do it.
She said—*as if I cared*—that she was through with me.

access — excess   The second syllable of both words comes from a Latin root meaning "to go." Etymologically, *access* means "a going toward," hence "approach" or "admission" [The auditor has access to the records]. *Excess* originally meant "going out or beyond," hence its present meaning of "beyond what is necessary or desirable" [He worries to excess; a tax on excess profits].

accusative case   In modern English, the objective case.

acronym   An abbreviation which is pronounced as a word and is made up of the first letters of the title or phrase being abbreviated [CORE (Congress of Racial Equality); snafu (situation normal, all fouled up)].

ad   Clipped form of *advertisement*. Appropriate in informal styles, but the full form, *advertisement,* is preferred in formal writing, especially in letters applying for a position.

A.D.   Abbreviation for Latin *Anno Domini* (in the year of our Lord). Opposite of B.C. (before Christ). Used to distinguish dates before and after the beginning of the Christian era [He lived from 31 B.C. to A.D. 12; from 100 B.C. to A.D. 100 is 200 years]. A.D. is properly written before the figure; B.C., after it.

adapt — adept — adopt   *Adapt* means "adjust to meet requirements" [The human body can adapt itself to all sorts of environments]. *Adept* means "skilled" or "proficient" [He is adept at various sports]. *Adopt* means "to take as one's own" [He immediately adopted the idea] or—in parliamentary procedure—"to accept as a law" [The motion was adopted].

adjectives and adverbs   Adjectives and adverbs can often but not always be distinguished by their forms as well as their functions. Most adverbs end in *-ly*, but so do a few adjectives (*silly, lively, manly*). A few (*clean, far, fast, straight,* etc.) do not have *-ly* endings, and some have two forms (*late–lately, loud–loudly, slow–slowly,* etc.). Adjectives and adverbs are best recognized by their function in a sentence: adjectives modify nouns or pronouns; adverbs modify verbs, adjectives, or other adverbs. See **comparison; modifier.**

advice — advise   The first form is a noun, the second a verb [I was advised to ignore your advice].

affect — effect   Words often confused because of similarity of sound. Both may be used as nouns, but *effect,* meaning "result," is almost invariably the word wanted [His speech had an unfortunate effect; the treatments had no effect on me]. The noun *affect* is a technical term in psychology. Though both words may be used as verbs, *affect* is the more common. As a verb, *affect* means "impress," "influence," or "disturb" [His advice affected my decision; does music affect you that way?]. As a verb, *effect* is rarely required in student writing, but may be used to mean "carry out" or "accomplish" [The aviator effected his mission; the lawyer effected a settlement]. For students who have chronic difficulty with these words, a useful rule is to use *affect* only as a verb, and *effect* only as a noun.

affective — effective   See **affect—effect.**   The common adjective is *effective* [an effective argument], meaning "having an effect." The use of *affective* is largely confined to technical discussions of psychology and semantics, in which it is roughly equivalent to "emotional."

aggravate   Distinguish between the formal meaning, "to make worse" [His remarks aggravated the dispute], and the informal meaning, "to annoy or exasperate" [Her manners aggravate me]. Dictionaries classify the second meaning as colloquial. It is appropriate in very informal writing, but in some contexts *exasperate, irritate, annoy,* or *provoke* will be more precise.

ain't   Unless a student is attempting to record nonstandard speech, the use of *ain't* is not acceptable in college speech or writing.

alibi   In formal English the word is a legal term used to indicate that a defendant was *elsewhere* when the crime was committed. Colloquially *alibi* is used to mean excuse [I'm not worried about being late, I have a good alibi]. This usage is common in informal writing.

all the farther, further, quicker   Colloquial in some areas but generally unacceptable in college writing. Use "as far as," "as quick as."

all together — altogether   Distinguish between the phrase [They were all together at last] and the adverb [He is altogether to blame]. *All together* means "all in one place"; *altogether* means "entirely" or "wholly."

alliteration   Repetition of the same consonant, especially an initial consonant, in several words within the same sentence or line of poetry [The *m*urmuring of *imm*emorial el*m*s; *T*ippecanoe and *T*yler *t*oo]. Alliteration is a common device in poetry and in slogans, but it should be used with restraint in ordinary prose since its overuse or inappropriate use may seem affected.

allow   When used to mean "permit" [No smoking allowed on the premises] *allow* is acceptable. Its use to mean "think" [He allowed it could be done] is nonstandard and is not acceptable in college writing.

allude — elude — refer   When we *allude* to something we make an indirect or casual reference to it [He never actually identified himself as an officer, but he frequently alluded to details of army life as though he knew what it was to command troops in the field]. *Elude* means "to escape or avoid detection" [By these means he eluded the police for years]. *Refer* means "to direct attention" to something [The instructor referred us to the *Oxford Dictionary*].

allusion — illusion   Words sometimes confused because of similarity of sound. An *allusion* is a reference [The poem contains several allusions to Greek mythology]. An *illusion* is an erroneous mental image [Rouge on pallid skin gives an illusion of health].

alot   Although *a lot* is idiomatic and is appropriate in informal writing, it must be written as two words.

alright An established variant spelling of *all right,* but there is still considerable objection to it. *All right* is the preferred spelling.

altho Now accepted as a variant spelling of *although,* but the longer form is preferred.

A.M., P.M., a.m., p.m. Abbreviations for the Latin phrases *ante meridiem* (before noon), *post meridiem* (after noon). A.M. is used to indicate the period from midnight to noon; P.M., from noon to midnight. These abbreviations are used only when a specific hour is named [The first watch on a ship is from 12 P.M. to 4 A.M.]. The use of these abbreviations to stand for *morning* and *afternoon* when no hour is named [He gets up late in the a.m. and goes back to bed early in the p.m.] is a slang use not acceptable in college writing. Notice that either capital or small letters may be used in these abbreviations.

amount — number The occasional confusion of these words in college writing creates awkwardness. *Amount* suggests bulk or weight. [We collected a considerable amount of scrap iron]. *Number* is used for groups, the individual members of which may be counted [He has a large number of friends; there is a number of letters to be answered].

ampersand The sign &, an abbreviation for *and,* is used in some company names [G. & C. Merriam Co.] and in various types of notations. Except in statistical tabulation it is not acceptable in college writing.

an Variant of indefinite article *a.* Used instead of *a* when the following word begins with a vowel sound [an apple, an easy victory, an honest opinion, an hour]. When the following word begins with a consonant sound, or with *y, u,* or a pronounced *h,* the article should be *a* [a yell, a unit, a history, a house]. Such constructions as *a apple, a hour* are nonstandard. The use of *an* before *historical* and *humble* is an older usage which is dying out.

angle The use of *angle* to mean "point of view" [Let's look at it from a new angle] is acceptable, but the word is so overused in college writing—and so often used inaccurately—that many instructors object to it. Use it sparingly.

antonym A word opposite in meaning to a given word. Thus, *love* is the antonym for *hate.*

anybody's else An old form of *anybody else's.* It is no longer conventional.

anywheres A nonstandard variant of *anywhere.*

apposition In grammar, two constructions are in apposition when the second follows and identifies the first, as in "Mr. Botts, *the chemistry instructor,* has resigned." Most frequently the appositive is treated as a nonrestrictive modifier (see pages 405–06) and is therefore set off by commas, as above. When, however, the appositive word or phrase is felt to be so closely related to the construction with which it is in apposition that the two cannot be separated, it is treated as a restrictive modifier and written without commas [*Secretary of State* Rogers].

apt See **liable.**

Arabic numerals The numbers 1, 2, 3, etc., as contrasted with Roman numerals [I, II, III; i, ii, iii].

around The uses of *around* to mean "about" [He arrived around four o'clock], "near" [That is how they pronounce it around Brooklyn], and "throughout" [We traveled around the country] are colloquial. They are generally acceptable in college writing.

as . . . as The use of *as . . . as* in a negative statement [I am not as old as she is] is sometimes censured on the assumption that this construction should be used only for affirmative statements and that the correct negative form is "not *so* old as." In a very formal style the "not so . . . as" form may be preferable; but both forms are educated usage, and either is appropriate in college writing. In an affirmative statement, use *as . . . as*.

as = because Although it is accepted standard English, *as* is weaker than *because* to show causal relation between main and subordinate clauses. Since *as* has other meanings, it may in certain contexts be confusing [As I was going home, I decided to telephone]. Here *as* may mean *when* or *because*. If there is any possibility of confusion, it is wise to use *because* or *while*—whichever is appropriate to the meaning.

as = that The use of *as* to introduce a noun clause [I don't know as I would agree to that] is colloquial. This usage would be hopelessly inappropriate at a formal level and would be rejected by most college instructors at an informal level. Unless you are deliberately aiming at a colloquial style, use *that*.

as if = as though Synonymous constructions. The first is slightly less formal, but either is appropriate in college writing.

as to = with respect to Although *as to* is unquestionably standard usage, many instructors object to it on the ground that it is jargon (see page 150). Certainly its overuse should be avoided, and in an informal style *about* would be more appropriate than either *as to* or *with respect to*. For example, "I am not concerned as to your father's reaction" sounds stilted. It would be more natural to say, "I am not concerned [*or* I do not care] about your father's reaction."

assonance The similarity of vowel sounds in words which do not rhyme [we—weep, fine—white].

asterisk The sign *. A single asterisk is sometimes used as a footnote marker or to indicate items in a list which deserve special attention. A row of asterisks is sometimes used to indicate that the action of a story has been broken off or to suggest an interval of time.

at Avoid the use of the redundant *at* in such sentences as "Where were you at?" "Where do you live at?"

auxiliary verb A "helping" verb which combines with another to form a verb phrase [I *am* going; he *has been* talking]. The most common auxiliaries are *be, can, do, may, must, ought, shall, will*.

awful, awfully The real objection to *awful* is not that it is colloquial but that it is worked to death. It is inappropriate in a formal style unless used to mean "awe-inspiring." As a utility word it has become almost indispensable in informal speech, but the more deliberate nature of writing and the opportunities it allows for revision make the overuse of this word objectionable.

back of = behind The latter is the more formal usage, but both are generally acceptable in college writing.

bad The ordinary uses of *bad* as an adjective cause no difficulty. As a predicate adjective [An hour after dinner I began to feel bad] it is sometimes confused with the adverb *badly*. After the verbs *look, feel, seem,* the adjective is preferred. Say, "It looks bad for our team," "I feel bad about that quarrel," "She seemed bad this morning." But do not use *bad* when an adverb is required, as in "He played badly," "A badly torn suit."

badly = very much   *Badly* is used in informal and colloquial writing as an intensifying word [I wanted badly to be asked; he was badly in need of a shave]. When it is used in this way, care should be taken to avoid misleading word order. In "I wanted to play very badly" the adverb may be interpreted as a modifier of *to play,* which the writer did not intend. In college writing it would be safer to avoid this use of *badly* and to use one of the various possible synonyms. For example, "He was obviously in need of a shave," "I was eager to play."

balance = rest of, remainder   Now accepted as established usage in all dictionaries, though *rest of* or *remainder* would be preferred in a formal style.

bank on = rely on   In college writing the more formal *rely on* is generally preferred.

because   See **reason is because.**

being as   The use of *being as* for "because" or "since" in such sentences as "Being as I am an American, I believe in democracy," is nonstandard and is not acceptable in college speech or writing. Say, "Because I am an American, I believe in democracy."

between, among   In general, *between* is used of two people or objects and *among* for more than two [We had less than a dollar between the two of us; *but* We had only a dollar among the three of us].

The general distinction, however, should be modified when insistence on it would be unidiomatic. For example, *between* is the accepted form in the following examples:

He is in the difficult position of having to choose between three equally attractive girls.
A settlement was arranged between the four partners.
Just between us girls . . . (Any number of girls)

Bible   When used to refer to the Scriptures, "Bible" is always capitalized, but not italicized. When used metaphorically [*Das Kapital* is the bible of the Communists], the word is not capitalized.

blame on   This usage [He blamed it on his brother] is accepted without reservation by some dictionaries but labeled colloquial by others. The more formal usage would be "He blamed his brother for it," but either would be generally acceptable in college writing.

blond — blonde   In French the first is the masculine form, the second the feminine. This distinction is largely, but not always, preserved in English when the sex of the person is clearly known, but when the adjective refers to groups of persons of both sexes, use *blond* [All the children are blonds].

broke   When used as an adjective, *broke* is a slang synonym for "bankrupt" or "out of funds." This usage is common in informal, educated speech, but in college writing it should be restricted to papers clearly colloquial in style. The use of such circumlocutions as "financially embarrassed" is generally more objectionable than the slang itself. Simply say, "I had no money."

When used as a verb, *broke* is the simple past tense of *break* (past participle, *broken*). Do not confuse the past tense with the past participle. Say, "He has broken his leg," not "He has broke his leg."

business letters   All business letters follow a relatively standardized form which is illustrated by the example given below. For convenience, the various parts of the letter have been numbered.

115 Ohio Street   *1*
Galesburg, Illinois
December 28, 1971   *2*

3   Fisher Paint Company
        212 West Madison Street
        Chicago 7, Illinois

4   Gentlemen:

        In your advertisement of Colopake in recent issues of
        <u>Time</u> you say that the superiority of Colopake over
        other paint products is achieved by reducing the size
5   of the pigment particles. Since I am making a compar-
        ative study of various paints I should like to have
        more information on this point. Would it be possible
        for me to obtain a copy of the comparative data which
        were the basis of your advertising statement?

6   Yours truly,

                       John A. Baker

7   John A. Baker

     As the example shows, a business letter consists of at least seven parts:

1. The Return Address. This part will be omitted, of course, if stationery containing a printed letterhead is used, since the letterhead itself is the return address. The form used in the example is called a *block* heading with *open* punctuation. In a block heading the lines are not indented; each line begins flush with the one preceding. In open punctuation no marks are used at the ends of lines, but elements within the lines are separated in accordance with the usual conventions.

2. The Date Line. The date line is written as part of the first heading.

3. The Inside Address. This heading consists of three or more lines and follows the form established in the first heading. Abbreviations such as *Co.* and *Inc.* are used only if these terms are abbreviated in the letterheads of the companies being addressed. When the title of the addressee is given, it is usually placed after his name on the first line [Dr. David D. Henry, President]; but if this practice would result in an awkwardly long line, the title may be given as a separate line.

4. The Salutation. When an individual is being addressed, the salutation usually takes one of these forms: *Dear Mr. (Mrs., Miss,* or *Ms.) Blank, Dear Sir (or Madam).* Such an informal salutation as *Dear Bob* is acceptable only in writing to a personal friend. The form *My dear Mr. (or Mrs.) Blank* may be used in distinctly formal letters. When the letter is addressed to a company, rather than to an individual, the accepted salutation is *Gentlemen*. The form *Dear Sirs* is seldom used in modern business letters. If the company is known to consist of women, the salutation may be either *Mesdames* or *Ladies*. A colon follows the salutation.

5. The Body. The body of the letter usually consists of one or more paragraphs of single-spaced text, with double spacing between paragraphs. There is a marked preference for starting all paragraphs in a business letter at the left margin, with no indention to mark the opening of a paragraph. However, the older style of starting the first paragraph under the colon of the salutation and thereafter indenting the first line of each paragraph seven spaces from the margin is still common.

6. The Complimentary Close. The most common endings are *Yours truly, Yours very truly, Very truly yours, Yours sincerely*, or *Sincerely yours*. Such closes as *Cordially*, or *Cordially yours*, are used only when the writer is on familiar terms with his addressee. *Respectfully* is a formal close used chiefly in submitting a formal report to a superior. A comma is used at the end of the complimentary close.

7. The Signature. The signature consists of two parts: the written signature, and below this the writer's name and official position, if any, typed in. Both parts are necessary. The written signature is the legal identification of the writer; the typed name is a safeguard against misreading of the signature. Since it is conventional in business to address a woman as *Miss* unless she signifies that she is married, married women often enclose *Mrs.* in parentheses before their typed signatures:

Helen White   *Helen White*

(Mrs.) Helen White   (Mrs. John White)

When a letter is typed by someone other than the author, the typist puts first the author's initials, then his own (with a colon between them) flush with the left margin and below the author's signature.

can = may   The distinction that *can* is used to indicate ability and *may* to indicate permission [If I can do the work, may I have the job?] is a stylistic distinction. It is not generally observed in informal usage. Either form is acceptable in college writing.

can but   A formal variant of *can only* [I can but hope you are mistaken].

cannot but   A formal variant of *cannot help* or *must* [We cannot but accept the verdict]. In most college writing "We must accept the verdict" would be preferred.

cannot (can't) help but   While this construction is accepted in informal usage, it represents a confusion between the formal *cannot but* and the informal *can't help*. In college writing, the form without *but* is preferred.

can't hardly   A confusion between *cannot* and *can hardly*. The construction is unacceptable in college writing. Use *cannot, can't*, or *can hardly*.

can't seem   A colloquial short cut for "I seem to be unable." Acceptable at informal levels.

caret   The symbol ($\wedge$) used to identify the place in a printed, typed, or written line at which something is to be inserted.

case = instance, example   There is no question that this usage [In the case of John Jones . . .] is established, but a widely read essay labeling it jargon has created some objection to it. Like most utility words, *case* (meaning *instance*) may be overused, but its restrained use in college writing should be acceptable.

censor — censure   Both words come from a Latin verb meaning to "set a value on" or "tax." *Censor* is used to mean "appraise" in the sense of appraising a book or a letter to see if it may be made public [All outgoing mail had to be censored] and is often used as a synonym for "delete" or "cut out" [That part of the message was censored].

　　　　Censure means "to evaluate adversely," "to find fault with" or "rebuke" [The editorial writers censured the speech; such an attitude will invoke public censure].

circumlocution   Literally, "round-about speech." An attempt to avoid a direct statement by a circuitous reference, as in "She is expecting a little stranger" for "She is pregnant."

cite — sight — site   *Cite* means "to refer to" [He cited chapter and verse]. *Sight* means spectacle or view [The garden was a beautiful sight]. *Site* means "location" [This is the site of the new plant].

claim = assert *or* maintain   All dictionaries accept this usage [I claim that the assignment was never announced] as established. Despite continuing protests by Fowler, Bernstein, and others, there would seem to be no valid objection to the construction in most college writing.

cliché   A synonym for "trite expression": an overused or threadbare expression, or an observation which lacks originality.

clipped words   Shortened forms [auto, exam, gym, plane] which are considered whole words rather than abbreviations of the longer form. Clipped words do not require a period to mark abbreviation and are more appropriate to informal than to formal styles.

coherence   The quality of being logically integrated. In composition, chiefly used to refer to the integration of sentences within a paragraph. See page 92.

collective noun   A noun which refers to a group or class of individuals: *army, audience, committee, team,* etc. For the agreement of a collective noun and its verb, see page 390.

combine = combination   This use of *combine* [Several fraternities have formed a combine which will present its own slate of candidates] is colloquial. It is acceptable at informal levels of college writing. The more formal statement would be "Several fraternities have combined to present a common slate of candidates."

common case   In Modern English, nouns have the same form for nominative, dative, and accusative cases. This form is called the common case. Modern nouns, therefore, have a common case and a possessive or genitive case.

compare, contrast   *Contrast* always implies differences; *compare* may imply either differences or similarities. When followed by a preposition, both verbs usually take *with* [Contrast the part of the lawn that has been fertilized with the part that has not; the handwriting on the lease compares with this signature; if you compare the old leaves with the new you will see that the old leaves are darker]. However, the past participial form, *compared,* usually takes *to* as its preposition [Compared to her mother, she's a beauty].

comparison   Modern English adjectives and adverbs have lost the inflectional endings of Old English except those to show comparison. There are three degrees: positive, comparative, and superlative. There are three methods of indicating comparison in adjectives and adverbs: (1) by adding *-er* for the comparative and *-est* for the superlative; (2) by prefixing *more* for the comparative and *most* for the superlative; (3) by using different words for each degree. Methods (1) and (2) are regular; (3) is irregular.

Positive	Comparative	Superlative
(1) strong	stronger	strongest
(2) beautiful	more beautiful	most beautiful
(3) good, well	better	best
bad, ill	worse	worst
far	farther, further	farthest, furthest
little	less, lesser	least
much, many	more	most

complected   Nonstandard form of *complexioned*. Not acceptable in college writing.

complement   Literally, a completing construction. Used in grammar chiefly to refer to the construction which completes a linking verb. See next entry.

complement of "to be"   In formal usage, the complement of the verb *to be* takes the subjective case (It is *I*. Was it *she?*). In colloquial usage the objective is more common in the first person (It's *me*). The choice, therefore, between *It is I* and *It's me* is not a choice between standard and nonstandard usage but between formal and colloquial styles. This choice seldom has to be made in college writing, since the expression, in whatever form it is used, is essentially a spoken rather than a written sentence. Its use in writing occurs chiefly in dialogue, and then the form chosen should be appropriate to the speaker.

The use of the objective case in the third person (That was *her*) is less common and should probably be avoided in college writing except when dialogue requires it. The use of the objective case in a clause containing a subjunctive form of *to be* is especially to be avoided, because the subjunctive is a fairly formal construction, and the contrast between formal and colloquial usage points up the inappropriateness of the pronoun form:

Inappropriate	Appropriate
If I were *him,* I should resign.	If I were *he,* I should resign.
Would you do it, if you were *her?*	Would you do it, if you were *she?*

But notice that when the infinitive form of *to be* is used, its subject and complement both take the objective case:

She wants *me* to be there. (Pronoun is subject of infinitive.)
I wouldn't want to be *her.* (Pronoun is complement of infinitive.)

complex sentence   See **sentence.**

compound-complex sentence   See **sentence.**

compound sentence   See **sentence.**

compound words   Combinations of two or more words into a combined form, the parts of which may be written solid [blindfold], hyphenated [father-in-law], or separately [blood bank]. When in doubt about the spelling, consult your dictionary.

conjunction   A connecting word or phrase. A coordinating conjunction joins elements of equal rank. The coordinating conjunctions are *and, but, for, or, nor, yet, so,* and the correlatives *either . . . or, neither . . . nor,* and *not only . . . but also.* They join words, phrases, or clauses.

A subordinating conjunction joins subordinate clauses to main clauses. The principal conjunctions used to join adverbial clauses (adverbial conjunctions) are *if, as, when, where, why, while, how, since, because, although,* and *whether.*

If it rains, I shall study tonight.
Because it rained, I studied.
We act *when we believe.*
Whether we believe or not, we must act.

considerable   The use of *considerable* as a noun [I have spent considerable on this enterprise] is acceptable at a colloquial level. In a formal style, the preferred usage would require a noun after *considerable* [I have spent considerable money on this enterprise].

context   The environment—usually the verbal environment—in which a word occurs. Thus the other words in a sentence, paragraph, or page provide a context for a particular word. The context may also include the whole situation in which the word is used—the time, place, and attendant circumstances.

contractions   The use of contractions [I'll, can't, couldn't, didn't, he's, shouldn't] is appropriate in informal and colloquial styles but not in a formal style.

copula   See **linking verb.**

could of = could have   Although these two constructions have almost the same sound in informal speech, *of* for *have* is not acceptable in college writing. In writing, *could of, should of, would of* are nonstandard.

cute   A word used colloquially to indicate the general notion of "attractive" or "pleasing." Its overuse in writing shows haste or lack of discrimination. A more specific term will generally improve communication.

His girl is cute. [lovely? petite? pleasant? charming?]
That is a cute trick. [clever? surprising?]
She has a cute accent. [pleasant? refreshingly unusual?]
She is a little too cute for me. [affected? juvenile? demonstrative? clever?]

data   Since *data* is the Latin plural of *datum* (given or admitted as a fact) it has long taken a plural verb or pronoun [These data have been double-checked]. This requirement is now often ignored, so that in informal English "This data has been double-checked" is acceptable. *Data* is thus losing its foreign characteristics and being made to fit the general pattern of English nouns. The requirement of a plural verb is still observed, however, in scientific writing and in a formal style. For alternative pronunciations, see dictionary.

dative case   In Old English and in some other languages, generally the case of the indirect object.

demonstrative   *This, that, these, those* are called demonstratives when they are used as pointing words [This is the man; that coat is mine].

dialect   A pattern of speech habits shared by members of the same geographic area or social level [New England dialect; the standard dialect].

didn't ought   Nonstandard for "ought not" [You didn't ought to have told her] and not acceptable in college writing or speech. Say, "You ought not to have told her" or "You should not have told her."

dieresis   A diacritical (distinguishing) mark consisting of two dots placed over the second of two like vowels to show that they are to be pronounced separately—*reëntry, coöperation, coördination.* In Modern English the dieresis is so little used that it is not included among the characters on a standard typewriter keyboard. Such vowels are often separated by a hyphen without a dieresis—*re-entry. Cooperation* and *coordination* are now commonly written without either a dieresis or a hyphen.

different than   The preferred idiom is *different from,* although all dictionaries recognize *different than* as established usage. *Different to* is British usage.

digraph   Two letters pronounced as a single sound, as in bl*ee*d, b*ea*t, *th*in, sti*ck*, *p*sychology, gra*ph*.

diphthong   A combination of two vowel sounds run together to sound like a single vowel. Examples are the *ah-ee* sounds combining to form the vowel of *hide, ride, wide* and the *aw-ee* sounds combining in *boy, joy, toy.*

disinterested — uninterested   The distinction between these words is that the first is a synonym for *unbiased,* the second for *apathetic* or *not interested.* A disinterested critic is one who comes to a book with no prejudices or prior judgments of its worth; an uninterested critic is one who cannot get interested in the book. In recent years this distinction has lost ground, and so many speakers and writers have used *disinterested* to mean *uninterested* that the dictionaries have accepted this usage.

don't   As a contraction for "do not" it is appropriate in informal and colloquial styles, but not acceptable in college speech or writing as a contraction for "does not."

double negative   The use of two negative words or particles within the same construction. In certain forms [I am not unwilling to go] the double negative is educated usage for an affirmative statement; in other forms [I ain't got no money] the double negative is uneducated (nonstandard) usage for a negative statement. The objection that "two negatives make an affirmative" in English usage is a half-truth based on a false analogy with mathematics.

dove = dived   Both forms are established usage. *Dived* would be preferred in a formal style.

due to   The use of *due to* to mean "because of" in an introductory adverbial phrase [Due to the icy roads, we were unable to proceed] is an established usage to which some people object. The objection reflects personal preference rather than the facts of usage.

economic — economical   *Economic* refers to the science of economics or to business in general [This is an economic law; economic conditions are improving]. *Economical* means "inexpensive" or "thrifty" [That is the economical thing to do; he is economical to the point of miserliness].

editorial "we"	A practice employed by editors and authors of referring to themselves as *we*, even when the reference is to only one writer.
effect	See **affect.**
e.g.	An abbreviation for the Latin phrase *exempli gratia* (for the sake of example; for example). Used to introduce an example in publications, such as dictionaries, in which space must be conserved. Seldom used in freshman writing.
either	Used to designate one of two things [Both hats are becoming; I would be perfectly satisfied with either]. The use of *either* when more than two things are involved [There are three ways of working the problem; either way will give the right answer] is not generally accepted. When more than two things are involved, use *any* or *any one* instead of *either* [There are three ways of working the problem, any one of which will give the right answer].
elicit — illicit	The first word means to "draw out" [We could elicit no further information from them]; the second means "not permitted" [an illicit love affair].
elliptical constructions	A construction which is literally incomplete but in which the missing terms are understood [*I am taller than he* (is tall); Who told him? (It was) *Not I* (who told him)].
emigrant — immigrant	An emigrant is a person who moves *out* of a country; an immigrant one who moves *into* a country. Thus, refugees from Europe who settled in the United States were emigrants from their native countries and immigrants here. A similar distinction holds for the verbs *emigrate* and *immigrate*.
enormous — enormousness — enormity	*Enormous* refers to unusual size or measure—*huge, vast, immense* [an enormous fish, an enormous effort]. *Enormousness* is a noun with the same connotations of size and can be applied to either good or bad effects [The enormousness of their contribution is only beginning to be recognized; the enormousness of the lie almost made it believable]. But *enormity* is used only for evil acts of great dimension [The enormity of Hitler's crimes against the Jews shows what can happen when power, passion, and prejudice are all united in one man].
enthuse	Colloquial for "to be (become) enthusiastic." The more formal phrase is preferred in college writing.
epigram	A short, pithy statement, usually witty or cynical, in either prose or poetry:

Yes, the meek shall inherit the earth—six feet of it.

> Here lies our sovereign lord, the King,
> Whose word no man relies on,
> Who never said a foolish thing,
> And never did a wise one.

equally as	In such sentences as "He was equally as good as his brother," the *equally as* is a confusion of *equally* and *as good as*. Write, "He was his brother's equal," "He was as good as his brother," or "Both brothers were equally good."
etc.	An abbreviation for *et cetera* (and so forth). Should be used only when the style justifies abbreviations and then only after several items in a series have been identified [The data sheet required the usual personal information: age, height, weight, marital status, etc.]. Avoid the redundant *and* before *etc.*

etymology   The study of the derivations of words.

euphemism — euphuism   A *euphemism* is a word or phrase used as a substitute for an expression which is felt to be crude, improper, or vulgar. Examples are "a lady dog" for "a bitch," "pass away" for "die." *Euphuism* is a name given to an ornate and affected literary style which was popular in England at the end of the sixteenth century and to any modern style which shows similar characteristics.

exam   A clipped form of *examination*. Although classified as colloquial by some dictionaries, it is accepted at all but the most formal levels of college writing.

expect = suppose *or* suspect   This is a colloquial usage. In college writing, use *suppose* or *suspect* [I suppose you have written to him? I suspect that we have made a mistake].

expletive   In such sentences as "There are two answers to the question" and "It seems to me that you are mistaken," the words *There* and *It* are called *expletives*. In such sentences the order is expletive, verb, and real subject, the expletive occupying the normal position of the subject.

fact   Distinguish between facts and statements of fact. A fact is something which exists or existed. It is neither true nor false; it just *is*. A statement of fact, or factual statement, may be true or false, depending on whether it does or does not report the facts accurately. But there are no true or false facts. Also, avoid padding a sentence with unnecessary use of "The fact that" as in "It is a fact that all the public opinion polls predicted Truman's defeat in the 1948 election." The first five words of that sentence add no meaning. Similarly, "His guilt is admitted" says all, in fewer words, that is said by "The fact of his guilt is admitted."

famous, notorious   *Famous* is a complimentary and *notorious* an uncomplimentary adjective. Well-known people of good repute are famous; those of bad repute are notorious (or infamous).

fare — fair   *Fare* comes from the Old English verb *faran* (to travel) and is related to the expression *fare you well*. It is most commonly used today to indicate the cost of transportation [The fare to Chicago is $10.40]. *Fair* has a variety of meanings [a fair decision, a fair copy, a fair skin, just fair, fair weather, a fair profit, a county fair].

farther, further   The distinction that *farther* indicates distance and *further* degree is now less widely observed than it used to be. All dictionaries consulted recognize the two words as interchangeable. But to mean "in addition," only *further* is used [Further assistance will be required].

feature (verb)   The use of *feature* to mean "give prominence to" [This issue of the magazine features an article on juvenile delinquency] is established standard usage and is appropriate in college writing. But this acceptance does not justify the slang use of *feature* in such expressions as "Can you feature that?" "Feature me in a dress suit," "I can't feature her as a nurse."

fellow   As a noun, *fellow* for "man" or "person" is appropriate in colloquial and informal styles. As an adjective [fellow students, a fellow traveler] *fellow* is acceptable at all levels.

figures of speech   Metaphors, similes, personifications, allusions, and similar devices are grouped under the general name *figures of speech*. See page 141.

fine writing   In college, often used as an uncomplimentary term for writing which, because of its attempts to be "literary," is artificial, pretentious, or wordy.

finite verb   A form of the verb capable of serving as a predicate, as distinct from the non-finite forms, called verbals.

fix   As a noun, *fix* is colloquial for "predicament" [Now we *are* in a fix!]. As a verb, it is colloquial for "repair" or "adjust" [My pen is broken and I can't fix it]. Both uses are appropriate in an informal style. The verb *fix*, meaning "to make fast," is acceptable at all levels.

flaunt — flout   *Flaunt* means "to display conspicuously" [Here comes the Easter Parade, with the women flaunting their new dresses]. *Flout* means "to scoff at" or "to treat with scorn." It is used chiefly for open rejection of social or moral conventions [They seem to want to flout every custom which the community respects].

flunk = fail   Not suited to a formal style, but so commonly used in college that there would seldom be objection to its use in an informal paper.

foreword — forward   Despite similar spelling, these two words have quite different meanings. A *foreword* is a prefatory statement at the fore or front of a book—a preface. The common use of *forward* is well known; it is also used with unfavorable connotations to mean *bold* or *presumptuous* [a forward girl, a forward manner].

formally — formerly   *Formally* means "in a formal manner" [They dressed formally]. *Formerly* means "previously" [He was formerly with A. C. Smith and Company].

funny   The use of *funny* as a utility word [She gave me a funny look] is greatly overdone in college writing. Although appropriate at informal and colloquial levels, its constant use makes for vague diction. Select a more exact synonym:

She gave me a funny look. [hostile? alarmed? annoyed? scathing? perplexed? baffled?]

gender   A grammatical division of words into masculine, feminine, and neuter categories, which is important in highly inflected languages and is only partly related to differences in sex—for example, *nauta* (sailor) in Latin is a feminine noun, *das Kind* (child) in German is neuter. Except for personal pronouns (he, she, it) and a few feminine forms of nouns (actress, niece), English makes little use of grammatical gender.

genitive case   The possessive case.

gentleman, lady   These are good words, but avoid their use as synonyms for "man" or "woman" in expressions in which the latter terms are normal [manservant, man of the house, women's building, woman's point of view]. Also avoid their euphemistic use to designate the sex of animals [bull, tomcat, mare, ewe].

gerund   The *-ing* form of a verb when used as a noun [Sewing entranced her].

good   The use of *good* as an adverb [He talks good; he played pretty good] is not generally acceptable in writing. In both writing and speaking, the accepted adverbial form is *well*.

This discussion does not apply to the use of *good* as an adjective after verbs of hearing, feeling, seeing, smelling, tasting, etc. See **bad.**

good and   Used colloquially as an intensive in such expressions as "good and late," "good and sleepy," "good and ready," "good and tired." The more formal the style, the less appropriate these intensives are.

gotten	Leading dictionaries now accept *gotten* without comment as one of two past participles of *get*. The other one is *got*.
guess	The use of *guess* to mean "believe," "suppose," "think" [I guess I can be there on time] is accepted by all dictionaries on which this glossary is based. There is still objection to its use in formal college writing, but it should be acceptable in an informal style.
hackneyed diction	See **cliché**.
had have, had of	Neither form is appropriate in college writing. Use *had*.
had (hadn't) ought	Nonstandard for *ought* (*ought not*). Not acceptable in college writing or speech.
hanged, hung	Alternative past participles of *hang*. When referring to an execution, *hanged* is preferred; in other senses, *hung* is preferred.
headword	The chief word in a phrase: a noun modified by adjectives, or a verb modified by one or more adverbs, or the noun in a prepositional phrase [a very tall *tale;* they *danced* mechanically and routinely; at the *beginning*].
height — heighth	The form *heighth* is nonstandard and probably reflects a confusion with the final *th* in *breadth* and *width*.
historical present	Also called *dramatic present*. The use of the present tense in narrative style to record action in the past [His friends try to persuade him to escape, but Socrates reasons with them and shows them he must die].
home	Used colloquially and informally for "at home" [We have been home all afternoon; if you arrive too late, we will not be home]. In a formal style "at home" would be preferred.
homonyms	Words which are pronounced alike [air, heir; blew, blue; plain, plane; sail, sale].
hopefully	This adverb is not favored when attached loosely to a sentence to mean "I hope" [Hopefully, the plane will arrive on schedule].
idea	In addition to its formal meaning of "conception," *idea* has acquired so many supplementary meanings that it must be recognized as a utility word. Some of its meanings are illustrated in the following sentences:

The idea [thesis] of the book is simple.
The idea [proposal] he suggested is a radical one.
I got the idea [impression] that she is unhappy.
It is my idea [belief, opinion] that they are both wrong.
My idea [intention] is to leave early.

The overuse of *idea*, like the overuse of any utility word, makes for vagueness. Whenever possible, use a more precise synonym.

idiom	An idiom is a usage characteristic of the language or dialect in which it is used. We say, "How do you do?" Frenchmen say, "How do you carry yourself?" Neither of the expressions is more logical than the other. One is an English idiom, the other a French idiom.

Because idioms are traditional rather than logical, they can be learned only by experience, not by rule. There is, for example, no rule that will tell us in advance what preposition to use with what verb. We say aim *at*, abide *by*, account *for*, move *on*, and meet *with*. A foreigner who knows what *get* means will find that knowledge of little use in interpreting the meaning of *get ahead, get along, get away, get by, get on, get over, get through, get with it.* Most dictionaries list these verb-adverb combinations as sub-entries under *get.*

The following short list illustrates some common English idioms:

all in all	hard and fast
be taken in	in any event
by and large	keep up with
catch a cold	make no bones about it
catch fire	makeshift
come in handy	mull over
do away with	put up with
do up	set about
give and take	strike a bargain

These and similar idioms are all part of the common vocabulary of people whose native language is English and are in common use in informal and colloquial styles.

i.e.   An abbreviation of the Latin phrase *id est* (that is), used to introduce a restatement or an explanation of a preceding word or phrase. Its use is generally confined to publications in which space must be conserved; it is rarely used in freshman writing.

illusion   See **allusion.**

immigrant   See **emigrant.**

imply — infer   The traditional difference between the two words is that *imply* refers to what a statement means, usually to a meaning not specifically stated but included in the original statement, whereas *infer* is used for a listener's or reader's judgment or inference based on the statement. The dictionaries are not unanimous in supporting this distinction, but in your writing do not use *imply* as a synonym for *infer.*

in back of   See **back of.**

individual   Although the use of *individual* to mean *person* [He is a fascinating individual] is accepted by the dictionaries, college instructors frequently disapprove of this use, probably because it is overdone in college writing. In its formal uses *individual* signifies "single" or "separate" [The instructor tries to give us individual attention].

Indo-European   The ancestral language of most of the modern languages in India and Europe. Of the nine main branches of Indo-European, two are of special interest to us: the Germanic, from which modern English, Dutch, German, Icelandic, Norwegian, and Swedish are descended; and the Italic, from which, through Latin, modern French, Italian, Portuguese, Romanian, and Spanish have come.

inferior than   Possibly a confusion between *inferior to* and *worse than.* Say "inferior to" [Today's workmanship is inferior to that of a few years ago].

infinitive   The form of the verb usually preceded by *to: to see, to believe, to fear.* See **verb.**

in regards to   The only acceptable form is *in regard to.* The *-s* ending is not uncommon in speech, but it is not acceptable in college writing.

inside of   The use of *inside of* to mean "in less than" [I'll be there inside of an hour] is accepted as established usage. There should be no objection to it in college writing.

intensives   Such modifiers as *much, so, too, very* merely add emphasis to the words they modify [much obliged, so tired, too bad, very good], but the overuse of intensives (especially *very*) is more likely to result in wordiness than in emphasis. The pronouns *myself, yourself, himself, herself, themselves* may also be used as intensives [You yourself are the best judge; he built the cabin himself].

intransitive   See **verb**.

irony   A mode of statement in which the writer implies almost the opposite of what he explicitly states. The writing proceeds on two levels at the same time. Ostensibly, the writer is developing the literal meaning of his message, but he counts on the reader to see the implications of each statement in the total context and so to respond at the implied level. The most famous example in English is Jonathan Swift's *A Modest Proposal*, which, under the guise of suggesting a workable plan for improving the economy of Ireland, makes an incisive criticism of England's exploitation of the Irish. Irony is difficult to handle, and for that reason many teachers of freshman English prefer that students read it rather than write it. But as the essay "Why We Need More Westerns on TV" (page 9) shows, it can sometimes be handled effectively by an able student.

irregardless   A nonstandard variant of *regardless*.

irrelevant — irreverent   *Irrelevant* means "having no relation to" or "lacking pertinence" [That may be true, but it is quite irrelevant]. *Irreverent* means "without reverence" [Such conduct in a church is irreverent].

its — it's   The confusion of these two forms causes frequent misspelling in college writing. *It's* always means "it is" or "it has." The apostrophe is a sign of contraction, not of possession [The dog wagged its tail; it's (it is) too difficult a problem; it's (it has) been raining all night].

it's me   This construction is essentially a spoken one. Except in dialogue, it rarely occurs in writing. Its use in educated speech is thoroughly established. The formal expression is *It is I*.

jargon   A name applied to diction which is wordy and unnecessarily abstract. The name is also applied to the technical vocabulary and usages of special groups—the jargon of the medical profession, legal jargon. See page 150.

kid   Colloquial for "child," but often applied to young people of any age, even by parents to their married sons and daughters. Appropriate in informal but not in formal writing.

kind of, sort of   Use a singular modifier and a singular verb with these phrases [That kind of person is always troublesome; this sort of attitude will get us nowhere]. The use of *a* or *an* after *of*, in this construction, is colloquial and is avoided by most careful writers.

kind (sort) of = somewhat   This usage [I feel kind of tired; he looked sort of foolish] is colloquial. It would be inappropriate in a formal style and should be used sparingly in an informal style.

learn = teach   The use of *learn* to mean "teach" [He learned us arithmetic] is nonstandard and is not acceptable in college speech or writing.

leave = let   The use of *leave* for *let* [Leave us face it] is slang and is not acceptable in college speech or writing. Say, "Let us face it," "Let (*not* leave) us be friends."

let's A contraction of *let us*. The expression *let's us* is redundant and not acceptable in college writing.

liable, likely, apt *Liable* to mean "likely" or "apt" [It is liable to rain; he is liable to hit you] is a colloquial usage to which instructors sometimes object. *Liable* means "subject to" or "exposed to" or "answerable for" [He is liable to arrest; you will be liable for damages]. In formal usage *apt* means "has an aptitude for" [He is an apt pupil]. The use of *apt* to mean "likely" is accepted colloquially [She is apt to leave you; he is apt to resent it].

like = as, as though The use of *like* as a conjunction [He talks like you do; it looks like it will be my turn next] is colloquial. It is not appropriate in a formal style and many people object to it in an informal style. The safest procedure is to avoid using *like* as a conjunction in college writing.

likely See **liable.**

line The use of *line* to indicate a type of activity or business [What's your line? His line is dry goods] is accepted as established usage; its use to indicate a course of action or thought [He follows the party line] is also accepted. However, the overuse of *line* in these senses often provokes objection to the word.

linking verb (copula) A verb which is neither transitive nor intransitive, but is followed by a complement, usually a noun, a pronoun, or an adjective [That man is her father; they seem happy; we became ill]. In such sentences the complement both completes the verb and modifies the subject. See **verb.**

loan, lend Both forms of the verb are accepted in educated American usage.

loath — loathe The form without -*e* is an adjective meaning "reluctant," "unwilling" [I am loath to do that; he is loath to risk so great an investment] and is pronounced to rhyme with "both." The form with -*e* is a verb meaning "dislike strongly" [I loathe teas; she loathes an unkempt man], and is pronounced to rhyme with "clothe."

locate = find This usage [I cannot locate that quotation] is established, but its extension to mean *remember* [Your name sounds familiar, but I cannot locate your face] is not acceptable.

locate = settle This usage [He and his family have located in San Francisco] is colloquial. In college writing *settled* would be preferred.

loose, lose The confusion of these words causes frequent misspelling. *Loose* is most common as an adjective [a loose button, a dog that has broken loose]. *Lose* is always used as a verb [You are going to lose your money].

loose sentence A technical term used to describe a sentence in which the main thought is completed before the end. The opposite of a *periodic sentence.* Loose sentences are standard sentences and should not be thought of as faulty.

lot(s) of The use of *lot(s)* to mean a considerable amount or number [I have lots of friends] is colloquial. This usage is common in informal writing.

lower case (l. c.) Printer's terminology for small letters as contrasted with capitals. Frequently used by college instructors in marking student papers.

luxuriant — luxurious These words come from the same root but have quite different connotations. *Luxuriant* means "abundant" and is used principally of growing things [luxuriant vegetation, a luxuriant head of hair]. *Luxurious* means "luxury-loving" or "catering to luxury" [He finds it difficult to support so luxurious a wife on so modest an income; the appointments of the clubhouse were luxurious.]

mad = angry or annoyed   This usage is colloquial [My girl is mad at me; his insinuations make me mad]. In formal and informal styles, use *angry, annoyed, irritated, provoked,* or *vexed,* which are more precise.

majority — plurality   Candidates are elected by a *majority* when they get more than half the votes cast. A *plurality* is the margin of victory that the winning candidate has over his leading opponent, whether the winner has a majority or not.

malapropism   A humorous, though unintentional, confusion of words similar in form and sound [Henry VIII died of an *abbess* on his knee; one of the most momentous events in early English history was the invasion of the *Dames*]. The error is named for Mrs. Malaprop, a character in Sheridan's play *The Rivals,* whose speech often illustrated this kind of confusion.

math   A clipped form of *mathematics.* Appropriate in a colloquial or informal style but not in formal writing.

may   See **can.**

mean = unkind, disagreeable, bad-tempered   These uses of *mean* [It was mean of me to do that; please don't be mean to me; that dog looks mean] are colloquial. They are appropriate in most college writing, but their overuse sometimes results in vagueness. Consider using one of the suggested alternatives to provide a sharper statement.

might of   See **could of.**

modifier   A word, phrase, or clause which describes, changes, or limits the meaning of a word or other element in a sentence. Basically, an adjective modifies a noun, and an adverb modifies a verb, but an adjective may modify a pronoun or a verbal noun, and an adverb may modify an adjective, another adverb, or a connective. Both kinds of modifiers can be phrases and clauses as well as single words. A sentence modifier modifies the main clause [*If worst comes to worst,* we can go to work].

mood   Of the three moods of English verbs—indicative, imperative, and subjunctive— the indicative is by far the most common. A verb is in the indicative mood unless:

     1. It expresses a command or entreaty [*Sit* down! Please *listen* to me] in which case it is in the imperative mood.

     2. It is used in one of the following ways, in which case it is in the subjunctive mood:

       a. To express a condition contrary to fact [If I *were* you, I would go].

       b. To grant a concession [Be it as you say].

       c. To state an improbability [If this *were* the end of the matter, I'd be happy].

       d. To conduct certain parliamentary proceedings [I move that the committee *go* on record; it is moved and seconded that this measure *be* adopted].

     The form used for the imperative mood is always the same as the first principal part. The subjunctive, once fully inflected, is so little used in modern English that we need consider only the forms for the simple present and past tenses of the verb *to be.* These are *be* for all persons in the singular and plural of the simple present and *were* for all persons in the singular and plural of the simple past.

moral — morale　　Roughly, *moral* refers to conduct and *morale* refers to state of mind. A *moral* man is one who conducts himself according to the conventions of society or religion. People are said to have good *morale* when they are cheerful, cooperative, and not too much concerned with their own worries.

most = almost　　This usage [I am most always hungry an hour before mealtime] is colloquial. In college writing *almost* would be preferred in such a sentence.

must (adjective and noun)　　The use of *must* as an adjective [This book is must reading for anyone who wants to understand Russia] and as a noun [It is reported that the President will classify this proposal as a must] is accepted as established usage by the dictionaries.

must of　　See **could of.**

myself = I　　This usage [John and myself will go] is not generally acceptable. Say, "John and I will go." *Myself* is acceptably used: (1) as an intensifier [I saw it myself; I myself will go with you]; (2) as a reflexive object [I hate myself; I can't convince myself that he is right].

myself = me　　The use of *myself* as the equivalent of *me* [He divided it between John and myself] is not generally accepted. The preferred usage is "He divided it between John and me."

neither　　See **either.**

nice　　A utility word much overused in college writing. Avoid excessive use of it and, whenever possible, choose a more precise synonym.

It was a nice dance. [enjoyable? exciting? genteel? well-organized?]
That's a nice dress. [attractive? becoming? fashionable? well-made?]
She's a nice girl. [agreeable? beautiful? charming? friendly? well-mannered?]

nice and　　See **good and.**

nominative absolute　　An introductory participial phrase which is grammatically independent of the rest of the sentence [*All things being considered,* the decision is a fair one; *the interview having been ended,* the reporters rushed to the phones]. This construction is common in Latin but should be used sparingly in English, partly because it is sometimes unidiomatic, and partly because it may result in a dangling modifier. The first example given above is idiomatic English; the second would normally be written, "When the interview was ended, the reporters rushed to the phones."

nominative case　　Another name for the subjective case.

not . . . as, not . . . so　　See **as . . . as.**

notorious　　See **famous.**

noun　　A part of speech usually inflected for number and case and generally used as subject, object, or complement in a sentence [man, wife, house, flower]. It may be used in the possessive case as an adjective [the *man's* wife].

noun clause　　A subordinate clause serving usually as the subject, object, or complement in a sentence—that is, used in the positions in which a noun is normally used:

(What he needs) is more exercise. [Noun clause as subject]
He predicted (that it would happen). [Noun clause as object]
His actions were (what you would expect). [Noun clause as complement]

nowhere near = not nearly   Established usage, but *not nearly* is often preferred.

nowheres   Nonstandard variant of *nowhere*.

object   An object is a noun or pronoun which completes the action of a transitive verb [We bought the *car;* I asked *her*] or completes a preposition [She smiled at *me;* it is lying on the *table*]. An *indirect object* identifies the recipient of the action indicated by a verb-object combination [We bought *Dad* a car; the children gave *her* a party].

off of   In such sentences as "Keep off of the grass," "He took it off of the table," the *of* is unnecessary and undesirable. Omit it in college speech and writing.

OK, O.K.   Its use in business to mean "endorse" is generally accepted [The manager OK'd the request]. Otherwise, it is colloquial. It is a utility word and is subject to the general precaution concerning all such words: do not overuse it, especially in contexts in which a more specific term would give more efficient communication. For example, contrast the vagueness of OK at the left with the discriminated meanings at the right.

The garagemen said the tires were OK.	The garagemen said the tread on the tires was still good.
	The garagemen said the pressure in the tires was satisfactory.

one . . . he, his   The feeling that the repetition of *one . . . one's* [One must do what one can to ensure one's family a decent standard of living] makes for a stilted style has led to the permissible shift from *one, one's* to *he, his* [One must do what he can to ensure his family a decent standard of living]. In general a shift in the number or nature of pronouns is undesirable, but this particular shift is established usage.

only   The position of *only* in such sentences as "I only need three dollars" and "If only Mother would write!" is sometimes condemned on the grounds of possible ambiguity. In practice, the context usually rules out ambiguous interpretation, but a change in the word order would often result in more appropriate emphasis [I need only three dollars; if Mother would only write].

out loud = aloud   Generally acceptable in college writing. In a formal style, prefer *aloud*.

outside of = aside from, except   This usage [Outside of his family, no one respects him; outside of that, I have no objection] is colloquial. It would be inappropriate in a formal style, but not objectionable in an informal one.

over with = completed, ended   This usage [Let's get this job over with; she is all over with that romance] is informal. It should be generally acceptable in college writing.

part, on the part of   This usage [There will be some objection on the part of the students; on the part of businessmen, there will be some concern about taxes] often makes for a wordy and flabby style. Simply say, "The students will object," "Businessmen will be concerned about taxes."

participle   See **verb.**

party = person Colloquial, and generally to be avoided in college writing. In telephone usage, however, party is the accepted word [Your party does not answer].

past — passed Although both forms may be used as past participles of the verb *to pass, past* is primarily used as an adjective or a noun [in days past, the past tense, she is a woman with a past]. *Passed* is a past tense or past participle form [They have passed the half-way mark; he passed all his examinations].

per = a This usage [You will be remunerated at the rate of five dollars per diem; this material costs $1.50 per yard] is established. As the second illustration shows, the *per* need not be followed by a Latin noun. This use of *per* is most common in legal and business phraseology. For most purposes, "five dollars a day" and "$1.50 a yard" would be more natural expressions.

per = according to, concerning This usage [The order will be delivered as per your instructions; per your inquiry of the 17th, we wish to report] is business slang which is unacceptable in both college and business writing. Use "according to" or "concerning," whichever is appropriate.

per cent, percent Originally an abbreviation of the Latin *per centum,* this term has been Anglicized and is no longer considered a foreign word. It may be written as one or two words and no longer requires a period to indicate abbreviation [There is a ten percent markup; interest is at four per cent].

periodic sentence A sentence in which the main thought is not completed until the end. See page 116.

personification A figure of speech in which animals, inanimate objects, and qualities are given human characteristics [Death cometh like a thief in the night; the breeze caressed her hair].

phonetics The science dealing with the sounds of language. These sounds are represented by phonetic symbols which ignore the appearance of a word and record only its pronunciation [Phonetically, *schism* is transcribed sɪzəm]. When words are spelled as they are pronounced, the spelling is said to be phonetic; thus, *tho* is a phonetic spelling, *colonel* is not.

photo Colloquial clipped form of *photograph.* In a formal style, use the full form.

plagiarism The offense of representing as one's own writing the work of another. The use of unacknowledged quotations.

plan on When *plan* is used in the sense of "arrange" [I plan to be in Columbus on the seventh], the accepted idiom is *plan to.* When, however, *plan* means "intend" or "hope" [I plan to see that picture whenever it comes to town; they are planning on saving enough money to buy a new car], either *plan to* or *plan on* is acceptable. The safer usage is *plan to.*

plenty The use of *plenty* as a noun [There is plenty of room] is acceptable at all levels. Its use as an adverb [It was plenty good] is colloquial and would not be appropriate in college writing.

plurality See **majority.**

précis A summary which preserves the organization and principal content of the original.

predicate	That part of a sentence which makes a statement about the subject. The predicate may consist of an intransitive verb, with or without modifiers; or of a transitive verb and its object, with or without modifiers; or of a linking verb and its complement, with or without modifiers.
predicate adjective	An adjective completing a linking verb [His mother is *sick;* oh, it is *beautiful!*].
predicate noun	Same function as *predicate adjective* above [His mother is a *writer;* her brother became a successful *lawyer*].
prefix	A word or syllable placed before the root of another word to form a new word [*anti*bodies, *mono*syllabic, *un*natural].
preposition	A connective word which links a following noun or pronoun to another word in the sentence, usually a noun or a verb [He sat *on* the desk; there is room *at* the top].
principal parts	See **verb.**
pronoun	A pronoun is a word which stands for a noun. The **personal pronouns** are inflected for gender, number, case, and person, as follows:

Number	Case	1st Person	2nd Person	3rd Person		
				mas.	*fem.*	*neut.*
	Subjective	I	you	he	she	it
Singular	*Possessive*	my (mine)	your(s)	his	her(s)	its
	Objective	me	you	him	her	it
	Subjective	we	you	they	all genders	
Plural	*Possessive*	our(s)	your(s)	their(s)		
	Objective	us	you	them		

The **relative pronouns** *who, which, that,* and *what,* and their compounds *whoever, whosoever, whichever, whatever,* introduce adjective clauses. Only *who* and its compounds are inflected: *who,* subjective; *whose,* possessive; *whom,* objective. The **demonstrative pronouns,** *this* (plural, *these*) and *that* (plural, *those*) should agree in number with nouns they modify: *this kind, that kind,* not *these kind, those kind.* **Reflexive pronouns** (*myself, yourself, ourselves,* etc.) are objects referring to the subject of the sentence [I struck myself; he blamed himself]. They should not be used as objects when the subject is not the same person, as in "Give it to myself." Prefer, "Give it to me."

proven	Alternative past participle of *prove.* The preferred form is *proved,* but *proven* is permissible.
providing = provided	This usage [I will go, providing you accompany me] is established. Either form is acceptable in college writing, though *provided* is more common and more widely accepted.
real = really (very)	Unless the style is intentionally colloquial, use *really* [It was a really (*not* real) difficult assignment].
reason is because	Although Bryant offers impressive evidence (*Current American Usage,* pp. 170–71) to show that this is an established idiom, there is still some objection to it. In a formal style, "The reason is that" would be preferred.

redundancy   Repetitious wording. For an example, see the next entry.

refer back   A confusion between *look back* and *refer*. This usage is objected to in college writing on the ground that since the *re* of refer means "back," *refer back* is redundant. *Refer back* is acceptable when it means "refer again" [The bill was referred back to the committee]; otherwise, say *refer* [Let me refer you to page 17].

referent   The *thing* as contrasted with the symbol which refers to it. The person, object, event, or idea to which a word refers. The word is pronounced with the stress on the first syllable.

reflexive   See **pronoun.**

relative pronoun   See **pronoun.**

respectfully — respectively   *Respectfully* means "with respect" [Respectfully submitted]. *Respectively* means roughly "each in turn" [These three papers were graded respectively A, C, and B].

Reverend   *Reverend* is used before the name of a clergyman and in formal usage is preceded by *the* [I met the Reverend Alexander White]. It is not used immediately preceding the surname [the Reverend White], but must be followed by Dr., Mr., or a Christian name or initials [Rev. Dr. White, Rev. Mr. White, Rev. A. L. White]. In informal written usage, the *the* is often omitted and the word *Reverend* abbreviated.

Formal	Informal
The Reverend Alexander L. White	Rev. A. L. White
2472 Bancroft Street	2472 Bancroft Street
Toledo, Ohio	Toledo, Ohio

right — rite   A *rite* is a ceremony or ritual. This word should not be confused with the various uses of *right*.

right (adv.)   The use of *right* as an adverb is established in such sentences as "He went right home," "It served him right." Its use to mean *very* [I was right glad to meet him] is colloquial and should be used in college writing only when the style is colloquial.

run-on sentence   A sentence which consists of a number of main clauses loosely joined together by *and*'s and *so*'s. The ideas in the sentence lack organization. See page 356.

said (adj.)   The use of *said* as an adjective [said documents, said offense] is restricted to legal phraseology. Do not use it in college writing.

same as = just as   The preferred idiom is *just as* [He acted just as I thought he would].

same, such   Avoid the use of *same* or *such* as a substitute for *it, this, that, them* [I am returning the book, since I do not care for same; most people are fond of athletics of all sorts, but I have no use for such]. Say, "I am returning the book because I do not care for it," "Unlike most people, I am not fond of athletics."

scarcely   In such sentences as "There wasn't scarcely enough," "We haven't scarcely time," the use of *scarcely* plus a negative creates an unacceptable double negative. Say, "There was scarcely enough," "We scarcely have time."

scarcely than The use of *scarcely than* [I had scarcely met her than she began to denounce her husband] is a confusion between *no sooner . . . than* and *scarcely . . . when*. Say, "I had no sooner met her than she began to denounce her husband," or "I had scarcely met her when she began to denounce her husband."

seldom ever The *ever* is redundant. Instead of saying, "He is seldom ever late," "She is seldom ever angry," say, "He is seldom late," "She is seldom angry."

-selfs The plural of *self* is *selves*. Such usages as "They hurt themselfs," "They hate theirselfs," are nonstandard and are not acceptable in college speech or writing.

semantics The science of the meanings of words as contrasted with phonetics (pronunciation), morphology (form), and syntax (function).

sensual — sensuous Avoid confusion of these words. *Sensual* has unfavorable connotations and means "catering to the gratification of the senses" [He leads a sensual existence]. *Sensuous* has generally favorable connotations and refers to pleasures experienced through the senses [The sensuous peace of a warm bath; the sensuous imagery of the poem].

sentence English sentences are classified by structure as follows:

Simple: one clause, a main clause [Charlie shot a squirrel].

Compound: two or more main clauses [Charlie shot a squirrel, and Beth cried].

Complex: one main clause, one or more subordinate clauses [When Charlie took aim, Beth wrung her hands].

Compound-complex: two or more main clauses, at least one subordinate [Charlie shot a squirrel and Beth cried, while the dog barked loudly].

series Parallel constructions arranged in succession [He was *tall, tanned,* and *lean*]. The elements of a series may be single words, phrases, subordinate clauses, or main clauses, but all elements must be in the same grammatical form. See page 359

shall — will For a long time the schools have attempted to enforce the distinction that *shall* is used in the first person and *will* in the other two when the verb is expressing future action, but *will* in the first person and *shall* in the other two when the verb is expressing determination rather than futurity. This distinction has little support in American usage, except in northeastern New England. In all other areas of the country, *will* is the preferred form for all persons, whether the verb is expressing futurity or determination.[2] This *shall-will* distinction cannot be accepted as an accurate description of educated usage in America, Scotland, or Ireland. It is primarily a description of the usage of educated Englishmen, but the following quotation from a celebrated speech by Winston Churchill shows that the distinction is not consistently observed even in England. Churchill was speaking on a very formal occasion (an address to the House of Commons after the evacuation of Dunkirk in World War II). There can be no doubt that he was expressing determination rather than simple futurity, yet he consistently uses *shall* in the first person:

. . . we shall not flag or fail. We shall go on to the end, we shall fight in France, we shall fight in the seas and oceans, we shall fight with growing confidence

[2] See Margaret M. Bryant, *Current American Usage* (New York: Funk and Wagnalls, 1962), p. 183.

and growing strength in the air, we shall defend our island, whatever the cost may be, we shall fight on the beaches, we shall fight on the landing-grounds, we shall fight in the fields and in the streets, we shall fight in the hills; we shall never surrender . . .

In view of this diversity of usage, any concise statement is bound to over-simplify, but the following summary should meet most of the needs of American college students:

1. To express simple futurity only, *will* is used in the second and third persons and either *will* or *shall* in the first person, *shall* being the more formal. *Shall* is not used in the second and third persons when the sentence implies futurity only.

2. To express determination, resolve, or compulsion, *shall* is used in the second and third persons and either *shall* or *will* in the first person. But if the context clearly implies determination rather than futurity only, either *shall* or *will* may be used for all persons.

3. Shall is predominantly used in statements of laws [Congress *shall* have the power . . .], in military commands [The regiment *shall* proceed as directed], and in formal directives [All branch offices *shall* report weekly to the home office].

4. In questions, *shall* is often used in the third person as well as in the first [Where *shall* he be tomorrow? *But also:* Where *will* he be tomorrow]?

should — would   These words are used as the past forms of *shall* and *will* respectively and follow the same pattern [I *would* (*should*) be glad to see him tomorrow; he *would* welcome your ideas on the subject; we *would* (*should*) never consent to such an arrangement]. They are also used to convert a *shall* or *will* in direct discourse into indirect discourse.

Direct Discourse	Indirect Discourse
"*Shall* I try to arrange it?" he asked.	He asked if he *should* try to arrange it.
I said, "They *will* need money."	I said that they *would* need money.

In addition, *should* and *would* have specialized uses:

Should is used:

1. To express obligation, necessity, or duty [I really *should* go to her tea; the two sides of the equation *should* balance].

2. To express probability [She *should* be home by then; these tires *should* be good for another 5000 miles].

3. In a subordinate clause, to express a supposition [If I *should* be late, will you hold dinner for me?].

Would is used:

1. To express a customary action in the past [During those years he *would* write once or twice a year and send a card at Christmas].

2. As a synonym for "were willing" in conditional clauses [He could do it, if he *would*].

3. As a polite form in requests or commands [*Would* you mind making three copies of this letter?].

Avoid the overuse of the auxiliary *would*. Repeating *would* in a compound sentence is often awkward or wordy.

Awkward	Revised
If they *would have done* that earlier, there *would have been* no trouble.	If they *had done* (or *Had* they *done*) that earlier, there *would have been* no trouble.
We *would want* some assurance that they *would accept* before we *would make* such a proposal.	We *would want* some assurance of their acceptance before we *made* such a proposal.
If I *would be* in your place, I *would apologize*.	If I *were* in your place, I *would apologize*.

should of See **could of.**

show = chance This usage [Give him a fair show] would be appropriate only in a colloquial style. In formal and informal style use *chance* or *opportunity*.

show = play, motion picture Generally acceptable in college writing, but the other terms may be more precise.

show up The uses of *show up* to mean "expose" or "appear" [This test will show up any weaknesses in the machine; I waited for an hour, but he didn't show up] are established. The use of *show up* to mean "prove much superior to" [The girls showed up the boys in the spelling bee] is colloquial but would not be objectionable in college writing.

sic The Latin word *sic,* pronounced *sick,* is used in brackets to indicate that an error in a quotation appeared in the original source and was not made by the person copying the quotation. Example: "The significant words in the paragraph are these: 'No person will be allowed on the premises unless he is duely [*sic*] authorized.' "

sick = disgusted This usage [All these pious platitudes make me sick] is now recognized by the dictionaries. It should be acceptable in most college writing, but not in formal style.

simple sentence See **sentence.**

so (conj.) The use of *so* as a connective [She refused to exchange the merchandise, so we went to the manager] is thoroughly respectable, but its overuse in college writing is objectionable. There are other good transitional connectives—*accordingly, for that reason, on that account, therefore, for example*—which could be used to relieve the monotony of a series of *so*'s. Occasional use of subordination [When she refused to exchange the merchandise, we went to the manager] would lend variety to the style.

some The use of *some* as an adjective of indeterminate number [Some friends of yours were here; there are some questions I'd like to ask] is acceptable in all levels of writing. Its use as an intensive [That was some meal] or as an adverb [She cried some after you left] is slang and should be avoided in college writing.

somebody's else Say, "somebody else's."

somewheres Nonstandard variant of *somewhere*. Not acceptable in college speech or writing.

sort (of) See **kind (of).**

split infinitive   An infinitive is "split" when one or more words come between the prefix *to* and the verbal word [to *wholly* comprehend]. Usually the intervening word or expression can be placed elsewhere, but occasionally a split infinitive avoids ambiguity [The strike was sure to *further delay* production].

strong verb   A verb which uses a change in the vowel rather than inflectional endings to distinguish between present and past tenses [sing, sang, sung]. Weak verbs [walk, walked, walked] are regular, strong verbs [break, broke, broken] irregular.

subject   A word, phrase, or clause which performs the action expressed by the finite verb in the active voice [John left]. The subject of a verb in the passive voice receives the action [John was expelled]. Subjects are generally nouns or pronouns, but may be phrases or clauses. See **noun clause.**

suffix   A syllable added at the end of a word to make a derived word, as in *like + ly = likely, child + hood = childhood.*

suit — suite   The common word is *suit* [a suit of clothes, follow suit (in cards), suit yourself, this doesn't suit me]. *Suite* means "retinue" [The President and his suite arrived late], "set" or "collection" [a dining room suite, a suite of rooms]. Check the pronunciation of these words in your dictionary.

sure = certainly   This usage [I sure am annoyed; sure, I will go with you] is colloquial. Unless the style justifies colloquial usage, say *certainly* or *surely.*

swell = good, fine   This usage [It was a swell show; we had a swell time] is slang. It is generally unacceptable in college writing.

symbol   A word, signal, or sign. The word as contrasted with what it stands for. See **referent.**

synonym   A word having the same meaning as a given word. Thus, *patio* is often a synonym for *courtyard.*

syntax   The relationships of words within a sentence. The chief units of syntax are the subject, verb, object, and modifiers.

take and   This usage [In a fit of anger he took and smashed the bowl] is not acceptable in college writing. Simply say *smashed* [In a fit of anger he smashed the bowl].

take sick   This usage [He took sick and died] is disputed. Authorities differ in classifying it as established, dialectal, or regional. It would generally be safer to avoid it in college writing.

tense   Tense is the system of form changes in verbs which indicate time. Although it is possible to recognize some thirty different tenses in English, not counting idioms which do the work of tenses, six tenses are considered basic. These are

Simple present: They object	*Present perfect:* They have objected
Simple past: They objected	*Past perfect:* They had objected
Simple future: They will object	*Future perfect:* They will have objected

terrible, terribly   An overused colloquialism for *very* [She was terribly nice about it]. Its restrained use in informal papers is not objectionable.

terrific   Used at a formal level to mean "terrifying" and at a colloquial level as an intensive. Overuse of the word has rendered it almost meaningless.

theme
Used in two ways in composition courses: (1) the dominant idea of an essay [The theme of this essay is that self-deception is the commonest of vices]; (2) a general name for a composition assignment [Write a 500-word theme for Monday]. The first meaning is synonymous with *thesis* as it is used in this book.

thesaurus
A reference book which groups together in the same entry words with the same general meaning—for example, under **obedience:** *compliance, acquiescence, dutifulness,* and so on. In a dictionary you begin with the word and find its meaning; in a thesaurus you begin with an idea and look for words to express it. The best known is *Roget's International Thesaurus,* which groups words under broad concepts such as *Goodness, Badness, Health, Disease, Success, Failure, Victory, Defeat.*

thesis
As used in this book, the dominant idea of an essay.

tho
A variant spelling of *though.* The longer form is preferred in formal usage.

through = finished
This usage [Aren't you through with that story yet?] is now accepted by all dictionaries consulted. "Finished" would be preferable in a formal style [Haven't you finished (*not* finished with) that story?].

tough
The uses of *tough* to mean "difficult" [a tough assignment], "hard fought" [It was a tough game], "hard to bear" [It was a tough blow for all of us] are accepted without qualification by reputable dictionaries.

toward, towards
Both forms are acceptable. *Toward* is more common in America, *towards* in Britain.

transitional connective
Sometimes called conjunctive adverbs, these words link independent clauses not joined by a coordinating conjunction: *however, moreover, therefore, nevertheless* [Spring came late; nevertheless we planted our flowers hopefully].

transitive
See **verb.**

troop — troupe
Both words come from the same root and share the original meaning, "herd." In modern usage *troop* is used of soldiers and *troupe* of actors [a troop of cavalry, a troop of scouts; a troupe of circus performers, a troupe of entertainers].

try and
Try to is the preferred idiom. *Try and* would generally be acceptable in informal and colloquial styles.

understatement
The opposite of exaggeration. The device of deliberately saying less than one means, as in Winston Churchill's comment, "My life so far has not been entirely uneventful." Understatement is often used for ironic or humorous effect.

unique
The formal meaning of *unique* is "sole" or "only" [Adam had the unique distinction of being the only man who never had a mother]. The use of *unique* to mean "rare" or "unusual" [Spinal anesthetics allow the patient the unique experience of being a witness to his own appendectomy] has long been popular and is now accepted. But *unique* in the loose sense of uncommon [a very unique sweater] is generally frowned upon, especially when modified by an intensive adverb.

up
The adverb *up* is idiomatically used in many verb-adverb combinations which act as a single verb [break up, clean up, fill up, get up, tear up]. Often *up* adds a note of thoroughness to the action of the verb. Compare "They ate everything

on their plates" with "They ate up everything on their plates." Avoid unnecessary or awkward separation of *up* from the verb with which it is combined, since this will have the effect of making *up* seem to be a single adverb modifying the verb rather than combining with it. For example, "They held the cashier up" is subject to misinterpretation; "She made her face up" is simply awkward. Say, "They held up the cashier," "She made up her face."

used to   Notice the final *d* in *used*. We do not pronounce it in informal speech because it is elided before the *t* of *to.* But the phrase is written *used to,* not *use to.*

used to could   Nonstandard for *used to be able.* Not acceptable in college speech or writing.

verb   Such words as *be, do, walked, was, wrote, said, scolded* belong to a large class of words which name actions, states of being, or conditions, and are inflected to show number, person, voice, mood, and tense. Every verb has four principal parts from which its many other forms are derived. In **regular verbs** the third and fourth principal parts are the same, and are formed by adding *-ed, -d,* or *-t* to the first. In **irregular verbs** the third and fourth parts are different, and the main vowel often changes.

	Present Tense	Present Participle	Past Tense	Past Participle
Regular	conquer	conquering	conquered	conquered
	talk	talking	talked	talked
Irregular	speak	speaking	spoke	spoken
	see	seeing	saw	seen
	am	being	was, were	been

A **transitive verb** is followed by an object, which completes its predication [He wants sympathy. I wrote a letter]; an **intransitive verb** has no object but makes a complete predication by itself [The girls have left. Tomorrow our new term begins]; a **linking verb** connects the subject to a complement which may be a noun or an adjective [Judy was a cheerleader. The children were sleepy. He felt sick. The crowd became angry].

verbal   A verb form used with an auxiliary verb or used as a noun or an adjective in a sentence. The verbals are the infinitive [*to run, to have run*], the present participle or gerund [*running*], and the past participle [*run*].

very   A common intensive, but avoid its overuse in writing.

voice   English verbs have two voices: **active** [A girl *opened* the door] and **passive** [The door *was opened* by a girl]. When a verb is changed from active to passive, the object of the active verb becomes the subject of the passive verb. The passive voice is formed by adding the past participle to the appropriate tense form of the verb *to be* [The door *is opened, was opened, will be opened*].

vulgate   Synonymous with *nonstandard.* Any usage characteristic of uneducated speech.

wait on   *Wait on* means "serve" [A clerk will be here in a moment to wait on you]. The use of *wait on* to mean "wait for" [I'll wait on you if you won't be long] is a colloquialism to which there is some objection. Say *wait for* [I'll wait for you if you won't be long].

want for The use of *for* or *should* after *want* in such sentences as "I want for you to come," "I want you should come," is not acceptable in college speech or writing. After *want* in this sense use the objective case plus an infinitive [I want them to go at once]. When the sentence does not require an object, the infinitive is used immediately after *want* [I want to go home].

want in, out, off This usage [The dog wants in; I want out of there; I want off now] is colloquial. In college writing it would be safer to supply an infinitive after *wants* [The dog wants to come in].

want = ought This usage [They want to be careful or they will be in trouble] is colloquial. *Ought* is the preferred idiom in college writing.

ways Colloquial for *way* in such sentences as "You must have come a long ways from home." Except in a colloquial style the accepted form in college writing is *way* [You must have come a long way].

when (in definitions) Avoid the use of a *when*-clause in defining a term [A comma splice is when you put a comma between two separate sentences]. Instead of *when* use a noun phrase or clause (A comma splice is the use of a comma between two separate sentences].

where (in definitions) Same comment as for **when** above.

where . . . at, to The use of *at* or *to* after *where* [Where was he at? Where are you going to?] is redundant. Simply say, "Where was he?" "Where are you going?"

where = that The use of *where* in such sentences as "I heard on the radio where there was a violent storm in Chicago," "I see in the paper where the sniper was caught," may be occasionally acceptable in a colloquial style, but it is inappropriate in formal or informal writing. Use *that* [I heard on the radio that there was a violent storm in Chicago; I see in the paper that the sniper was caught].

which *Which* is not used to refer to persons. It is used to refer to things [The house which he built]. When referring to persons use *who, whom,* or *that* [The man who is talking, the girl whom I love, the doctor that I called].

who — whom In informal and colloquial writing *who* is often used instead of *whom* when the pronoun is in subject territory—that is, when it comes at the beginning of the sentence [Who is she marrying? Who are you looking for?] This is the colloquial and informal usage of educated people, but in a formal style *whom* would be required [Whom is she marrying? For whom are you looking?].

-wise Avoid adding the suffix *-wise,* meaning "concerning," to nouns to form such combinations as *budgetwise, jobwise, tastewise.* Some combined forms with *-wise* are thoroughly established [*clockwise, otherwise, sidewise, weatherwise*], but the fad of coining new compounds with this suffix is generally objectionable in English classes.

Xmas Pronounced "Christmas." An informal abbreviation much used in business and advertising.

you = one The use of *you* as an indefinite pronoun instead of the formal *one* is characteristic of an informal style, but be sure that this impersonal use will be recognized by the reader; otherwise he is likely to interpret a general statement as a personal remark addressed to him. Generally avoid shifting from "one" to "you" within a sentence.

Index

Correction Symbols

adj	Use adjective instead of adverb (p. 397)
adv	Use adverb instead of adjective (p. 398)
agr	Make circled words agree (subject-verb, pp. 386-91; pronoun-antecedent, pp. 354-56; tenses, pp. 380-83
apos	Use apostrophe (p. 416)
bib	Check form of bibliography (pp. 264-70)
cap	Use of capital letter(s) (pp. 429-31)
case	Case form (pp. 383-86)
chop	Choppy sentences (pp. 109-11)
cs	Comma splice (pp. 357-59)
d	Indicated diction needs revision
det	Details faulty or inadequate (pp. 85-86)
det?	Details not pertinent (pp. 84-85)
dg	Dangling modifier (pp. 361-62)
fn	Check form of footnote(s) (pp. 280-83)
frag	Sentence fragment (pp. 354-55)
gen	Diction or statement too general (pp. 138-40)
id	Incorrect idiom (p. 453)
lc	No capital. Use small letter(s) (pp. 429-31)
lev	Confusion of stylistic levels (pp. 134-37)
log	Faulty logic
no	Use numbers (pp. 434-35)
ns	Nonstandard usage (p. 135)
¶	Begin new paragraph
no ¶	No paragraph
p	Punctuation needed
no p	No punctuation needed
ref	Clarify reference of pronoun (pp. 394-95) or modifier (pp. 375-76)
rep	Undesirable repetition
sep	Undesirable separation (pp. 376-77)
sp	Consult dictionary for correct spelling
t	Use correct tense form (pp. 380-83)
wo	Revise word order
wordy	Reduce wordiness (pp. 124-26)
wr	Write out: do not use abbreviations (p. 428) or numbers (pp. 434-35)
ww	Wrong word
?	Illegible word
∧	Something omitted
/	Remove word, letter, or punctuation so slashed
x	Careless error
, / ; /	Provide punctuation indicated
Additional Symbols	_____
	_____